shattered

memoirs of an amnesiac

SHATTERED

Memoirs of an Amnesiac

A.E. HAYES

Terra Publishing

Shattered: Memoirs of an Amnesiac

Copyright © 2017 by A.E. Hayes

The author has tried to recreate events, locales and conversations from her memories of them. In order to maintain their anonymity, in some instances she has changed the names of individuals and places. In addition, she may have changed some identifying characteristics and details such as physical properties, occupations and places of residence.

Editing by Michael Dell
Cover Design by Carrie Miller
Cover Photograph © ccaetano
Author Photograph © Katie Venezia

Terra Publishing
an imprint of Stars and Stone Books

starsandstonebooks.com/terra-publishing

Digital Edition 1.0

Print ISBN: 978-0-9989514-1-6
Digital ISBN: 978-0-9989514-0-9

❋ Created with Vellum

This book is dedicated to Toby, who held on when he could have let go. Thank you for loving all of me, exactly for who I am (and as I am).

AUTHOR'S NOTE

As an amnesiac, it's been quite the challenge to write a memoir about my experiences in a way that doesn't sound like a disjointed or falsified mess. However, in the interest of the truth, I've had to rely on many sources to accurately write this story—from old journal entries and police reports to firsthand accounts of my own life as told to me by friends and doctors. And since the truth is something different depending upon who happens to be telling it, I can promise that, no matter the situation, everything portrayed here occurred in some form. These words are my truth, even if some of the details remain unclear or still hidden from my fragmented brain.

However, some of the names and characteristics of certain individuals have been changed to protect the innocent (as well as the not so innocent). The details are all true, but the identifiers have been turned from nonfiction into creative nonfiction.

When you're an amnesiac, the truth matters more than almost anything else. In my life, the search for who I really am will linger until my dying day. I'm getting closer, but I'm confident I'll never find out everything I believe I should know.

Hence this note. Hence my desire to engage you in what is the most honest story I could ever write about myself.

Please proceed into the madness.

What are the roots that clutch, what branches grow
Out of this stony rubbish? Son of man,
You cannot say, or guess, for you know only
A heap of broken images, where the sun beats,
And the dead tree gives no shelter, the cricket no relief,
And the dry stone no sound of water.

— T.S. ELIOT, THE WASTE LAND

The truth has always had three sides—
Mine, yours, and how it went.

— QUEENS OF THE STONE AGE, "3'S AND 7'S"

INTRODUCTION

There are ghosts that live within these walls, and they aim to take permanent possession.

―――――――――

I don't know how old I am—three, perhaps, or slightly older—but there he stands, by the doorway, near my closet and giraffe growth chart and collection of Sesame Street posters. The streetlights that scream their golden shards of warning through my bedroom window don't seem to be illuminating as much as they should.

But I want to know. I need to know who has come to visit. I turn toward the bears, the Smurfs, the large plush cats that watch over me in the disturbed nighttime stillness. They'll know what to do. They are my guardians. But instead, they betray me. They stare back at me, beaded eyes glazed with the harsh truth that their sewn-together mouths can never shout: "This is your issue now, so you get up and handle it. You're not some dumb little kid."

I am some dumb little kid.

That's when, for the first time, I hear the voice. Her voice. I look at the figure, but it still appears to be male. The voice seems to have come from some other place. I glance back at my stuffed animals, my once-defenders and now-betrayers, but they remain quiet.

"Get up. Get up now. It's been worse than this before."

I get up, because I don't have another option.

"Move. Go. Run past the door. Go to your mother. *Go*."

The voice speaks with a demanding certainty. It is one that cannot be ignored. But I know that voice now. I know that voice as I know myself, a precocious three-year-old who shows off her reading skills at the local McDonald's by opening the newspaper and spouting off world disasters and editorials to anyone who will listen. I read and sing for these strangers. I tell them that I should be known. My mother is proud of me.

I'm a show pony.

("Of *course* you are. You are for show. My show. And if you learn to keep them wanting more, you'll have access to everything you could ever want. That way, when the time comes, you'll know what it means to have control. You will finally understand power.")

I approach the figure, and it doesn't move. Can I see the door through the figure? No, that must be a trick, some sort of discrepancy with the lighting. I look up, try to gaze into the eyes of my visitor, and see nothing.

I do as I've been told, as I've always been told, and as I'll always be told by the sly, sultry, worldly voice.

I run.

When day descends into night, I feel it within my bones. There are colors in the air that whisper from the crickets, the wind, the passing cars. As the chill eventually settles, my memories ebb and flow like the rapid tide.

The voice always knows that I'm here, but she doesn't seem to need me as much as I need her. She does not want me to exist in this manner. And so, I run. I run too quickly. I cannot be caught. The sunlight will not always reflect my shadow. Only the darkness can.

I run from men who gather me onto their laps and demand one more song.

I run, skirt ripped, dignity torn, from the frigid bed of an unknown pick-up truck.

I run from one bar into another bar, and then into another, until I find false salvation.

I run from stage to stage, performance to performance, in case I am caught in the act.

I run from closets I've slept in and from rooms that render me rigid and complacent.

I run from the light, because I'm terrified that you can find me there.

I fall in love and marry a decent, respectable man, and I find a series of decent, respectable jobs for college-educated, decent, respectable girls. All is silent.

("*Show pony.*")

The doctors say, "There's a chance that you could be dead soon." I roll my eyes and ignore their words. They hand me chemotherapy and platitudes. I hand them indignation. I begin to crumble.

I say to other doctors, "I will be dead soon." They roll their eyes and ignore my words. They hand me pills and a straightjacket. I hand them nothing, because suddenly, I am nothing. I am breaking.

A beautiful man—my Starlight Boy—tells me he can fix me. My mind accepts the challenge. I hand over a stable marriage to this promise. He hands over his heart. We ruin everything.

I am broken.

But after the break, there is a miracle. I go away, and when I come back, I come back to rebuild. I publish and perform. I reunite with my husband. Somehow, I am forgiven. Somehow, I exist as fractured and whole.

And after almost a decade of loss and agony, my husband and I find out that we are going to have a son.

Son. Sun.

There cannot be shadows now.

And for the first time, I refuse to run.

This is my melody. It may be uneven, split, and cacophonous, but it is mine.

This is how it goes.

These are the ghosts that I yearn to set free, away from my body and mind, before they dare take up their highly sought-after residency.

This is how I must let them roam, reckless and carefree, to repair what has been shattered.

THE AFTER

August 24, 2010–August 30, 2012

AUGUST 24, 2010

There was a Before—capital letter necessary, because the Before was my possession. It contained a life that once belonged to me. The Before may be lost now, but from October 27, 1981 to August 24, 2010, it had a place, a time, and a definitive name.

But the Before died in a matter of seconds. Sometimes, that's all it takes.

In the early morning stillness of August 24, 2010, I had been sleeping, supported by a mattress that had taken up occupancy in the living room because I was unable to climb stairs following a moderately routine surgery. But I woke up, in pain, and in need of the bathroom. Apparently, I made it there just fine.

But when I had finished, I stumbled back into the living room. Into the dark. Into a void that completely took over everything around me.

There was a desk nearby—a beautiful roll-top desk that once belonged to my beloved grandfather, Doo-Da—and as the dizziness grabbed me, I reached for that desk.

I missed and slammed my head into the corner of the cherished possession.

For a moment, there was stillness and peace. There was a warm sense of calm that embraced me, and I'd been so cold that I allowed myself to be bathed in that warmth.

But in the nighttime sky of this strange, warm reality, there were stars and airplanes. I heard music, off key and humorous, coming from behind me as I saw a boy and a girl standing on a small porch, elbows touching, shivering outside in the cold. I flashed into a new vision then, the stars and airplanes still surrounding me, of a little girl with dark hair and green eyes, sitting at the top of the staircase in my house. She cried out for me. "Mommy!" was her only word. I wanted to get up to grab her, this beautiful girl who was my daughter, but I was unable to move. Something within me was cracked, and it wasn't possible for me to understand what was happening.

And then, the voice. The voice I'd always heard, ever since I was a scared, helpless three-year-old.

"You've been captive far too long," she whispered. "So I'm releasing you."

The universe was bathed in white light, and as I touched the azure and ruby stars dancing above my head, the crack within me split and fractured into madness.

I felt the shatter. But I was powerless to stop it.

And then, as I called out for my non-existent daughter, a seizure took hold.

That was the end of the Before, and the tumultuous, disconcerting beginning of the After.

"MY NAME IS... RUBY," I SAID. TWELVE HOURS INTO THE AFTER, I woke up in a hospital room, surrounded by people. I knew what people were.

But I didn't know any of these people.

However, one of the people asked me for my name, and Ruby seemed right. I uttered it, and a warm feeling spread throughout my chest. Something was clear. Finally. But the words were difficult to speak because words didn't make any sense. They sounded like odd patterns, jumbles of noises that lacked meaning. I saw colors when I spoke. It hurt to talk.

"That's not your name," one of the people said to me. "Can you try again?"

I had no understanding of what this person was asking me. Try again for what? What was so wrong with Ruby?

That was when I noticed a person—a man, my brain discerned—sitting next to me. He was crying. My brain tingled. Was I supposed to feel sad for this man, even though I didn't know who he was? I looked over at him, which caused him to cry even more. Something inside of me whispered, "This is the time to hurt," and so, I listened. I hurt.

"You must be a doctor," I said to the crying man. My words were scrambled and nearly unrecognizable.

"No," the man said. "I'm your husband."

I had no idea what that meant. A husband sounded like a serious thing, especially a crying husband, but I had no idea what I was supposed to feel for this man besides hurt.

There were odd things hooked to me. If I moved in certain ways, they pulled against my body and neck. Something above my eyes throbbed.

Nothing made sense. I was so overcome with confusion that, despite hearing a strange and sultry female voice in my head, I allowed my eyes to roll back.

Once again, I let go and fell into the darkness.

ACCORDING TO MY HUSBAND, TOBY, I HAD BEEN SLEEPING IN THE living room, gotten up to use the bathroom, and then, when I returned, collapsed and smashed my head into my grandfather's desk. When I hit the ground, I had multiple seizures, each one more intense than the previous, until I eventually stopped moving. At that point, I was rushed to the hospital in a coma.

Nothing Toby said resonated with me, but I noticed that people didn't seem as worried when I nodded in mock understanding, so I nodded. Yes, I thought. Of course. All of that made perfect sense.

But none of it actually did.

At one point, Toby said, a doctor had asked if a priest should come in to bless me, just in case. What was a priest? Was that a special doctor? But I simply nodded as Toby said he didn't invite one into the room. I just remained hooked to machines until my eyelids eventually fluttered and I woke up to the After. And that was when I was asked my name. But I'd been wrong. It hadn't been Ruby.

Then where had that name come from, in all the time I had lost to darkness?

Tons of people came in and out of the room. Toby—the crying husband—stayed the entire time. At one point, as I tried to figure out what was happening, I heard a buzzing sound.

"That's your phone," Toby said.

"What is it for?"

"For talking to other people who aren't in the room. You can say hello with your voice or by writing them a message. You are a writer, you know. Do you remember that? You wrote an entire novel in two weeks last year."

"Then I'm pretty cool," I said, and Toby laughed. Nothing he said sounded logical, but his tone was so upbeat and hopeful that I had no choice but to believe that I was worth something more than the emptiness inside my head.

Toby handed me the phone, and I studied the rectangular device. It seemed farfetched and inhuman. I used one of these things? I pressed down on a few of the buttons, and when I did, the screen lit up, showing me a string of letters.

"You got it," Toby said. "What do you see?"

"Words." I looked at them. I studied them intensely.

And then my body lurched forward. I was going to throw up, but I didn't know what that meant, and I didn't know why.

"What? What is it?" Toby asked me. I looked at him, at the man who claimed to be my husband. But if "husband" was a term of importance, a term of hurt and love and obvious dedication to some sick, confused girl in a hospital bed, he wasn't telling me the truth. He wasn't my husband, because the words on the phone's screen indicated something that conflicted with his version of the truth:

"Where are you? Haven't heard from you. I miss you and love you always."

I handed the phone to Toby. "Is that a husband, too?"

He looked at the screen, rolled his eyes, and shook his head.

"No," he said. "Don't worry about that. I am your husband. I'm going to take care of you. You're going to be okay."

"Am I in love with that—phone person?"

"Slow down." Toby reached for my hand. It felt right when he held it, as though I'd felt the sensation a thousand times before, but couldn't recall when or where. "It doesn't matter. That phone person is just a friend of yours. Don't worry about him. You'll remember all of this soon. I know you will."

"Remember what?"

I didn't understand a damn thing. What were all these machines? Who were all these people? What in the hell did I look like? What was my name? Where did I live? Who, exactly, did I love? What were these words that I heard in my head but that I absolutely could not articulate?

Toby must have sensed I was overwhelmed, so he came up with a plan. "I want to play a song by your favorite band," he said. "The band's name is Coheed and Cambria."

"That's a thing?"

"They are a band. They make music. Listen. Maybe you'll know the song." Toby pressed a few buttons on the phone and, just like that, music began to play. It was the most amazing thing I had ever witnessed in my new life. Making music come from that tiny device seemed like some form of magic, and Toby was somehow able to do it.

But I had no idea what the song was. It felt good as the music surged through my body, but I didn't know the song.

And then, suddenly, I did.

"Pray for the broken, no one can fix us," I said, right as the singer of the song said the same words.

Toby's eyes filled with tears. "You remember!"

"A little." But I guessed that a little was enough. Memory was such an important thing to these people. It made them feel some sense of excitement. I knew I would have to continue to fake it.

And at that moment, some part of me knew that, by faking it, the remainder of my life was going to be a tremendous lie.

A NEUROLOGIST WHOM I HAD APPARENTLY BEEN SEEING FOR seizures and other neurological conditions came to visit, and within a second, she dashed my ability to lie my way through life.

"What is this?" she asked, holding an object in front of me.

"It's bright." Of course that was the right answer. The object was bright.

"Well, that's a start." She looked at Toby and frowned. "Now really think about it this time. What am I holding in my hand?"

She sounded annoyed as hell. At that moment, I was some sort of race that she could not win. But she didn't understand that I didn't want her to lose. I wanted her to make me better. I wanted what everyone else seemed to have: knowledge.

I glanced at Toby, hoping he would tell me what the object was. But he didn't. He simply looked eager for me to respond. I couldn't, though. And I couldn't lie and say it was a phone, because I knew it wasn't. It wasn't a song, either. It was just this bright thing that she held. I shrugged my shoulders and admitted defeat.

"It's an umbrella," the neurologist said. "It's a yellow umbrella." Then she said to Toby, "Well, she's definitely had a brain injury, that's for sure. I can't be certain what she does or doesn't recall at this moment. But I wouldn't say this is a good start. She's going to need a lot of rest, therapy, and time to get this right."

Toby nodded, his eyes focused on the floor. Why were they talking about me as though I didn't exist? I was right there in the room. I could hear them. Did I cease to matter if I was injured in some way? Was this how people spoke about those who were hurt?

"One more question," my neurologist said. "What's your name?"

"It's Ruby. I know it is. That's what I know."

"Okay." She looked at Toby again, shook her head, and left, closing the sliding glass door behind her. I could see her talking to a doctor on the other side, but I couldn't hear a word she said. But the look on her face was ominous.

I've let everyone down, I thought. I didn't know what that yellow umbrella was. I have had a brain injury. Everything I was saying was wrong.

"More music," I said to Toby, falling back against the bed. He played song after song. In some cases, I recognized some of the words, but most of the time, everything sounded foreign. But I couldn't understand why.

And I kept wondering about the phone person. Who had sent me those words— "I miss you and love you always"?

There were no answers, though. Only questions. I allowed myself to give in to music, and I rested, hoping that whatever had been broken inside of me would repair as quickly as possible.

Since I could breathe and talk, and nothing was broken (brain aside), I was allowed to leave the hospital with Toby that evening. But before we departed, a doctor arrived and said a lot of words that made no sense.

"This seems like retrograde amnesia," he said. "Perhaps some of her memories are also being repressed due to a highly traumatic past. Her memories may be recovered in time, but it's too soon to tell. She may never remember anything that happened before this day."

Why did these people keep talking about me as though I no longer existed?

And what in the hell was retrograde amnesia?

After Toby signed a stack of papers, a different person put me into a wheelchair, and Toby took me out to the car. When I stood up, my legs shook. I started to fall, and that was when I realized I couldn't feel my legs.

"You have a wheelchair of your own, just in case," Toby said. "You'll probably need it for a few days."

Why did I need it before?

My phone buzzed. On the screen, it said "Mom."

"Your parents are calling," Toby said. "I'm sure they are worried sick about you. I've been trying to keep them up to date, but—it's been a busy day. Just answer the phone. It's okay."

I hit a green button and a woman started talking to me. My mom. She said a lot of things that didn't make sense, but since I knew that memory made people happy, I pretended to understand, and I said yes, of course we would come over to visit. I assumed I lived close enough for that to be possible, and Toby told me that we were only a few minutes away.

On the drive to their house, Toby told me a bit about my family. It all sounded pretty good, and so, I told him that I understood.

"I remember about... sixty percent of everything now," I said. I had no clue if he believed me, but I figured that it was worth a shot. I had to convince him I wasn't lying.

I was exhausted, and the visit with my parents and brother exhausted me further. They asked me a lot of questions, and I made up answers, pretending that I knew what they meant. When they told me about an upcoming event, I nodded and laughed as though I knew why that event had meaning. But what choice did I have? If I was hurting Toby by not answering his questions, I didn't want to hurt these parent people, either. That didn't seem fair.

The voice entered my head again. "Good girl," she said to me. "I can help you."

And I was reassured, even though the woman's voice made no sense. Where was she? Was she just for me, or did everyone get some sort of helper voice if they had been hurt?

Life was simply one giant question, and I had to pretend to know most of the answers.

Before Toby and I left my parent's house, we all watched a movie. The girl in the movie had long black hair and pale skin, just like mine. She struck me as familiar. I asked Toby if that girl was me.

"No," he said. "That's an actress. You have been on stage before, but this girl isn't you."

But that couldn't be. I knew that I had dressed like that girl before. I knew that I had said some of the things that this girl said. I began to grow dizzy, and the voice came back.

"She is with you. She's helping you. Remember, you're a good girl."

I felt reassured again, and I smiled. Even though Toby and I left to go back to a place that he called our house, and helped me to a spot that he called our bed, I smiled and accepted it as though I wasn't living with someone who was still a stranger. I allowed myself to be positioned on the mattress, and Toby handed me my phone.

He left the room, and when he did, I hit the button to light up the screen. I found the message from earlier. And I found the button that would allow me to reply to it.

But I didn't know how to reply.

It took me a long time to respond, but I was finally able to slowly type, "I hurt my head. Badly. And I love you, too."

That seemed like the right thing to say.

"He does love you," the voice said to me. "And you have us. We'll get through all of this."

I smiled and closed my eyes.

Of course I would get through this. I had the voice. And she was the only one who seemed to be completely on my side, despite a lifetime of events, situations, and people that my brain no longer wanted me to remember.

AUGUST 25–SEPTEMBER 30, 2010

I n the newness, in the After, I began my life by sleeping for two or three days. I didn't understand that there were other things that I could do. I could have showered, eaten, worked on my writing, or conversed like a human being. But none of that made sense, and I felt as though it never would. I slept, and let my brain rest instead of allowing it to consume me.

Only one word connected with me: death. And sleep was the closest I could get to that state.

The person who had been sending me messages on my phone was another man I loved—as much as I loved Toby, the voice told me. Maybe even more. But he wasn't my husband, and confusion surged through my body as I pondered what to do.

His messages were so loving. "When you're ready," he said, "I will help you get pieces of yourself and your life back. Only I can fix you. I love you."

Toby knew about this man, this person I had, apparently, always referred to as my Starlight Boy. And Toby wasn't happy with the texts that were being exchanged.

"He's manipulating you," Toby said to me. "You may not see that yet, but he's using you."

I clutched my phone to my chest. "Prove it."

But he couldn't.

That same night, my parents called to tell me that our family cat of ten years had died. I told them I didn't understand—I had a cat? I didn't know that I had a cat. There were two cats living in my house with Toby, but they were both very much alive. Where did this third, mysterious cat come from? In an effort to help my memory, my parents brought the deceased cat, Marley, over to my house. I looked at the cold body, and I felt nothing.

The next day, my parents came back over to my house. Both of them, along with Toby, said that I needed more help than they could offer. My dad suggested that I was hiding something. I had no idea what he meant, but I could tell I was hurting everyone who cared about me. I couldn't lie my way out of this. When the voice seared through me, sharp and swift, and said, "You know what to do now, you've done it before," I listened to her. I slowly reached over to the table beside me, grabbed a pair of scissors, and held them to my throat. It was a primal action, a way to tell everyone to back away, and they did.

Then, someone quickly snatched the scissors from my hand. As I sank into the couch, defeated, Toby and my parents gathered some of my belongings.

And then they took me back to the hospital.

Now, I knew the truth. It all made sense. I was just like that Coheed and Cambria song Toby had played for me: I was The Broken. No one could fix the damaged person that I had become.

It was too late for me to ever live a normal life again.

BROOK LANE WAS A PRIVATE MENTAL INSTITUTION NESTLED IN THE mountains of Western Maryland. The pricey facility was about two hours away from my house, but the distance didn't seem to matter to the county social workers who deemed that I needed long-term care. Our local hospital, they told me, didn't have the resources to help me. But Brook Lane did.

And that was going to be my new, albeit temporary, home.

Toby and I both cried as a social worker called for an ambulance to take me to the facility. He promised that he would come and see me every day, no matter what, even if that meant four hours of driving despite a full-time job and his undergraduate classes. He held my hands in that empty, concrete room and sang with me until the ambulance arrived.

I'd been overmedicated on Valium and some other drug—I could feel the dizziness that only a strong cocktail of psych meds could provide—but that was standard, a doctor had told me. After all, I had threatened to slit my throat and then dug my fingernails into my wrists so furiously that they had bled down my arms. But what they didn't understand was that I had to feel something. I didn't know who I was, or what I was doing. And the pain felt real. It felt so incredibly good, and with that feeling came the sense that I was alive.

When the ambulance finally arrived to transport me to Brook Lane, I cried even more. I screamed for more Valium. I couldn't do this—I couldn't leave Toby, despite the two days we'd spent locked in that cold, windowless room. I didn't want to be in a place where there wasn't a single person who knew me. I needed the familiar, and going away wouldn't solve the problem.

But one of the techs took a bag that Toby had packed for me, and then I was loaded into the back of the ambulance. Stunned, I looked down at my pale arms, the gashes on my wrists, the bandages that only covered half the wounds I had inflicted upon my skin. I reached up and touched my short, black hair.

This was all real. This was happening. This was me, going to live in a hospital that would teach me how to do things like eat, tie my shoelaces, and interact with other human beings again.

Had I ever been more terrified in the past than I was in that moment? I couldn't remember.

But then again—who would want to?

The hospital was small and looked old. It sat next to a pond.

It was pretty on the outside, and I immediately saw the appeal of the new situation as we pulled into the driveway.

The inside wasn't so awful, either. There were three wings on the main floor—one for the doctors, one that had fifteen private rooms for adult patients, and one that had fifteen private rooms for children seventeen and under. When I saw the sign for that wing, I felt sick. What had happened to those kids that would force them to be placed here? Had they harmed themselves, too? Had they lost their memories, or just their minds?

Even worse—had I once been like all of them?

My private room was large, with a plush carpet and a sizeable closet. There were chairs for visitors. My desk and bed were both bolted to the floor, but otherwise, this seemed to be a reasonable home. William, the main nurse on duty for the evening, told me to unpack and settle in before he took a case history and my vital signs. I needed to relax and get used to my living situation, he said. Then, he closed the door, and left me alone.

That was the first time I'd been alone in almost three days.

I began to unpack. Toby had provided many items—clothing, toiletries, and even a box of protein bars. I had learned that I had a medical condition called Celiac Disease, which meant I had to adhere to a strict diet of certain types of food, so I assumed that he knew the hospital might not have those items ready for me right away. I was grateful. And in my gratitude, I missed my husband. He was still a stranger, but he was the nicest stranger I knew.

Toby had also packed a composition notebook and a pencil, as well as two books for me to try to read. They were favorites of mine, he had told me—works I had loved and then studied in undergraduate and graduate school. I recognized one of the books immediately, as it had been on my side table in the living room. But the second book was more mysterious, as it was bent and frayed, and I assumed it to be something important from my childhood.

The tattered book intrigued me so much that I sat down on my new bed to look at it. It was a book of poems by T.S. Eliot, with "The Love Song of J. Alfred Prufrock" marked up by tons of little notes that, at some point in history, I must have written. This book had to have been mine in college, I thought. I did go to college. And Toby must have known that it might trigger memories for me, or at the very least, bring me comfort.

But there was a surprise located in the middle of the book.

There were parts of my life in there, and I was certain Toby didn't place those items into my poetry collection. I must have stashed them here for safekeeping, I thought, especially since this book was so important to me. It must have been my hiding place.

The items were odd because I couldn't give them any context. There was a picture of two cats on top of a bookshelf. There was a letter from my college friend, Catie, that said she loved me and that my novel should absolutely be published. There was a picture of four people at my parent's house—me, my brother, Toby, and the person who had been texting me. This was my Starlight Boy. And it was obvious from this photo that we were in love. I was placed in between him and Toby, and Starlight Boy's hand was on my hip, clutching onto me in a protective manner. His head was tilted toward mine. And I was smiling. My hair was also longer, but it didn't look like real hair—was I wearing a wig? Why? And I had been that large? I hadn't realized that I once took up more space than I currently did. I looked down at my body then, and saw that it was smaller.

"You can smile for real now," the voice told me. "We worked very hard for this."

I smiled.

There was also a note from Starlight Boy in the book—a copy of a message he had written me that was dated back to March. In his letter, he said that he loved me, and that nothing could ever change that. My marriage couldn't change that. Nothing about me could every change that. I cried as I read the words, and then, at the bottom of the note, I saw a phone number. It was written in pen. I must have jotted it down at some point before my brain injury. But why would I have done that? If this man and I were in love, and we had clearly been together— maybe I'd had to get rid of his number from my phone at one point? But if that were true, how was he able to continue to send me messages that Toby called "manipulative?"

I placed the items back in the book and started to sob. Everything was so confused. Everything was a manipulation.

A knock on my bedroom door startled me. I didn't say anything, but William entered anyhow. I realized that I wouldn't have privacy here, and I didn't care.

"What's going on?" William asked, and sat down in the chair next to my bed.

"I don't know my name," I sobbed. "My clothes don't fit—they're all too big. And they don't look like mine. I think that I'm in love with two men, but I'm only married to one of them. Something happened to my head. Did you know that? Did you see the scans? And someone in my brain wants me to hurt myself. I don't know what's happening. I'm not even allowed to eat!"

William told me that I had been taken to Brook Lane for the exact reasons I had mentioned. "There isn't a cure for the amnesia that you have," he said. "But if you do have some repressed memories somewhere in there, we can work to recover those. You have to accept, though, that there are some things you may never understand or remember. It's good to have mementos, or objects. They'll help you piece bits of your life back together. No one here wants you to be unhappy. No one wants you to kill yourself, okay? We're all going to help you. But it's going to take time. It's going to be a lifelong process. And I need you to be patient."

I nodded. "Okay. I will."

"Now, let me give you the grand tour—show you where your bathroom is, where the payphone is, and where we'll line up for meetings," William said. "Oh, and by the way, you'll have your own bathroom. You're the only female patient here right now, so you'll have a lot of privacy. I'll make sure of it. I'll also make sure to write your name on everything so that you know what is yours."

"But what if I forget my name?"

"Then we'll help you remember it."

William ushered me out of the room to show me around my wing of Brook Lane. As we walked, he told me that he would make sure to wake me for therapy, as well as for meetings with social workers, doctors, and occupational and physical therapists. He also said he would wake me in time to take all my medications. There were a few new drugs I needed to try, he said, but that was fine. He wanted to help me. Everyone did.

When I got back to my room to rest for a while, I heard her voice.

"You have journals at home," she told me. "They contain all your memories. Get the fuck out of here. You're going to die in here. Go back. Get back to Starlight Boy. We all need him."

Who in the hell were *we*? But I knew that I wouldn't receive an answer.

But the voice allowed me to ponder yet another question: if there was a *we*, then how could there possibly be an *I*?

ONE DAY TURNED INTO ANOTHER AT BROOK LANE. MOST OF THE patients stayed for a couple of days, but only two of us remained for an extended visit—myself and a man in his thirties named Thomas. Something about his name made me feel uneasy, but I shook away that feeling. Maybe I had been with a Thomas in the Before?

I liked him, though, and I didn't have enough details of my past life to care otherwise. All I could discern was that he was my friend, and I was the youngest patient on the adult ward by about ten years. I was also able to learn about flirting—the voice helped with that. She told me that most of these men were flirting with me and that I would be wise to smile.

If they were flirting, maybe I wasn't an awful person? Did their words somehow improve me?

Dr. Patel was patient with me as I asked myriad questions in his office twice a day. I often stumbled over my words, and he and I discovered that I only had three or four actual memories that could be verified. Nothing from my childhood existed.

When I told him about the voice, he prescribed another medication, an anti-psychotic called Risperdal. I took the pill, allowed it to give me heart palpitations and severe visual distortions, but the voice didn't go away. She was as clear as ever. She somehow knew how to beat back the medication. But I decided not to let Dr. Patel know.

This was the man who taught me how to hold a fork properly so that I could eat. He talked to me about how to apply eyeliner—not around my lips, but right around my eyes, there, just like that, just to make them more beautiful. He taught me how to talk to people without being rude, selfish, or confrontational. In essence, he taught me how to be myself—the *I* that I had been constantly worried about retrieving.

When Toby and my parents came to visit, I practiced being myself. It took effort, and I was certain that they knew it, but I tried. During one visit, my mom brought me some more clothes. She had noticed that my other outfits were falling off my body, and decided I needed something that fit. When I slipped on the new jeans, I looked at the size on the tag. I was close to being in child-sized clothing. And something about that tiny number made my brain shiver.

The next morning, Thomas and I went down to breakfast, but I refused to eat. He worried, but he promised not to tell my secret. We were keepers of secrets and had stories to share that no one would believe. While mental illness was our connection, confidence was our ally.

But Dr. Patel was far more watchful, and for a while, I wasn't allowed to go down to breakfast. I had to eat in my room while someone watched me. And then I couldn't go to the bathroom in private after eating, just in case I decided to throw up. I told him that I wasn't a prisoner and that he was being barbaric. He shrugged and said, "You lived through a brain injury. You want to die by not eating eggs? I don't think that is how it's going to work."

In a way, Dr. Patel felt like a father to me. He cared. He was determined to help me live a normal life. And he wasn't the only one. The other patients were kind to me as well. In group sessions, they allowed me to pick songs to sing so that I could work on practicing my speaking skills and my memorization. When we were asked to draw self-portraits in an art therapy class and I forgot what I looked like, another patient asked the therapist if someone could take a picture of me so that I could know I was beautiful and that I was real. I felt like a child, the product of several watchful parents, and I knew I was safe.

It scared me to realize that I didn't ever want to leave.

THOMAS KEPT ASKING TO HEAR ME SING, BUT EVERY TIME WE WERE alone, an orderly told us that we needed to be separated. We hadn't done anything, but there was a rule: no female patients inside of rooms belonging to male patients. But I was the only female patient. And Thomas was my friend. I had no one else.

I promised him that I would make sure to sing something before I left, whenever that was. Neither of us knew our departure dates, but I was learning the basics of life in all those days at Brook Lane. I knew I wouldn't live there forever. I'd even grown proficient at mundane tasks, such as putting on makeup. One morning, as I was applying eyeliner and mascara in front of my bathroom mirror, a male patient with whom I'd become friendly walked by and said, "Well, hey! There's our movie star. You really should be a model."

"You were," the voice said to me. Maybe she was telling the truth? I soaked up the praise.

After an early afternoon medication call, in which patients stood in a line, waiting to be handed their cups of pills and water, Thomas was called away for a family meeting with his wife. He had told me that his bipolar disorder had been getting in the way of their relationship, and that he was certain she would leave him. She was simply waiting for the family meeting to tell him. But I assured him that he was a good person. No one would leave him.

While he was away at his meeting, I sat on my bed with the poetry book, trying to make sense out of the words that had once come so easily to me. But nothing resonated. I pulled out the note that Starlight Boy had written, and I took it down to the payphone. I called the number, my heart pounding—what if he didn't remember me, what if he was the awful person Toby said he was? —and when he picked up and said hello, I immediately started sobbing.

Starlight Boy cried as well. "I love you so much," he said over the phone. "I had no idea where you were. I'm so glad you're safe. And I don't want to overwhelm you with anything right now. You've been through hell. Just know that I'm here for you. And I love you."

"My doctor wants me to rip up a picture that I have of you," I said.

"I don't think you're suppose[...]
are a part of my life. I don't u[...]

The voice tried to talk ove[...]

"This is so unfair to you," [...]
do, but know that I haven't h[...]
It's *his* fault. *He's* the monster. [...]

I didn't know for certain. B[...]

"I love you," Starlight Boy [...]
you. But I do have to tell you [...]
dad called me a few days ago. [...]
conflicting memories, and he a[...]
thinking that maybe you had a[...] ...ow I know
better. I've been a wreck. I've missed you. I want to be able to call you,
no matter where you are. Is that okay?"

I felt an incredibly powerful surge of rage shoot through me. Both
Toby and my dad had, essentially, tried to stop me from talking to
this man.

"You are not a possession," the voice said. "Do what you know
you must."

"I can't believe them," I said. "I trust you. And no one has the right
to tell me if I can talk to you. Or whom I can love or hate. I'll call you
when I damn well want, just as you can call me."

"You're amazing," Starlight Boy said. "You are so strong. But just be
careful. Don't let them know. Our love is so different."

When I headed back to my room, fists clenched, my desire to
punch something so strong that I was afraid I would harm someone, I
saw Thomas. He was sitting in the hallway, right outside of his room,
and he was sobbing. I relaxed my hands and my heart let go of
the anger.

I sat beside him. "I take it that the meeting didn't go well."

"She hates me," he sobbed. "She hates me for this—disease. For
who I am. I just wish I could be dead! I wish I could forget everything
about my fucking life!"

"Don't wish for that," I said quietly, staring at my torn-up wrists. So
many days had passed—weeks by this point, since time had blended
together and the only schedule that mattered was the one Brook Lane

provided me—but my wris[...]
tore at my wrists in m[...]
and the orderlies d[...]
couldn't remem[...]
"Oh, Go[...]
don't wa[...]
want[...]

...ts still were bruised, scraped, and scarred. I
...sleep, the orderlies told me. I had night terrors,
...dn't know what I was so terrified about when I
...er anything.

...d," Thomas said. "I'm so sorry. I didn't mean it like that. I
...nt to forget my wife. I don't want to start over. I just don't
...things the way they are now. I don't want to hurt."

"I know," I said. "Everything hurts, all the fucking time."

"Everything *is* a waste of time."

I nodded, and he buried his head in his hands and sobbed.

I pulled Thomas' hands away from his face. I took his head and
rested it against my shoulder.

And I sang.

I sang songs that I knew the words to. Songs by Snow Patrol,
REM, Queens of the Stone Age, Disturbed. A flood of music came
back to me as Thomas rested against me, shuddering with sobs.

When he eventually calmed down, he hugged me and told me I was
the best friend he had ever had. And if we ever left, if we ever could,
we would always remain best friends.

That next morning, I was told that my insurance company didn't
want to pay for more inpatient nights at Brook Lane. Despite Dr.
Patel's appeals, the need for more money won out over the need for me
to have more time to recover.

I had twelve hours before I was going to be sent home.

———

Dr. Patel had tears in his eyes during our final meeting. I
don't know if he felt the fatherly connection that I did, but there was
something there. After all, he had helped me learn the basics. He had
taken me and allowed me to be human again. I could have an adult
conversation without stuttering, and I could write in a journal in a way
that sounded poetic and logical. I still didn't eat, but I could, at the
very least, hold a fork correctly.

"I know you'll be fine," he told me. I glanced over to my chart,
which he had spread open on his large, dark desk. There were so many

papers. How many notes had he kept on me? What did they all say? How many records, conversations, medication changes, revelations?

"And the voice? Her voice?"

"I want you to keep seeing all your outpatient doctors," he said. "And if you do that, I think she'll go away in time. You just—need a way to cope for now. And you are coping. That should make you feel happy."

"You're not happy," the voice said. I couldn't help but agree. She was, as always, correct.

Dr. Patel wasn't supposed to, but he hugged me goodbye before I stepped out of his office and into the hall. When he closed the door behind me, I walked over to the whiteboard that listed all the patients' names and room numbers.

I knew my name now, but it didn't feel as though it belonged to me. But it didn't matter. It was just a title, a placeholder. And it no longer existed on the whiteboard.

According to Brook Lane, I was officially gone.

———————

A FEW MINUTES BEFORE TOBY AND MY MOM ARRIVED TO DRIVE ME home—both so excited that I was leaving after all that time, and both optimistic that I was doing better—I noticed the line for dinner was forming. That was my best chance to say goodbye to the other patients. Those people were, for the most part, my family. They had come to know me more than I was able to know myself. I hugged each one, said something nice, and heard something kind in return.

I wanted to go home with Toby, but I hated leaving this family behind. I wasn't ready for the world outside Brook Lane. It was too open, too wild, too bright. It held secrets.

Thomas was at the end of the line, as usual. He leaned down and engulfed me in an enormous hug. We both began to cry.

"I love you," I said to him. "Please stay safe. Please always stay alive for me."

"I love you, too," he said. When we pulled away from each other, he took my hands into his and looked into my eyes. "I know you may not remember the movie *The Wizard of Oz*," he said. "Do you know what the Scarecrow said at the end?"

"No," I said. "What did the scarecrow say?"

"I'll miss you most of all." Thomas leaned down and hugged me again, and then the line began to move. We parted, and with a quick glance and a wave, he was gone.

But I saw Toby only a few minutes later, and I fell into his arms. "Are we going home?" I asked. He nodded. He looked so confident, so certain, that I relaxed and smiled. The worst must be over now, I thought.

I was incredibly wrong.

DURING MY ABSENCE FROM THE REAL WORLD, TOBY HAD STARTED TO make a wise decision. He had been looking for a new house for us to rent but hadn't chosen one until I was back to agree upon the decision. We found a nice, accommodating rancher, and when I looked at it, I was thrilled. This was where I could start my new life, I thought. If I had to leave the past behind—including Starlight Boy, who was forbidden to call my cell phone—then why not choose a new home? Why not choose to make everything new?

But when we moved into the new house, with friends and family members assisting us as much as possible, the voice got louder. She never stopped talking to me. At times, she talked for me, and it surprised me to hear certain things come out of my mouth.

And she had memories—not many, but a few. She had somehow been able to hold on to events she thought I should know. I was unable to put those events into context, and they didn't seem to relate to my life, but I accepted them as mine, especially when Toby was able to verify some of them. I was surprised. Most of my memory was gone, but somewhere in there, the voice had kept some memories for me to have. I felt grateful to her, even though she was within me.

I had learned to use my computer again a few days after coming home from Brook Lane, and I was able to check my email. I waded through the long list of messages until I saw one from a person I most definitely recognized.

It was from Starlight Boy. It had been sent only two days prior and was emotional and abundantly sweet. He told me the details about how we had met, how we had connected through music and past memories, and how, in time, we had fallen in love. Our love was meant to be from the start when we'd met years earlier, he said. The timing had never been right in the past, but when my mind was ready, maybe it could be our time?

I saved the email and hid it in a folder on my computer. I didn't have a reply yet.

A doctor that I saw the next day told me that my physical health was declining. I had, she said, been diagnosed with Lupus a year before the amnesia, and the medication I had been on for that wasn't working as well now. The fertility medication I had also been taking wasn't helping me do anything other than lose weight. All of this arrived as a shock. Lupus? Infertility? Were those treatments part of the twenty-pills-per-day regimen that I had been put on in Brook Lane? Why hadn't anyone told me I was so physically destroyed?

And then my therapist dumped me. She said that while she liked me, my case was well beyond the scope of her training. She needed to refer me to a different, male doctor who specialized in "unique circumstances."

All at once, everything changed. I thought I was ready for change, but I wasn't. My mind couldn't process it. I couldn't keep up with the phone calls, the noises, the lights, the flashbacks.

I stepped back from the confusion, and while Toby slept, I opened up a package of razor blades. In the bathroom, I took one to my wrist, clenched my teeth, and cut. Then, I took the blade to the other wrist and repeated the process. I watched in fascination as the blood seeped out of me and onto the tile, and then, dizzy, I rested my head against the bathroom rug and lost consciousness.

"JESUS CHRIST," A SOCIAL WORKER SAID TO ME IN A PSYCH HOLDING cell located within our county hospital. "You're having—quite the time, aren't you?"

"Yeah," the voice muttered, coming out of me before I could stop her. "The time of my life. If you don't mind, you can unhook me from these fucking machines and get me out of here."

"That's not going to happen," she said. "And unfortunately, your insurance company won't send you back to Brook Lane this soon. Luckily, we do have plenty of rooms open here. They're right upstairs. Your husband can come visit you every day, and you'll be safe."

"Get the fuck out."

"Now, we don't really work with people who have—your conditions," she said. "But we are able to help people who have PTSD and Borderline Personality Disorder."

I snapped back into reality. "I have what?"

I knew those names, and the acronym PTSD—which stood for Post-Traumatic Stress Disorder—had been tossed around while I was at Brook Lane, but how did I suddenly have a personality disorder? Who was the genius that decided that?

"A few days of therapy and rest here will help you," the social worker said. Then she asked me to voluntarily sign myself into the psychiatric ward.

I was shaken. The room that I had been placed in for about twenty-four hours—they had needed time to stabilize me and bandage my wounds—was tremendously cold, and even though six blankets covered my body, I couldn't stop shaking. My wrists ached every time I tried to bend them. I looked around at the grey walls and felt like passing out.

"There is no way that I'm staying in this hellhole," I said. "I've stayed here before. You people put me in here against my will! No way. No. Fucking. Way."

The anger in my voice scared me. The social worker sighed, turned away from me, and looked over to the corner of the room. I glanced over as well and saw Toby, despondent and uncertain, attempting to relax in a hard-backed chair.

"She has to stay," the social worker said. "She can either voluntarily commit herself, or I can have her committed involuntarily for at least seventy-two hours."

"Fuck you and your paperwork. I'm not staying," I growled.

I ended up with the involuntary stay.

THE DARK, DIRTY PSYCH UNIT WAS ONLY TWO MILES AWAY FROM Toby, and he came to visit me twice a day. But I didn't care. I knew we loved one another—or, if we didn't now, we did once—but if I had no idea who I was, then how could I truly love anyone at all? It would have been smarter, I thought, to have cut ties with everyone and start over, by myself, in a new state. I should have run away after I left Brook Lane.

But instead, I was placed in a tiny, private room, where I bled through my bandages and tried to shut out the screams of the man down the hall who was detoxing.

That state-run psych ward wasn't the place for trauma patients. If anything, it was a holding tank for alcoholics and addicts. One of the people I met had been diagnosed as bipolar, but when I was wheeled up to the ward on my first night and my story started to spread, I was immediately treated like an outcast. I was nobody's child, nobody's golden girl like I had been at Brook Lane. I was a certifiable nut job who couldn't remember her name. Even the nurses were afraid of me. They still ordered me around when it came to medication and meals, and they told me when it was time for therapy, but otherwise, they never forced me to go to groups or to socialize.

"Good," the voice said. "Fuck those people. You are so much more than they will ever be."

Toby brought me my poetry book, so I had my picture of Starlight Boy, along with his note and phone number.

In my cold, windowless room, as I watched the early fall spiders and beetles climb up the sides of the wall, I took out the picture and stared at it—those four, smiling faces, from a time in my life when love made sense. And then, I ripped Starlight Boy out of the picture and tossed his image into the trashcan.

But I refused to get rid of the note and number.

I SPENT AN OVERMEDICATED FIVE DAYS IN THIS FACILITY, AND IT WAS clear that the goal was to push people out once they stopped saying "I don't want to die." This was a game, and by day three, I learned not to ever verbalize what I was actually thinking. I would not say "I feel like dying," even if I still did.

Dr. Kail, my psychologist, was willing to discharge me on the fourth day, but he had an interesting theory.

"There's no doubt that you have amnesia due to the brain injury," he said. "And that can actually cause radical personality changes. But the voice you've been mentioning, and the fact that you can still flash back to a few select memories—well, I wonder if we should perform a special kind of MRI."

"For what reason?"

"To see if the lesions we last saw in your brain have gotten worse," he said. "But I have a sense that there's more to this than just a knock to the head."

On my last day, I was taken from the psych ward into the main hospital for the fMRI. I was told some things while being placed in the machine, and the voice wanted to cry out, but I knew that if I spoke, they'd have to restart the entire two-hour test. And by the time hour one had passed, I was exhausted and in pain. I closed my eyes, told the voice to shut up, and stayed still.

After the test, I was sent back to my room to pack. I wasn't allowed to call Toby to pick me up until Dr. Kail received the images, so once I finished packing, I started pacing the halls.

And then I remembered that I had my phone card and Starlight Boy's phone number. I called him while I was waiting.

"Are you going to be okay?" he asked me. "You're always in the hospital, and I never know where to find you. You're never at home. I'm so worried about you. I'm worried about what people are telling you, and how those things may not be true."

"Are you still in love with me?"

"Yes," he said. "You always have my love. And I think you're being overloaded by people trying to force all your memories back on you. Just remember that you are a beautiful, creative, attractively eccentric person. How could anyone *not* love you? But I'm just worried. I need to see you. I'm supposed to be there."

"When I get out of here, take a sick day or something. We should talk in person." Starlight Boy did something for the government—he had told me as much during one of our phone calls while I was living in Brook Lane—but I couldn't remember the specifics.

He agreed just as a nurse came to tell me that Dr. Kail wanted to meet with me in his office. I hung up the payphone, my last words a promise that I'd message Starlight Boy once I was home and settled.

Dr. Kail was pacing around his office, and when he saw me, he asked me to sit down. I did so, and Dr. Kail slid some papers in my direction.

The fMRI showed that I did have lesions in my brain that were associated with both trauma and, potentially, Multiple Sclerosis. But the more intriguing part, Dr. Kail said, was that different regions of my brain had lit up during the scan.

"And they shouldn't have," he said. "In a brain that's—well, not like yours—those regions wouldn't have lit up in that manner."

"What does that mean?"

But Dr. Kail said I should see my neurologist and my new psychologist about the results. They'd be able to offer a better perspective and to give me a definitive diagnosis. Then he signed my discharge papers and told me to call for a ride home.

The final paperwork given to me by the hospital said that, besides amnesia, depression, PTSD, a traumatic brain injury, and Lupus, I had a "highly questionable personality disorder." I ripped up the report and tossed it into a bathroom trashcan on the way out of the ward. And I ignored the voice when she said to me, "You did the right thing. You know who we are."

In the car on the way home, Toby asked me if I was okay.

I felt a smile creep up on my face, and I was unable to control it. "Fantastic," I said, leaning back against the seat.

But that wasn't true. My past was neatly tucked away somewhere, lost inside the fragments of my broken brain, and now, I knew I had reason to fear the day that some of that past started to leak out and reveal who I truly was.

DESPITE BEING DISCHARGED FROM THE HOSPITAL, I HAD BEEN ASKED to come back for an Intensive Outpatient Therapy program (or, as we all jokingly called it, IHOP) that ran from eight a.m. to three p.m. It was school for the mentally ill, and I was to be a two-week pupil. My new therapist, Ron, said I should probably go, and even though he didn't know me very well yet, I agreed. After all, if I hated it, I'd just stop showing up. Insurance would love that.

But I didn't hate it. In fact, I loved it far more than I had any reason to. Every day was a chance to be someone different and interesting to the seven other people in the program. I was thin enough that, in a random heat wave that fall, I could get away with wearing skimpy tank tops and tight jeans to make sure all eyes were on me. I wore a different wig every day to cover up my too-short, growing-out hairstyle. On one of the days when I wore a long, curly blond wig with a lingerie top and a pair of tight jeans, random men asked for my number. I gave it to them without hesitation. It seemed right. My head was far quieter when I gave in to the demands of men, and the quiet was a nice change. But the doctors in the program didn't care for my antics, and they told me to cover up.

"You're not a whore," one of the doctors told me.

"How do you know that?" I said slyly. He blushed and turned away.

A blond-haired guy in the program chuckled, as he'd overhead the conversation. Then he handed me his sweatshirt.

"Honestly," he said, "you should be able to wear whatever the hell you want. They're taking away your right to be you. And you're really cute. I hope someone has told you that today."

I put on the Vans hoodie and smiled. "I think someone just did."

Frank—the owner of the hoodie—and I were both discharged from the program on the same day, and he asked for my phone number. I gave him a fake one. I'd grown bored with him in ten days, and knew I didn't need him for anything.

When I arrived home that last day, I sent an email to Starlight Boy.

"I'm out of the hospital and free from their repressive treatments. I really need to talk to you. Tell me when you can be here. I can feel it now—I know I shouldn't be without you."

"I'll be there Monday during the day," he replied. "Keep yourself intact. I love you."

I smiled. I jumped, ready and eager, and he jumped right along with me.

OCTOBER 1–DECEMBER 31, 2010

Ron called my forty mg a day Valium use an addiction. I crossed my legs over the arm of a chair in his small, third-story office and allowed my short skirt to ride up just enough so that he could see the new lace panties I'd purchased.

"I'm an addict," I said. "What are you going to do about it?"

He did nothing but stare at my panties, and then leaned forward to slide his hand up my leg.

He smiled. "Whatever you want me to do."

He was an old hippie, all about peace and love and sex. If anything, I thought, he might call my psychiatrist, but all she would do was give me a slightly smaller dose of Valium, thirty mgs or something good enough, and that was fine. I would score pills elsewhere. I had sources now. Stays in those psych wards meant that I had connections. The visits were hell, but the perks were bountiful.

I was never myself—or, at least, the self that I was trying to become during my tenure at Brook Lane. As my twenty-ninth birthday approached, I didn't understand what that number really meant. I didn't look twenty-nine. And I knew I didn't act twenty-nine. Besides, I was watching my life as though I were in a perpetual dream—I was stuck behind a plate of glass, with every action controlled by the voice.

She seemed to know some things I had yet to learn—not necessarily memories or life skills, but how to get men and women to do whatever she wanted them to do.

When Starlight Boy came over that Monday in the late morning, we both fell into each other's arms as though we had done it a million times before. And we had, he told me. I just didn't remember. The voice allowed me to be there for that, but only for a moment. Then, she threw me behind the glass again as Starlight Boy picked me up, kissed me, and held me on the couch, our limbs tangled and woven together.

Why was I allowed to watch this? When had I lost all control? When had my brain become so separated from itself?

Since I hadn't seen Starlight Boy since the amnesia, we spent the entire day on the couch, cuddled up, conversing and kissing. It didn't go further than that. He worried about my physical and mental health once I told him about the occasional paralysis in my legs and the voice that sometimes entered my head. And I thought to myself that he would run away. If so, then I needed to push him away. But I couldn't. I could tell we loved each other and that the love went far beyond physical attraction. We had a history, and no matter what other people told me, Starlight Boy was not manipulative and cruel. He loved me and wanted to keep me safe.

"Don't listen to Toby," he said when I expressed concern about loving two men at once. "I'm closer to being your real husband than he is. You can consider me your husband, you know. I've done so much more for you."

Was he? Had it all been a lie—Starlight Boy was my husband, and Toby was a kidnapper?

"He's keeping you caged up in here," Starlight Boy continued. "And I would never do that to you. I love you so much. No one that I could ever meet or see will change that. You're the only one. I'd be lying to both of us if I said otherwise."

As I wondered who this man truly was, he pulled me against him and kissed me. And my heart told me one answer: Starlight Boy was the one. He was my husband. No one else mattered at all.

DESPITE CONSTANTLY THROWING UP FOR REASONS I COULDN'T explain, I decided to throw a Halloween party. Toby wasn't sure that I was making a wise move, but pictures and journal entries didn't lie: I was the queen of throwing excellent parties. I invited forty people I barely knew over for a costume party, and Toby took me shopping for alcohol, food, and decorations.

When I needed to find a very short black skirt to complete my costume, Toby and I hit up a department store. And a new obsession kicked in: shopping. When I realized that I could finally fit into clothing from the children's section, I went on a spree. I bought everything short, tight, and cute. I bought clothing that was slightly Victorian or Steampunk in design. I bought new lingerie and marveled that I could see my ribs jutting out underneath my bra line. And when I decided to buy four skirts, not just one, I was able to rationalize the decision to Toby: I was giving myself an early birthday gift. This was, after all, my very first birthday. What was five hundred dollars in clothing during one's first year of life?

The next morning, I received an odd phone call from an attorney. Apparently, I had filed for disability due to Lupus and a few other medical conditions, and my attorney was calling to let me know that he had added PTSD, amnesia, and depression to the list of reasons why I could no longer be gainfully employed. He also told me that we would have a verdict within a matter of days. I felt hurt. Who had made the choice that I was unable to work? But then I thought about it. If two hours of shopping made me feel so dizzy and sick that I had to lie down for a few days, how could I go to work? I was dismayed, but I had visions of my life floating in and out of my head: work would send me to the hospital. I'd forget something easy and I'd get fired. This was for the best.

But being sick and having those disorders meant more than just acronyms and labels that my doctors kept tossing around. They were a new and disturbing way to live, and I had to relearn that, slowly and painfully. I'd had to relearn everything, from the names of my best friends to the difference between right and left. My life would not be the same.

When I saw Ron again, he told me that I was spirited and eccentric. When I laughed, he pulled a tarot card from a deck he kept in his office.

"The Queen," he said.

"But of course."

He put his hand on my knee-high boot and slid it up the leather. He had just done that a week ago, I thought. But then, I blacked out. I didn't remember what happened after his hand started moving, but something clearly happened, because when I left the building after coming to post-session, the voice said, "Keep flirting until they all pay. And they will. We're preparing." I had no idea what that meant, but it scared me.

I had no more than ten memories, no idea how to control my impulses, and a voice that wouldn't stop talking to me.

But a party was on the horizon, so when I arrived home from therapy, I tried on my costume.

"That's right," the voice said, her tone sly as always. "That look will get them."

I wondered who we were getting. But by that point, I had learned it was best not to question her. She ran the show. And I was nothing more than her puppet.

My TWENTY-NINTH BIRTHDAY ARRIVED WITH A SURPRISE—A LETTER in the mail from the Social Security Administration. They were, according to the verbiage, pleased to inform me that I had been approved for permanent disability, or SSDI. My back pay would be a solid, five-digit figure that would grant me a bit of financial security—it would be enough to pay off some medical bills, old debts, and for the fertility treatments Toby and I kept trying. I didn't know if I really wanted a baby yet, but that had been part of the plan prior to the amnesia, so I hadn't said no.

But I was told that I would not be in control of my money—not the upcoming back pay, nor the monthly payments. As someone who had been deemed mentally ill, I was therefore unfit. Toby would be my representative payee. All the funds would go to him, kept safe in an account bearing his name only, and he'd have to withdraw them every month for us to use them.

"They're using *you*," the voice told me. "This was a plan. Keep you locked up, all cute and pretty in this nice house, away from your own fucking money. Do you plan to put up with that?"

No, I thought. I was tired of other people telling me how I should live my life.

Before I could do anything about the monetary situation, Halloween arrived, and nothing mattered more to me than preparing for the gathering. Toby had told me that Halloween had always been my favorite day of the year—a day when I could be whomever I wanted to be—and I embraced that as though I remembered what Halloween was actually like.

People came in and out of the house like a rough tide. I couldn't remember any of them except for the few friends I'd seen after coming home from Brook Lane. But it didn't matter. The music was loud, Guitar Hero was on the Xbox, and a late-night run to the store across the street provided plenty of attention and entertainment. A group of strangers asked to take my picture, and I obliged. I laughed, I flirted, and I was happy.

But I was so confused and tired.

Back in my bedroom, the party raging behind me, I downed a handful of pills and checked my phone. Starlight Boy had sent a text message.

"There are a lot of beautiful girls at this bar, but none of them hold a candle to you. I can't stop thinking about you, and I wish I was allowed to be there with you. It's not right that we can't be together on Halloween. I am just seeing through these other girls and I know what I want. So now, I'm outside, under the stars, thinking about the time we need to spend together."

I felt dizzy. I needed to put down the phone. Toby and I had been trying so hard to be happy.

But the voice. She told me to text Starlight Boy or I'd be rude. I complied.

"I'm glad I'm the only one for you," I wrote. "We'll make this work somehow. I know we will somehow. I know that we can be together. I love you."

The stars had always belonged to us. When Starlight Boy had mentioned being outside, standing under the stars, I saw a brief flash, similar to the one I saw the last night of the Before: two people, a boy and a girl, outside together, gazing at the night sky. The girl wore a black dress and shivered in the cold, and the boy, in his thick jacket, stood next to her to keep her warm. They studied the constellations. They wanted to admit their love.

I sent another text to my Starlight Boy. "Come over this week," it read. "Help me find a way to be yours forever."

"That's what I wanted you to say," he replied. "You're mine. So I'm coming for you."

"DID YOU JUST HEAR THAT?" I WHISPERED.

"What?"

"The front door. The goddamn fucking front door."

Starlight Boy and I were in my bedroom on an early November morning and, without even realizing it, I had stripped down to a matching bra and panty set. When had I removed my clothing? And why did I remember that some of Starlight Boy's clothing was in my living room?

"It's probably one of the cats," he said.

But then we heard footsteps.

"Or fucking not," I replied.

Up until that moment, there had been no part of me that was paranoid. I was not at all concerned with getting caught.

But I was a stupid girl.

There, in the foyer, was Toby. He could see Starlight Boy's backpack and clothing. He noticed me with barely any clothing on my body. I stood there with my hands on my hips, but I couldn't ignore the look on Toby's face. It was fair—a look of complete betrayal.

I panicked. And that was when the voice took over, and I got to watch the showdown, silently screaming from behind the glass where she had placed me.

"So the hell what? Like you didn't know? You knew. It's not like you even care about me. You are not my husband. You don't even know who I am. Just leave. Leave us alone!"

"He needs to go," Toby said. I heard a noise behind him and peeked around the corner. It was my mom, who stood there with a stunned look on her face.

"Tell him to come out here and confront me," Toby said. "Then he'll leave. For good."

I went back into the bedroom and saw Starlight Boy sitting on the edge of the bed.

"I can't leave you here," he said. "And all of my stuff is in the other room. I don't know what to do. I don't know what he'll do to you."

"I'm going to get your stuff." My words felt directed, focused, as though I was still a puppet and someone else was tugging my strings. "And then, you'll go out the back door. You don't have to see anyone if you don't want to. When my mom leaves and Toby chills out, I'll call you. Do not leave town. If you still want me, then I'm yours."

"You'll leave with me?"

"Yes," I said. "There's no other choice."

I exited the bedroom again, still in my lingerie and nothing else, and went into the living room to grab Starlight Boy's belongings. But Toby was outraged, and he stopped me.

"You tell him to come out here and face me!" he said. "He owes me that much!"

"He owes you absolutely nothing." I grabbed the backpack and clothing. "Now shut up and give me a minute."

Toby stood there as I returned to the bedroom with Starlight Boy's stuff. I helped him dress as his hands shook. I put on a T-shirt, kissed him, and took his face in my hands.

"I can handle this," I said. "Just stay close. I will call soon. Come on —out the back door."

The back door was always dead-bolted as a safety precaution, but the key was located right above it. However, today, the key was missing.

Toby had known all along. He took the key so that Starlight Boy would have no choice but to confront him. We'd been set up.

I marched back into the living room and threw a string of obscenities at Toby. I told him I wanted a divorce, but first, I wanted that fucking key. I wasn't screwing around. He was a spy and a monster, just like Starlight Boy had said, and if Toby didn't give me the key, I would make sure the entire world knew he was keeping me locked away as a prisoner in my own home.

Judging by the look on his face, Toby had no idea how to respond. He handed me the key. I ran from him, unlocked the back door so Starlight Boy could leave, and locked the door behind him as he sprinted toward his car.

Back in the living room, my mom asked a simple question.

"Is this really what you want? Do you want to leave Toby?"

"Yes. I do."

She left the house as Toby started to cry. I stayed bizarrely still. I had no idea how to react. There was a part of me that ached, that knew everything I had done and was doing was wrong. But there was another part of me that urged me forward. I wasn't Toby's prisoner. I was a new woman. And I could be free.

Toby told me he loved me so much, amnesia and weird actions included. We could work through this with time and therapy. He believed that. He knew the real me would come back. But I said no—it was too late. I had planned to meet Starlight Boy for the night, and then, in the morning after my therapy session, I would make my decision—to stay married or to leave town forever. But tonight was my night, and Toby was not allowed to interfere.

My heart hurt. I felt like a horrible person. But my brain told me to soldier on. So, as Toby watched, I packed two large bags that would hold everything I deemed important—new clothing, my laptop, some photos, my phone, a few books, my makeup, and my medications.

It was a lot to pack, but as I prepared to head out the door, it made sense.

I would not be going home to Toby again.

STARLIGHT BOY MET ME AT A RANDOM LOCATION DOWN THE STREET after I had called for him to come get me. When I climbed into his car, he took my hand. He told me he had checked into a hotel for the night so that we would have a safe place where we could work out our future plans.

But I was paranoid that Toby would go to the bank, take out all the money from the joint checking account I was still able to access, and leave me with nothing but the credit cards in my wallet. And since Starlight Boy was still new to his job, I know he couldn't afford to pay for the both of us to live together. My medications, therapy, and doctor visits set me back about a thousand dollars a month. I slumped against the seat of the car, temporarily defeated.

Starlight Boy told me not to worry. He had everything figured out. While we were out getting food, water, and other things deemed necessary for the evening, we also took a detour by my bank. We walked in together, and as I filled out a withdrawal slip, taking as much from the joint account as the bank would allow, I became dizzy. The day had been difficult, and I sensed, in that moment, that Toby had crashed as well. He was somewhere, sobbing on the floor, and that was my fault. I knew it. As I walked up to the bank teller to get the money, I had a hard time talking. Starlight Boy put his hand on my back and rubbed it. I leaned against him.

"Didn't you once worry about people seeing us out together like this?" I said.

"That was stupid. I should have always been proud of you and shown you how much I love you. But it doesn't matter. I have you now. You belong to me."

Back at the hotel room—a dilapidated mess of yellow wallpaper and stained sheets—I decided to go to the front desk to pay for a second night's stay, just in case. I pulled on my boots and headed out the door.

After I paid for the second night, a man outside the hotel asked me how much I cost. Offended, I told him to fuck off. But then I looked at myself—at the tight orange tank top, the tight black pants, the knee-high boots. I did look cheap. I looked exactly like the type of girl that one could pay for by the hour.

I didn't know this girl at all.

THE NIGHT FLEW BY IN A BLUR OF TEARS AND SOBS. STARLIGHT BOY agreed to accept whatever I decided with my therapist, but I told him that if I decided to stay with Toby, I could only be with Toby. I felt my heart burst as Starlight Boy and I held on to one another, crying in the hotel bed. We slept on and off. We didn't leave each other's arms, not even to shower, just in case that last night was indeed the last.

But despite the flare-up of emotion, there was a practical side to the evening. Even if I decided to stay with Toby, Starlight Boy and I had figured out the logistics, just in case. He would have to come clean to his family. I would need to live with him in a place that had close access to a hospital. And I would have to figure out how to receive my SSDI money in my own name, but if I could get to it, we would have thousands of dollars of back pay to use.

After a night of not letting go, I got dressed the next morning and gave Starlight Boy a gift. It was a bracelet with a stone on it, similar to one he had said he'd bought for me in the Before. He cried and immediately put it on his wrist. No matter what, he said, we were connected. And I would figure that out in therapy.

But during the therapy session with Ron, I made the tough decision. I would go home and work out everything with Toby. I would say goodbye to Starlight Boy and start over. After tonight, he and I would never talk again. For my mental health, and for my safety, Ron said, it was the smart thing to do.

My sobbing as I entered the hotel room immediately alerted Starlight Boy of my decision. I sat on his lap and clutched onto him, desperate to explain that I loved him, but there was no way we could end up together.

"You are so beautiful," he said through his tears. "Please don't leave me."

Despite Ron having told me to cut Starlight Boy out of my life for good, I knew that I couldn't. I told him I would find a way for us to keep in touch, even if I sent an email every now and then. Starlight Boy stared at me and told me that he was terrified Toby would hurt me or have me locked away.

"He's a controlling monster," he said. "You deserve better. I can give you more."

Twenty-nine hours after we had checked in to the hotel, Starlight Boy packed his belongings. My plan was to stay in the hotel room for one more night, just so that I had the time to emotionally wind down. Toby knew about this plan, and he understood my choice. But in the parking lot, standing next to Starlight Boy's car, I buried myself against his jacket and sobbed. He kissed me—my cheeks, my forehead, my lips —over and over again. He told me that he loved me and would always love me.

"If you need me," he said, sobbing, "I will be here. I will come back in an instant for you."

"I know," I said. "I love you."

We released one another, and then Starlight Boy got into his car. He rolled down a window, and I leaned in to kiss him one last time.

"I love you, too," he said. I held up three fingers—my thumb, pointer, and pinky—and kept them raised to the starry night sky as my Starlight Boy drove away. Then, I walked over to the hotel sidewalk, slumped down on the curb, and sobbed uncontrollably.

Goodbye, I thought. No one could ever love me as much as you did —or do.

I called Toby an hour later and asked him to pick me up. I couldn't stay in that hotel room, I thought—it contained memories amnesia wouldn't erase. Luckily, Toby obliged, and when he saw me standing by the open door of the room, he gathered me into his arms. We both cried and promised to make it work, no matter what. We had to find our spark—something we'd lost after my brain injury—and then, we'd be okay. We'd go to therapy and out on special dates. We had been together for seven years, and would be together for the remainder of our lives.

But my heart ached. It was over, I thought. All the horrible things I had done had been burned to ashes, but from that pile of wreckage, I would never be able to rebuild who I was.

As November's warmer temperatures began to give way to a colder, harsher December, I found myself at a random spot in the woods. I had no idea how I had arrived there, but there I was. I was losing track of time and space. I didn't even know that I had been sending emails to Starlight Boy through a secret account, but one afternoon, I opened my computer and found the electronic paper trail. Starlight Boy had told me that he knew me too well to let go. He knew that I loved him, and if he came to get me—would I go with him?

I had, apparently, responded with an enthusiastic yes.

But I had no memory of sending any of those emails.

That night, I sliced through one of my wrists with a razor blade and bled all over the living room carpet. The next night, I took a hammer to my other wrist and then broke a kitchen chair. I didn't recall doing those things, but my wrists and that chair—as well as Toby—told the stories.

I had slipped. This wasn't the life Toby had hoped for. I couldn't be the wife he wanted.

During the first frigid week of December—nearly one month after saying goodbye to Starlight Boy—I disappeared.

Nobody, including me, had known where I was.

But when I came back, I told Toby that my name was Shilo, and that a girl named Ruby had sent me. Petrified I had been injured, or that another form of amnesia had seized my brain, Toby took me to the county hospital, and within hours, they deemed my situation an emergency and transported me back to Brook Lane.

I could not recall that I had been in Brook Lane before. I was no longer myself. Whoever I had been, whoever I had been trying to recover, was gone. I was a complete stranger.

It took a team of doctors a full week to convince Shilo that she was not actually real, but was a manifestation of my brain's desire to help me cope with reality. Apparently, through the meticulous journal entries Shilo kept during that week, she believed herself to be a real person, inhabiting a body that both did and didn't feel like hers. And during my absence, she had poured the contents of an open glow stick into the wounds on my wrist in an effort to "feel better."

When I came to as myself, and realized where I was and what had happened to me, I collapsed in shock. There were journals, pictures, and notes that Shilo had left for me. The handwriting was vastly different from my normal, illegible scrawl. There were three different names listed in that journal, and none of them were mine.

And that was when the doctors told me.

"Children of trauma often create alternate personalities to cope with the things that happened to them. Their brains rely on creativity to survive, so different personalities are brought to life to help deal with the trauma. You needed them, and apparently, you still do. They may be with you for the rest of your life. And in the past, you probably knew they were there in some form. However, the brain injury from your fall and seizures made you forget. But these personalities are coming through to tell you that you're not alone. They're trying to help. That voice you have always claimed to hear? That is one of them."

In 2005, I had been officially diagnosed with Dissociative Identity Disorder—or DID, as it was more commonly known after the change from the previous name, Multiple Personality Disorder. I didn't remember that diagnosis, and I assumed I hadn't told anyone. But that explained the voice. It wasn't just a voice—it was a separate personality living inside me, telling me how to deal with my life.

Now, the diagnosis was confirmed. I wasn't just myself. I was also Ruby, a twenty-eight-year-old model and rock star who knew how to handle the men who had raped and abused her. I was Madeleine, a twenty-three-year-old mother figure who kept the peace and who was, apparently, the good girl. And I was seventeen-year-old Shilo, who came out when I felt sick or weak and needed extra help to get through the day. She was the one who had been sneaking out into the woods at night.

I looked up at the doctors standing by my bedside, and then looked at the journal with the different handwriting. I examined my hands and studied the wounds and scars on my wrists.

And then, I threw up all over the bed.

That night, a voice fueled me—Ruby's, I learned. The one who had been with me since I was three. But she wasn't just a voice. She was her own entity, renting space inside me. And that entity was pissed. She fed me rage and anxiety, so much so that, when I came to as myself, I rushed out of the room and collapsed at the feet of a nighttime orderly. He took my blood pressure and, concerned with the reading, called the psychiatrist. He was ordered to immediately give me Risperdal, but it didn't work. Then he gave me Valium and Seroquel. But those didn't work, either. Not even an intensely high dose of Trazadone could calm me enough for me to go to sleep or lower my blood pressure. I screamed and tore at the flesh on my wrists.

Cliff, my favorite nurse, stared at me. "Who are you? Are you Ruby?"

"No! Fuck you!" I screamed. "I know who I am! Please, just help me. I can't breathe. I don't know what's happening to me. Please don't let me die here." I stumbled and fell into Cliff's arms, and he quickly paged another nurse for help. They carried me into a small, concrete room with a pad on the floor. Cliff pushed a pill into my mouth and helped me attempt to swallow water. When I started to choke, he coaxed me to keep drinking. Water splashed out of my mouth and onto the floor, but eventually, I swallowed the pill. Then, he helped me lie down on the pad, and out of what I assumed to be duty, sat with me, holding my hand.

"This pill is supposed to help you forget things," he said. "Tonight, you're safe. No DID. No past. Just rest. Please rest. You need it."

Thank God. I had been granted a chance to forget, because this time, I did not want to remember.

WHEN I ARRIVED HOME A FEW DAYS LATER, TOBY WENT WITH ME to visit Ron. He told Toby that he believed me to be a gifted actress. DID wasn't a real diagnosis; it was pop psychology, the stuff of movies and soap operas. Even though several doctors had agreed I had the condition, Ron remained unconvinced. Toby told him to fuck off, and through bouts of dissociation—being trapped behind that glass that I thought was just part of my amnesia, that glass that allowed me to watch myself but never interfere—we began to look for a doctor who could help me. But DID wasn't common, and the ability to find the right specialist for it was rare.

In the meantime, however, we prepared for Christmas, trying to maintain some semblance of normalcy. I briefly thought about Starlight Boy—what would he think about this diagnosis? I had to tell him. It would explain so much. I sent him an email, and he replied, grateful to hear from me. We worked out a place to meet—a medical complex only a block away from my house—and I told him that we needed to just sit in his car and talk. He agreed without hesitation.

And that was what we did. I told him about my DID, the most recent hospital stay, and how I couldn't keep track of who I was. My mind was deteriorating, just like my body.

Starlight Boy stared at me and asked if I had ever loved him.

"Tell him what he wants to hear," Ruby said.

"I was the one who loved—loves—you," I replied. "But to be fair, the others in me do, too."

We stepped outside of the car for a few minutes and walked behind the complex. The sun was going down, and I needed to run home before Toby arrived and assumed the worst.

"This is actually goodbye this time, isn't it?" Starlight Boy asked. I nodded and brushed my fingers against his wet cheek. Then, he took my face into his hands and kissed me. It was a kiss I wasn't meant to forget. It was a kiss for me—not for Ruby, or Madeleine, or Shilo.

"Please remember me," I said as he started to walk away. "Remember me as the person I really am." Starlight Boy ran back to me for just a moment, gathered me into his arms, and held me against him. He promised to love me, just as I was. But as the sky turned black, we pulled apart, and we said goodbye. I watched him walk away, and I knew I could not follow him.

He was gone for good now, my Starlight Boy. My shooting star was gone. And I would not give in again. He was now an official part of the past.

JANUARY 1–MAY 25, 2011

Life posed a new challenge now that I knew I had to deal with dissociative amnesia on top of retrograde amnesia. Not only were doctors telling me that I might not regain my full memory, but that the little I could regain would be severely unpleasant. Ruby, Madeleine, and Shilo probably held most of my memories regarding trauma. And that seemed to be true, from the tiny snippets of memory I was able to confirm: Ruby knew about rape and affairs, Shilo knew about being used and being sick, and Madeleine knew about trying to keep the peace so that my body wouldn't be used to lure people into my bed.

This wasn't real, I thought. This diagnosis? It was fake. DID wasn't a real thing—it couldn't be. Everything was stemming from the brain injury, as well as from an odd past. There could only be one form of amnesia, and I'd had that for months now. It had been confirmed. But the notion that there were memories that other parts of my brain could access? Absurd.

I talked to at least six doctors. They all told me that DID, though rare, was real. I was fragmented, split, shattered. I needed to learn to stay in control of myself—the person I was learning to become, for the most part, since waking up on the afternoon of August 24, 2010.

As Toby and I ushered in a quiet new year, greeting 2011 with a kiss and a promise we would put the worst behind us, I began to worry that he wouldn't be able to handle a mentally and physically ill wife. I had been horrible to him—the worst sort of person anyone could be. I stayed up for several nights in a row, panicked, unable to sleep next to the man who claimed to love me.

"I can handle all of this. You know it." The voice—the one I now knew as Ruby—was strong in her convictions. She was steady and secure. She could be my guide.

I allowed her to take over, and I took my spot behind the glass. I could watch, and every now and then, I could step in and act, but I was going to be okay.

Ruby was there now.

TOBY NOTICED THE CHANGE IMMEDIATELY BECAUSE OF ONE horrendously unutterable fact: Ruby hated him. After all, he had forced Starlight Boy out of our lives. But since a pill could not reverse or sedate DID, there wasn't much he could do but wait it out. He still went to work, but nervously so. There were a few occasions that he arrived home to discover Ruby had gone across the street to hook up with random men at the convenience store.

All I could do was watch and pound on the glass separating us. But she wouldn't let me out.

Ruby confessed that one of the reasons I'd never been able to stay pregnant—and why I had been vomiting and rapidly losing weight—was because she drank dish soap and laundry detergent daily. I heard myself scream. It echoed around me but never exited my mouth. I shouldn't have allowed her to take over. She wasn't there to help. She didn't want me around.

And she didn't seem to care that if she killed me, then she would kill herself as well.

AT SOME POINT DURING THE FIRST WEEK IN JANUARY, RUBY WAS still raging, and Toby had no idea how to handle her. If he took me—or her—to the hospital, it would involve explaining DID, and our county hospital had already told us that they didn't treat "complex cases." Other treatment options were too expensive. He had no choice but to wait for her to leave.

There were a few hours, however, when she allowed me to come out. No one was home, but she hated the mundane, and someone had to pay the bills, talk to my parents, and research treatment options. There was an option at a well-known Baltimore hospital that looked promising, but the waiting list for the exclusive trauma unit was long, and it would take months before I would be able to secure a bed. Even when I called to explain the situation, sobbing into the phone that I knew I'd be dead by the end of the month, the intake coordinator said she'd try to expedite my case but couldn't promise anything.

When I checked my email, I saw a message from Starlight Boy. He and Ruby had arranged for him to visit the next day.

I refused to delete the message. Perhaps I had wanted Toby to find it, but something—or someone—within me told me to hold on to it. And I did. To be fair to Starlight Boy, I thought, it would be best for him to come over. Then, once he witnessed how horrible things were, and how easily he would provoke Ruby to come out, he would never want to see me again.

On the day of his arrival, I learned that Ruby didn't always come out because she wanted to but because she could be triggered to. Certain words, phrases, or injustices were upsetting to her, and she would come forth—perhaps to protect me, or perhaps to take revenge upon everyone who stood in her way. She had never physically harmed anyone except me, but it was clear she could do damage. And she made it clear that if she didn't want to come out, she had the capability to push Madeleine or Shilo out in her place, as they were weaker.

I was living in hell and had no way to avoid the flames that scorched my feet.

But Starlight Boy was coming. Despite my dizziness, I focused on my breathing to stay in control. I dressed and readied myself. I would not be triggered. The madness was going to end.

But then he arrived, and the true madness began.

It was impossible for me to keep track of who came out when. It started with me—I hugged Starlight Boy at the door and ushered him inside, asking him if he wanted something to drink. He mentioned how sexy I looked, and I felt Ruby. I heard her voice as she urged me to let her be with him. She loved him, she told me. So that meant I did as well.

As Starlight Boy and I sat on the couch, we held hands. I began to tell him everything about what had been happening to me, but he could not stop commenting on my appearance. He told me how much I turned him on. His words were gorgeous, as though he knew exactly what to say, and when he kissed me, there was a buzzing in my brain. Suddenly, I couldn't hear. I was shut out of my life again and Ruby had come back.

And she was not playing around. She straddled Starlight Boy, rubbed her body against his, and scraped her nails down his arm as he moaned. I knew—somehow, or at least Ruby told me—that I had talked to him about BDSM in the past, but it seemed she had involved him in the practice. The pain she was causing clearly turned him on. He asked for more. She demanded he remove his clothing, and he listened. And there, in the living room, she bent him over the couch and beat him so badly that he bruised and bled. He wanted it—he kept screaming for her to beat him—but all I could see was the blood seeping onto the floor and the sofa.

I came back. He pulled me into his arms and kissed me, and I tried to tell him to wait a moment. But he was too invested by then. He had that right. After all, he'd just been given the experience he wanted.

"I'm glad that you were my real first," he said. "We missed too many other firsts together."

"First what?"

"You're absolutely infertile now, right?" he asked. "Or do I have to wear a condom?"

"Wait, what? I told you I'm infertile? When? And what condom?"

He kissed my neck. I couldn't pretend that it felt awful—it didn't. But I knew it shouldn't be happening. I promised Toby this would never happen again, but Starlight Boy kept kissing me and told me how beautiful I was and...

...Ruby came back. I watched as she undressed, climbed on top of him, and allowed him to slide inside her. Both moaned, and I screamed. I was infuriated—I had loved him first, as my friend and confidante, and she did not have that right. But a bigger part of me was terrified. That wasn't what I wanted. That wasn't me. And he knew about Ruby—I had told him less than a month ago. If he knew about her, then he knew she could come out. But as they moaned and shook and bucked together as Starlight Boy eventually released himself inside her, she laughed. At one point, I swore I heard her tell him no, but there she was, laughing. There was blood on the couch, semen on her fingers, and clothing on the floor. She was the vessel for his pleasure and my pain.

There had once been actual love in my life, I thought, and Ruby had made a mockery of it.

I WAS FULLY COHERENT AT THE END OF STARLIGHT BOY'S VISIT. HE asked for two simple requests before departing—for us to stay in touch, even if he couldn't visit, and for something that struck me as odd.

"Can we dance together? We never have. And I always wanted to."

I told him yes. He picked a song on my computer—a Coheed and Cambria song, as he knew my favorite band and could use that to his advantage—and there, in my living room, we held each other and danced. It was a perfect goodbye song, and I couldn't help it when I began to cry. I was confused and lost. Starlight Boy kept dancing but kissed my tears as we moved.

It was getting late and he had to go. We hugged and kissed and said our goodbyes, and as he departed, I closed the door and turned back to the living room.

It was a mess. What had I done?

But I didn't get to answer that question because Ruby came back, and I watched in horror as she licked the blood that still remained, dark and sticky, on the leather couch.

Toby heard about Starlight Boy's visit from Ruby, who defiantly told him that he couldn't control her. But he convinced her to get into the car, and from there, we went to the trauma unit in Baltimore. There were no rooms available yet, so Ruby was taken to the general psych ward.

But Ruby had no desire to be there. She had already been told by one nurse that DID wasn't "a thing," had been sexually assaulted by a male patient, and watched another patient throw a chair through the window of the nurse's station. She faded away and forced seventeen-year-old Shilo out to deal with it.

According to her journal, Shilo had hid in her room for four straight days. She refused to eat and would only come out for therapy or to see Toby. Her writings were manifestos of illness and fear, and she wanted to go home. But she knew that if she didn't listen to Ruby, Ruby would hurt her body. My body.

Our body. I was told by one of the psychologists to use the term "our," because I shared both a body and a mind with my personalities. But I, as myself, could not do it.

On the fifth day, I returned and entered the psych ward as myself. I had no idea what had happened, as I had been shut out of everything. But Shilo's detailed journal mentioned some older memories that the brain injury had not deleted—a rape in 1996, for example. The night a nurse forced her to take six pills against her will when she had come out of her room, crying, looking for comfort. She had been told that she wasn't a real person and had been ignored. She had wanted to die but didn't want to upset anyone.

A nurse found me and told me I had a phone call. On the line was a doctor from the trauma unit who said that she had a bed in the DID/PTSD ward, and the opening was immediate. I could easily move over there within the hour. The average stay, she told me, was a minimum of twenty-one days, and since I was already in the same hospital complex, it would be best for me to come over. She had already called Toby to explain everything.

But I, as myself, had been gone for weeks. I was in severe pain from a menstrual cycle so horrid that I was throwing up blood, and none of the doctors were willing to give me standard Motrin to dull the pain. And since my psychologist had told me that I could go home since I was back "to normal," I turned down the trauma unit offer and asked if I could return at another time. The doctor said that I would go back on the waiting list but should consider calling sooner rather than later. I wouldn't get better without their help.

Toby cautiously took me home, and he stared at me throughout most of the forty-five-minute drive. I told him that, no matter what I'd done, I was okay. I had a new medication to try to ease my anxiety, which had the chance to quell some of the triggers that caused me to switch. I had been given the name of a psychologist in our city who specialized in trauma-based disorders, and that would be helpful to me. For a person who had just been locked in an abusive psych ward, I was strangely optimistic.

After all, the hospital psychologist had said that I was back "to normal." I didn't believe that we'd ever know what "normal" was again, but I invested my entire future in that convoluted, ridiculous, self-serving word.

MY NEW PSYCHOLOGIST, DR. VEE, WAS WITHIN WALKING DISTANCE of my house. Toby was understandably nervous about my ability to walk there and back without Ruby coming out, but the arrangement was convenient, so he let me go. He had missed so much work as it was; carting me to the doctor would just waste more time.

And this doctor was helpful. I saw her twice a week, and while she wasn't an expert in DID, she was an expert in trauma and had a great desire to hear everything I had been through. She was intrigued by the alternate personalities and, within a few sessions, told me Ruby had played a huge hand in my affair with Starlight Boy. Was I still to blame? Yes, of course. He and I had fallen in love two years prior, according to journals I always brought along during my visits. But all the sexual encounters, when Ruby had trapped me behind the glass and forced me to witness what she wanted to do with him? I couldn't have known. Starlight Boy knew how to coax her to come forward with very specific patterns of words, and Ruby had turned my life into chaos when she took over. All I could do was bear witness. And all of that, Dr. Vee proclaimed, was why Ruby was currently outraged. Her love had been taken away from her, and she had no say in the matter. There was a chance she would never forgive Toby and would always see him as a monster. But if we found a way to convince her that it was best to cooperate, and that she would be allowed another pleasure to focus on, there might be peace.

Ruby stayed quiet for a while, but both Madeleine and Shilo made appearances. Madeleine did chores around the house and hummed as she folded laundry. Shilo showed up at my neurologist's office in a Victorian-style nightgown. My neurologist was confused—she had diagnosed me with a brain injury and amnesia, not DID. She could handle the former concerns but not the latter. She released me from her care with the notion that I had conversion disorder, but nothing "quite like DID."

That was an all-too-common theme in the medical world. I wished I had some way to tell doctors that no actress in the world could fake the amount of hell I had been going through. I hadn't had any major breakthroughs with memories yet, but yes, the personalities somehow knew some things that I didn't.

With retrograde amnesia? Those memories were gone. But dissociative amnesia? We were still looking to discern where the line between the two forms of trauma existed.

FOR A WHILE, THERE WAS PEACE. TOBY AND I RECONNECTED AND decided to host a small party. We hadn't seen our friends recently, and we wanted to do something routine and fun. We invited two other couples over to the house for dinner, drinks, Guitar Hero, and cards, and the gathering went well. I'd just had my hair cut and dyed green and black. I looked exactly like the character Ramona from the movie *Scott Pilgrim vs. The World*, and while the people I knew who didn't understand DID worried that I had formed a new personality, I hadn't. DID didn't work like that. Alters could latch on to figures that struck them as familiar, but no, I did not dye my hair because a new personality had come forward due to a movie. I was trying to find myself.

Before our friends left for the night, we all decided to play a card game called Apples to Apples. The game required you know your players well enough in order to win, and considering I wasn't even four months post-amnesia, I knew I was at a severe disadvantage. But I refused to let on, and we played. I even managed to win one round.

During one hand, I held seven cards that all seemed to connect. The theme was right there, shoved in my infertile face. The words on the cards said, "Toys," "Changing the World," and "Having a Baby." I took a picture of the cards, just in case.

After everyone left, I showed Toby the picture.

It was January 23, 2011. He asked me, almost shyly, if I was ready. He asked me if I was myself. I nodded, and we went back to the bedroom.

And I, as myself, made love to my husband. It wasn't a rushed, painful, furious love like what Starlight Boy and I had had. It was calm and patient. It made my body tingle without making my mind ashamed. It was true that I didn't feel like the beautiful model Starlight Boy always claimed I was, but he had always had a strange way to get me to obey his orders. With Toby, however, I wasn't required to obey. I didn't have the need to put on a show in order to impress or tantalize him. I was simply required to do what made me comfortable. We connected and flourished together, and the world felt infinitely brighter.

That was family, I thought. Finally. That was actual love.

TOBY AND I MADE LOVE EVERY NIGHT FOR A WEEK, BUT MY physical health stopped me by knocking me down with a painful Lupus flare. I couldn't stop passing out, and I was nauseated and dizzy. I had forgotten how painful flares were. Besides that, my head was starting to feel dark again. I could feel Ruby lashing out about the fact I had been with Toby instead of Starlight Boy. She was trying to take something wonderful and resurrect it into a nightmare.

I ignored Ruby as best as I could until one night, on the way home from a doctor's appointment, she came out and tried to take the steering wheel from Toby. Her intention was to drive off the road and kill us. But Toby remained in control, and within minutes, I returned. And we couldn't determine the cause of Ruby's brief visit.

A few days later, on Super Bowl Sunday, I felt particularly ill. I felt my period starting, and the nausea knocked me over in waves. But Toby and I still went to a party at my parents' house. I was dressed in Shilo's Victorian clothing, and that created conflict, both internally among the alters and externally among my family. My parents had tried to support me, but they still didn't seem to believe in the disorder that took away their daughter. I could tell that they were trying to hide from the truth and that, despite the fact I was finally the pretty, thin child they had always wanted, I was an embarrassment. I didn't work, I was sick, and I had just spent four months in and out of hospitals. I had slept with a man who wasn't my husband. I was no one to emulate.

Toby and I left the party early because I felt unwelcomed by the stares and questions. I shouldn't have worn Shilo's clothing, even if it made me feel attractive. Everyone kept asking why I decided to begin dressing that way. In the few photos that were taken, I looked like I was on the verge of crying.

On the way home, I apologized to Toby. "I've messed up your life," I cried. "You didn't sign up for this. Everything that's happened and that's been happening is entirely my fault. I don't know how to say I'm sorry for all of this in some way so that you know I mean it."

"I do know," Toby said. "I know some of the things that have happened were out of your hands. I just wish I had understood sooner."

Inside our home, we cried and held each other all night. Despite the hell, the raging storm, we were going to manage. I wasn't a perfect person and never would be. But I would continue to learn how to control my disorder, no matter what.

But something triggered Shilo, and when she came out, she had a seizure. Her legs—my legs—were paralyzed. She couldn't talk.

There was no reason for this. But we were still managing. Our wayward family of five somehow carried on, because there were no other remaining options.

SHILO'S ARRIVAL, SEIZURE, AND PARALYSIS CAUSED TOBY TO STAY home from work for two days. He and Shilo both tried to determine what had caused the loss of her voice, as well as the trigger for me to switch over to her. Maybe it was stress from being at my parents' house? Maybe it was exhaustion? Perhaps a memory that Shilo had but wouldn't discuss? But she said no, shaking her head silently. Instead, they watched movies, because there was nothing else to do.

On Tuesday, February 8, Shilo and I did something miraculous—we shared consciousness. I couldn't maintain the connection with her, but there were moments where we co-existed. I could hear her, and she could hear me. And when I thanked her silently inside my head, I noticed the feeling in my legs had returned.

But there was a heavy feeling in my stomach, and I knew what it was right away. Ruby had forced Shilo to drink dish soap, and Shilo's desire to share consciousness with me was her way to tell me she had been poisoned.

My voice had yet to return, but I wrote down everything that was happening. Toby looked at me and, puzzled, said I seemed okay—I didn't look ill at all. I didn't throw up, and Shilo didn't return, so we couldn't assume Ruby had made anyone sick.

"I think I know what's happening," Toby said. And without a word, I knew as well. I went to the bathroom, grabbed a pregnancy test from the years and years I had stored them, those little pink boxes lined up that shouted "miracle!" in bright, bold colors. It had been seven and a half years, and we had been without a miracle.

When I exited the bathroom, I held the pregnancy test.

On it were two little pink lines. I was, after all that time, pregnant.

Toby held his hand to his mouth and started to cry. I cried without sound, my voice still lost, and we hugged each other. Yes, the lines were faint, but it was early into the pregnancy. And it was still too soon to fully rejoice. But that was the first time we'd seen a positive test together. Former pregnancies that I had learned about were handled by me, or by Ruby, in secret. But this wasn't a secret. It was a first. We had actual proof that we were going to be parents.

I cleared my throat, and the words came out.

"I'm a mom. I'm going to be someone's mom."

I had never been happier than I was in that moment.

THAT APPLES TO APPLES GAME HAD BEEN STRANGELY PROPHETIC, and Toby and I laughed about the coincidence. We determined I must have gotten pregnant that same night, and therefore, I was only four weeks along. It was still so early. We needed to wait, to see the OBGYN, and then, once I had safely passed the twelve-week mark, I could tell the world.

But we couldn't wait. We had a feeling about this baby. We knew.

I called the OBGYN first, and he ordered two blood tests per week for the first five weeks. That was really all we could do at this stage, he said. We had to hope that this baby, after all those treatments, would stay with us.

He said "baby." I wanted him to say it again. I had a baby. I had a baby growing inside me.

Then we called my parents. I was terrified that they would be pissed off. I knew that I had been unstable, and unstable was a kind way to put it. What if they questioned my ability to be a mother? What if they assumed that the way I had been was how I would always be?

But when I told my mom that I was pregnant, and that she would finally be a grandmother, she screamed in excitement. My dad was nearby, and they both celebrated over the phone with me. The fact that I had their support was almost as good as being pregnant.

Toby's parents were, without hesitation, elated. Their oldest son was to have his first child. After all we'd been through, we'd been granted our miracle. Every doctor had said no, and yet, here we were. And the more happiness that I heard, the more normal I felt. Normal people got pregnant and had kids, I thought. This might be the way for me to be like them.

It was far too soon to share the news with anyone else, but I took a second pregnancy test that read, in bold letters, "pregnant." The word stared at me, clearer than anything. I posted an announcement on Facebook, and the world began to offer hope and kindness.

There was also a long road ahead of us, but finally, the odds had been defied.

I WAS IN THE HOSPITAL FOUR TIMES DURING MY PREGNANCY'S FIRST trimester. I was sick, I bled often, and I was in constant agony. I had to come off many medications, and I went through a withdrawal so painful that I switched personalities at an alarming rate. When I was myself, I could say that it was worth it. If the baby was going to make it, I had to make it. Ruby didn't feel that way, but I sometimes shoved her aside, not fully certain of how I could do that.

I had to be on bedrest, so Toby bought a sleeper sofa. It was time to get rid of that old, bloodstained couch, anyhow. This was the time for new beginnings.

Since my pregnancy was deemed high-risk, I was unable to do much for almost three months. My OBGYN started to tell me things such as, "I wouldn't keep my hopes up. This doesn't look good." His constant negativity and fear caused me to switch personalities and grow hostile, so I found a new OBGYN—right in the same medical complex across the street where my psychologist was located. I met with him, and after he reviewed my file and talked to me about the number of miscarriages I had had in the past, he confirmed the necessity of bedrest. But we were at the nine-week mark, and, he said, he might be able to find a heartbeat. That would definitively determine if the baby was alive.

Dr. Miller, that wonderful new beacon of hope, found my heartbeat

—a racing 110 beats per minute. But then, I heard a sound. It was a horse, galloping across the doppler against me.

"That's your baby's heartbeat," Dr. Miller said. "It's strong. That's a wonderful sign."

My thyroid function was out of control, I was stuck in bed, and I was having panic attacks, but the baby was healthy. All I could do, he said, was rest until the twelve-week mark.

Back at home, my restlessness and sickness caused Shilo to come forward. We shared a conscious space in my head, and there, she told me about an incident that had happened back in 1996—an incident my doctors, friends, and journals were all able to confirm. A man named Thomas had sexually assaulted me on numerous occasions, and during one of those occasions, he told me that if I spoke up, he would kill his wife, my parents, my brother, and then me before putting a gun to his own head and pulling the trigger.

When the flashback faded, I did not return. Instead, a new alter emerged.

"Wanna play cards?" she asked Toby. "I'm really good. You'll never beat me."

Toby had no idea who this alter was. We were not prepared for a fourth. But he indulged her, and, true to her word, she won game after game of Blackjack and Gin Rummy.

"I can count cards," she said. "I see them all in my head, and I know how to beat everyone."

"How old are you?" Toby asked.

"Thirteen," she said. "And you don't know my sister yet! She's only three. She's a baby. Her name is Alex. She uses her hands to talk, not her mouth."

"She speaks in sign language?"

The alter nodded. Toby knew I didn't know sign language whatsoever, with the exception of my name and "I love you."

The alter revealed her name. "I'm Carmen," she said. "And I know everything that Ruby does. You should watch her. And check her emails. That guy—the one she loves so much? He had a big fight with her when she told him to leave her alone. But he keeps sending her messages. And she loves him, but she is so annoyed by him now."

"My guess is that Ruby wasn't the one who told him to stay away," Toby said to Carmen. "This body—the one you're in? There's a baby in there. The baby is going to be born in the fall, so no, we don't want this other guy to interfere." Then he looked through my laptop. Sure enough, there were messages from Starlight Boy. He wanted to see me. He was upset that I chose a baby over him. He even assumed that the baby was his.

"Oh God," Carmen said, rolling her eyes. "He totally sucks at math." She looked at the ceiling and then continued. "There's no way that baby is his. Shilo said she had that bleeding thing in the bad hospital before there was even a baby, so he's kind of stupid. But he loves her."

"Loves who?" Toby asked.

"Ruby. Or this body. Something like that. Hey, did I tell you that I can count cards?"

She was young, and a tattletale, but she was knowledgeable. She had come into our lives at just the right time. But she had no memories before the age she told Toby she was. Everything had been there once, she said, but now, it was all dark. That confirmed the brain injury for certain, and it gave us the line we had been looking for—the dissociative amnesia kicked in around age fourteen, when I had been raped. But my entire childhood was gone.

When I came to, I had a horrendous headache. Toby told me about Carmen and that, somehow, she was a mathematical genius. Then, he told me about Starlight Boy. I checked my messages, and sure enough, he hadn't backed away. I also noticed a strange IP address from his current state of residence, and that the IP address had been checking my email account several times a day.

I'd been hacked.

I took a breath and held myself together for the sake of the baby. My friends and family members told me Starlight Boy was sick, a narcissist, and would try to win me back.

I'd had no desire to believe them. But now, we had proof of his obsession.

I WAS ON AND OFF BEDREST UNTIL THE END OF APRIL. AS I PASSED through the first trimester, Dr. Miller made it a priority to have a maternal fetal medicine team from a well-respected hospital come see me once a week to check on the baby's health. Luckily, the baby flourished. I was hanging in, but the doctors noticed that something was wrong with my kidney function. And I wasn't gaining much weight.

"Your baby is taking resources from you," Dr. Contag, the specialist in charge of my case, told me. "As the baby grows and needs more, you're going to get weaker."

There was a risk that I wouldn't make it through the pregnancy and delivery, and that risk remained unspoken every time I visited Dr. Contag and his team. But there wasn't a way to turn back now, and we didn't want to. We were almost halfway there. The baby was due around October 24, and we'd now seen plenty of images of a little body and head. A doppler I'd purchased for home use picked up on the heartbeat every day. We were so close.

While things remained perfectly unbalanced, Toby and I kept investigating the fact that Starlight Boy had been tracking me. I changed all my passwords, and then, Ruby invaded. She was Hannibal riding over the mountains, aimed at total occupation. While Toby worked, she began to feed me memories of the things she and Starlight Boy had done together. I felt loss and disgust. I hated that she had taken an emotional connection and made it all about conquering me.

"I was the one who pushed Shilo out while having sex with him on the couch," she wrote in a journal. "That last time together? She said no. And he didn't care. He just wanted to fuck you."

I couldn't handle it. I saw blood on the floor, Toby's stunned face when he caught Starlight Boy and me together. I thought there had been love. And there had been, for a while. Ruby hadn't the power to change that, but she was hellbent to make everything about her.

I couldn't be a mother like this. I couldn't go through what she was doing to me.

I told Toby that I was worried about being a mother with DID. I had alters ranging in age from three to twenty-eight, and I had no clue how many others were hiding out. What would happen if I gave birth and never returned—if I was permanently shut out from my own child?

The next day, Toby picked up the phone. Given my circumstances, health, and critical mental state, as well as the terrifyingly vivid flash-backs, would the trauma unit in Baltimore please take me while I still had the chance?

He received a positive response. There would be a bed for me within two weeks. And there, during a bulk of my second trimester, I was going to rid myself of the alters.

Or at least that was the lie I told myself.

MAY 26, 2011–AUGUST 30, 2012

I had a few weeks to prepare for my stay at the prestigious trauma unit, and my family, friends, Toby, and I kept those weeks as occupied as possible. We started to set up the nursery in what had been our guest bedroom. It was a small space, but babies were small things, I figured. But this one already had a ton of stuff—everyone who had been waiting more than seven years for this child had given us an abundance of presents. We were spoiled and grateful.

My best friend Carrie came over to tell me some big news: she was pregnant with her second child, a little girl, who would be born about a month before my baby. We talked about raising our babies together as we hugged and cried. And we compared horror stories.

Toby and I went to our local Starbucks almost daily, because I craved coffee more than any other substance on the planet. We became fast friends with baristas and regulars, and within a week, we were known by name and drink orders. The fact that we found a little community right in the middle of chaos was yet another unexpected, surprising gift.

And then, something strange occurred.

During some lab work at the beginning of my nineteenth week, a beautiful tech inserted the needle into my arm to fill vials. Since there were so many to fill, we chatted, and I told her that I was nervous about becoming a mother. And I hadn't even picked out a name for a girl yet.

"Honey," the tech said, her deep brown eyes shining in a way that enchanted me, "you're having a boy. And he's not gonna just be your boy. He'll be the world's boy. That child will be more than you could ever imagine. You keep that in mind, no matter what happens during the upcoming years."

I couldn't help but to keep her words in mind. They seemed prophetic—a voice of wisdom hidden inside of a tiny, beautiful lab tech with a giant needle in her hand.

In only a few days, Toby and I would be finding out if we were going to have a daughter or son. We didn't care about gender. I just needed to satisfy my curiosity, especially after what the tech had said. But our main goals were that this child would be safe, loved, accepted, and protected from the things I dealt with as a child and teenager. This child had a chance.

The greatest gift we could give our baby was a chance.

○ ○ ○

ON THE NIGHT BEFORE THE ANATOMY SCAN, I WAS UNABLE TO RID myself of every worry in the world. What if the baby had a horrible disease or a cleft palate due to my Valium use? What if the baby would be ill because of my outrageous thyroid problems? I doubted myself; I shouldn't have become pregnant. It had been a risk. Why had I taken it? I called Dr. Contag, who graciously called me back after I left a frantic voice message with his service. My fears, he said, were normal. My circumstances were quite odd, yes, but my fears? Common. I hadn't hidden any disorders, physical or mental, from him. He knew the challenges Toby and I faced. And he reassured me I was not a horrible person for wanting a healthy child.

As usual, I turned to music for solace. I found it in Green Day's album, *American Idiot*. The concept behind the album had been turned into a Broadway musical about a year before, but I hadn't been able to see any of the performances. But, for some reason, I felt a deep connection to the themes behind the songs. There was something there below the surface—something more than just the political viewpoint that so many people used as a rally cry back in 2004 when the album had been released.

And then, it clicked.

The album wasn't just political. It was personal. It was about running away from pain and turning to something else—or into someone else. The main character in the musical, Johnny, takes on a repressed alter ego, whom he calls St. Jimmy. St. Jimmy does the things Johnny didn't do, and lives the wayward, artistic life Johnny wants until Johnny can learn to cope with his own existence again.

The album was shouting at me. "This is dissociation!" it screamed. "Don't you get it?"

I got it.

Toby and I had planned to name our baby James if he was a boy, but now when I stared at my swollen abdomen and felt the steady kicking, timed perfectly to the music, I knew.

"You're my St. Jimmy, aren't you?" I asked. "It's a big burden, but I think you're going to save me."

I was kicked in reply. Repeatedly. The baby never rested, remaining fearless and strong.

TOBY, MY MOM, AND I SAT IN THE LABOR AND DELIVERY WAITING room the next day, attempting to come up with female baby names if, in fact, the scan told us I was having a daughter.

But we were called to a room before we could decide on anything. Dr. Contag and an ultrasound tech were waiting for me.

"This is a big day," Dr. Contag said. "I'll let the tech take all of the images, and then I'll review them and we can talk. But I'm sure everything will be great." He left, and I pulled up my shirt. I was so amazed by my body at that moment. It was holding a life inside it, and it hadn't let go. The eating disorder demons were happy that I could still fit into a size four pair of pants, but I was able to push them aside to marvel at the fact that I was, indeed, growing. And I had to eat. If I didn't, both my life and the baby's life were at risk.

But today, we focused solely on every moment. The tech smiled and placed the wand onto my abdomen.

"Let's see what we have," she said. "The skull looks good. Head size is above average—must be a smart baby." I laughed. "And I don't see any signs of a cleft palate, or even the formation of one. There are no abnormalities. Weight and height at this stage are perfect—the baby is long, but that's not bad. Look at how tall your husband is. Be prepared for that, Mom."

It was so weird to hear that word. Mom? I had never believed it would happen.

"Oh, and it looks like the rest of him is perfect as well. Right on par, or above. Wonderful."

"You have no idea how relieved I am right now," I said.

"Yes," the tech repeated. "The rest of him is perfect. Him. You're having a boy."

Toby, my mom, and I stared at the ultrasound screen for a few moments, and then all three of us started to cry. I rubbed the area where my son kicked me and said, "I knew it. Toby—I knew. We have a son. Hello, James. Hello, my St. Jimmy."

Dr. Contag was pleased and said the tech had been correct—the scans were better than he could have imagined. James was healthy. However, he said, I was pale, anemic, and not gaining much weight. I had to rest and take care of myself, and the doctors in the trauma unit would be receiving a call about how to handle my care. I nodded, and the tech printed out tons of pictures as St. Jimmy showed off for the camera. We headed over to Target to buy clothing and fun gifts, something I had desperately wanted to do before leaving for Baltimore.

Those few weeks before the trauma unit sped by, though, and before I realized it, I was twenty-two weeks pregnant and about to become a resident of a live-in psychiatric facility. I cried the night before, certain I had made the wrong choice, but Toby calmed me. I was doing the right thing. James was healthy, and I needed to be healthy for him. Nothing would happen between the next two months that could jeopardize our baby. I had to be released by my thirtieth week to have twice-a-week scans and to go back on bedrest, so I only had to stick it out for two months. That was it. Not two years. Just two months.

"OK, St. Jimmy," I said to my son. "You be the rebel now. I have to learn to keep the peace."

He kicked me, as always. And the next day, bags packed, Toby and I headed to my new home.

———————

I KNEW THAT, THROUGH COUNTLESS JOURNAL ENTRIES AS WELL AS MY more recent visits, I had stayed in psych wards on and off since the age of eighteen. But going to live in one for months was vastly different. I had my own room, just as I did at Brook Lane, but it was stark. I was allowed to decorate, and visitors were welcomed twice a day. Therapy would be intense, and I was told that, given my history and my pregnancy, I would have to weigh in every morning.

In the long hallways, I passed by several people, all female, ranging in age from twenty to sixty. I felt both old and young at my age of twenty-nine, as well as both scared and fearless. I wouldn't become another crazy patient. Not this time. I couldn't.

On that first night, during intake, nurses searched me for drugs. They had to explore every orifice of my body, even though their touches made me cringe. But I laughed and told them that I didn't do drugs—I was pregnant. They obviously could see that.

"You'd be surprised," a nurse said to me, handing me my underwear. "Alters will smuggle in anything for you if they so desire. We've found drugs taped under breasts. Or hidden in pubic hair. Like I said, you'd be surprised."

More than anything, I was surprised that she was giving me ideas. But I pushed them away.

I was clean, so I was allowed to settle in. As I unpacked, I began to cry. I was allowed an iPod Shuffle and a tiny dock—the cord connected to it no longer than four inches just in case I decided to strangle myself —and so, in the privacy of my room, I turned on Green Day's "St. Jimmy," sang along, and told myself that this stay was for the best.

But it wasn't. I switched constantly and without warning. Everything was a trigger, and I had no way to hide. Because I was pregnant, I couldn't be medicated for night terrors that came about as the alters talked about rape, an experience involving a murder, miscarriages, stillbirth, sleeping with men for money, and forbidden love. Entries were scrawled in my journal that shocked me. I still didn't know my past.

And I couldn't eat. It made me too nervous. There were eighteen other patients in the unit, and eating in front of them, especially while pregnant, did not sit well inside my head. Plus, I couldn't trust the food to be gluten-free. If it contained wheat, I could go into shock and die. I refused until the staff eventually relented and let Toby bring my protein bars over so I could eat at least twice a day, in the privacy of my own room.

The way that patients stared at me was considerably unnerving. I was treated as a Mother Mary figure when I was myself, but when I switched, both patients and doctors had a hard time handling a pregnant girl who said her name was Carmen—a thirteen-year-old card shark.

But I couldn't blame them. I wouldn't want to handle me, either.

My therapist, Dr. White, was a slim, hard woman, and she gave me straight replies. "DID and PTSD are forever," she said. "I can't give you some magic pill to cure you. But if you can learn to become co-conscious with your alters, to let them see what you see so that they don't push you away, that would be a good step. Work with them. And know that you might continue to discover new alters as you learn more about your past. The goal is to keep you in your life, not locked out of it. Not behind that pane of glass you've talked about. You need to know as much as you can, from the incredible to the traumatic. The alters may have helped you, but this is still your life."

"I'm doing this for my son."

"No," Dr. White said. "Do it for yourself. He can't exist without his mother."

Maybe she was right. As time passed and I learned new, slightly odd—but also useful—coping skills, I thought that maybe I'd be okay. I learned how to ground myself—if an alter was going to come out and make a scene, locking me away from my own life, I was to hold a frozen orange to stay in the present moment. The past was simply that: the past. Nothing could hurt me now, especially if I felt the current cold of that orange or saw the vivid color in front of my own eyes. And while it wasn't a cure, it helped.

But I still could not sleep at night. Finally, I was prescribed some Benadryl—just a small, safe dose. And since I was told it was safe, I took the pills that were given to me.

The next morning, James didn't kick me. And on the following day, he didn't kick me.

"You've killed my baby!" I screamed in the common room. "You made me take those pills! I need a hospital. You're murderers!"

Within minutes, a nurse and two staff members rushed me out the back door of the trauma unit to the closest hospital. They called on their way and explained the situation in hushed, panicked tones as I screamed in the backseat.

And all I could do was scream, because somehow, I knew what it meant to not feel an active baby kick in two straight days.

We were so close, I thought. And my selfishness, my illnesses, had ruined everything.

———

"You can breathe," the doctor in Labor and Delivery said to me. "He's alive. But he's very deeply asleep, and his heart rate is low. He's been sedated. What have you been taking?"

"Just Benadryl," I replied. "The doctor said it was okay. It was safe."

"What dosage?"

"I don't know—three of the pink pills?"

"Jesus Christ." The doctor looked at the staff member who had been required to stay in the room with me in case I'd decided to kill myself. "You were giving her seventy-five mgs of Benadryl a night?" Her face grew pale as the doctor continued. "Twenty-five mgs may have been fine. But seventy-five? And with a baby not even in the third trimester? Who decided that this was okay? This is criminal!"

When I was finally allowed to leave the hospital—after several hours, many exams, and hearing my son's heart beat increase to 130 beats per minute—I spent all night on the payphone with Toby. That wasn't allowed, but the nurses were treading lightly. I cried into the phone, and I pleaded my case. Toby was worried, but he agreed and respected my decision.

In the morning, I petitioned a social worker for my release. When she asked on what grounds, I shoved my hospital records from the night before at her. Her eyes grew wide, and within half an hour, everything was in order.

That afternoon, my two-month stay was cut short. Toby came to get me, and we headed back home, prepared to safely greet my soon-to-be third trimester.

THE REAL WORLD WAS TOO LOUD. I NEVER REALIZED HOW SHELTERED I'd been in psych wards until I arrived home after a prolonged stay to face people, dogs that barked nonstop, cars that rushed outside the living room window. I was in sensory overload, and for the first time in several days, I switched. Carmen wanted to play cards and talk about Ruby. Ruby told Toby that she'd always hate him, and even more so now that he wrecked the body with a baby. Alex signed her name with her left hand and cried when Toby tried to approach her. Madeleine allowed us to get through the days by doing laundry and singing lullabies to the baby. And Shilo handled the Lupus flares and medicine changes. DID was awful, but I wasn't alone. I had an army with me.

James was flourishing and growing. I went to the hospital twice a week for scans and labs, and they all were wonderful. He was doing so well, but because of my traumatic past and history of miscarriages, both Dr. Miller and Dr. Contag decided that I needed to have a C-Section. That would involve a needle going into my spine. I started to shake as Ruby said to me, "That's why you have nerve damage in your leg; doctors fucked you up during a spinal tap for MS."

Shilo came out, and she worried that every single person in that room would think ill of her.

But they didn't. The doctors explained that everything would be different this time, and between their calming words and wet wash-cloths, Shilo left.

"I can do it," I said, fully myself again. "I'll do anything for James."

However, there wasn't much I could do about my physical health. My kidneys weren't holding up well, and my Lupus-related lab work was poor. There was no option. The C-Section in mid-October would happen. If the doctors waited, there would be a chance I'd die.

All the plans were in motion. A suite was booked for an October 17, 2011 birth, and I continued to have my twice-weekly scans. I saw my therapist. I helped decorate the nursery. My mom and two friends threw a huge baby shower during my thirty-fourth week, and Toby and I were stunned and grateful by the diapers, clothing, and toys. James will want for nothing, we thought. Nothing material, nothing food-wise, and obviously, he wouldn't long for love. He'd have it, all of it. He already did. He was the most loved unborn baby ever.

A week before the C-Section, I was on my computer in bed and received word that I would be published. Three of my short stories were to be featured in an upcoming anthology. I reviewed the contract and pay rate, signed on the lines, and scanned the documents back to the publisher. Things were in place.

And then, an hour later, I went into labor.

"IT'S TOO SOON, AND YOU AREN'T DILATING," THE ON-CALL OBGYN told me. "Your due date is only six days away. If we performed the C-Section right now and, somehow, one of the doctors or techs was wrong about the due date? Your baby might be premature. You are having contractions every five minutes, but if you can hold out for those six days, it would be best."

"You want me to do *this* for six days? Fuck you!"

In the end, I was sent home. Both Dr. Miller and Dr. Contag agreed—it might be too early. And since I wasn't dilating, I had to stay in bed twenty-four hours a day and breathe through it.

I didn't breathe, because I couldn't. But I sang. I sang with rage, contractions knocking me back against the bed. But singing was all I had as James kicked me, looking for release.

Those six days were a blur, because, despite the agony, October 17 wasn't that far away. And it started off with two wide-eyed, exhausted almost-parents sitting in the living room at six in the morning, waiting to go to L&D at 9:30. We tried to play cards, but I was too distracted. Plus, I wasn't the card player Carmen was, and that bothered me.

Besides, the house cleaner was coming at 8:00 am. The piano tuner was coming at 9:00 am. I needed to shower, to try to look semi-decent for the pictures I knew would be taken, and fight through the contractions. I also had to write checks. And were we packed? Were we ready?

We were. And at 9:20 a.m., my dad came over to the house to stay with the piano tuner so that Toby and I could go to the hospital.

Things were fine until I was taken back for the spinal. Despite the Valium that had been given to me to help me relax, I experienced a major panic attack. I switched briefly, and Shilo came out to cry about the 2009 lumbar puncture. When I arrived back, I screamed in her place.

"You have to calm down," the anesthesiologist told me. "I will not hurt you. I promise. Your son is trying to get out and say hello to the world. You can do this."

"I can't," I sobbed. "Put me under. I want anesthesia. I was told that was an option."

"It would be in some cases, but with your health? It's too risky. We could lose both you and the baby. You can do this." He nodded toward a nurse, who injected something into my IV. As the anesthesiologist proceeded to push a few needles into my spine, I told him I couldn't breathe. The nurse pushed another injection into the IV.

"It's Versed," she said to me. "You'll be okay. Toby can come in very soon."

I couldn't feel anything from my lungs to my toes. Who elected to have a C-Section? I hadn't wanted this. But luckily, before the panic made me pass out, Toby walked in, clad in thin blue scrubs, and Dr. Miller followed him shortly after. It was time.

I asked the anesthesiologist if I could breathe. He told me that if I could just keep talking to him, I could breathe. He'd sit beside me and be my friend. He held my hand, and then I felt a sharp tug, as though a vacuum had been placed inside of me and was cleaning me out.

I screamed, and as the nurse put more Versed into my IV, I heard crying.

My son. James was here.

"I can see him!" Toby said, and he started to cry as he gripped my hand.

"He's here," Dr. Miller said. "And perfect. His vitals are one-hundred percent. You did it."

A nurse brought James over to Toby and me, but I couldn't move my arms. I was growing dizzier by the moment, and I began to choke. But I kissed my son's head and told him that I loved him. Then, I looked over at one of the nurses and whispered, "Something isn't right." My eyelids fluttered as Toby took James into his arms. I looked at my son one more time.

And then, I lost complete consciousness.

I WOKE UP IN SMALL STINTS. DURING ONE OF THE TIMES I WOKE, I saw Toby giving James a tiny, two-ounce bottle of formula. I was shaking and wanted to hold my own child, but I couldn't talk. I passed out again.

Another time, I found myself in an emergency room back in Labor and Delivery, where doctors and nurses were pumping Fentanyl into me and trying to keep me conscious. At one point, I overheard, "We had no choice but to give her high doses of Versed. That's part of this. But it's likely her kidneys, too. She's going to stay hooked to these machines for a while. And if her kidneys don't do well, she'll need dialysis. She probably won't remember much."

And that was a fair statement. I didn't recall the first eight hours of my son's life. When I did eventually wake, fully conscious but in complete agony and shock, we were moved into a birthing suite the size of a huge hotel room. Six people could sleep in there, I thought.

"She's doing okay. Thank God." I don't recall who said those words, but they were said. I would live.

A nurse placed a tiny, blanketed bundle into my arms. "He's so much smaller than we expected," she said. "But he's absolutely perfect. He's so gorgeous. He's the most gorgeous baby I've ever seen. I know I'm supposed to say that, but I mean it this time. Look."

I stared at this miracle baby, this child who wasn't supposed to exist but, somehow, defied every odd placed against us. My little St. Jimmy stared up at me with wise, deep blue eyes. He took calm breaths and didn't cry once. I took his tiny hand and held it in mine, and then, we stared at one another.

That was when the bond hit. Those first eight hours that I'd missed didn't matter, because my son and I had a connection that transcended everything and everyone.

"I love you so completely," I said, kissing his head. "I will not fail you." His eyes remained open, and he never stopped staring at me. I was in love in a way I'd never felt before. And in those moments, the past melted away, allowing for that sublime experience in which a mother's love for her child surpassed everything else.

It was all worth it. He was here. And my life had changed for the better.

———

TOBY TOOK TWO WEEKS OFF FROM WORK TO HELP ME WITH JAMES. After four days in the hospital, I was still shaky, and I'd caught a nasty virus. Coughing against C-Section stitches made me double over in pain, but I still smiled.

Ten days after James was born, I turned thirty. My grandmother, who was ninety-one, visited with me and marveled at "this good baby" as she stroked his head. James was so calm. How, of all people, did I end up with such an even-tempered child? And how had we ended up with a baby at all? He was a miracle.

But Toby had to return to work. Family stopped coming by as often. And that was when the depression hit. No matter how tightly I held onto my son, I could not shake the feeling that I would never be good enough for him.

My therapist told me I was a prime candidate for post-partum depression, but I didn't accept her diagnosis. I was sick and over-whelmed. And I still loved my son: it was amazing to watch him grow, change, laugh, and play.

"But you can still be depressed," Dr. Vee said to me. And I ignored her.

Right before Thanksgiving, my rheumatologist told me that I needed to go back on Methotrexate because of the damage that had been done to my body. By the time James, Toby, and I were celebrating our first Christmas together as a new family, all my hair had fallen out, and most of my days were spent throwing up and sleeping. I knew I was an inadequate mother.

As 2011 turned into 2012, Madeleine gave me a small reprieve. She was there for the new year, and even though I had expressed concerns about switching in front of James, Madeleine didn't bother him. She was far too nurturing for him to know the difference. She gave me the strength to get out of bed, to change and feed James, and to do tasks around the house. I was bald, sick, and shaking, but James thrived as Madeleine pushed me forward. I'd never felt so grateful for DID as I did then—knowing that, somewhere inside of me, I had created a personality with a warmth and strength I myself did not possess.

I fought through the darkness, saw my therapist regularly, saw a wonderful psychiatrist named Dr. Housel, took all my medications, and did everything I was told might help me. I couldn't be selfish: I had a child. And my love for him never faded, even when I switched. In the back of my mind, that love was there.

But we couldn't seem to settle into a routine. Like his mother, James was a child of the night. He would sleep soundly all day, wrapped in someone's arms, but by 9:00 pm, he would be ready to interact with the world. Toby and I tried everything to reverse his sleeping patterns, but nothing helped. Finally, I just accepted things the way they were. In the morning, Toby would bring James into bed with me, as well as a few diapers, wipes, and two pre-mixed bottles. He made sure we were safe and prepared before he left for work. And James and I slept for hours on end. He woke occasionally to eat, but he never cried for food. In his typical, placid nature, I'd find him staring up at me, or occasionally knocking against my arm as though to say, "Oh, hey, I'm hungry, so you might want to help me out here."

He was content. And as I snuggled him, I thought that maybe, just maybe, there was a chance that I wasn't the worst mother in the world after all.

MY THYROID CONDITION, KNOWN AS HASHIMOTO'S THYROIDITIS, was getting worse, and after an ultrasound in March, my endocrinologist told me I had several large nodules on my thyroid. He briefly mentioned a biopsy but decided on a different course of action. My medications were increased as I sat in his office, shivering from the cold and my mostly bald head.

A few weeks later, I tripped and fell into a bookshelf. By some miracle, I didn't hit my head. But my shoulder dislocated, and I was alone with James, screaming for help. I crawled on one arm toward my phone, sobbing in pain. But I heard James start to cry, and so I did the worst thing I could have done—I jammed my shoulder into a doorframe to try to put it back in place.

I became a new mother on chemo wearing a full arm brace and a sling.

I was failing at life after all. And while I felt grateful that Toby came home often to help me, and that my family only lived five minutes from my front door, I tried to avoid help. Why couldn't I do this like everyone else? Twelve other people I knew had had babies in 2011. They all seemed to be doing just fine. What was wrong with me?

"I don't want this, and neither do you," Ruby said. She didn't dare come out while James was awake, but we were co-conscious now, and I could hear her distinct voice and see the world through her eyes. "Don't you miss the days when you were free, when Starlight Boy would come around and we'd just spend all day in bed together? You miss that."

"I don't miss him," I said. "I don't even remember much about him. Just lies."

"I'm going to email him. Maybe he can get us out of this mess."

"No," I said. "No deal. I have amnesia. Isn't that enough? Stay out of my life."

"Oh, honey. You made me who I am. I *am* your life." She laughed and then locked me back out of her choices. But she wasn't able to lock me away from her emotions.

I wasn't aware of what her email to Starlight Boy said, but as the months passed, I began to miss him. I knew he had used me, had lied to me, had manipulated me to get what he wanted, but I missed him. And Ruby fed me good, idyllic memories—napping together under a cool sheet in the spring; long, slow kisses as our legs intertwined; laughter about politics and poetry. She allowed me to see that night under the stars again, cold and in love on our friend Paul's porch. Had my life really been better in 2009, when my biggest conflict had been love?

No. I knew better. James was my priority, and Ruby's idyllic view of my past couldn't change that. I couldn't let her remain in control.

But I also couldn't help but wonder what she recalled that I could not. I hadn't been a saint—far from it. And while Starlight Boy had manipulated me, the deception had run both ways to some degree.

Did he still love me? And if so—did I honestly want to find out?

Despite the new baby, pain, and personalities coming in and out like unwelcome house guests, I decided to direct a shadow cast dedicated to one of my favorite cult films. Within months, our small group had talented, eager cast members, and I played an active role as the lead female—a sickly young girl who spends her life caged up inside her home. The rehearsals were shorter than the after-parties. Fortunately, my parents always watched James on the nights when people streamed into our home to sing loudly before passing out drunk on the living room floor.

But it fell apart when, come early August, people stopped showing up for rehearsals. We had a show booked at a major Steampunk festival, but were down to five cast members. I couldn't even control a small theatre group, and that had been a huge part of my past. That had been my life in my teens and twenties, but now, I couldn't manage it. I claimed illness as our failure and put the company on hiatus. I wasn't getting paid—in fact, I'd spent several thousand dollars to bring the group together—but I hadn't minded. Without being a performer, I had been reduced to a few simple terms: mother, wife, and chronically ill. I needed more.

More was serendipitously offered in the form of a horror convention in Gettysburg, PA, during the last week of August. The creator of the beloved cult film that I had so desperately tried to emulate would be at this convention, along with two other actors from the film. Without hesitation, Toby and I, along with Carrie and her husband, booked a hotel room in the same location as the convention. My parents were more than willing to take James for three days so that I could get away for the first time in years. Carrie and I worked furiously on costumes, my hands cramping as I sewed, but it didn't matter. I saw an out, and I was going to take it.

But I didn't consider one factor: I hadn't been in a car for more than ten minutes since my brain injury. Even five-minute car rides made me panic. How would I make the hour-long trip?

"You'll be fine," Toby said as we loaded the car with our clothing, makeup, and my medications. "James is safe with your parents, and remember what the anesthesiologist said when you gave birth—if you can still talk, you're breathing. We'll just talk. And if you do need a hospital, there's one only three miles from the hotel. In one hour from this moment, we'll be having fun."

"Oh, I plan to have fun," Ruby said. Toby looked at me, and my eyelids fluttered. She'd come out that quickly, and then, without another word, disappeared. We climbed into the car, and as we started the drive, I could feel it: she had plans. But I didn't know what they were.

As we drove up to the crowded hotel in Gettysburg, I was myself, and mostly calm. The building was overflowing with people, but we had pre-registered, so we grabbed our bags and costumes and walked in. We had made the drive in one of our costumes, and people immediately pointed to us and shouted kind words. And suddenly, the little panic that had resided within me lifted. I was with my people.

These people weren't going to hurt me. I was safe. I was accepted. We were all there for fun, theatrics, and a good time. We shared a love of campy horror flicks and industrial music. We were in this together.

And when I looked out of the window of our incredibly large handicapped suite, I felt a true sense of something—as myself, and no one else—that I hadn't felt since the amnesia took hold:

Freedom.

I WAS DRESSED AS THE NAMESAKE OF ONE OF MY MANY ALTERS—IT was obvious how she had chosen her name—but luckily, she stayed inside. She didn't like crowds and wouldn't come out.

Ruby, however, was a different story. And as Toby and I headed into the convention hall, people staring at my somewhat revealing outfit, it took all my strength to hold her back. I sensed that, at some point, she would attempt to make a scene.

That first evening was exceptional. We met the film's actors, and they quickly became friends. My costumes were deemed eerily authentic by the very person who had created the movie. He didn't stop staring at me, even when Toby and I left him to go explore. There were things to buy, new people to meet, and midnight karaoke on the horizon. And even as we waited for Carrie and her husband to arrive, I was still in my element as I propped open the window of our hotel room to watch a fire-breathing show.

I could live like this, I thought. This life could be mine. I needed to fight for this—for more freedom. More time to be myself. That would probably keep me grounded.

At the bar that evening, I drank water while everyone else got wasted. Two of our new actor friends entered the bar, spotted me, and remarked that I was a carbon copy of their creation. I could be on screen, they said. I was flattered, and Ruby pressed me to flirt. I did so, without shame, and before I knew it, one of the actors was so drunk that he asked to sleep in our hotel bathtub. But thankfully, nothing happened. Toby was there, as was Carrie, and they didn't allow things to get out of hand. Still, it was a drunken, entertaining game, leading the wasted actor back to his hotel room.

I woke the next morning with a massive headache—unfair, I cried, since I had been the only one without alcohol—as well as a Lupus flare. My body couldn't have chosen a worse time to betray me. But we had plans, and a long day ahead of us, so I put on my costume and makeup, and we headed down to the convention to promote the film, as well as to hopefully revive the now-dead shadow cast.

The film's creator, stunned by yet another costume, joked about chaining me to the bar that night to have sex with me. I looked like his creation, he whispered. I should live up to her namesake for his benefit.

Ruby screamed in my head. "Fuck this! I thought he would love me, but no. He lied to me!" Feeling the same rage, I said no, disgusted by his behavior. I was there for my friends, and to have fun. I couldn't go back to a life where I was sneaking around, having sex with strangers, living behind a plate of glass put up to keep me away from my traumatic past.

Later that night, as I was in the bathroom to prepare for another night at the bar, I became dizzy. A war inside my head began to consume me.

"There are others out there who want to sleep with you," Ruby said. "Just have fun with them. What's one night? You're keeping *me* caged up like an animal. Fuck that."

"Fuck your rage," I said back to her, the words all internal. I fought all her demands.

"Rage? Oh, there are more of us in here, born from rage. You'll find out."

I was scared by her words, but rage had been a theme in my life. I had been a child born to a raging birth father. I knew enough to know that those others she had mentioned were more than likely his fault.

But I silenced her screaming. And I knew I was an idiot. I had never been who anyone had hoped I would be. DID had ruined that. And dressing like someone else, no matter how fun or sexy, wouldn't help. I'd been jaded by a world that raised me to be jaded.

And it was too late to turn back.

THE BEFORE

1982-August 24, 2010

1982–1989

He comes to me at odd times, in flashes and bursts of need and obligation.

A lot of what I initially know about him is hearsay. He likes pictures of teenagers wearing cheerleading uniforms, the kind of magazine girls who look like they are leaning forward and waving their pom-poms just for him. He is a musician who locks himself in the basement with a case of cheap beer. He hurts my beautiful mother, and he apologizes by ignoring her.

He distributes and engages in drugs and child pornography.

When I am less than a year old, I become a strange target. I am not old enough to be a cute cheerleader; I'm no musician, not yet; I'm not able to do more for him but say simple words like "dada" and "kitty."

"It's so nice to hold my naked daughter against me," he says to my mother. She grabs me from his arms, inspects me, checks for the signs that she doesn't want to see.

She is as smart as she is beautiful, and perhaps she wanted a baby—I know she did, I know that she wanted me, as she had lost others before my arrival—but life would be easier without me in it. I am nothing but a product of her want and his anger. And now, no matter my age, I will bear their desires and angers like tattoos carved into my flesh, heavy-handed, never fully healed. I will always be part him, that dark part that suppresses her.

But still, in her worst hour, she takes us to my Grandmama's house, away from this man who wants too much and steals our bodies and spirits.

This man is my father. Dada.

Even once I'm away from him, enclosed in the master bedroom at my Grandmama's townhouse, I think about him, and when I do, my brain shivers. I hear a voice, and it tries to argue with me. It invades my sleep.

His harm has torn me apart, and I know it.

And I'm not even three years old.

THE BRAIN SHIVERS PERSIST AND GROW AS THE YEARS GO BY. THERE is a voice that emanates from the core of me, but I never open my mouth to hear her. When I do open my mouth, it's to show off—to read editorials from the newspaper, to tell stories that I've concocted, to sing complex lyrics to songs that I've heard on the radio. Music and stories lull me into complacency. They stop me from crying.

But I see things—ghosts, I believe. My mom swears one visits us every so often, and when I wait for the arrival, I'm not sure if I see anything at all. Once, I think I do. But it could have been something else. Or someone else. At night, it's easy to see anything if you believe in it enough to make it real.

My birth father is granted Wednesday night visitations. My mother, wary and vigilant, tells me that someone always watches me and my birth father go out to eat dinner, go to the park, buy a toy. I don't think she's lying to me, but there are times no one is watching. I know no one is.

This man—not a father, really, but a Toy Daddy, a man who comes around every now and then to buy me things and treats me like a doll until it grows dark and he drops me back home—holds me on his lap. I'm scared, trying not to cry when it doesn't feel right as he rubs my back and my thighs.

"You like that," he says. It's not a question. It's a declaration.

I don't move. His hand moves, but I remain still. I try not to squirm, because if I fidget, he'll be angry with me. And if he's angry, he could tell my mother I was bad. Then, he might not buy me a toy. I want him to love me, and when he buys me things, he says he is buying them because he wants to show me how much he loves me. I nod and clutch my new My Little Pony figures.

But it's so different when his hand moves. He does this under tables in McDonald's, in his car, and in those moments when we're somehow alone, with no one watching.

How do I wish him away? How do I turn him into just another story?

MY MOM IS HER OWN BOSS FOR A WHILE, AND THAT MAKES HER A superhero. I'm impressed by the way she tells people what to do without sounding harsh and unpleasant. Men flock to her, and then they compliment me, and I love those days, those mother and daughter times when everyone wants us and gives us the things we desire. But then, she switches careers, and someone else becomes her new boss.

Then that someone else becomes her husband, and my new father. During their casual backyard wedding—my mom shimmering in a simple gown while I, the four-year-old flower girl, the new daughter, scratches at her tights and begs to get out of her dress so that she can roll in the grass and play—a helicopter drowns out the ceremony. Someone has come to watch the wedding from afar. We laugh and wave. Cameras capture us as we smile, frozen in our new lives and new roles. We are all safe. There are people, there is cake, and I have a dad now.

He's a good man, and an honest man, and I could sense that from the day I met him. He doesn't scare me or ask me to do things that my birth father does. And he has his own house. We move away from my Grandmama—even though I know I'll miss her crass sense of humor, the sips of coffee she gives me off a spoon, her generous love, her eyes that change color just like mine—and settle into a real family home. And since I have a new daddy, I can—and want to—call him Daddy, and call my birth father my Toy Daddy. My birth father is unhappy with the moniker, so I try not to talk about my new situation. I am almost five.

I know how to keep secrets.

I don't like to tell people that I have two fathers, because people ask questions. And one of those fathers makes the voice come into my head more often than the other does. The voice also likes to sing, so I quickly learn all the words to every song I hear. One listen is all it takes. I know what happens when I don't pay attention to every detail.

"I'm *singing*," I say to people as I belt out Air Supply's "Making Love Out of Nothing at All." They stare at me, a mixture of surprised, impressed, and concerned.

I want everyone to like me. I want them to like me so much.

I want my Toy Daddy to go away.

PLEASE LET THIS BE A DREAM. THIS IS A DREAM BECAUSE IT HAS TO BE a dream. I tell myself it's a dream, and therefore, none of it matters. The voice inside my head isn't screaming. She doesn't know that this is a dream. She can't tell what is and isn't real.

My birth father and I are in a local bar, only minutes away from my mom and dad. He's drinking and holding me on his lap. Other men look at me and call me beautiful. I don't like the way they say that word. They slur their speech; they pluck at the fabric of my clothing; they tickle me and think it's okay to keep going because I'm laughing so much.

There are drugs here. I know what drugs are, just as much as I know what cigarettes and bottles of beer are. I've been taught these things. I'm supposed to know.

There is also music—loud music. Jukebox music. I don't know all these songs, these twangy and cacophonous tunes, just as I don't know all these men. But my birth father doesn't care. It's his night with me, and he has plans. And I'm not an inconvenience.

I'm here to close the deal.

This must be a dream.

"It's not," the voice says. "But I can handle it. Use me."

Small baggies of cocaine pass between the men, breaking up the thick smoke that permeates the room. They don't weigh or measure it; there is an unspoken trust between them. Cash exchanges hands. One man pulls me onto his lap and asks me to test his batch, just to make sure it is clean. When I say no to the detergent-like powder held in front of me, he scoffs, rubs it into his gums, and pushes me off his lap.

I wander off as my birth father conducts his business. The men get louder and louder. I can see them, as though I am floating outside my body, but I don't understand how or why. Nothing feels real. I'm both there and not there.

But there's still no escaping them. I'm five. I should know that escape is not an option.

Waitresses and patrons stare at me as I approach the jukebox. A random man hands me some change, and I stand on my tiptoes, trying to read through the song selections. I have just enough money to pick three songs. I choose three that seem familiar, and then, knowing I must, I trudge back over to my birth father and his friends.

The mood has changed. Everyone is so happy. They love everything. They love me. I smile, but I don't mean it.

"You gonna sing for us, right?"

I look at the man, some friend of my birth father's, his semi-toothless smile scaring me into silence.

"Sing. Do it now," the voice tells me.

And I do.

The men are amused because I am their puppet. They love that a little girl, barely tall enough to reach the jukebox, can sing along to the music they enjoy. But I'm free from them when I sing. Their hands and words and drugs can't hurt me when I have music.

But we're in a side room, and no one is paying attention. No one watches as more cocaine is cut. No one watches as the men pass me back and forth, from lap to lap, brushing my long brown hair with their rough fingers.

"I have you," the voice says.

I slip into an alternate state when one of the men asks me to lie down on the table.

This is a dream.

I watch my body. I watch everything that happens. I watch myself smile, even though I don't feel like smiling. I can see everything.

There is no cocaine on my body. They don't snort cocaine off my body. People don't do that. People don't gang up on you, snort drugs, touch you, place their fingers inside of...

"Yes. Just stay still," the voice says. Her voice. It's safe and worldly. I'm so glad I have her.

I focus on her and let them have their way. I sing the songs from the jukebox in my head.

My nightmares and screams about the random pain in my body let on that Wednesday nights are the worst nights of the week. But I don't talk. And no one asks.

And therefore, no one knows.

"MY TOES HURT!" I SCREAM INTO THE NIGHT. MY MOM COMES INTO my room and looks at me.

"Growing pains," she says. "If only you'd had more milk when you were little. I'll go get you some cheese. This is normal. There's nothing wrong with you."

There is so much that is wrong with me, but I can't let her know that.

I say my favorite words in my head: Fuck. Shit. Goddamn. I know I can't say them out loud or someone might smack me, but I love to say them in my head. I say them to the neighborhood boys, to Ryan and Matthew and Duke, as we torment the little nerd who lives a few doors away from me.

"Fuck this kid!" I yell as we chase him from yard to yard.

I don't want to hurt him, though. I just love the rush from seeing the terror on his face. And it doesn't matter: we're never able to catch him. He's far too agile.

"Fuck you," I say to my mom in my head. I love her, but I want her to help me.

Everything hurts.

Every fucking thing hurts.

I START TO LAY OUT MY CLOTHING ON THE FLOOR A FEW HOURS before I'm supposed to get up for first grade. If I can run away, no one will bother me. Sometimes, I slip on the clothing and start to head for the door, but then I realize that I haven't packed any food or books, so I go back to bed.

Then, I voluntarily move myself into the basement. There's a little toy closet down there, built under the staircase, and I sleep in a sleeping bag, kept safe by my dinosaur posters and action figures. I don't like dolls. Not yet. I don't like the breasts that I could accidentally touch.

When I begin to watch Alfred Hitchcock movies at three in the morning in the basement, my parents make me sleep upstairs again. I want to tell them that Hitchcock isn't scary. I love his ideas. They make real life tolerable. Things stop hurting when I watch his movies.

But my mom is pregnant with a baby boy, so I listen to her because I desperately want a brother. And on the day we go to tell my Grandmama the big news, we enter the townhouse and see a static-laden television. It plays the emergency broadcast alert. The air is still.

Something is wrong.

My dad goes upstairs, and when he comes down, he quickly ushers me out of the house. But I notice that my mom's face is deathly pale as I'm sent off to a neighbor who gives me cookies, lemonade, and platitudes.

My Grandmama has had a stroke, and since she was on that bathroom floor for several hours without help, she won't recover. She's only in her forties, and she loves me more than anyone. But she's practically braindead. We've lost her to hospitals and nursing homes.

And suddenly, I start to understand death. I understand the permanence of injury, of harm, of slipping away and never coming back.

And with that understanding comes the feeling that I want it. I'm six years old, and I want to die.

MY BIRTH FATHER DOESN'T SHOW UP AS OFTEN FOR HIS WEDNESDAY visits because, as he tells me, "You have a new family now." I shrug. A few weeks later, he takes me to McDonald's for ice cream, and on the way home, tells me that he never wants to see me again. He doesn't need me anymore, and in fact, he doesn't want me, either. He slaps the side of my leg like I'm a racehorse, and I exit his car, running down the hill toward my house.

You are a motherfucker, I think to myself. I hope you die.

I should be relieved, but all I hear are his words, over and over: "I never want to see you again."

I roll those words around in my brain for a few days. The voice tells me to forget him. He's a perverted asshole who loves drugs and porn more than his own kid, she says. I nod and agree.

"Who are you talking to?" my mom asks.

"My stuffed animals." They are my cover. I write poems for them, even though those poems are really for the voice. And I start to keep secret journals, hidden on scraps of paper, for my eyes only. I don't want anyone to know me.

A few days later, I sneak into the kitchen, pull out a pair of scissors, and go upstairs to the bathroom. Quietly, I examine the blades. I think about what they would feel like against my skin.

Then, I take my nearly waist-length brown hair, smooth and soft between the blades of this miraculous instrument, and with a harsh whispering sound, the hair falls around me on the floor. I have never felt so much control, or so free. No one can hold this hair, or tug on this hair, or tell me this hair is pretty. They'll never do that again.

My parents are pissed. And I believe they are equally as pissed when I sneak all my toys outside one Saturday morning and hold a yard sale without their knowledge. I raise more than a hundred dollars, and everything that is childish is now gone. A baby is coming into the house. I'm going to be seven. It's time to put away childish things.

But I do feel remorse when I see the confused looks on my parents' faces. I write a book of poetry for them to try to make up for the hair cutting and the yard sale. I give it to them for their anniversary, and they seem to love it. But my mom is sick, desperately sick from this pregnancy. She's sleeping, or irritated, or stuck in bed. I guess she likes my words, but I'm only used to seeing her in pain now. It's not her fault; I know that. I just don't recognize her the same way any longer. It's like not having parents when my mom is in bed and my dad works late nights.

And this gives me every reason in the world to act as though I don't have parents. The thought of being on my own gives my brain shivers. The voice tells me that living alone would be for the best, anyhow. I want to live alone so badly. Then, I can go to school, find people who understand me, and have a boyfriend. I know that men like me. I can see it on their faces.

I don't want to miss out on having a brother, though, so I choose to stay. But the thought lingers. Leaving as soon as possible is my new childhood goal.

———

THAT CHRISTMAS, MY BROTHER ARRIVES. HE IS TINY AND WRINKLY, the most perfect gift that any of us could ever receive. I love him so deeply that I tell myself that my new goal is to protect him for the rest of my life. I'm scared someone will hurt him. I hold him as often as I'm allowed, and my parents are happy to see me give him his bottles of milk and juice.

"Just like a little Mommy!"

My mom's friends often say this when they see me holding my brother, feeding him and singing to him. Everyone seems so proud. But I don't understand why there is pride in taking care of a baby. Isn't that what a person is supposed to do?

My mom must have done all of this for me when I was a baby. She must have cradled me, sang to me, fed me, made sure I was safe. I'm certain she did.

But we were living with my birth father then.

I won't let anything happen to my brother.
Ever.

I DON'T LIKE THAT MY FRIENDS ARE ALL MY AGE. MY PARENTS SAY
that I'm smart—too smart sometimes, really—and hanging around
with other kids who are seven and eight is boring.

But there are exceptions. Melinda is my best friend, and has been
since we were both four, trudging up snowy hills with our sleds and
matching jackets. Matthew is my crush, and we kiss in secret in
between rounds of Super Mario Brothers at his house. Kissing a boy
like this is funny, and I don't know if I'm any good at it. But he doesn't
seem to mind. And since he doesn't mind, the voice tells me to go on.
This is, she says to me, excellent practice for later.

Adelle is my other best friend, and she knows everything. When
I'm around Adelle, I let the sultry inside voice come out, because
Adelle knows about kissing and sex. I know the basics, of course—my
birth father had seen to that well before my parents could give me any
sort of talk about the subject—but she knows all the fun things that
make more than just my brain shiver.

Adelle and I go roller skating at a rink where my grandfather, Doo-
Da, used to work, and then I attend basketball practice that same
afternoon. I want to be a singer—even the guy who builds our neighbor's deck that summer tells me that he plans to see me on stage one
day after I spend an afternoon singing to him—but I like sports as
well. I'm not particularly worried about getting knocked to the floor,
because I'll just knock everyone back down. Put a microphone or a
basketball in my hand, and I'm in charge. But take away the basement
closet I still like to sleep in, and I can cry for days.

I don't even make sense to myself.

The confusion lingers into that evening, when Adelle and I make
up the sleeper sofa in the basement. After we know my parents are
upstairs in their bedroom, we break out a hidden stash of Oreos, turn
on horror movies, and talk about boys.

"I've had one of them touch my nipple before," Adelle tells me. I lap at the Oreo frosting, eat the cookie, lick my fingers. I try not to think about breasts.

"So what?" I say. "I actually have a boyfriend. He can do whatever he wants."

"Has he touched your boobs yet?"

I don't want to talk about this. Breasts make me think bad things. They make me think about the men at the bar. I hate that I crave someone touching them and making me feel good, but the only people who have touched them have made me feel horrible.

I start singing in my head as Adelle keeps talking. I recite all the words to Billy Joel's "We Didn't Start the Fire." That takes concentration. If I can focus on those words, I'll be fine.

"Oh, here," Adelle says, breaking my concentration. "Let me show you. It's really fun."

"This is stupid," I tell her. "I don't want to."

"Just lay on your back. It's really easy, and then you'll want all the boys to do it. I swear."

I lay back and she lifts my shirt. She gently places one finger on top of my nipple. It tickles, so I giggle, and she tells me to shut up. My face grows serious. I know that tone. I shut up.

Adelle moves her finger around. It still tickles, but there's a warm sensation between my legs, like a fire but without the burn. I like that fire. But I don't like that she's causing it. I keep singing in my head as she plays with my breasts. I don't move under her, because I know that squirming could mean getting hurt. I don't want her to hurt me. I let her touch me.

"Feel this!" Adelle says, and then puts her mouth on mine while she keeps her hand on my breast—on the almost flat area where, soon, real breasts will grow. Her mouth is soft, much softer than her fingers. I kiss her back, because that's what I've been taught to do: comply. But after a minute, I push her off me, because the feeling between my legs has stopped and my heart is beating so quickly I can't breathe.

"Why did you do that to me?" I ask her. "I didn't want you to kiss me."

"You are *so* young," she says, shaking her head. She's only a few months older than I am, but I've been shut down. She's right. I don't know anything.

But I just wanted her to get off me, because I didn't want to think about her in the same way I think about my birth father.

I vow never to get that close to anyone again.

And that night, as she sleeps soundly beside me, I begin to plan my suicide.

1990–1996

Planning a suicide is really easy, I think to myself. All I need to do is make it look like some freaky childhood accident. Kids get hurt all the time.

Inside my head, the wheels turn. I have created inventions in my room vastly more complicated than a suicide and am especially proud of the way I'd rigged some string and coat hangers together so that I could turn off my bedroom light without getting out of bed. Creation isn't a new concept.

Creation leading to destruction, however, is.

Then it clicks. My window is on the second floor, and there is a metal shed beneath it. All I have to do is jump out the window, miss the shed, and land on the ground. I'm eight, almost nine now. That impact will harm me, I guess. If it doesn't kill me, it will at least render me unconscious. And then maybe people will listen to me and take me seriously.

We have an outdoor cat, Lucky, and I love her so much—as much as I love the snakes, fish, mice, and hamsters that come and go from the house. But Lucky becomes part of the set-up. I feel badly that my cat is going to watch me die, but I hope she forgives me for it.

THE EVENING IS WARM, AND THE SUN IS SETTING, LEAVING VIOLET and orange trails behind as it descends behind the trees. I open my window, hear the crickets, and feel the slight breeze. This is the right way to do it, I think. This is how I can die.

"If you're ready, so am I," the voice says. "Let's get the fuck out of here."

I wait to see Lucky, and when I do, I begin to lean out the window. My heart is pounding. I'm sweaty. But it's time.

I lurch forward, and when I do, something causes me to scream. It's not the voice; she wants this as much as I do. But I scream, and I scream loudly enough to attract attention.

My mom rushes into the room as I'm halfway out the window, seconds from falling. She grabs me with a force I've never known and pushes me back inside.

"What happened? What were you doing? You—oh my God."

I'm on the floor, sobbing. She hugs me as the sun sets, and I want her to hold me.

But despite the random scream, I want to die even more. And now, I know I am a failure.

THE NIGHT TERRORS INCREASE AFTER MY SUICIDE ATTEMPT. IN dreams, I fall from everywhere—planes, houses, rooftops, anything that is more than a story high. I wake up, still falling.

"Calm down. Be a good girl. Don't let them know."

My dad puts a wooden plank against my window to keep me safe. I can't fall, but I also can't see outside very well, either. My failure gives my parents reason to believe I could accidentally fall again, and they make sure it won't happen.

But I feel like a prisoner. I take anything nearby—pens, markers, pencils—and write on that wooden plank. I leave messages to myself about being trapped. Logic tells me that they are happy that I'm trapped. I am a good girl to them, yes, but maybe not good *enough*.

"You aren't their child," the voice says. "You're her child, but not his. They have their own baby now. You are not a top priority."

The voice leads me to believe that my parents want nothing to do with me.

If they don't want me, I think, then I will find somebody who does.

I AM TEN, ALMOST ELEVEN, WHEN I FINALLY GET TO MIDDLE school. I love school—it's an escape. I can show off in plays and musicals; I can earn high grades and receive praise for them; I can make friends and ditch them within the same day. My constant, steady friends, Melinda and Danie, make life tolerable. We play softball together and have sleepovers, and when we do, I feel like a kid. I feel as though life is supposed to be about silly crushes and staying up until three in the morning, eating cheese out of a can and weaving friendship bracelets.

When no one is around, I sing at the top of my lungs, trying to drown out the voice. I'm discovering new music, new bands that my parents don't love. I'm becoming a child of the grunge era, with Kurt Cobain and Chris Cornell as my guides and gods. But at home, around my parents, I still sing along to Amy Grant and pop tunes from the eighties. They like that. I couldn't care less, though I am very good at faking to try to make them happy.

I'm dating now, too, even though my parents don't like it. I go from Jeb to Tim to Shawn to the next guy. There is no being alone in my universe—with the exception of being inside my head. But even there, the voice finds me. She always does.

At dinner one night, as I sit next to my beloved grandfather, Doo-Da, I notice that I am bleeding all over myself. Shit, I think. Did I actually cut myself instead of imagining that I did?

"Well, look at you," my mom says, leading me upstairs to the bathroom. "You're not even eleven, and you're menstruating."

I wasn't even shaving my legs yet, but somehow, I was no longer a kid.

She gives me some of the details, but I learn most of it through

Adelle. We aren't as friendly as we once were, but she still tells me things. And I know she tells the truth.

"If you have sex now, a man can put a baby inside of you," she says one afternoon. "You better be careful."

I'd had an orgasm already—reading over a section in Stephen King's *Needful Things*, of all books, but between the thrill of stealing it from my dad's collection and rubbing myself on the floor as the couple kept touching one another, it couldn't be helped. And I liked that feeling. I know how to make myself feel good. I don't need someone else to do anything but love me.

But I don't want to have sex. I just want a guy to come and take me away.

"What do you think a guy's gonna want to do?" Adelle asks. "Just look at you?"

And she's right. How do I get someone to get me out of my house forever, away from people who don't understand me, but not have him do things to me that I don't want?

"It doesn't work like that, little girl," the voice says. "You'll find that out. Keep it up."

I don't know what she wants me to keep up, but despite my awkward, middle-school appearance—this weird stage where I'm not pretty, but not really ugly, either (disregarding the stupid haircuts my parents like me to wear)—I figure it out.

Flirt with everyone until someone old enough takes me home and gets me the hell away from everything the voice tells me to hate.

———

MY MOM AND I FIGHT. A LOT. SHE REINFORCES WHAT MY BIRTH father showed me: I can't trust anyone.

Some days, she praises me. She brings me into her college classes and has me read poetry for her professors, and they claim it is dark and complex for a twelve-year-old girl. I must be special, they tell me, and therefore, that makes my mom special, too. We bask in the glow of special. We flirt with the concept, swirl it around throughout our bodies. I'm a gifted and talented student with perfect grades. I'm a singer, a pianist, and a writer. I play two sports. I have a lot of friends. When my mom tells her professors this, and the other students in the class ask me what it's like to be "different," I don't know what to say.

"You're better than they are, and they know it," the voice says to me. "They secretly hate you for everything you can do. Just smile. They're worthless—all of them."

But I am the one rendered worthless on the days when my mom's praise vanishes and her anger comes out. I provoke it—I'm sure I do—but I don't know how to stop her from slapping me or telling me to shut up. When we both meet with the same piano teacher, and I'm told that I'm a natural pianist while my mom is simply "good," my ego flares. But I have no idea my mom knows about that conversation, and on the ride home from a recital we are both in, she screams at me and kicks me out of the car into the thirty-degree weather.

Well, fuck you, too, I think.

"What's wrong with you?" is my mom's favorite question.

"Yeah," the voice mocks. "What *is* wrong with you?"

And the truth is that I don't know. I feel it—I feel that I am wrong, that I am damaged, that I am useless despite the gifts that are sometimes praised—but I can't verbalize it. How can I write poetry that astonishes adults, but I can't seem to tell anyone what's wrong with me?

One night, I'm sitting at my computer—an old, beat-up thing that is still luckily mine so that I can type poetry and homework assignments, even at three in the morning when my parents think I should be sleeping—and a string of words comes out. When I glance at the clock again, it's almost time for me to get up for school.

Almost four hours go by and I have no memory of them. I look at the words on the screen, pages and pages of everything that is wrong with the world, wrong with my parents, wrong with me, and I feel sick.

I didn't type this.

I delete the document, quietly turn off my computer, and climb into bed. I stare at the wall, waiting for someone to come wake me—or for someone to come tell me how I've become so completely broken.

THE NIGHTMARES ARE VICIOUS—SO MUCH SO THAT MY SCREAMING wakes my parents. When they ask what's wrong, I admit to them that yes, I have nightmares. They make me feel glued to my bed. I see figures standing over me and I feel cold after these visions. My body feels violated and sore. I'm helpless.

For a while, they don't say or do anything but observe. Convinced that they don't care, I rebel. I wear makeup that they tell me to wash off, but then, I put it back on once I'm in school. I wear flannel shirts and boots and chokers—clothing my parents dislike—and when they ask me to change, I refuse.

And I smoke. My friend at the bus stop, Ellen, has an older brother, and he scores smokes for us. Every day while walking home, Ellen and I smoke together. She gives me three to take inside for me to smoke "whenever," and I try to sneak off as much as I can. My parents aren't home in the afternoon, and my brother is in elementary school, so it's not hard to hide behind a tree and light up. The smoke fills me, calms me, makes me feel whole.

"I wonder if we'll get caught," Ellen says to me one afternoon while walking home. "My parents would kill me. I'm only thirteen."

I'm only twelve, I think. And I don't give a shit. So what if they find out? What are they going to do? There's not much left for them to take away besides books and music, and even if those were removed, I'd still find hook-ups. I have good, kind, considerate friends—the type of friends parents dream their children might have—but I also have friends who knew how to score whatever I want and would give it to me for free. And I had good hiding places. I could not have cared less. The voice tells me not to care and where to hide my contraband, and I listen to her.

But despite the smoking, the careless attitude, the frequent orgasms I allow myself to experience when I talk to my male best friend on the phone (he knows; he's proud to be the voice of the fantasies I let roam inside my head), the nightmares persist. And finally, my parents take me to my first therapist.

"What do you dream about?" she asks.

My parents are in the room. I'm dressed in clothing they have chosen—a white shirt with a blue checkered vest and shorts to match.

I look hideous, and feel worse than hideous. I can't tell her what I see: my birth father, children being attacked, strange figures holding me down and experimenting on my body, the voice as an actual person who tries to lure me toward her, her fingernails painted a bright, ruby red. I cannot say anything with my parents in the room.

"Stuff," I say, and cross my arms. "Just—people dying. My grandmother is sick, so, there you go. I don't know what else I'm supposed to tell you. They're nightmares."

I'm told to keep a dream journal, so when I wake up after a nightmare and am able to move again, I should write down the time and the dream. Then, the therapist says, she can look for patterns in my journal and get to the cause of "why I'm like this."

But I make it all up. Before I go to bed at night, I write out two or three entries about death, fire, my teeth falling out, those kinds of things. I can't tell the truth. I write the lies, hide them under my pillow, and wait until the morning, when I can claim that my dreams are breaking me and can produce the evidence of a crack within my system.

There is a crack, yes. But it's not the one I present. The therapist gives up. I smoke, stare at my computer screen, plan different ways to kill myself, and wonder if I'm ever going to feel like a real person—not some fractured, broken monster of a wayward girl.

MY FAMILY GOES TO THE OUTER BANKS QUITE OFTEN. I AM fortunate that my grandmother owns a family beach house only a few steps from the ocean, so at least twice a year, we make the seven-hour drive to the property. When I'm on the beach, standing by the water, my heart doesn't race. The nightmares subside. My poetry is clear and sharp. Something within the sea calls my name, and I make nightly visits to watch the moon shimmer off the ripples in the water.

I feel as though I need to grab my dad's kayak, go out, start paddling, and never come back. And though I find myself close to fulfilling this need one night, I don't follow through. The kayak is too heavy for me to lift by myself. It never happens. But I dream of it. I dream of seeing nothing on all sides of me. I dream of freedom, in a place where I respect the ocean and the ocean, in turn, respects me. I won't think of ways to kill myself. Thoughts of razors and needles and pills wouldn't be necessary, because I'd be on my own. I wouldn't feel burdened by what is expected of me, as well as what I expect from myself. And no one could touch me out there. I could sail, fish, feel the wind in my hair, and sing, and not a soul could stop me. No one could abuse me. And if I got caught in a storm and died in the ocean? That would be okay. That, after all, is where I want to be when I die.

During my eighth-grade year, as one of my teachers takes a great interest in my mother, another of my teachers takes a great interest in me. When I go to the beach during a massive hurricane, he asks a classmate to call me to make sure I'm safe because he is so concerned. He hovers over my shoulder, his chin almost resting against me, and watches as I do projects. At first, this is a joke—my friends and I all laugh about it. He's a perv! What a weirdo! But when he calls me into his classroom at the end of a school day, when no one else is around and my dad is supposed to pick me up, I know what's going to happen.

I go into the lion's den. In my short flannel dress and black boots, I look unstoppable. I fear nothing. I don't fear this man—this man who sat in superglue and tore his hideous khaki pants during a prank a bunch of us pulled. He is nothing to me but a loser.

"Oh, but he is something," the voice says. "Maybe he can free you. Did you ever think about that? Think about why your own mother is so close to your other teacher. They aren't just in the PTA together. Stupid girl. Learn something. If you want out, this man is giving you a way."

I sit upon a desk, cross my legs, and smirk. "What do you want?" I ask. "I'm a perfect student. I get along with everyone. What is it?"

"You," he says and walks over to me. "And I can tell you want me, too."

I let him brush my dark hair away from my face and run his finger down my cheek. It seems innocent enough. But then, as I look into his eyes, I see something that scares me—a hunger, a lust. A need. I've seen this look before, and not in the eyes of the random boys I date in middle school. I've seen this look from men.

I push away and go over to the door. "Don't you fucking touch me again," I say calmly. But I don't feel in control. The voice is helping. Otherwise, I wouldn't know how to act.

"Don't say a word about this," the teacher replies. "You can't."

"Then fucking leave me alone."

I walk out of the room, head held high, but when I get home, I go into the upstairs bathroom, sit on the edge of the bathtub, and cry. He didn't want to save me. He didn't want the real me at all. He just wanted something to fuck.

I'm thirteen and am shaving my legs now. In the bathroom, I have razor blades.

I take my razor from the side of the tub and stare at the metallic blade. I touch it gently. If it can take the hair off my body—can it remove skin?

It's winter. No one will see. So quickly, I hold the blade against my wrist, and I scrape. It hurts a bit, and I wince, but when I look down, I see a faint line of blood. I do it again. Same result—little cat scratches. Nothing major. Nothing life or death. Just a feeling of being alive again. A feeling of power.

"This is how you get power," the voice says. "This is how you get people to stop betraying you."

This is when only two things consume my mind: how to get away from this town to go live on the water, and how to cause myself just enough pain to feel alive.

TOWARD THE END OF MY EIGHTH-GRADE YEAR, I'M SELECTED TO join the advanced chorus group in the high school I'll be attending. This is, to me, a great honor—I want nothing more than to sing my heart out on stage, and I know I'll have more chances in high school than I did in middle school—and I participate in a county-wide music festival.

I take my seat as an alto, despite the fact I have already studied music for years and am a soprano. A girl sits beside me, humming something in a strong, beautiful tone.

"What's that song?" I ask her.

She introduces herself as Carrie. We find out that we both will be attending the same high school and will be in the same music program together. On stage, we stand next to each other, and bizarrely, despite barely knowing each other, we make future plans. We're going to write a musical together. We're going to sing duets that will put everyone to shame.

And I feel like I've found my soulmate. This is a person who understands me and who wants to feel free somehow, too. She doesn't say as much, but I sense a darkness inside her, something that remains as unspoken as mine. And yes, maybe she'll grow up differently—this I know, I can already tell—but our passions and our worries unite us. We will be friends for life.

I leave eighth grade happily, with two new friends—Carrie and a girl I call "Bob"—and the sense that life will only get better. The voice may never shut up, but I'll be wanted now.

Bob and I go to the beach together that summer, and we sit by the water, listening to Green Day and talking about guys. And as we talk, I realize something else that is odd within me: I don't like all the guys my friends like. Everyone thinks Brad Pitt is hot, and I don't. I like funny guys—Jim Carrey, for instance—and within these funny men, I feel as though they do what I do. They act because they don't want to reveal what lies inside of them. Brad Pitt may be multifaceted somehow, I think, but people like Jim Carrey lay it out on the line. I know he is like me. I know his brain is as broken as mine. And I feel the same way about Billie Joe Armstrong, the lead singer of Green Day, despite the fact I know very little about him. The Internet has just come to our town, but we don't have it yet—we're not slated to get it until the fall of my first year of high school. The only way I learn about these men is through magazine articles and by listening to the specific inflections in their voices. There is so much to be learned through the voice. I wonder if people can hear it in mine—if they can hear my stories, too.

Bob and I meet two boys on the beach, and they invite us to sneak out with them late one night. I'm ready to go, but Bob decides against it. She doesn't want to get in trouble. Frustrated by her concern, her need to adhere to rules, I lock myself in the bathroom.

"You lost your chance because you listened to people," the voice tells me. "And you can't trust people. You are more than just common like they are."

I sometimes see red when she speaks. Red flashes and sparks literally blur my vision, and I wonder if, in her wisdom, she's also a harbinger of something unspeakable. But I don't defy her. She's kept me safe with her enigmatic presence.

But Thomas—the husband of a secretary who has been recently hired at my dad's law firm—doesn't allow me to think about the voice at all. Thomas is twenty-four and handsome, and on the first day we meet, I have absolutely no doubt in my mind that this will be the man who will love me for the rest of my life.

———

MY NEW HIGH SCHOOL IS ENORMOUS—FIVE WINGS, TWO THOUSAND people (not including teachers), with a projected graduating class of seven hundred students. At first, I'm intimidated.

"These are *children*," the voice says. "You are not going to let them break you down."

Thomas is around all the time—he and his wife, Jen, have become fast friends with our family—and when I come home with stories about guys I find attractive or how I'll be performing a brief solo in a concert, he always listens. He never demeans a thing I say; in fact, he wants to hear about my life. With the exception of Doo-Da, who warns me that people are not always as they seem, Thomas is my *only* confidante.

I do, however, find solace in Carrie's friendship. We sit across from each other in the chorus room, with our amazing instructor, Bev, usually in between us, but we still talk and pass notes constantly. Along with our dear friend, Phil, we dominate the air with our voices. Hers is a strong, commanding alto; mine is a sultry, rich soprano. When we sing duets from *Les Misérables* together, people stop and stare.

And because I play softball and basketball and am in advanced academic classes, I seem to blend in. The typical high school cliques don't really apply to me. I'm not just a chorus geek, or an athlete, or a nerd. I get a free pass to roam, and that makes high school life infinitely easier.

When basketball season begins in the winter of 1995, Thomas asks my dad if he can be an assistant coach. "I used to play," he says. "I'd love to help, especially on your daughter's team." I'm more than excited when my dad agrees, and so, I see Thomas almost every day. I'm not the greatest player, but I'm fast, and I'm efficient with my moves. Despite a tendon in my ankle that I've screwed up a few times playing softball, I run, and I glide, and I pivot, and I notice that Thomas watches.

One night, we decide to get dinner after practice, and Thomas and I ride in his car together while his wife rides with my parents and brother. "We should discuss some strategies," he says, and it makes sense for me to be with him. As we drive to the restaurant, he puts on Hootie and the Blowfish's "Only Wanna Be With You," and instead of talking, we sing.

"You're so good," he says to me and pats my arm. "I hope you have people telling you that every time you sing."

"They don't," I reply. "But I'm glad you like it."

"I've seen your writing, and heard your singing and piano playing," he says as we pull up in front of the restaurant. "You're going to go very far in this life. Don't let people hold you back. I know that they are. I know what happens when people don't let you live your life. Jen does that to me sometimes—she doesn't allow me to be free. But we've been together since we were fourteen—the age you are now. What can I do?"

I feel awkward. But I understand him. He feels trapped, just as I do. He gets it. We are inexplicably tied together despite an eleven-year age difference.

"You can trust me," he says as we get out of the car. "You can tell me anything. Promise."

"I know I can," I reply. "I'll keep that in mind."

But high school occupies most of my life. I move from one boyfriend to another—Scott, Kevin, John—and realize that these guys aren't mature enough. They want to make out after lunch or take me to winter formals. They don't want to take me away from my life.

I fall in love with a friend of mine named Ian. He's only a year older than I am, but for the first time, I feel something serious toward someone my age. But there's a problem: he doesn't like me. And my fourteen-year-old brain doesn't know what to do with that.

In January of 1996, as I'm on the basketball court, another player slams into me. The referee, however, does not call a foul. I stand there on the court, upset about Ian, watching Thomas stare at me, and hearing the voice.

"Tell them exactly how you feel," she says. "Do it. Quit pretending this shit is okay."

There, in front of my family, friends, and fellow teammates, I let the ref have it. I call him every name I can get away with before he ejects me from the game. And when he does, I storm out of the gym, down the hall, and sink down next to a water fountain.

"I'm not going to cry about this," I say out loud. "This is fucking stupid."

Then I see Thomas. And when he sits beside me and puts his arm around me, I sob against him.

"This isn't about basketball, is it?" he asks, holding me. "It's about something else."

"It's about my life!" I say. "Why is it that I'm not good enough for my family? Or my teammates? Or myself? Why won't the guy I love feel the same way about me?"

Thomas looks at me and brushes the tears off my face. "Oh, I bet he does," he says. "I honestly think he does. He couldn't overlook how talented you are."

"I must not be that talented if he doesn't want me."

"Give it time. Maybe he's waiting to make his move. Or..." Thomas lets his voice trail off as I stare at him.

"Or what?"

"Or you could make your move. You're not a dumb kid. I've seen how you handle yourself. You can always go get what you want. I believe you can have anything you want."

I lean against him and cry for a few more moments.

It scares me to realize that I might be in love with this man.

IAN AND I DON'T GET TOGETHER—HE'S IN LOVE WITH A MUTUAL friend of ours, he tells me in a letter. My heart is devastated, but Doo-Da and I drive around together one day, and while we're belting out jazz—music to soothe my soul, he says—he tells me that he sees potential in me.

"You are not just a beautiful face," my grandfather says. "Don't market yourself that way so that boys or men will like you. You are a very gifted musician. You are an excellent student. You have been the best big sister that your brother could ask for. Those are the things that matter."

"I'm twenty pounds overweight and I'm unhappy," I reply. "I don't know what's wrong with me."

"There's nothing wrong with you," Doo-Da says. "And you're not overweight. You play sports. That body has muscle in it. Stop doubting yourself. I don't doubt you."

But his words, though reassuring, don't stop me from taking the razor blade to various parts of my body. After a piano recital in which I missed a few notes, I curl up on my bed and sob, and then, in the privacy of my bathroom, slice three gashes into my upper thigh where no one will ever see them—three gashes for the three notes I missed in the sonata.

The voice threatens to come out when, one night, my mom presents me with a ring that I'm supposed to wear as a symbol of trust —I'm not to have sex until I'm married. With that ring comes a dinner and several letters. One of those letters is from Thomas.

"I waited until Jen and I were married to have intercourse," he says. "And I'm glad I did. It was a very special moment for both of us."

"But they married at nineteen," I tell my mom. I know more about Thomas than anyone.

"Too young," she replies. And while I don't disagree, there's a lot of hypocrisy in this evening that makes me feel queasy. I can't tell her about my life, past or present. I nod, accept the beautiful emerald ring, and go on my way. But I still feel lonely.

"You're not alone," the voice says. "We know more than we're letting on."

Her use of "we" bothers me tremendously. Besides the fact I'm still hearing this voice—this voice that has guided me since I was basically a toddler—does she mean we as in her and I? Or as in her and someone else? But how could she know anyone if only I can hear her?

I dare not ask those questions. But I forget about it one evening, when my parents are away and my brother and I are home together, playing Sega and cursing at the TV.

I especially don't think about it when Thomas comes through the door and says he is dropping off something for my parents. Then, he sits down on the couch, right beside me, and asks how things are.

My Baltimore Orioles shirt is five years old and ratty. I'm wearing boxers. I look like total crap. And I feel embarrassed. That's how things are, I think. But I say fine, and let him read the newest poem in my collection. He gives it praise, and then, as my brother misses a jump in Sonic the Hedgehog and gets upset over it, Thomas pokes him in the side and makes him laugh.

"Don't do that to him," I say. "That's mean!"

"Okay," Thomas says, smiling. "I'll just do it to you."

And then, he is on top of me, pinning me to the couch, tickling me so hard that I can't breathe. He invites my brother to join in, but he doesn't. He sits there, playing Sega, as Thomas runs his fingers all over my body. I'm bucking from laughter, pushing up against him, trying to twist away as he scrapes his fingernails over my ribs. I'm trapped. He doesn't stop.

When I finally scream out that I'm going to get sick and scare my brother, Thomas gets off me. I look over at him to see that he has a very large erection.

"I have to go," he says, but he's smiling. "Tell your parents I was here. See you at softball!"

Did I want him to do that? I didn't ask him to. I didn't tell him no.

But he wanted to touch me. And that type of new pain both scares and intrigues me.

I tell Carrie and Phil a little of what happened, but they mostly brush it off as innocent. And I do, too. So what? Friends mess around all the time. Thomas knew I was in a bad mood. He was just trying to cheer me up.

I'm an awful, disgusting pig, I think, staring into the mirror that night. I need to lose weight. I need to stop thinking that I saw Thomas with an erection. He's married. He and Jen want to have a baby. What the fuck is wrong with me?

That's the night I stop eating unless I'm in front of my parents or friends. And the voice urges me on as my freshman year comes to an end—as I go to a senior prom with a boyfriend who thinks he's mature because he knows how to "finger a girl," and as I create amazing English projects with my good friend Erin about King Arthur and Shakespeare plays we'd read that semester—the voice is there, and she guides me into the summer, telling me that, by not eating, I am finally, at last, in complete control.

———

THE SUMMER IS CALM, AND IT'S A WELCOME REPRIEVE. I GO TO THE beach a few times. I get my hair cut in a style that I actually find flattering. I work on a musical with Carrie. And I notice that my weight is dropping. Clothing that was tight on me two months ago now hangs off me. And it's so easy, I think. Eat one meal a day, and weigh myself every few hours. That's all it takes.

It doesn't occur to me that this may be problematic.

Thomas visits us often during the summer as well—mostly just to say hi or to bring Jen over for dinner. The dinners are calm and welcoming. The basketball games Thomas and I play in the driveway after eating are not.

"If you lose, you have to go play piano for me for twenty minutes," Thomas says, trying to steal the ball from my hands. "And you can't miss a note or you'll have to start over."

"And if you lose?" I ask.

"Come up with a way to punish me." Thomas winks, steals the ball, and makes the shot.

On August 18, Thomas and Jen come over to jar pickles with my parents. It's a smelly hobby of my dad's, and I keep to myself, mostly watching the tenth anniversary concert of *Les Misérables* on PBS and working on new poems. I'm going into tenth grade in two weeks, and I want to start writing for our literary magazine. I need to up my game.

When the concert ends, I go into the living room to play piano and sing. Thomas comes in, places his hands on my shoulders, and says, "I wish you lived at my house. I'd be able to hear this all the time."

"I can record it for you," I say. I stop playing and look down at my clothing. What is he seeing from his angle? Can he see down this green, V-neck shirt? Can he see that my overalls are hanging off my body? Can he see the skin of my knees or my tanned legs and feet?

"Nah," he replies. "Not the same. Hey, want to go play pool? I'm not really into this pickle-jarring thing."

"Sure," I say. "I haven't played in a while, though."

"You'll be fine."

Thomas and I go into my parent's basement and set up the table. My brother rushes downstairs, wanting to play, and he does. It's a mess of a game—my brother is seven, I have forgotten some of the skills I'd picked up when we first bought the table, and Thomas is clearly able to beat us without issue—but we have fun. Things don't feel awkward. Even when Thomas stands behind me, showing me how to correctly hold the cue, his body pressed up against mine, I'm not bothered. He likes me, and he praises me, and he wants me to do well.

My brother grows bored and wanders upstairs. When he does, I sit on the basement couch, and Thomas sits beside me.

"I really think that I should tell you something," he says.

My heart pounds. "Oh yeah? What's that."

"Here you go," says the voice. "And you knew this was coming."

"Ever since I saw you last year, I thought you were really cute. Pretty. And then I heard you sing and play and noticed your attitude out on the ballfield, and I thought to myself, 'That's a girl who doesn't take no for an answer.' And I know I'm right. I—I really like you."

Thomas almost seems shy with his admission. I try not to feel sick. But he's just telling me how he feels, I tell myself. He isn't doing anything wrong, and he isn't hurting me. He likes me.

He does want to take me away. The thing I had wanted can actually happen now.

But that thought is interrupted when Thomas leans over and kisses my neck.

I pull back. "What the hell?" I say. "What are you doing?"

Thomas puts an arm around me and then, slowly, runs his hand across my breasts. "I don't know yet," he says. "I'm trying to figure it out. But I'm only doing what I know you want."

I don't want this. I want him to take me away, to hold me when I cry, to praise me. I don't want him to kiss me or touch my breasts. I never, in any fantasy I had of him, wanted this.

Thomas reaches into my shirt and begins to fondle me. "Oh God," he says. "Jen never lets me do this. You are amazing."

"What are you doing?" I say. He keeps touching me and moaning, and when he removes his hand to place it on my lap, wiggling his fingers underneath my overalls, I repeat myself. I don't know what else to say.

When he shoves me back on the couch, straddling me, I think about screaming. My parents and his wife are only one floor away. They could come down these steps in three seconds. This could stop. I look up at the ceiling, and Thomas notices.

"Don't you fucking say a word," he says. "If you talk about this..." his voice trails off and, suddenly, he begins to cry. He's on top of me, so I can't move—couldn't move even if I wanted to, which I do, but I feel so paralyzed—but now, something has changed. But he finishes his thought, and that changes everything.

"If you talk about this," he says, glaring at me, "I will kill your brother first. And then your parents. And then Jen, and we're trying to have a baby, so I may end up killing the baby. And then, you're next—after everyone else. And then, since I'll have no one left, I'll kill myself. All that blood will be on your hands. Do you want that?"

I shake my head no.

"Then you can't tell anyone about our love," he says, and as he begins to unsnap my overalls, he slams my head into the arm of the couch.

I black out. I lose time. When I come to, my overalls are

unsnapped, and my body aches. I have a bruise on my thigh and blood on my mouth. Thomas is sitting next to me, crying, and mumbling something about being a "good Christian man."

"What did you do?" I ask. I wipe my mouth clean, fix my clothing, and sit up.

"Where did you go?" he says. "You weren't even paying attention! I told you I loved you!"

"What are we doing?"

"Nothing. Go upstairs. You're fine. Nothing happened."

I want to believe him, but everything on my body tells me otherwise. Still, I run upstairs to the bathroom, clean up, and come right back out. My parents will think I'm being rude if I hide for too long, and I don't want them to die.

It's almost two in the morning. My brother is asleep, and Thomas and Jen are about to pack up to head home. But the plan is to finish the rest of the jarring next weekend, before I start tenth grade. Thomas smiles and winks at me, and says, "More pool next time?"

I nod, and when they leave, I go up to my room. I sit in the middle of my bedroom floor, turn on the radio, and wonder if what I know to be true is, in fact, the truth:

I have been raped.

THE FOLLOWING WEEKEND PLAYS OUT IN THE SAME MANNER. Thomas molests me in my parents' basement, but this time, my brother walks in. I am horrified, coherent about what is happening, but fortunately, I'm able to sit up and smile before he sees anything. We had been wrestling, I say. I'm fourteen and covering up the tracks Thomas is leaving behind. But he'd leaned against me this second time, before he began, and reminded me that he'd kill all of us if I didn't comply. He loves me. I have to cover everything.

I am so good at keeping my mouth shut about the big things. No one even caught on that past week. I did ask Bob if she thought I'd been raped, and she'd said yes—a conversation my mom overheard that prompted her to ask what had happened in the basement—but I brushed it off and only mentioned that Thomas had held me to him while teaching me to play pool. She didn't know. And I didn't tell. I didn't want her to die.

But that next weekend, after Thomas is finished with me in the basement, things get worse. I go into the living room to watch TV, and he sits down on the couch only inches away from me. Our thighs touch. His wife and my parents are in the kitchen, less than fifteen feet away, and he doesn't seem to care.

"What are you doing?" It's the only thing I can say. I want to say no, but I know what will happen if I do.

"It's fine," Thomas says, and he finds a baseball game on TV. "No one cares." He grabs a blanket from the back of the couch and places it on our laps. Then, he takes my hand and shoves it down into his pants.

"My parents," I whisper. "They're right there."

"No one will know," he says, and he rubs my hand up and down against his penis. But when I don't do exactly as he wants, he sighs, and removes my hand. Then, he reaches under the blanket and into the waistband of my panties.

His hand is warm, and as he puts his fingers inside me, I jump.

"Stay still," he says. "You like this."

But I squirm. It hurts, I know my parents will walk in, and I want him out of me. However, he doesn't want to stop. He digs his pinky nail into the side of my inner thigh as a warning, and I feel blood seeping onto my leg. He's cut me. But I don't scream. I let him finger me until he makes a loud noise, and then, he gets up to go to the bathroom.

I go upstairs to check my leg. He's gashed my thigh, and it's still bleeding. It's also bruised from the way he was holding it down. I wash the wound, bandage it, and go back downstairs, my walking stilted from being sore due to his rough fingers.

Thomas doesn't touch me the rest of the evening. He got what he came for. That's what matters, and I know it.

"You're damaged goods now, honey," the voice says. "But you've been that way for a decade."

I start tenth grade two days later, plastering a fake smile on my face for the pictures my parents take that morning. The smile doesn't move. I wear it throughout school and I talk about my amazing summer. When people ask if I hooked up, I just smile.

"You better embrace being fake," the voice says. "I'll help. All those times you've been blacking out? I've been there. I know what Thomas does to you. I can handle him."

I don't care how crazy I am. If the voice can take over? I'm now willing to surrender.

————

IT ENDS, FOR THE MOST PART, ON LABOR DAY.

We're at Thomas and Jen's house, having a cookout. My parents play tennis with them in the community lot; I watch my brother, and I watch Thomas watch me.

When we go back into the house, Jen mentions that she has to switch her laundry from the washer to the dryer. I volunteer, and I go to the basement to complete the chore. But Thomas follows me down. And after I start the dryer, he shoves me up against the basement wall.

Where is the voice? Didn't she say she'd be here?

"What are we doing?" I ask—my standard reply. But Thomas says nothing. He kisses me forcefully and shoves his hands into my shirt. And I stand there, a coward, waiting to be saved.

But before dinner, as I'm in the kitchen grabbing plates to take to the dining room, Thomas walks in. And suddenly, I hear her. I hear the voice. She tells him to back off—she knows everything. But Thomas only smiles and hugs me from behind. He holds me to him, fondles my breasts for a moment, and then starts to sway back and forth, as though lulling me into some form of complacency.

"Smile," the voice says. "Just smile."

I do. I plaster the fake smile on my face.

And my mom walks into the kitchen as Thomas has me pressed against him.

I almost start to cry. She's here to save me, I think. I wasn't wrong. Someone was coming to save me, but I had to wait. She's here!

My mom stares at us for a moment, and then turns and leaves the kitchen.

Thomas only chuckles. "See?" he says. "She doesn't care. She can see our love."

That night, after an awkward dinner, my parents confront me. What had Thomas done? What had I done with him? I looked content, so should they call the police or not?

I want them to call the police. But they didn't watch him cry against me before mentioning that he'd kill all of us if I told the truth. They hadn't been scarred or threatened or slammed against a wall. They hadn't been led to believe that they were special when they weren't.

I say no. It's nothing. Yes, I am upset, but it's nothing. And they let it go.

Or so I think.

A few months pass, and as we enter the Christmas season—I haven't seen Thomas since that day my mom walked in on us—my mom tells me that Thomas is coming over. He has something he wants to say to me, she tells me.

I'm not feeling well—my throat is dry and I have a slight fever—but I don't say anything. I just accept this. And when he arrives, he's in tears. He delivers a half-hearted apology, shuffling his feet on our blue and white kitchen floor, about "the things your mom has seen." He only, deliberately, brings up the indiscretion that my mom witnessed. I mumble my reply: "It's okay." A few minutes later, he leaves, but as he does, he turns and stares at me. I know that stare.

He's going to kill me.

That night, I can't breathe. I can't stop coughing. My fever rises, and the next day, I'm diagnosed with pneumonia. And I don't care. I don't want to move, or think, or be awake. I want to die. I think about dying when I'm lucid. When I'm asleep, I miss out on five days of the world—a chorus concert in which I was supposed to have a solo, a party thrown by some friends to celebrate the holidays, passing Algebra II—but none of those things matter now.

My brother, who is about to turn eight, comes into my bedroom after a week. "My birthday party's tonight," he says to me. "I really, really hope you feel better because I want you there."

And my heart breaks. For the first time since Thomas attacked me, I feel something other than hatred or indifference.

"I'll be there," I say. "I swear I will."

After he leaves the room, I sit up in my sweat-soaked bed. I'm still broken, but the only traces of physical illness are a cough. I can go. I can be there for him.

But as the year ends with my beloved brother's party and a large Christmas celebration, the hatred returns to my heart. My mom walked in on me with Thomas—she saw—and she did nothing? Why? Because I'd been told to smile? Why was Thomas allowed to get away with this?

"Honey, I have it," the voice says. "I told you—you can go away. I'll handle them."

I do as I'm told, and I begin to witness my life the way I want to—detached, uninvolved, a spectator in a horrendous game that I had never, in my entire life, thought I'd have to play.

1997–1998

I can't undo what Thomas did, but at the beginning of 1997, I make plans. I can show off and gain attention in a way that doesn't involve people touching me. If I lose twenty-five pounds, I'll be perfect for any role. I'll be a size zero, not a size six. I know I'll be cast in something.

Not eating often is easy, especially when I look at my very slender friends like Bob. When I tell her I only eat one meal a day—dinner, in front of my parents—she says she is worried, but she doesn't force me to eat with her.

Plus, I don't have much of an appetite these days. Thomas took that away, too. A lot of the things that I thought were amazing about the world seem to be childish. I'd been a fool, but I definitely wasn't one now. And it helps, I think, that the voice knows how to guide me. I can't fail with her protection. If I tell anyone I hear her, I will fail—I know what mental illness is and how it's perceived, and I know I'll be medicated to make her go away. I remain silent.

But I harbor resentment. The resentment grows when my mom tells me what's about to happen one week in February:

"Thomas is coming over to do some work in the upstairs bathroom," she says. "But I'll be home, and you won't be alone with him. Nothing will happen between you two."

Everything has already happened between us. Some of it happened in front of her eyes. What the fuck? Why is he allowed in our house? I'm already angry that Jen still works at my dad's firm, but I understand that she can't be fired for her husband's indiscretions. But to allow Thomas here? My mother truly doesn't care about me. The things she saw are things she denies.

I try to make plans to stay after school that day, but they fall through, and when I arrive home, I stop breathing. His car is in the driveway. He's in my house. He's going to see me.

My mom tells me he's upstairs, finishing up the work she paid him to do. I think about sneaking down to the basement, but I don't want to be alone down there. I don't go into the basement much these days unless I'm with a friend or am throwing a party. I'm safe among thirty people. But by myself? I know better.

I quietly make my way upstairs into my bedroom, but before I can go in, Thomas spots me.

"Well, hi," he says quietly. I examine him. He looks exactly the same—dark hair, bright eyes, thin build—and doesn't look as though he wants to kill me. I nod and head into my room.

"No, please, come here," Thomas says. And it seems as though I have no choice. I feel pushed forward, and I find myself only a few feet away from him.

"What? What can you say to me?"

"Jen is pregnant. I'm going to be a father. So—I'm sorry. About us. I still like you, but I can't be with you. Not now, anyway. I did want that until—you know."

More than anything in the world, I want to run downstairs, grab the phone, and call my dad's office to get in touch with Jen. I want to scream, "Your husband raped me and is still in love with me, and he's going to kill us." But I don't. I can't. I simply nod again and say, "Congrats. Don't be sorry. You don't want to be with a girl like me."

Then I walk into my room, shut the door, and against what my parents normally ask of me, I lock it. I need to be contained. I need to process what I've just heard.

I go into my closet, shut that door, and in the silence, bury my head in my arms and sob.

I REFUSE TO DATE ANYONE UNTIL MAY, WHEN THE GOOD NEWS arrives: I will be in Vocal Ensemble in the fall, which is our high school's most prestigious singing group. It's not common for a fifteen-year-old student to be accepted, but Bev, our chorus director, believes in me.

But I can't tell her that the voice sings for me sometimes. And I start to think: maybe I'm not real. Maybe the voice is real, and I'm just an odd vessel. If so, then it doesn't matter what happens to this body. I can cut it, burn it, and bruise it all I want. I can starve it so that I can see my ribcage. None of that matters if I, as myself, don't exist.

Carrie hosts a large birthday party, and I attend with my new boyfriend, Dave—a guy who'd been a friend of mine, and someone I'd hooked up with at a dance that spring. We sneak into a shed to make out, and it all feels so innocent. This doesn't hurt. It's simple. It involves no thought. Sure, he's not as experienced as I am, but that's what I like about him. He doesn't have the capability to hurt me. We make out, sing and play the guitar for friends, and for just a moment, I feel normal. I think that this is how a fifteen-year-old should feel.

It doesn't work out between us, however. Once I tell Dave about the rape—a huge topic for a sixteen-year-old boy to handle—he says that he doesn't know what to do with that information. So even though we like each other, and we remain good friends, we call off the relationship.

Is *that* how the rest of my life will be, I wonder? If I tell, will people run?

As always, keeping my mouth shut remains the best policy, and as I finish a successful tenth-grade year, I vow never to reveal my secret to anyone.

I WEIGH 115 BY THE SUMMER, BUT NEXT TO MY TALLER FRIENDS LIKE Bob, or my naturally slender friends like Melinda or Christina, I still look huge. I don't know what to do. My breasts have always been large, and they betray my thinner waist. My thighs are muscular from a decade of basketball and softball. I'm never going to win this game.

But I don't know how to quit playing.

That summer, I spend a lot of time with Bo, a member of my vastly large group of friends, and he and I flirt the entire time. Bo is inexperienced, I'm told—he's never had a girlfriend and has never had much of an interest in one. But I'm different, and I know it. I tell him that he'd be lost without me. I tell him that I will make his life perfect.

I go to the Outer Banks with my parents and Bob while Bo deliberates a potential relationship. Bob and I spend our days by the water and our nights on the pier, and we soak up the whistles from the guys who walk by us just as much as we soak up the sun.

A letter arrives at the beach house from Bo. It's long, and the handwriting is hard to read, but after spending two weeks away from me, he knows that he can't use his brain in this decision. He must follow what his heart tells him, and his heart tells him that he likes me. He wants to be with me, and only me, and there is no one else for him.

When I arrive home from the Outer Banks—a few pounds lighter and my hair almost blond from the clay-scented Sun-In I'd dumped in it at the start of the trip—Bo comes over and we hold onto one another. And something about him feels right. He's inexperienced, like Dave. I can run this show, and because of that, he won't hurt me.

"I really don't know how to date," Bo says. "What do we do?"

"Just—this," I say. "Hang out. Kiss. Go to dances and all of that."

"I haven't kissed a girl yet. And I hate that public stuff."

"You won't hate it with me. And we'll be with our group of friends. It's easy."

That night, on my front porch, I show him how to kiss me. It's awkward and fumbling, the way his honest first kiss should be. It's not like the kisses I'd experienced with older men or with other guys who pushed me up against walls to thrust their tongues against my teeth. It's slow and gentle, and it offers a promise: I will not harm you.

There's magic in that summer, as Carrie is dating a guy she loves, and Jim is dating a girl he cares about. The six of us go to a cornfield a few times a week and lay there, watching the stars, talking about the future—and then we go to our separate spots among the stalks to make out. I teach Bo how to touch me, and I touch him in a way he's never experienced.

"How do you know what to do?" he asks, gasping for breath.

I can't tell him. I kiss him, and I let my fingers explore his body.

But I notice that he still stares at other girls—thinner girls, especially those at the somewhat frequent pool parties we attend. My body is fine, he says. I'm not fat. I'm just not—you know.

"I know? I know what?"

But he's so gentle. I can't lose him.

It's easier to distract him. One afternoon, while my parents and brother are away, Bo comes to my house, and I give him a blow job. But as he orgasms, my mouth filling with bitterness, my parents and his dad pull into the driveway.

It's an awkward teenage moment, and I almost laugh at it. What are they going to do? Tell us we can't see each other? Bo starts his senior year of high school on the same day I start my junior year. We'll see each other all the time. I hold in my laughter, afraid to spill the contents of what's in my mouth, as Bo rushes to sit up and zip his pants.

I run to the sink, spit, start laughing, and rinse out my mouth.

"This isn't funny!" he says. "What is wrong with you?"

This is the most innocent thing that could happen to me, I think. What is wrong with *you*?

Bo and I aren't supposed to see each other for a week—my parents are pissed to find us alone in the house—but he sneaks over constantly. I don't care. Their rules are inconsequential.

To keep me occupied one Saturday before school begins, my dad drags me out of the house to run errands. It's 10:00 am, and I don't want to get up, but I throw on a tank top and a pair of shorts and head out the door.

"Where are we going?"

"Hardware store first," he says. "I need to grab some outdoor stuff and some parts for the riding mower."

My heart stops. Thomas works part-time at the hardware store. He has since he moved to our town, just to bring in extra money. And by now, Jen must have had their baby, so they need that income. I haven't asked my dad, because talking about Jen and Thomas is not allowed in the house. And that's fine with me—I know they won't believe anything I say to them as it is.

We arrive at the store—a larger chain which has all but shut down the smaller store we used to frequent when I was a child—and I feel sick. I can feel Thomas in here. I know he's here.

I'm not wrong—he is here. He's right by the lawnmower section. And when he sees us, he freezes. But then, he grins.

And then he tries to kill me.

THERE'S NO WAY HE COULD HAVE PLANNED WHAT HE WAS GOING TO do. But as always, he acts in a way that allows no one to catch on and that makes me look as though I am to blame.

As my dad wanders through the outdoor section, Thomas asks me how I've been. I tell him I'm fine—I'm in the top choral group at high school, I have a decent boyfriend, and my life is fantastic.

"You know that cliché about how living the best life you can is the ultimate revenge?" the voice says. "Well, it's bullshit. He doesn't care."

I know he doesn't care, and as he pushes a ladder up against a display to secure some push mowers, he says, "Your hair is blond now. It looks good."

"Yeah."

"Oh, and in case you didn't know, Jen lost the baby. If you were the one praying for our baby to die, well, you got your wish." Thomas has his back to me, chaining the mowers as he speaks, and I look around. No one could have heard him.

I killed their baby. I had prayed that it wouldn't be born—that any son or daughter born to Thomas would be an easy target. I didn't want that child to suffer. I had sobbed, prayed to every god I could name, and written dark journal entries about how much I didn't want her to have that baby. And she hadn't. She'd miscarried.

"I'm sorry for her," I say. "But not for you."

Thomas turns around, smiles, and lets go of the chain that secures the mowers to the display.

One of them is directly above me, and I have about two seconds to move before impact.

Every survival skill I have kicks in. Every move from my years of sports comes into play. Adrenaline—and the voice—helps me pivot my heel, turn, and throw myself on the ground in the other direction.

The mower misses my body by less than twelve inches.

"Oh!" Thomas says, loud enough for others to hear. "The display!" He climbs down and tries to help me get up.

"Don't you fucking touch me," I mutter. I roll over and sit up. I'm no worse for the wear—just a small scrape on my knee and a bit of pain in my ankle and my elbows—and I know exactly what he tried to do. Did this store use security cameras? If so, I was going to report him.

"Don't you ever talk to me again," he says, and at that point, a customer rushes over to help me up. A moment later, my dad is back, and Thomas says that I tripped while he was putting up the mower display.

Back in the truck, my dad tells me that I shouldn't have stayed there with Thomas. "You claim he harmed you, but you willingly stood there with him? Are you dumb?"

I was trying to avoid murder, I think. And I was trying save your ass. But I'm done. I'm done with all of you. If he follows through, the blood is no longer on my hands. Why do I have to be the fucking adult in this situation?

That night, Bo comes over, and in tears, I hand him a letter. In it, I've written everything Thomas did, and the events of the day. And maybe Bo will run. Maybe he'll think I'm a whore. But whatever happens, he'll know, so that when eleventh grade starts, I'll either have a reliable boyfriend or a clean slate.

Bo holds me to him and says how sorry he is. He didn't know. But he won't let anyone hurt me again. He won't let me out of his sight. I cry against him.

He didn't run.

"I love you," I say to him. He stares at me, unsure at first, and then he replies.

"It's hard for me to say out loud," he replies. "But I love you, too. A lot."

I can't get the thought of what Thomas did that day out of my head. But at least, for now, I'm safe. Someone knows, and while he may not understand, at least he knows how to love me.

Eleventh grade seems easy, minus a particularly difficult Advanced Placement Spanish course I signed up to take. But if I pass the class and take the AP exam, I won't have to take Spanish 101 in college, and I can study in Spain for the summer. And there are two perks to this plan: one, I'll be away from my hometown, and two, Bo is in the same class, so we'll be in Spain together. Nothing can go wrong. Between Spanish, Drama, Shakespeare, and all my music classes, it's a relatively easy year. I can focus on singing and performing, because I know that college applications are due the following fall. I need to prove myself this year.

I try not to think about dying, but during a party I throw at the beginning of the school year, my mom comes outside. "You need to see this!" All of us rush in.

Princess Diana has died in a car accident. She'd been with a man in a car, and someone had caused their car to crash.

The only celebrity death I had ever cried about was Kurt Cobain. I grieved for him for weeks, though I didn't speak about it often. My parents wouldn't have understood why I felt so connected to this grunge-rock god who thought that suicide was the only way out of his life. But with Princess Diana? Everyone could mourn. She was beautiful and kind. She was a universal idol. We all sat there, stunned, not ashamed to let tears stream down our faces.

"You're no princess," the voice says as Bo holds me. "No one's gonna mourn you."

She's right. And as I feel a sadness settle into my bones, I remember that Bo wants me to lose more weight, and that I am worthless—an object, a vessel, something people use for pleasure and then cast aside.

That night, in the bathroom, I examine the inside of my thigh where Thomas had scarred me the year before, when he'd held my leg down to shove his fingers inside me. There's a white, almost circular scar there, and it hasn't faded. It's bright against my tan leg.

I take a pair of fingernail scissors and, delighted by the intense pain, try to cut out the scar.

But no matter how I try, or how hard I bleed, the scar remains. I bandage it, come out of the bathroom, and begin pondering other ways to die.

———

Bo's not a fan of crowds, but he likes to be seen in public with me, so we go to homecoming, football games, and costume parties. I feel safe among tons of people, and safe with Bo at my side. And now that we've been together for a few months, I can see how much he loves me. He writes me letters almost every day, expressing how deep his love is, how he worries when I don't seem to sleep at night, and how he couldn't ask for a more talented, beautiful girlfriend.

But when he writes his college entrance essays, he writes them about me. And normally, this would thrill me, except for the fact that he mentions I'm generally a failure. The thoughts he shares with me in person are tainted with beautiful lies; the way he actually feels is spelled out on the page for the world to read.

And he asks me to edit the content.

"My girlfriend is my inspiration. Sure, she's not the brightest person I know, but when she received a B- on a Spanish test and I received a B, she was there to boost my spirits. She's a natural care-taker, though, and will one day be a good mother."

What in the fuck is this shit? I think to myself. I edit the hell out of it, to prove I'm far brighter than he is when it comes to the English language, and then I berate the living shit out of him when he tells me that he'll be sending these essays to colleges across the country.

"Do you actually have anything nice to say about your stupid girlfriend other than the fact you think I'll 'be a good mother?' How do you know I even want to be a mother?"

"You love everyone. You'd love kids. And I didn't actually say you were stupid."

I don't speak to him for a few days. He is the only person I have shared my secrets with, but I won't take insults. Thomas was good at backhanded compliments. I didn't want to fall for that with Bo. But my sixteenth birthday is approaching, and I don't want to be miserable when it comes time to celebrate, so I forgive him, and he decides to write about something else.

I just wish I meant something more to him than an idea for a college essay.

―――

MY LUCK CHANGES AS I'M CAST IN A MAJOR ROLE IN A MUSICAL. ONE more goal is off my list, and 1997 is nearly over. I'm almost at my target weight, I'm in the best vocal group in school, I went to NYC to see a musical, I'm in a musical, and I'm dating someone who isn't a rapist.

Not bad, all things considered.

One night during a rehearsal, I mess up. I'm sick to my stomach—a virus, I'm sure—but I push through it, and because I push, my voice suffers. The director screams at me and tells me that if I don't get my shit together, I can easily be replaced.

I go home, cry, throw up, and shove a pair of fingernail scissors into my inner thigh. And then I throw up again.

I'm sick for several days, but I'm not replaced. The musical comes and goes, and even though I wanted to feel like a star, I don't feel anything. I've already been tapped to sing a solo for the winter concert, and the praise this musical receives mostly focuses on the pivotal male characters, so I don't care.

But my changing moods scare me. One day I care so much, so deeply. But then the next day? Nothing has any meaning.

"This is nothing," the voice says. "Don't tell anyone. You'll live in an insane asylum."

Some part of me wonders if that would be preferable to my current life, but as always, I stay silent.

Bo goes away for the new year, and I'm disappointed that I still have ten pounds to lose. I know he'll say something. I begin to make better plans.

I weigh slices of lunch meat and give up snacks. I don't drink anything but water. I throw up the meals my parents make, claiming that my stomach is always hurting. The claim isn't a lie—I've had digestive issues since I was a child—but the fact that I'm so good at vomiting silently and then saying it's just a stomachache definitely is. But I don't care. I also smoke more—never in front of Bo, who condemns anything dealing with drugs, tobacco, or alcohol—and that curbs my hunger. I buy cigarettes from Ellen, and even though I don't take the bus home these days, I still see her at school, and we have a secret exchange. It's an easy system.

At night, I cry, and I wait for good things to come. When they don't, I try to make good things happen. I petition for a spring musical but learn that it's going to be a play. I go to New York City to see a musical with some friends, but someone steals the cash out of my purse. I try to get along with my parents, but the voice holds me back, and every encounter is just a fight.

And I can't stop thinking about Thomas. The scar he left on my body remains. The things he did are wedged into my head. The notion that I killed his unborn baby wakes me up at night. I put on head-phones and try to sleep, but sleep eludes me.

So, I give up sleeping, too. I don't need food or sleep. I remain awake until I see the sun, and then Bo and I begin a morning ritual of meeting up at 6:30 am to take a walk together before we have to head home to shower and prepare for school. My parents are less than pleased, but since they think I'm sleeping every night, they don't say much. I know my mom still comes in to see if I'm sleeping sometimes —usually at the same time each night—so I make sure to put down whatever I'm doing, and even if the light is on, I climb into bed and close my eyes. Maybe she knows, but if so, she doesn't say a word.

Maybe she's the person from whom I learned to keep secrets.

And that thought chills me more than anything.

MOST OF MY SENIOR-YEAR FRIENDS ARE GETTING ACCEPTED INTO colleges across the country, and I'm just preparing for the SAT. I feel so behind—I'm only sixteen while they, at eighteen, are thinking about career paths—but my friend Jon stops me one day, sits with me in the school lobby, and tells me not to worry.

"You are one of the smartest people I've ever met," he says. "My sister talks about you all the time since she sees you in the chorus class you help out with. You're going to get there like the rest of us. I promise. I mean, you already teach voice and piano to kids. How cool is that?"

Jon is an actor, much like most of my other friends. The Creatives —those of us in music, band, journalism, and drama—seem to hover around one another, always attending the same parties and hanging out together before and after play rehearsals. And I feel grateful that these are my friends, and that, despite the madness, these friends provide a loving outlet.

Jon is in a play that is about to open, but on opening night, I'm not feeling well, and I miss it. My other friends will be there, so I ask them to tell me about it the next day.

I don't expect a phone call from Bo at 10:00 p.m.

"I don't know why he's calling this late," my mom says, handing me the phone. "But phone cut-off was at nine. Keep it short."

On the other end, Bo is crying. "Jon died on stage," he says to me. "We don't know what happened. Something with his brain. Or his heart. He died immediately. I'm coming over."

Methodically, I pull the sheets back, climb out of bed, go to the bathroom, and go into my parents' room to hand them the cordless phone. "Jon is dead," I say, my voice flat. "Jon died on stage. Bo is coming over."

My mom starts to cry—she's known their family for a while now and is rightfully devastated by the notion of a mother losing her eighteen-year-old child. But for a moment, I'm blank. Jon is dead. Jon is— dead? People my age, people who are very talented, people who are named top of their senior year class, don't just die.

But apparently, they do.

Bo arrives with his dad, and I collapse into Bo's arms. The sobs come.

"I just talked to Jon," I say. "He told me I was smart."

I don't sleep at all that night, and going to school the next morning feels like a dream. How was I supposed to be okay with this? But when I arrive, I am told that Jon's friends are allowed in Bev's chorus room. There, we would learn about what happened to him, and we could talk together.

Fifty or sixty of us sit together on the floor—children lost to the mystery of death—when Bev tells us that Jon had a brain aneurysm.

"That's not common for someone his age," she says, trying to comfort us. "He was there and then—it just happened. I'm so sorry."

I hug Carrie and Bo. I sob when I think about Jon's twin sister.

And then, I'm not there. I can see what's happening, but I'm not in the room. I'm floating above it, over it, watching my body shake with sobs, but not feeling them.

Have I died, too?

I watch myself go to the main office, call my dad, and ask him to take Bo and me home. He agrees, and only when we get back to the house do I resurface as myself.

The funeral a few days later is beautiful, but watching Jon's parents and sister cry feels like a knife in my heart. I've never lost a friend before. And that's hard. But what's it like to lose a brother or a son?

As we exit the church to go to the interment, my mom stops me. "I don't want you to go," she says. "You don't need to see that. The funeral was enough."

In my fury of sadness, I lash out. "My friend is dead! And you don't want me to say goodbye? What is wrong with wanting to see him one last time? What is wrong with you!"

She eventually relents, and as I watch Jon's coffin go into the ground, I wonder what he would want from us. Would he want us to be happy—to keep acting and singing, studying, and go to college? Would he want us to have the families he would never grow up to have?

Would he want me to stop thinking about dying?

I think he would. And as a good friend of Bo's approaches me—a beautiful girl I thought had been trying to steal him away from me—and gathers me into a big hug, she echoes my thoughts. "I know that you've tried to hurt yourself," she cries. "Bo told me about the scars he's seen on you. But please don't. Remember Jon. Okay?"

Well, okay. It's not like I could forget him, anyhow.

MY JUNIOR YEAR, AND BO'S SENIOR YEAR, ENDS ON A SURPRISINGLY high note. I am the first to perform a solo at a brand new outdoor performance space and am granted high praise. My solo in Vocal Ensemble goes over so well that Bev asks me to be her Assistant Director in the fall and to use my senior status to help freshman and sophomores navigate the new world of high school music. I'm asked to perform in All-County Chorus, and I have an audition to win Maryland Distinguished Scholar in Vocal Music. My senior-year classes will all be music and English related, I'm going to Spain—without Bo, but still, I'm going to Spain—for part of the summer, and six of us rent a limo, buy the appropriate luxury wear, and go to the Senior Prom. Bo tells me that he can see us being married as we attend the after-party, and I agree.

Jon's death brings about an odd peace. Everyone is getting along. Good things are happening. And for the first time in a while, I wonder if there is a Heaven. It certainly feels as though Jon is watching over us, making sure that we get to do the things he never will.

And then, I leave for Spain.

The first two days of the trip—with only four adults trying to keep an eye on sixteen teenagers—are spent on airport floors. We get delayed by storms in Baltimore, but once up in the air, I take a few Xanax—my doctor tells me it's okay, everyone feels a little anxious sometimes—and puff on my inhaler due to the bronchitis I contracted right before the trip. The sky is cotton candy pink as the storm clears and the sun finally starts to rise. I could stay in the air for hours, I think. But then, we land at Heathrow before catching a hopper to Madrid, and we are, once again, grounded. We sleep on the floor, create puppets out of socks the airline gives us, and try to find food without getting lost. Heathrow is a city. We see nothing of London, but we see the entirety of that massive airport.

When we finally land in Madrid, I cry. Something about Spain feels like home to me. Erin, who is my roommate during the trip, sleeps soundly at night while I sneak out of the hotel room, go outside onto the hotel porch, and sob. I'm not even close to home—I'm oceans away—and yet, I *am* home. I want to get lost here. I want Bo to come here and live with me, because there is so much life. There is so much beauty. Walking the square at night, being handed roses and serenaded with beautiful Spanish songs, bartering in markets, drinking nothing but Fanta Limon and wine—how could anyone want a life that is different from this one?

"Don't go home," the voice says. "Get lost. They won't stick around for you."

It seems like a plausible notion, but two things stand in the way. One, we spend a night in Morocco, and I am slammed against a wall and groped by two men who find me to be an easy target. I feel as though it's my fault—we were told to cover up, and due to the heat, I'm wearing a sleeveless shirt with my long skirt—and I say nothing. I want to go back to Spain, where beauty was praised and no one kicked a dead bird around in the street as a makeshift soccer ball. And two, a student in our group loses his passport, which causes a major crisis. The crisis is not resolved by the time the group returns to the United States, and so, one of the teachers stays with this poor kid—and they desperately want to go home.

But as I sing on a radio station as part of a karaoke contest in Malaga, drop to my knees at the beauty of the Cathedral in Toledo, and stand on a cliff in Portugal, singing to the ocean, I know in my heart that I *am* home. Everyone else is eager to return to their families and loved ones, and with the exception of Bo, I see no reason to rush. I speak fluent Spanish and am making my way just fine.

When the last day arrives, I sob in the bathroom. What am I returning to? My senior year should be good, sure, but I won't be returning to peace. I won't stand by the water and sing. I won't have a reprieve from the voice, who has been mostly quiet during this amazing experience. I'll have the mundane. And I don't feel as though I am meant for the mundane.

Back at home, I have a hard time adjusting. I don't eat. I smoke, and I throw up.

"Spoiled," the voice says. "You're fucking spoiled."

"You know what? I am sick of whatever this bullshit is," I say out loud. "This ends now."

"I can end it right now," she says. "Say the word."

"End it."

And then I'm floating again, disconnected from my body and watching as every single thing in my life occurs without me saying a word.

SENIOR YEAR BEGINS WITH A LOT OF WONDERFUL THINGS, AND WHILE I'm witnessing them—shut out, not actively participating due to the voice —I'm at least able to take part. I win multiple music scholarships. I apply to six colleges, having toured most of them once I had returned home from Spain. Two colleges invite me to enroll early if accepted. One is three hours away, but the other is close to Bo. If I'm accepted, the choice is obvious.

"Don't choose a school based on a guy," Bev says to me. "Choose it based on your talents."

I consider the notion, but I'm not in control. The voice is. She says okay, but winks.

With Bo so far away, the voice commands that I flirt with every available guy. And I do. But it's mean and unrelenting. She urges me to flirt with guys that are too young, too dorky, too out of character. When a boy in my journalism class asks for me to meet him after school in the stairwell, I do, and he requests to stick his hand down my shirt. I let him and unhook my bra.

"Is that what you wanted to see? Well, there you go. Now, go and die happy."

I'm finally a size two, and even my mom has praised me for how thin I've become. Everyone has noticed that I'm not just athletic looking—last year and this year, I've become beautiful. People say it all the time. And if my mom says it, I know it must be true. I don't care what I do or show. My body isn't in my control, anyhow. It's in the hands of the voice.

The voice draws the attention of our new drama director, a guy who tried to make it on Broadway but failed. He asks me to spend time with him in his classroom, and I do, and I accept the fact that he's going to touch me. I don't even question it. I know it's wrong, but he keeps praising my voice. He says he'll write letters to every college I want to attend to help me get a good music scholarship. If he's willing to offer me something, I can stay quiet.

I do. After all, I've learned that there really is no other choice.

OUR CHORUS CLASS TAKES A FALL TRIP TO NYC TO SEE *JEKYLL AND Hyde*, and for a day, the voice lets me out. I sit on the bus with Carrie and Allen, and we sing all the songs.

We also talk about the upcoming musical that the new drama director will be taking over. There's one female lead, and it's a big one, and two large male leads as well. I am determined to get that lead, but I want Carrie to get it, too. Before the musical starts, I find Bev in the theatre and, since she's the music director, ask her if the lead role can be split into two parts.

"That's the plan," she says. "It's a big role. Two seniors will fill it. My guess is that you'll be picked without question. I hope Carrie is, too. But that's not entirely my call."

I report back to my friends, and we gossip about casting until *Jekyll and Hyde* opens.

And the musical is my life. Here is a man, lost in the darkness, trying to find a way to cure madness. But by trying to cure madness, he drives himself mad. He can be two people—the selfless, loving Dr. Jekyll, or the carefree, vigilante-justice-ridden Mr. Hyde. Dr. Jekyll does what he feels is right; Mr. Hyde gets what he needs.

Tears run down my face, but I try not to let on to my emotional display. This is exactly what's happening to me. Something has poisoned my brain, and I can be Jekyll and Hyde.

The songs never leave my head. I sing them as I drive to school. I sing them in the stairwells between music classes. I want to audition for the musical with one, but I'm told no—the drama director wants us to sing songs from the actual musical in order to prove we're good enough.

A few weeks before auditions, Bo calls me from college. He's crying, and my heart sinks. Another one of our friends is dead. I know that's what it is. I can hear it in his voice.

But it's not. Bo is addicted to the Internet. And while I say, "So what?"—hell, it's late 1998 and we all have the Internet now, and we all love it and use it to chat back and forth—Bo reveals to me that he's been spending up to fourteen hours a day looking at porn.

"I mean, I love you," he cries. "But I look at these girls and they just—they're everything."

And I know that I'm going to end things with him. And I will end them painfully.

I'm given two very good opportunities to break up with Bo, and I use both of them to my advantage. Despite several of my friends calling me callous, I start to flirt with a younger guy in our Vocal Ensemble class named Jess. He's a friend who hangs out with Allen and me, but I had only seen him as a nice guy. But when I lie for another friend, making a phone call to the principal on her behalf to get her out of class early, I'm caught—I pretended to be her mother on a school payphone, and they traced the line back to the one I had used. And I'm so upset by this, terrified that my parents will find out and verbally berate me, that I turn to Jess. I sob against him and tell him I'm worthless. I don't know why I'm like this. I tell him all about my Jekyll-and-Hyde nature—that I'm messed up and unworthy of love.

"But the thing is," he says, "I've liked you for almost a year now. You're perfect. An angel."

And with that, the first opportunity is complete. At a church concert a week later, Jess and I officially declare our love for one another, and I dump Bo with a cold, callous phone call.

That night, the voice is silent. I sit in my bathroom, humming

Christmas carols and the solo I'd performed at the church, and take the razor to my wrists. I am a horrible person.

"Oh honey," the voice interjects, coming in from nowhere. "You're just getting started."

I do have feelings for Jess—that's not a lie. But Bo is destroyed. He won't stop calling my house or sending emails. I ask him to stop, but he doesn't. Our mutual friends tell me that I should cut him a break, but I don't. I will not be some standby while he jerks off to porn.

A week before Bo comes home for winter break, auditions for the musical occur. I belt my heart out, and from the look on the drama director's face, it's clear—I've won the role. But Carrie isn't there. And I want to perform this female role with her. There's no better match; our voices mesh perfectly.

She's home with a migraine, and the drama director won't let her make up the audition. He casts a junior in her place—a friend of mine, and a decent singer, but not a senior as per Bev's usual guidelines—and everything is a bit disjointed. Jess doesn't get a role. And the drama director thrusts the blue books into my hands and asks me to write the harmonies for the other female part, since she's "not quite like me."

He strokes my arm with his finger. "I know you know what to do. But she's still so young. Can you please do this to help all of us out?"

I agree. And when Bo comes home for Christmas, he stops by. I'm buried in music books, banging out harmonies on the piano, and all he does is sit with me and cry. He's a failure. He's not doing well in college because of his porn addiction. He loves me and shouldn't have given me up. Look at me now—a thin, talented, beautiful girl who is so smart and so loving.

"I don't miss you," I say. "If you'd ever loved me at all, you would have shown it. Now go."

He leaves, and I get back to work.

The second opportunity to crush Bo occurs right after Christmas, when a friend throws a huge party. Some of the people there are still side-eyeing me for dumping Bo to be with the younger, not quite as popular Jess, but I couldn't care less about their opinions. They don't know the things Bo did and said. So those friends can shove it.

Ian—Bo's roommate and my former freshman-year crush—is at

that party. He asks to speak to me privately, and we go to his car. There, he tells me that Bo is contemplating suicide if I don't take him back. But as he talks, I notice that he's staring at me—at my tight red dress, at the green velvet bra I have peeking out. It's clear he's not really thinking about Bo at all.

"You're with that Jess guy," Ian says. "He's a year younger than you are."

"So what? I'm a year younger than you are."

"But I know you've liked me for a long time. Do you—want to try it? To hook up?"

At first, I say no. I want to betray Bo by being with his roommate, but I have no desire to hurt Jess. To Jess, I am still an angel. He calls me that every day. He listens to me when I cry about messing up a note on a piano concerto, or when my parents yell at me for no reason.

But then, the voice takes over. "Yeah," I say, feeling her rush throughout me—feeling Hyde take over as I lose control and am nothing but a bundle of impulse. "We should do this."

When Ian touches me, it feels amazing. He rubs the velvet of my bra, sticks his hand under my dress, and lets me enjoy it. When I reciprocate, he moans and calls out my name. But when we go to kiss—there's nothing. We laugh, and we try again. But still—nothing.

"So, we're meant to be friends," I say. "Funny. I cried about you for a year for no reason."

"I still liked this time together," Ian says. "But don't tell Bo. He'll kill himself. I know it."

"Yeah, sure thing."

I throw a New Year's Eve party, and people filter in and out. As Jess and I make out at midnight, promising that 1999 will be the best year in the world, I am filled with hope. This *is* going to be my year—graduating senior, star of a musical, and tons of music scholarships already under my belt. Despite all the trials of the past, things could be okay.

"They'll never be right," the voice says. "When will you ever learn?"

And the truth is I never do.

1999

B o's stalking is in full force at the beginning of the year—going so far as to sneak a note inside my house when no one is home and camping out in the snow on my front lawn. My dad, fed up, puts an end to it. And I am shocked. My parents are protecting me now? I can handle this kid. What I couldn't handle was the man who raped me in their house almost three years ago.

But in school, senior year is amazing. I'm in a great musical. I'm accepted to every college I'd applied to, and now that I'm with Jess—who will still be in high school when I'm off at college—I choose a college only thirty-five minutes from home. The college doesn't have a particularly large music program, though, and I want to study voice. But the admissions counselor promises me that I'll have tons of opportunities and that being a big voice in their small vocal pond will allow me to get ahead quickly. I like that notion, and despite my parents' reservations, they pay the deposit. I am officially a college student. The only time-consuming high school class I have now is Advanced Placement Literature, and that's not too challenging. If I pay attention, I'll earn an A. If I skip some classes and don't pay much attention, I'll earn a B.

I skip class often to hook up with Jess in the chorus room. Bev has allowed me to have a back office so that I can grade freshman-year papers, but when she's not there, Jess and I sneak in and make out on the desk. I teach him what I like—and what I like is pain. The Internet may have seen Bo as prey when it came to porn, but I could watch for just an hour and feel content. And I thank God for the Internet, because it allows something to click inside my brain: other people like pain as pleasure. They like to be hit, held down, tormented, tickled, smacked, and chained. All those times I thought I was sick? I wasn't. I now had validation.

I teach Jess how to do those things, and my seventeen-year-old self is fully, and happily, immersed in the world of BDSM—with limitations, of course, because I am seventeen, somewhat poor, and don't have enough privacy to really enjoy the practice.

"This is power," the voice says one morning while Jess has me held down against the floor. "You can tell him to get up, and he will. You're in control. He isn't. You won."

And she's right. I've won.

I just don't know there are upcoming battles that I'm on the verge of losing.

Rehearsals for the musical go extremely well, and despite a limited budget, the show is looking as though it will be a success. But a series of events occur that limit me: first, I sprain my ankle, and have to rehearse on a pair of crutches—proving to be a hindrance since I'm often climbing set pieces. A shy boy with starlit eyes in my Humanities class helps me carry my books. He tells me I'm a good singer. I'm intrigued by him, and I flirt, but nothing happens.

Then, a week later, as I'm sitting on a desk, slyly singing a song about adultery in the musical, a poorly-designed wooden set piece slams down and smacks the back of my head. I go flying off the desk and into the wall across from me.

I am not conscious when the drama director runs over and finds my shattered hair clip on the ground. I'm not conscious when someone calls 911. But I wake to find the drama director holding me in his arms, as though I am some tragic heroine to his hero, and whispering:

"Please don't be hurt. Please remember me. I need you. I'm in love with you."

I have a concussion, I think. He's not telling me these things. He's forty, for God's sake.

But it's confirmed by several other cast members. The director had rushed to my side, picked me up, cradled me, cried, and spoken several words to me.

I do have a concussion, but the show, as always, must go on. And as we near opening night, my ankle mostly healed, my head throbbing but functional, I keep an eye on the drama director. I pay attention to how he touches me and how the voice handles it differently than I do.

The night before we open, something is wrong. My throat is closing. My head feels like it's on fire. My mom examines me, hears my coughing, and tells me I have pneumonia again.

"But if I miss school tomorrow, I'll miss opening night," I say. "I'm a lead. No one can fill my place. We have everyone coming in from out of town!"

And it's true—the show can't happen unless someone sings my lines. We have family members from five hours away coming to watch. I will go to school, health be damned.

And I make it through opening night. My voice is raspy, but not terrible, and I'm praised with words, cards, and flowers. Things are successful. I can do this. A fever of 104 and a hacking cough will not keep this actress in bed.

But the next morning—a Friday, and a night that we all know will be a sold-out performance—I can't walk. My parents urge me to stay home, but I ignore them, get dressed, and have my dad drive me to school.

"If you can't drive, maybe you should be home," he says. But I tell him I can't miss AP Lit. And the rule is that if I can make it until 11:00 a.m., I can still be in the show that night. I just have to make it through half a day, and I'm through the front doors at 7:30 a.m. I can manage.

I pass out in the lobby fifteen minutes later, am taken to the nurse, and am sent home. I have pneumonia again. But this time, I'm not worried about what I'm missing, because I'm not coherent. I spend the day in and out of consciousness, hoping that they'll extend the dates.

They don't. Instead, the drama director decides to use his ego to fill my part. He puts on a tux and, for the Friday and Saturday shows, performs my part. On Saturday night, I'm coherent enough to know what's happening, and while our friends ridicule him for what he's doing, I'm livid. I can't breathe, and I can't stop coughing, but I want to hurt him for stealing what's mine.

But my voice returns the following week for the final three shows, and I belt out every note as though it will be my last. Closing night is a sold-out success, and as we take our final bows and pose for pictures, I cry. This is a taste of what my life will be. I will have this.

As I prepare to leave the auditorium, talking to friends and family about how wonderful the entire experience has been—sickness, injury, and all—the drama director interjects. He tells our group that I am a star and that he will never forget me.

And then he presses his lips to mine and shoves his tongue in my mouth in front of everyone.

This time, my parents have none of it. My dad yells at him as I press back. Did that happen? I keep thinking. Is my dad yelling at this man? Did he kiss me in front of a thousand people?

He did. And when I return to school after the weekend, Bev tells me to stay away from him. It's March now, and I'll be graduating in a few months. I don't ever need to see him again.

A week later, my thoughts about high school cease when my mom takes me upstairs to her bedroom. I'm on my way to the mall with Jess, and I'm irritated, but when she says it's urgent, I can tell she's not joking around to waste my time.

"It's Doo-Da," she says, holding back tears. "He has a brain tumor."
"Is it cancer?"

She nods and starts to cry.

I hug her—more for her comfort than mine, because I feel nothing. My beloved grandfather—my ally—has brain cancer. What am I supposed to feel? If I cry, it won't stop.

She tells me that he's going to have an operation to try and remove the tumor, but his mood and behaviors will most likely be different. And that's something I can understand, tumor or no. I know odd behavior. Nothing will alter my love for him—not even a new personality.

I go to the mall and tell Jess. He's almost in tears, but I'm emotionless.

I don't care what it takes, I think. I refuse to be upset, because I know this, God: Whatever I have to do, whatever I have to sacrifice, I will not let him die.

DOO-DA'S OPERATION LEAVES HIM WITH HUNDREDS OF STITCHES ON the side of his head. Back in his apartment, we listen to music and learn the truth.

They couldn't remove the tumor entirely. It had grown. His cancer, called glioblastoma, would take his life before the end of the summer.

But we go through the motions. Senior Prom is coming up, and two days after prom, I have my AP Lit exam. My uncle is also getting married on the day of prom, so there's no downtime. But if I can get through May 17—the year's last chorus concert—I am officially free. I have two weeks where nothing happens but a few small solos, nighttime concerts, and then, graduation.

Prom is a blur of gorgeous gowns and compliments, and the AP Lit exam is nothing. I pass with no issue, which means I can skip English 101 in college. Thank God, I think. Now, all that remains are some duties with the choir, and then, I'm free. High school, while wonderful, won't matter in only one week. And I'm already leaving school at 1:00 pm to go to 7-11: nothing is going on in the afternoon chorus I class in which I'm an aide, so Bev often tells me to head out. I listen to music and sit on my car, smoking and singing with the radio.

My final chorus concert is a whirlwind. I have a solo and a duet, and the duet is with Jess—a song from *Jekyll and Hyde*. We perform it well and receive great praise, but I feel as though I should have done more. When I act upon my Assistant Director duties, presenting Bev with end-of-year gifts from the musical as well as a jewelry set, we're emotional. This is it. Soon, I won't see her every day. I won't see Carrie, or Jess, or my newest friend, Allen. I'll be on my own.

I'm both intrigued and terrified.

But the responsibilities are now over. Our Vocal Ensemble sings at some small, evening functions, but seniors have no need to be anywhere. Some of us hang out at the 7-11. Allen and I sometimes hit up Burger King, where I eat and then go throw up in the privacy of the bathroom. I drive around, the radio blaring, and sing at the top of my lungs.

And I cry in private. Doo-Da is getting worse. And my other grandfather is now sick as well. My parents are stressed, and I'm living out the end of my high school career by handling everything myself. But I'm seventeen. It's a good transition into the adult world.

One night, after a softball game, my dad delivers some startling news.

"I know we don't talk about this much," he says. "But Jen just had a baby. It's a boy."

I hadn't known that Thomas and Jen were having a baby. Maybe I hadn't wanted to know. Maybe, if I had known, I'd somehow blocked it out. But now, my deepest fear has happened.

"I wish I could adopt that baby," I say. "They don't deserve it."

My dad sighs. In my mind, I wonder if he thinks back to the times when things seemed easier: when I was twelve and we'd go to Baltimore Orioles games every year, eating hot dogs and screaming at our favorite players. I wonder if I've failed him, despite my excellent grades and musical skills and college acceptances. But somehow, it always comes back to the trauma.

"He never believed you about Thomas," the voice says. "Neither of them do. You know it."

I do know it. Thank God I'm leaving this place.

Graduation is a three-day event at my high school, and it kicks off with an emotional ceremony as the principal points to me and mentions that there will never be another singer in this school with a voice like mine. And the next day at the Farewell Assembly, Bev presents the graduating Vocal Ensemble students with a gift, and the one she gives me is beautiful: a sapphire bracelet with matching earrings. As I sing my solo—I'd been selected to be one of a few people to perform at this final ceremony—I think about her. I wonder if we'll stay in touch when I leave town. I don't have plans to come back unless it's to see Jess or to visit for the holidays. I may feel homesick sometimes, but it's not for my actual home.

The next night, during a long, six-hour ceremony, our graduating class of seven hundred cheers. In my tiny white dress, covered by my oversized gown, I'm shaking. As our chorus sings together one final time, Carrie and I stand next to one another—not caring that she's an alto and I'm a soprano and that we're in the wrong sections—and we clasp hands. Our bond will not break.

But my graduation party the next day is a disaster. Doo-Da cannot attend, and we receive word that my other grandfather has been moved to the ICU. The mood is somber, and I feel broken. This is my one chance to celebrate life. Why does death do this? And why is death taking these people from me? I should have died before them.

That evening, after the party breaks up and Jess goes home, I slash my thighs with razor blades. If Doo-Da is going to die, I want to go with him. Maybe death really is home.

"Look at you, being tough," the voice says. "I told you I could handle it."

"Leave me alone. You're not real."

"I'm as real as you are."

The summer is a blur of depression. My grandfather dies in the middle of June, and my dad doesn't handle it well. I think about Jon— if he had lived, and his dad had died, would he have been this upset? And the answer is probably. I guess people cry at funerals.

Why can't I?

Since Jen is out on maternity leave from my dad's law firm, I serve as a secretary for the summer. I don't mind—I like studying law, and besides, the extra money will help me save to get my own place so I don't have to live at home again. Between the cash I make with my dad and the money I'm given for graduation, I have a nice amount set aside. My parents ask me to give it to them so that they can put it in a bank account, but I say no. The checks are mine. I want access to my money. Sure, I go on a spree to Victoria's Secret and buy two hundred dollars worth of lingerie—Jess is pleased to accompany me, and bra and panty sets aren't cheap, my parents should know that—but I'm saving. I just can't say why.

While I'm at work one day, with my dad out of the office and no one calling on me for anything, I type a letter to Bob. I tell her that, despite the fact we haven't spoken for a while, she's the one who needs to know. And even though I omit a few details, I tell her what happened with Thomas during the summer of 1996—and how I've seen him since, in this law office, still staring at me. Maybe, I tell her, it's because I'm thinner and wear really tight dresses, but still, he's an asshole. And he should die. I save and print the letter, and I mail it to her that night.

With trepidation, my family and I take a summer trip to the Outer Banks. Doo-Da is at home and under hospice care now, and we are on high alert: if a nurse calls and tells us to come home, we pack up and come home. I get it. Despite my love of the water, I will be there for him. My mom and I spend a lot of our nights at his apartment as it is, watching TV and making sure he's comfortable. During some of his lucid moments, he smiles at me and sings. When he's not as lucid, I quietly sing to him. My love for him is often contained in music, just as my love for the world is contained within the ocean I touch as it rushes to the shoreline.

Halfway through our trip, as I'm upstairs in my room, missing both Jess and Doo-Da, I hear the phone ring. My heart races. It's the hospice nurse, I think. Doo-Da's dead. I can feel it; inside of me, something is wrong. Something is changing forever.

But that's not it. When I wake—or, at least, pretend to wake after I slow my heart rate—I go downstairs and find my parents a disturbingly ghostly shade of pale.

"Doo-Da," I say. "He's gone."

"You wrote a letter on my work computer," my dad says slowly. "Jen returned to work to find a letter you wrote about her husband and what you said he did to you."

My heart disappears. It doesn't drop, or sink, or flutter. It simply vanishes. I cannot be weak.

"He did every one of those things," I say. "And good. She should know."

"Some of those things in that letter are lies," my mom says. "I know they are. Thomas said he didn't stare at you when he saw you a few weeks ago. He tried to avoid even seeing you."

Bullshit, I think. But what else can I expect?

"What now?" I say. "Now you know some of what he did to me."

"You never told us all of this."

"You never would have believed me."

The argument goes on until my mom, exasperated and upset, leaves the beach house. My dad and brother follow behind, and I stay back. I call Jess, unsure of what else to do.

"Well, now they know, so that has to be good," he says.

"This is far from good," I say. "They didn't care then. What gives them the right now?"

The rest of the vacation is awkward, and we play cards at night to keep the silence.

I don't want to do this anymore. I start to make a list of everything I should take to college so that, when winter break comes, I don't have to move home. I'll get an apartment as planned, be on my own, and cut ties. I'll have my money and Jess. What else could I need?

"Sanity," the voice says. "No health insurance from your parents, no sanity."

Like I've ever had any.

I SPEND MY LAST FEW WEEKS BEFORE COLLEGE IN TWO LOCATIONS: Jess's house or Doo-Da's apartment. I visit Doo-Da during the day—with Jen back, and with the drama, I no longer work at my dad's firm—and then promptly head over to Jess's where I break down into sobs. He sets up a tent in the backyard and we lay there, listening to crickets, trying to quiet my crying.

A few days later, I'm alone with Doo-Da, trying to help him to the bathroom. He falls and lands on his back in the hallway. I can't lift him —I weigh half of what he does, even in his sickly state—and instead, I call for help and we wait. But as we wait, his glazed eyes brighten and he turns to look at me.

"You have to promise me something," he says, his voice as clear as ever. "You have to promise me that you will keep singing. That you will create art. You are meant for this life. You are meant for so many great things. Keep singing. Always sing for me."

I cry and we hold hands. "I promise," I tell him. "Every song will be for you."

That night, I head home around midnight and am struck with the urge to compile every photo I have of my beloved grandfather. I want a collection. Soon, it's going to be time for a collection, and throughout the night, I go through every photo album and box I can find.

Seven hours later, my mom wakes me. "He died an hour ago," she says. "He's gone."

She hugs me and, I think, waits for me to cry. But I don't. I don't cry in front of her.

I visit my grandfather's apartment one last time that afternoon. "I'll do what you asked," I say to his empty bedroom, the sheets still wrinkled from where he had been sleeping. "I'll be your star. I promise."

I take one of his sweaters and I leave.

The morning of the funeral, my Aunt Jan comes into my bedroom to wake me. In her hands is a stuffed penguin—an animal I'd been collecting for years. "It's a tough day for everyone," she says gently and hands me the stuffed animal. "How are you feeling?"

No one has asked me yet. I don't know how to reply. But I thank her for the gift and get dressed and ready to go to Doo-Da's funeral.

Jess grips my hands as people come in and out. A softball jersey from my team is in my grandfather's open casket. Pictures—mostly ones I had gathered only days earlier—are displayed everywhere. I go up to the casket to say hello to guests, to hug them as they cry. I'm in a long black dress, prepared to sing for my grandfather. I will not be crying. That is not what performers do, no matter what—even when their best friends die from cancer.

I tuck a small note in Doo-Da's hand. "I love you for always," I say.

"With this note, you now know everything about me. I'm sorry if I let you down, today or twenty years from now."

My performance is flawless. I don't shed a tear. I'm too hardened now. And the voice says not to cry, so I listen. Crying won't bring Doo-Da back to life.

Once the funeral and wake ends and our out of town family members leave, I resume packing for college. I'm taking my entire life with me. Nothing will be left behind that bears significance. I'm not coming back.

The voice never stops talking. She's constant now. She talks over me. I burn myself, I cut my skin, I tear out my hair, and nothing stops her.

"Doo-Da, help me," I say one night in bed. "Please."

But the voice doesn't shut up. I don't think she ever will.

MY PARENTS DON'T WANT JESS TO COME UP TO COLLEGE WITH ME— they want to say goodbye to me alone, as a family. But I protest, and he climbs into the crowded van. My dad had joked the night before that I was taking my entire room with me. But he hadn't been wrong. I am.

Mount St. Mary's College, located in Emmitsburg, Maryland, is a short drive from my hometown, and when I arrive on campus, I marvel at the mountains and a shrine of the Virgin Mary. I frown at how tiny the theatre is, but hope that maybe, if I can make an impact, we can expand the music program. It only takes one person. I'm free now. I can do it.

But as I go into my dorm room and begin to unpack—my room-mate, Felicity, still hasn't arrived yet, though I know who she is and look forward to spending time with her—my parents take as much freedom from me as they can.

My car will not be here. I'm never to leave campus unless one of them takes me somewhere. I am to go to classes, spend time with female friends, do homework, and get good grades. I am to surrender my pager. I am to expect daily phone calls or emails. And because I am seventeen, not eighteen, I must comply.

When they leave, I cry only because I know I won't see Jess or my brother for a few weeks. Otherwise, I'm thrilled. They are gone. Their rules are bullshit; I still have the pager, and they won't know if I leave campus. A lot of people here have cars. It's not an issue.

Felicity and I bond quickly and set up our room the way we like it —green area rug, green curtains, pictures on the walls, two fridges for snacks and drinks. As I look at the pictures I've taped to the concrete of this tiny room, I mourn for my grandfather. But I can't let on.

Within the first week, I attend all my classes and am horrendously dismayed that the music program is not rigorous. There are two elite choral groups, and I can join the church choir, but I'm told there isn't an actual degree in vocal performance. The person I'd spoken to in admissions thought I wanted to study music education, not receive a musical education so that I could perform. But my advisor, Terry, tells me not to worry.

"If you want to make a name for yourself, start here," he says. "You can only move up."

I immediately fall in love with this man.

"He's yours by the end of the semester if you can act like a damn adult," the voice says.

And that I can do.

The liquor store within walking distance from the campus sells to minors. I only buy cigarettes, going through a pack a day. Felicity and I walk around campus, smoking, enjoying the freedom that comes with no one telling us no. We ride in our friend Collette's car to the grocery store or Wal-Mart or to restaurants. The four classes and two music groups I'm in are a breeze. College is nothing. And the guys are plentiful. They notice me. I wear either pajamas—a college staple when one has a class at 8:00 a.m.—or tiny dresses and skirts, and they notice. I'm not having sex with any of you, I think. I'm not betraying Jess. But I'll take the attention.

A guy from my freshman seminar class invites me to a party. He has a car, and if I want, I can drive. I tell him good—I don't drink much, so I'll be the designated driver, and he can have a good time. He hugs me, rubs my shoulders, and tells me I am the greatest person alive.

The night of the party, I dye my hair from blondish-brown to auburn. This is another no-go on the list my parents gave me: no hair dye, tattoos, or piercings. But fuck it. It's hair. What will they do—cut it off? Plus, it looks good. I borrow a tube top from a friend, and paired with my short black skirt and boots, I am ready for this party. Felicity is as well. But at the last second, Collette decides not to go.

"You guys go," she says. "I just—have a bad feeling. I want to stay in."

I shrug, and Felicity and I leave. But once we get to the party, Collette's intuition fills me, too. There are only three girls here, and Felicity and I are two of them. But there are at least thirty boys, and by this point, almost all of them are wasted.

One boy, Stone, takes interest in me. His friend Matt sent him over, he says. Both think I'm the hottest girl they've ever seen. Do I want a beer?

"No," I say. "I don't really drink."

Stone flirts without reprieve, even when Matt comes over to have an actual conversation with me about literature. And as much as I try to ignore Stone, I can't. He's constantly on me, grinding his body against mine, trying to get me to kiss him. I smoke, knowing he can't kiss me if something is in my mouth. Eventually, fed up with his antics, I go into the main house and hide in the bathroom, away from the raging outdoor party.

When I come out, Stone is waiting.

"You told me you'd give me your phone number," he slurs.

"Oh. Sure." I know I hadn't said this, but he's drunk. I make up a bullshit phone number, and he smiles, pocketing the paper that contains the deception. Then, he follows me out of the house and we begin to descend the steep driveway that leads back to the party.

I am not prepared when he grabs my long, newly-dyed hair and shoves me into the back of a pick-up truck.

"You fucking cocktease," he says. "You come here looking like this and act like you're Miss Intellectual? Like you don't want to get laid?" He jumps on top of me, and my head slams against the truck bed. I scream for help, but he shoves his fingers into my mouth.

"Try that again," he says. "I dare you."

But I'm choking, so I shake my head. He removes his fingers and then lifts my skirt.

"They're better off in here," he says, and he shoves his entire fist inside of me.

"I have this," the voice says. "Go away. Don't be here for this."

But I can't. She may pretend that this is okay, because she knows to shut up and go with it, but inside, I can't. I whisper no as he tears my skirt, smacks my face, and shoves himself into me with such force that I fly back farther into the truck bed.

When it's over, Stone smiles. "I'll call you," he says. And then he leaves.

My outfit is dirty and torn. My hair is a nest of tangles. I'm bleeding from several locations. But I stand up, wince, wipe myself clean, and head down to the party. I'll be safer there.

I see Matt. "Where's Stone?" he asks. But I don't say a word. Then Matt starts to cry. He tells me that he's drunk and wants to go home. Silently, I place his head on my lap and rock him back and forth. A bizarre, motherly instinct has kicked in, and I don't know why.

"Shh," I say, ignoring the blood streaming down my leg. "I have you. Nothing is wrong."

After the party, I climb into my bed, fully clothed. Felicity asks what happened, but I say nothing. I simply lay my head on my pillow, close my eyes, and go to sleep.

The next morning, I wake up to find that the room is empty. But there's a note.

"I think you have something to tell me about last night," it says, scrawled in Felicity's handwriting. "When you're ready to talk, I'm here to listen."

I stagger to the shower, smiling at my hall mates as I do so. They think I'm drunk. But I'm as sober as ever. I just want to wash the blood and semen off me. I want this day to end.

I want this life to end.

That night, Collette and Felicity sit on the floor of my dorm room, and they ask me what happened. I tell them about Stone. "But it's my fault," I say. "I did dress like a slut."

"You need to get help," Felicity says. "You have to go to the ER."

"But if I go, they'll call my parents. And I'll get in trouble. I can't."

"You were raped," Collette says. "I know you hate that word, but you were. Let's go."

Felicity and Collette push me into Collette's car and we drive thirty minutes to the nearest hospital. But once I'm there, I'm on my own. A volunteer from a local rape crisis center is called in, but otherwise, I'm alone with a male doctor and a male police officer.

"You're bruised up," the doctor says. "We have to take pictures. And collect evidence."

"Evidence?" I ask. "What evidence? My story?"

"Not just that, but samples—blood, semen, tissue, that stuff," the officer says. "If you want to catch this guy, we'll need you to do a rape exam."

"Please, no," I say. "I want to go back to school."

"Then you'll let him get away with it and you'll just be another statistic," the officer says.

I go numb. While the rape crisis volunteer holds my hand, the doctor reaches inside of me to take samples. He finds fingernail markings, torn skin, semen. He scrapes off blood.

And though I'm emotionally numb, the pain is unbearable. I scream. Who the fuck does something this barbaric after a rape? I should have stayed quiet.

When the doctor and officer have what they need, they give me some pills in case I have an STD. "I have to call your parents," the officer says. "You won't be eighteen until next month."

"I'll tell them," I say. "I swear. Please don't call them. Let me do it tomorrow."

But he says no. My rape is officially their business.

On the ride home, Felicity and Collette give me a card and a stuffed animal. I thank them and stare out the window, and I wonder how much trouble being raped again will cause.

I CONTEMPLATE CALLING MY MOM, BUT DECIDE AGAINST IT. Instead, I call my dad at work. Jen picks up, and the voice takes over, somehow blocking me out from my own words. "You tell my father that I was raped the other night," I say coldly. "And not by your husband this time. The cops have already called, I'm sure. But you tell him right now."

Shaken, unable to breathe, I sit on the floor of my dorm room. It's only a matter of time before my parents show up, and I know it. But Collette comes in and sits on the edge of my bed, and in the kindest gesture, she takes my long hair and starts to braid it. And it feels normal. She doesn't want to hurt me. She loves me.

My parents arrive as she's finishing the braids. "You say you were raped and you're just—letting someone braid your hair?" my mom says. "And you went off campus?"

"I did. And I was raped."

"Well, we don't know for certain," my dad says. "You hide a lot from us."

"I know for certain. You weren't there. But trust me, I damn well was."

An argument escalates, and when they eventually leave—my mom sobbing, my dad telling me that I'm disrespectful and irresponsible—I slam the door. I will not answer their phone calls. I will not reply to their emails unless they have to do with my nine-year-old brother. They are now dead to me.

I no longer care what I do. I go to class, because academia is a reprieve, and when Terry, my advisor, asks me what's wrong, I tell him. He sets up an appointment for me to meet with the school counselor and tells me that I am not to blame. Even if I don't want to identify the person who attacked me, I was harmed, and I have the right to mourn.

He's probably not supposed to, but he hugs me as I cry. I promise him that I'll get help. But when I leave, I smoke an entire pack of cigarettes, eat a box of Pop-Tarts, throw up, and then find a male college friend who beats me so hard, so bloody, that nothing else hurts any longer.

I receive a phone call from an officer who tells me that Stone is only seventeen. While I have identified him as my attacker, and despite that he admits he was with me, he will not go to jail. He's a minor. No one wants to ruin his college career. He's set free. Ruining his college career is, apparently, more important than ruining my life.

The school counselor I meet with immediately diagnoses me with depression and anxiety. "I can't believe you've never taken medication," she says. "But I have something for you. They're samples. You don't have to pay. They'll help you feel normal. I promise."

The little pink pills, called Paxil, do nothing. They don't quiet the voice or stop the panic. But I take them, because that's the night I start drinking, and those pills combined with alcohol make the world seem tolerable.

Jess keeps calling. I answer, and we talk, but not for long. I do go home once, mostly to see my brother, but I reveal nothing about my life to my parents. They don't know I get drunk every night now, or that I stash bottles of cheap Zima and Bud Lite in my dorm closet. They don't know that, in only a few weeks when I turn eighteen, I'll be opening a bank account so that my own money is safe. All they know is that their daughter is home for two days.

But I refuse to let them know anything about who I really am.

ONE NIGHT, I MEET A TWENTY-TWO-YEAR-OLD GUY NAMED ADAM through a college friend who throws tons of alcohol-fueled parties in her room. By this point, I'm forgoing class to sleep during the day, sing with the choirs in the afternoon, and party at night. My professors are far too forgiving: Terry has told them I'd been raped during that first weekend on campus, so as long as I turn in my homework, no one seems to care. I show up on occasion, but not enough to be noticed. It's only with Dr. Crew, my music professor, that I bother to make an appearance. I've already been bumped to the top choir in the school and have a spot in the women's choir. Plus, he wants me to be a cantor for the church services Wednesday and Sunday. On those occasions, I am the golden girl: I sing, I praise God, and I welcome everyone. But when music is not involved, I'm holding a bottle and a cigarette and am sitting on some guy's lap.

Adam and I immediately connect. When we go into an open music room one night and he plays the piano while I sing, we bond. He's a model—an actual model for an actual company—and while I feel self-conscious around him, he tells me not to. He tells me that I should model with him—beauty like mine shouldn't be overlooked. I pretend to believe him.

He asks to sleep with me that night, and while we do spend the night in bed together, I don't give in to his sexual demands. But when I wake up the next morning, it's 10:00 a.m., my panties are missing, my insides are sore, and he's gone. I suppose I was too drunk to remember.

The next time I see him is at another alcohol-fueled gathering—and Adam is already too drunk to walk. He tries to pull me onto his lap, but I refuse.

But later, Adam takes me back to my room and he starts to remove my clothing.

"I've wanted you from the night we met," he says. "And tonight, you'll be awake for me."

"Yeah, whatever." I don't feel fear. I want to fight. I want him to fight me so that I can punch him, because I'm angry at the way men use me—and angry at myself for allowing it.

A friend of mine named Vaughn pounds on the door, and when Adam opens the door and sees him, he laughs before punching him in the face. A fight begins as I stand there, half-naked, sobbing.

Eventually, the fighting ceases. Adam stands up and looks at me. "You fucking whore," he says. "You're not worth this!" Then he turns to the students who have gathered for the show. "Do you see why she's been raped? Look at her. If you want her, there she is. Take her."

When he leaves the room, I shut and lock the door. All I want is to die in peace.

THE NEXT MORNING AS I MAKE MY WAY ACROSS CAMPUS, I STUMBLE and collapse on my advisor's staircase. Terry, knowing I'm hung over, takes me into his office.

"You can't live this way," he says to me. "You have to tell your parents. You should go home and get help."

"I can't tell them shit. They hate me. I'm the worst. And they're right—it's true."

"You need to see a proper psychologist," Terry says. "Because what you see and what I see are two different things. You see a broken girl who has been seriously damaged by trauma. And you have been—that girl exists. But I see something else. I see a smart girl—someone about to be a woman—who has so much intelligence and talent that she's wasting it by subduing her pain with alcohol and cigarettes. I see a beautiful girl who could take that trauma and put it into her singing and writing. That girl could help others. You can do more than you think you can."

"Do you want to sleep with me?" I ask.

"What?"

"When people say things like that, they want to fuck me."

"No," he says. "You're a beautiful girl. But you're eighteen. I just want you to be well."

"You wouldn't fuck me if you had the chance?"

He shakes his head. "To be frank," he says, "I think you've been fucked over too much."

Terry's pleas eventually reach my parents, who agree that I need to see a proper psychologist. My mom comes up twice a week to take me to a doctor, and during our rides home, we talk. I tell her about the things I resent and how clouded my head is. I tell her that I haven't been faithful to Jess. I begin to open up in ways I hadn't been able to before.

Part of the plan to make me well is to move me into a different dorm—on a no-drinking, no-smoking wing. I agree, hoping that I'll be safer, and while painfully detoxing, I meet my new roommate, Ann. We get along immediately, and suddenly, college feels like college again. It's safe—just safe enough for me to resume going to classes and trusting the world may be okay.

But as finals approach, it's clear: nothing is safe. The world is not okay. And neither am I.

I WAKE UP ONE EARLY DECEMBER MORNING AFTER A 3:00 A.M. Denny's trip with some friends to find that I'm sick. I can't stop getting sick. I feel a lump on my body, in a place where a lump shouldn't be. Confused, I call my mom, who tells me to see a doctor. I do just that, and the doctor tells me it's a cyst caused by an autoimmune disease called Crohn's.

This explains why I've spent thirteen years of my life getting sick every day.

He does nothing for the cyst, saying it will go away in time. But he does give me painkillers. Lots of them. He says to take two a day, and if I run out, call him. We'll check on the cyst again after I finish my finals.

I go into a friend's room. "I'm sick," I tell her. "I have a disease. I need to take pills. Can I borrow your car?" I don't tell her why I want to, but she doesn't hesitate to hand over the keys.

I drive to the liquor store, load up on cheap tequila and whisky, and sneak it into my dorm room. There, I down five painkillers and drink a fifth.

And this gets me through the final week of classes. I appear in two chorus concerts, sing my solos without issue, perform a duet with my friend Amber, and star in a small, student-run production of *The Odyssey*. I'm the siren, singing men to their inevitable deaths, and as I put on my green dress, I notice something: it's too big.

But it's a size two. It can't be too big. I haven't lost more weight —have I?

I run to my scale and see a magic number: 98 pounds. Drinking and pills? Best diet ever.

The production goes perfectly. The walk back to the dorms with my fellow cast members is a smoke-filled, alcohol-fueled rage-fest. I am in agony—I haven't had painkillers in two hours—so once we get inside, I rush to my room, take a handful of pills without counting, and drain the rest of the tequila. Then, I climb into bed.

The nightmares are vivid—my beloved Doo-Da welcoming me into hell, a bright light being shoved into my eyes, Thomas holding me down and raping me. When I wake up, I get sick and notice my sheets are covered in sweat, vomit, and blood. Scared, and without any idea of what to do, I call my mom. She comes to get me, and when she arrives, I'm almost unconscious.

I'm in the hospital with sepsis and far too many painkillers in my system. I miss all of my finals as I spend a few days in and out of consciousness, and surgery is performed to remove the septic cyst. Luckily, I'll be allowed to make them up when I'm better, but I miss the last few days of college. And those are my last few days: I've decided not to return to Mount St. Mary's. The only good memories I have are of Ann, Terry, and singing in choir. Everything else was an alcohol and lust-fueled waste. I'd been on a rampage, and I knew I needed to stop.

A week later, right before Christmas, I slip on a tiny dress despite the freezing temperatures, drive up to the college, take all five of my finals, and then attend a chorus concert at my former high school. I cry when I see Bev, and Jess tells me to take it easy: I've just had surgery. And my parents don't want me out, anyhow—I have eighteen inches of surgical gauze packed inside of a still-open wound that could easily grow septic again.

My plans to be on my own for the winter have been dashed, so I revolt, angry that a disease made me septic and ruined my goals. I go to the concert. I dress in ways my parents don't like. I tell them I've opened my own bank account with my own money, so they don't own me. I go out at 10:00 pm to visit Jess despite a massive amount of snow on the road.

The night I visit Jess during the snowstorm is when I'm confronted.

"Who in the hell are you?" my mom screams. She smacks my face. I shout a string of obscenities at her, fearful I'll wake my brother, but knowing they must be said.

"You're living at home," my dad says. "You aren't living at college next semester. No way."

"Like fuck I am," I tell them. "I'm eighteen. Kick me out or get out of my life."

My mom slaps me again and pulls my hair. I smack her off me. "Don't touch me ever again," I say and go up to my room. But she follows me, and there, she grabs me by the hair and shoves me into my closet.

"Dad!" I've landed on the swollen surgical area and feel faint. "I need your help."

"*Dad, help me,*" my mother mocks. She smacks me again and tells me that I'm the worst daughter a parent could ever have. When she leaves the room, I sit in the closet, my chest heaving, and wonder if she's right. I *am* the worst. She *should* hit me and shove me into closets. I'm not worthy of her love. I'm only worthy of death. And I know now how to do it.

I pack one backpack with the things I need: clothing, makeup, pills, books, and music. At five in the morning, I sneak downstairs and go out into the snowstorm.

The plan is to walk to the Dunkin' Donuts three miles from my house. In normal weather, it's doable. But in a blizzard? I could die.

And that's exactly what I want.

But somehow, I make it to the store by the time the sun rises. And I call Jess, telling him that he has to get me before my parents find me. They've hit me, and I have the marks to prove it.

Jess and his mother show up just as my dad does. As he screams for me to get into his car, I refuse and go with Jess. He follows us back to their house and demands for me to come home. But I say no. I will not live like a caged-up monster. If they hate me, they need to let me go.

"You're a child," he screams.

"I'm eighteen. You cannot make me go back."

He leaves, and I sob on the couch.

A few days later, as 1999 is dangerously close to turning into 2000, I decide that I should make amends and at least go home to check on my brother.

"Don't do it," the voice says. "You've made it this far. You even got a job. Don't go back."

She's right: I had made it this far. I did just get a job. I don't need them.

I call my parents from a library payphone. My mom sobs and apologizes, asking me to come home. I shouldn't live with Jess and his family. I should live with my own.

Just as I am about to say yes, I remember how she told me she hated me. I remember how she hit me and shoved me into a closet. I say, "No deal," and hang up as she screams.

I climb into a car with Jess and his mom, and we head three hours away to visit his aunt and uncle. I have my backpack and nothing else. After a while, the three outfits I've packed will fall apart. And I'm running out of everything, including medication.

But Jess's aunt and uncle provide for me. His uncle, who came from a background of abuse and neglect, relates to my stories. We hold each other and cry. His aunt finds clothing in my size and gives me two bags to take back with me. They ask me to please eat—I look sickly and pale and too thin. They notice I'm still strung out from medication. By the end of the three-day visit, I find the family I want. And they welcome me back, just as I am—voice and all, because I decide to tell them the truth—without any hesitation.

Back at Jess's house on New Year's Eve, we sit in excitement. It's almost 2000.

With only four minutes left until midnight, there's a knock on the door. And it's for me.

It's a police officer—a friend of the family who used to date one of my relatives. "I'm just checking up on you," she says. "Your parents are worried sick."

"I'm here and I'm safe. I have made the choice to be here, and I'm eighteen. My mother hit me and threw me into a closet. I am not going back to that."

"Would you like to press charges? You do have that right."

I think about it for a moment, but then I consider my brother. "No," I say. "Just tell them to stay out of my life forever. That's my wish. I'll be fine without them."

The officer leaves, and when I go back into the living room, I've missed it. It's now 2000.

"You did the right thing," the voice tells me. "You're on your own now. No turning back."

I smile because she's always right.

I refuse to turn back.

2000

Living with Jess and his parents is easy. And I'm a good guest: I cook, I clean, I wash dishes, and I do laundry. College classes at the local four-year university begin in only two weeks, and I have my books. I dress more modestly around them, feeling content to be domestic. The voice rages inside my head, telling me to get out, but I ignore her. For now, I feel bliss.

And I work as a server in a popular local restaurant. My boss is a kind man, and he is always trying to feed me. "You need a cheeseburger!" he says, and I roll my eyes.

But he's not the threat. The head chef, Rick, is. He often talks about my ass—I hear him as I deliver plates of food to my customers—and one day, Rick asks to speak to me in private.

"Your pants are too tight in the—you know," he says. "The rear."

"They're a size zero. They fit. I don't have money for new clothing right now."

"I don't know about all that, but if you wear those pants, we're going to stare at your ass."

"Then fucking stare. You can't do anything about it."

He does when he pushes me into the freezer the next day and

shoves his hands under my shirt. I go blank and let him. I need this job. I don't want to get fired. I just stand there.

Rick asks me to date him. I say no and ignore him. When Jess catches on to the harassment, he begs me to quit, but I refuse. I have regular customers who love me and tip well. Despite my age, I'm serving alcohol, and that means larger tips as the hours grow later. And I'm so close to having enough money for my own apartment.

And it's about time I get one, because Jess's mother makes it clear to me that I need to live elsewhere. I'm too worldly for her son, she says. She loves me, and doesn't mind that I date Jess, but when he sees me in a towel after coming out of the shower, he's "thinking impure thoughts."

Jess's dad helps me find a small apartment only five minutes from work. I can walk to the convenience store, the liquor store, all the essentials. Rent is only four hundred fifty dollars a month for this apartment in a somewhat unfriendly neighborhood, but since I'm buying a car, I'll be safe to get to work. He kindly pays the deposit for me and winks. Within a week, I have furniture, food in my fridge, a working vehicle, the Internet, and a cat.

This is what I wanted, I think, wandering from my living room to the kitchen to the bedroom to the bathroom. This is all mine. No one can take it away. As long as I can afford rent and electric, I'm okay. I make more than five hundred dollars a month. I can maintain this. I'm free and on my own.

My parents discover where I'm living, and in a desperate afternoon conversation, my dad comes over. In tears, he asks me to move out and come home. They'll listen this time, he says.

I hug him, because I don't feel as betrayed by him as I do by my mom. But I shake my head.

My parents organize family therapy sessions, and while I'm not required to go, the voice urges me to. "This will be hilarious," she says. "You can tell them everything. No rules. Do it."

And I go. The first things my mom talks about are how I betrayed her rules.

"She dyed her hair. She went off campus while in college—and she was raped while disobeying me. She drank. What am I supposed to do with that?"

"Well," I say smugly, "I guess you hit me. Throw me in a closet. Ignore the fact I'm being raped by a family friend even though you walk in on the event. That's what you do with that."

The therapist looks at me, mouth wide open, as my mom cries and leaves the room.

Then the therapist files a police report. I'd been raped at fourteen, she says. She has to report it, even if nothing can be done legally. I consent and tell her the basic details.

The next day—only a week after I've started classes at my new college—there's a knock on my apartment door. I'm getting ready for school, and I've learned that a lot of drunks often look for a place to sleep around here. I'm not opening the door for anyone other than Jess.

"It's the Maryland State Police," a voice says. "You need to open the door."

I haven't broken the law—underage drinking aside. And a little shoplifting I did the week prior, when I realized I needed a phone but hadn't made enough money for one yet. But they couldn't put me in jail for that, could they? I barely remembered the incident. It was almost as though I hadn't been there. The voice said to steal it, and somehow, I walked out of the store with a phone and answering machine tucked under my shirt. I find other stolen goods—towels, food, toilet paper—in the trunk of my car as well. But I hadn't taken those. I know I hadn't.

I open the door, and a male police officer introduces himself and asks to come in. We sit across from each other, perched on two white chairs I'd bought at a county auction.

"It's been brought to my attention that you were sexually and physically assaulted as a minor," he says. "We took the perpetrator in for questioning, and he spent last night in jail."

I'm silent for a moment before I realize that he means Thomas. "Wait," I say. "Thomas was in jail? For raping me almost four years ago? He finally went to jail?"

"We can't keep him there," the officer says. "The statute of limitations has passed. But I need a full report from you. I need to know what he did, and then what happened the night you left your parents' house. According to another officer, you were bruised and scratched."

I tell him everything, my words falling out of my mouth in jumbles. Yes, Thomas raped me. He threatened to kill my family. A guy named Stone raped me in college, too. My mom did beat on me a little, but I got over it. I want to move on, and I feel as though I'm choking as I talk.

"I just want to go to school," I finally say. "I don't want to talk about this any longer."

"I'm going to see if we can do anything else regarding Thomas," the officer says. "What he did to you is atrocious, and the fact that it was never reported is even worse. You should have said something."

"I was fourteen. He said he'd kill my family if I spoke up."

"Then your parents should have reported it if they walked in on it. That's deplorable."

He leaves, and I skip time. I don't even realize it's almost time for me to go to work until my phone rings. But I don't answer. Blankly, I drive to Jess's house. He's the only one home, and he takes me up to his room. But I don't speak. I can't tell him what I'd tried to do.

On the drive over, I'd tried to drive my car off the side of the road. There was snow, and I swerved on purpose, attempting to hit a telephone pole and land in a ditch. But when I did so, my car spun around and pointed me right back in the same direction. I'd failed at suicide.

All this comes out in the two hours that I'm partly catatonic on Jess's bed. I moan drips of it into the air—car, death, suicide. When his mom arrives home and Jess tells her that I tried to kill myself after talking to the police, she calls my work and says I won't be in for a while.

And then they take me—unable to eat, completely unfocused, and suicidal—to the hospital.

I'M ALONE IN A GREY CONCRETE ROOM, SHIVERING. ON ONE WALL, there's a painting of a woman sitting on a windowsill.

Jump out, I think. Jump out of here, die while you're pretty and young, and save yourself.

When a doctor comes in, he asks me why I tried to kill myself. And I can't tell him. I am tired of talking about rape, abuse, death, starvation, and the voice. I'm just so fucking tired.

"Don't tell him you were pregnant," the voice says.

"What? That I was what?"

The doctor hears me. "What did you say?"

"I'm not talking to you. I'm talking to her."

"Who? There's no one else in here."

"That's nice for you, but for me, there is," I say. "And I need to talk to her right now."

He watches as the voice uncovers a horrible truth: the night that Adam had slept in my bed and stolen my panties, he had sex with me. I hadn't said no, but had been too drunk to consent and passed out halfway through. And because I'd been so drunk and had been starving myself, my birth control pills hadn't worked. I got pregnant, and about eight weeks in, miscarried the baby in the shower at Mount St. Mary's. It was only a few weeks later that the cyst developed.

"That's not true!" I scream. "I didn't miscarry a baby! I'm a virgin!"

The doctor shakes his head, "Not even close," he says. "Not according to any of your medical records. If your OBGYN has told you as much—it's not the truth. Now, I don't know about this pregnancy, and I don't know who you're talking to here, but you need help."

"Fuck you!" I say. "I don't need your help. Get out of here."

"You're talking to someone I can't see. You're sick. You're staying."

"Like hell I am!"

"You don't have a choice," he tells me. "You tried to commit suicide. You are dangerous and you hear a voice. You will be staying for at least three days."

I scream as he leaves the room, and I dig my fingernails into my wrist. I will not stay in a psych ward at eighteen. I have a job. I have a cat. I have a home. And this is bullshit.

But three hours later, as Jess and his mom watch me leave, their faces messy with tears, I stay. I'm screaming, clawing at my skin, and yelling, "I didn't lose my baby!" But deep down, I knew the voice is right: I miscarried a baby. I'd somehow been able to block the memory.

I'm taken to a private room in the hospital's psych ward. It's dark. I have nothing with me but the clothing I'd worn to Jess's, as well as my purse, which has been taken.

"I want my pills," I tell the nurse who checks me in. "And cigarettes."

"You can't have those here," she says. "We'll give you other pills after you meet with the doctor tomorrow."

"And what am I supposed to do tonight? Keep digging at my skin? Because I can."

"We'll give you some paper and a crayon so you can journal," she says. "That might help."

"I think a pencil would be better," I say. "I'm not five."

"But we know what you could do with a pencil."

Well, thanks for the idea.

The next morning, I'm woken at eight to meet with my new psychologist, Dr. Mau. He's an older man, friendly in demeanor, but I want nothing to do with him.

"So, you're having hallucinations and thoughts about ending your life," he says. "And it sounds like, from what I can gather, your behavior is rather—odd. You think you're invincible, and then, you want to die. You make yourself into a human rollercoaster."

"I don't *have* hallucinations," I tell him. "I hear a voice. And nothing about me is invincible. Though the human rollercoaster thing —I like that."

"You think that's an appropriate description of your behavior?"

"My behavior? It's who I am. I'm Jekyll and Hyde, just in girl form."

"No," he says. "What you are is a manic depressive. With anorexia and bulimia."

I sit there and stare at him. I'd heard manic depressive—or bipolar —mentioned by my psychologist in Emmitsburg, but hadn't been given a diagnosis. And now, I have one.

"What now?" I ask. "Medicate me to get the voice to go away? Because she won't."

"She will," Dr. Mau says. "I have a good combination of medications that will help you with the bipolar, as well as with your depression, anxiety, and what is a very clear case of OCD. You are obsessed with harming yourself. But we can end that."

"Whatever. Just get me out of here."

"You'll have to remain under observation for at least three or four days while you start these new medications," he says. "Then, after some therapy, we'll see how you function alone."

"I can't miss work. I have to pay rent."

He shakes his head. "Your focus now is on yourself. Nothing else."

The days pass in a blur as I'm overly medicated. All the Zyprexa, Lithium, Depakote, and Anafranil takes over my body. And I don't hear the voice. I don't hear anything, because all I can do is sleep. No one even bothers to wake me unless it's time for therapy.

I don't shower for days. Jess visits, and he cries, but I stare at the wall. My parents come to see me, and they are just as upset, but all I can do is stare. A friend of the family comes to visit, to bring me a Bible and to tell me that Jesus will cure my mental illness. I laugh.

"I can be treated," I tell her. "Not cured."

After all, I know better. You can't cure someone like me.

AFTER ABOUT A WEEK, I'M CONSIDERED STABLE, AND I START TO attend group meetings. People talk about their depression: lost jobs, husbands who have left them, those sorts of things.

When it's my turn, I mention rape, abuse, sexual harassment, hatred from my parents, and now a miscarriage. I can't come to terms with that, and I can't tell anyone outside this room.

"And you're how old?" another patient asks. "Sixteen?"

"Eighteen. What the hell does it matter? We're all here for shitty reasons."

I have to weigh in every day, but a fellow anorexic clues me in on how to trick the scale. If my doctors want me to weigh 110, but I weigh 102, I can sew objects into my panties.

"With what?" I ask her. "My fucking imagination?" But she smiles and reaches into a book. Between the pages are objects: pills, a few cigarettes, and a sewing needle with yards of thread.

"No shit," I say. "You're the queen of contraband. I am literally bowing to you."

"This is my fourth stay." She hands me the book. "Take what you need. They say they check everything, but not when visitors come. Anyhow, sew some bundles of plastic ware into your panties. You may not weigh what they want you to, but if you're close, you can go."

"Get out? How soon?"

"Just don't ever say you're crazy or you hear voices," she says. "Then you'll never leave."

I play the game. I smile and pretend to be fine. I interact with patients that I detest. And three days later, Dr. Mau deems me fit to leave. I have to go to an outpatient therapy program, and he wants me to find a psychologist and psychiatrist, but for now, he's written prescriptions for the four medications I've been on while in the hospital.

Jess and his mom pick me up and take me out to dinner to celebrate my release. I eat as though I've never eaten before. For the first time in months, I am famished. But my body doesn't know how to handle regular eating, so I get sick.

Back at my apartment, everything is fine. My cat is alive and well. Nothing is out of place.

But I am. I'm out of place. I don't belong here in this world, alone, keeping the secret of my new diseases. I don't want to be inside my head.

"Then don't take the pills," the voice says. "Get out of your head. Go out and live."

She's always right. I smile, grab my jacket, and head for the nearest bar.

———

LIFE ISN'T ENTIRELY CRAZY. I APPLY FOR A SECOND JOB AS A CHURCH choir director, and after a brief interview, they bring me on board. It's only two days a week: Wednesday rehearsals and Sunday services. For an additional four hundred dollars a month, it's more than worth it. And I'm back at my regular job, too, singing for customers, making good money, smiling as though I'm fine.

But at night, things change. I let Rick from the restaurant take me to a bar, and then he takes me back to his apartment. He asks me to strip for him, and I do. Despite the fact he leers at me, shoves my head against the wooden floor, and slaps me when I eventually tell him I don't want to have sex with him, I still stay with him. He sleeps at my apartment when I don't go to his place. At least I'm not alone, and he's old enough to buy all my alcohol.

Most of my money goes to rent, utilities, clothing, the piercings I start to get on my body, a different hair cut every week, and extravagant gifts for Jess and other friends. I can't stop myself. If I'm not out spending money, then I'm stuck at home. It's shopping or the bar, and soon enough, I realize that the former is costing me hundreds a month.

I swallow my pride and risk it.

"Okay," I tell Rick the next night at his apartment. "Here's the truth: I'm a prostitute."

"I knew it!" he says, delighted at the fact that he believes he's right. "I told the boss that! I knew you weren't just a waitress. Oh man. He is going to *love* this."

"Well, then, if you want me to fuck you, you're gonna have to pay up."

I am shaking and terrified. I am out of control. But I need the money.

"How much?" Rick asks.

"Three hundred a night for whatever you want."

"Fuck all," he says. "We don't get paid until Friday. But then—then, we'll do it."

"Can't wait," I say, and as Rick goes to sleep, I sit on the edge of his bed and sob.

At the local bar the next night, I am handed my normal rum and coke but am surprised to see that Rick isn't the one handing it to me. Instead, a handsome man with dark hair does. And he looks incredibly familiar.

"Your buddy over there told me what you like to drink," he says, smiling. "So, I decided to pay for this round. Cheers, pretty girl." He touches his beer bottle to my glass, and we drink.

"I know you from somewhere," I say, looking at Rick. He's staring at the floor, dejected.

"Don't worry about that guy," the man says. "He won't miss you. I told him that we were together, so he won't bother you again."

"What the hell? I work with him! I see him six days a week!"

"Well, he won't be bothering you. And yes, you do know me. You've probably seen me every day. And if you haven't, then you haven't been watching TV."

Ryan is a prominent newscaster in our state. And for some reason, he's in this shitty little bar on the same night I am. No wonder people stare at him. No wonder he could tell Rick to stay away without argument. This is a man people like and want to emulate.

This is a man with money.

"How old are you, anyway?" he asks.

"Eighteen. And you?"

"Thirty-four. It's not that big of a deal, is it? It's just an age. A number. What matters is that we met on this night. You're gorgeous. Have you ever thought about being on TV?"

"I'm a singer. I perform on stage in front of a live audience."

"I can get you on TV," Ryan says. "A girl like you? No problem at all."

It's a line, and I know it. Adam said the same thing about modeling, and all he did for me was get me pregnant when I hadn't even realized we'd had sex.

But Ryan asks me to leave the bar with him, and when I do, I see an impressive car.

"You'll be taken care of now," Ryan says to me. "Whatever's been happening to you? Wherever you're living? I'll take care of it."

Maybe he's an angel, I think. Maybe he can save me from myself somehow.

"Idiot," the voice says. "Enjoy your delusion."

"You're the delusion," I say in my head. "You're the one making me crazy. Without you, I'd be fine."

"Without me, you would have died a long time ago."

I ignore what I hear and focus on the ride to Ryan's house. And I feel carefree. He'll help me move out of my awful apartment and find something better. He'll hook me up with a better job that pays more. My cat will be just fine. Ryan has the power to take care of everything.

That's the night he kidnaps me.

───────────

I'M COMPLETELY OBLIVIOUS TO THE SITUATION UNTIL WE GO TO AN apartment—not the big, mansion-like house Ryan had been talking about for half the car ride. It's not a bad apartment, but it's not that different from mine: one bedroom, one bathroom, very minimal furnishings. Dishes litter the sink and they smell awful. The curtains are all black, and the room's only light comes from dim, overhead bulbs.

"Very funny," I say when he lets me inside. "Now, where's your house?"

"We're not going there tonight," he says. "For tonight, we'll stay here. Maybe tomorrow, too."

"I have to work tomorrow. I can't lose out on the money."

"But I told you I'd take care of you." He takes my purse from me—the only possession I currently have, which holds my keys, my wallet, some medication, and a bag of makeup—and while he leaves the room with it, I stand there, shivering in my red tank top and black skirt, wondering if this is a mistake.

I know that it definitely is when he comes back with a blindfold in his hands.

"Oh, hell no," I say. "Give me my purse. I want to go home."

"Not tonight," he says. "And I have cameras in this apartment. If you leave, I'll know immediately. An alarm will sound, and I'll knock you down the stairs before you get outside. So why not just stay in here with me? It's warm. We'll have a drink, watch some TV, and you know —have a chance to play."

I start to cry. "My boyfriend will know I'm missing if I don't call him. If I'm not back at my apartment, someone will look for me."

Ryan sets the blindfold down on the kitchen table and approaches me. He takes my hands—almost lovingly, almost like a father would—and says, "No one is looking for you. Rick told me your story. You're a big girl now, and you're on your own. I'm not going to hurt you. I just want to have some fun together. And I promised that I'd give you some money. I will. I swear."

I have two choices: try to run or play along.

Thomas taught me that running didn't help. And I hadn't been able to run from Stone, either.

It is decidedly safer to play along.

That night, we curl up on a threadbare sofa and look at a photo album of his family and friends. When I start to cry, he holds me and says, "I know no one loves you. But you know I will. I think I already do. We can make so many memories together to add to this book. We can fill it with outings, vacations, and maybe even a baby. Would you like that?"

No, I think. No, and go fuck yourself and die. But I simply nod.

Much to my surprise, he leaves me alone on the first night. I'm in his bedroom, sharing a bed, and he's asked me to sleep in only my bra and panties—telling me that I'm so sexy because I'm wearing a red lace set, so I must have known something good was coming my way. But he doesn't force me to have sex. He simply holds me and goes to sleep, and eventually, exhausted and too terrified to want to deal with the world, I follow.

He's making breakfast when I wake up, and he feeds me in bed. We watch movies throughout the morning. Then, around 2:00 p.m., he leaves, and he locks the door behind him. But before he goes, he says, "If you're not here when I get back, I will find you. I have connections. I already know where your apartment is. You are not to leave or there will be trouble."

"You don't know where my apartment is."

"You have a paystub from your job in your purse," he says. "So yes. I know exactly where you live. Now listen to me. Don't leave, or I will find you. And when I come home at nine, I want you on my couch in nothing but your lingerie. If you can do those two things, we'll have another pleasant evening. Do you understand? Do you know I'm going to help you?"

"Okay."

He smiles, kisses my cheek, and departs. I wait about ten minutes, hunt for my purse—cameras be damned, I doubt he has any at all—and find nothing. He must have put it in his briefcase or something. It's nowhere to be found.

But he has a phone. I run over to it, pick it up, and then realize there's no dial tone.

"Okay," I say to myself. "It's okay. If you play along tonight, it will all be okay. You can convince him that you need to go home for something tomorrow. Or that you need something he'll be embarrassed about—like tampons. Or psych meds."

I wander around the apartment, thinking about how easy it would be to just unlock the door, scream, and hope for help. That's what a strong person would do. And I don't.

Ryan comes back at 9:00 p.m., as promised. And as promised, I am on his couch in nothing but my red lingerie. He smiles, sets down his briefcase, and comes over to kiss me.

"You're such a good girl," he says. "You're the best girl out of all of them. You love me."

I nod.

"Say it."

"I do love you."

He hands me a bag with some food in it and I notice that his hands are scraped. He's also sweaty. But I'm so hungry. I try to ignore him as he watches me eat.

"I love to watch skinny girls eat," he says. "You have so much pleasure in your eyes."

"I haven't eaten in twelve hours. I'm hungry. I'm sorry."

"Don't be sorry." Ryan unbuckles his pants, pulls them down, and then sits beside me. He begins to jerk off as I'm eating, but I immediately put the food down.

"No," I say. "There's no way. I'd rather starve."

Ryan rips the bag of food out of my hands. "Then that's what you'll do," he says. "Here I am, trying to be nice, trying to show you I love you, and look at you. You ungrateful bitch."

"I'm not being an ingrate. I just don't want you to watch me eat. I like privacy."

"It's just us." He smiles again. "No one else is coming. We have privacy."

He zips up, carries me into the bedroom, and throws me onto the bed. He locks the bedroom door behind him. I scramble to the head of the bed and curl into a ball.

But he leaves me alone and puts a tape into a small stereo on his dresser.

"Self-help tapes," he says. "I saw the medication you have in your purse. You don't need that. Listen to people who know how to heal your soul. I'm going to give you some of these tapes soon, and when we get you into your nice, new apartment, you can listen to them."

"I haven't taken any meds since I've been here. I'll listen to the tapes."

Then the blindfold goes on and he pins me to the bed with his knees.

"I have been waiting for this," he says, and I hear him take off his clothing. I feel him grab my hand so that I can help him undress, and after some of his clothing is off, he takes my hand and shoves it into his pants.

"Tell me you want to fuck me," he says.

"I want to fuck you."

He slaps my face. "Bitch," he says. "Now say it like you aren't lying."

I grab his hand and place it on my breast. When he moans, I whisper, "I want to fuck you."

"I can tell you do. Good girl. This is the best night of my life."

He gets off me for a moment, and I hear him doing something with the tape player. He leaves the room, and I pull down the blindfold. He's gone. But I quickly pull it back up when I hear footsteps right outside the room.

"Okay," he says. "I have the tapes for you. For later. I can focus. I wanted your wellbeing to come first. Now, it's my time."

I feel him pin me to the bed again, and he takes off my bra. He gropes at my breasts, rough and unsure, and before he even has a chance to take off my panties, I hear him moan again. Wet, sticky fluid is on my thigh. I try not to cry and think about how relieved I am that this happened before he could come inside me.

He takes one of my breasts and twists it. "You fucking cunt! That wasn't the plan!"

"I'm sorry. I can't help what your body does. I'm sorry."

He squeezes my breast again, and when I cry out, he slaps me in the face and then climbs off me. "This is a fucking disgrace," he says. "But there's always tomorrow."

"Someone will be looking for me," I say quietly. "I should at least go to the apartment tomorrow to make some calls. You can drive me. We can go together."

Ryan removes the blindfold and smiles at me. "Okay," he says. "Maybe we'll do that."

Then he climbs into bed, still sticky, and pulls me toward him. He tells me that my auburn hair is gorgeous. He tells me that my body is beautiful. And then, he falls asleep.

I stay awake until a see a small stream of light peek through the bedroom curtains.

I risk it.

I get up, and silently, I locate my bra and clothing so that I can dress. I grab my shoes—I can't put them on, or he'll hear the heels on the floor—and tiptoe into the kitchen. I'm afraid I'm going to vomit and ruin everything.

Before I put on my clothing, I open Ryan's briefcase. Sure enough, my small purse is inside. Everything is there—keys, credit cards, cash, medications. He's taken nothing. But he does know where I live.

And now, I can't live there.

I take the purse, shut the briefcase, and go back to the kitchen where I've left my clothing. I'm ten feet from the door. I can do this.

All I've put on is my bra and skirt when I hear movement. I quickly grab my clothes and purse and make a run for it.

But I'd heard nothing. And as I enter the February air, I realize there are no cameras or alarms. He knew how to trick me. And it had worked.

I take one last risk: I sneak back inside, grab the self-help tapes he'd left on the kitchen table, and take them back outside. I put on my shoes, and there, on the doorstep of the apartment, I crush the tapes with my heel. I reach into my purse, grab a pen and a scrap of paper, and in bold, capital letters, leave a note tucked under the pile of destruction:

"GO HELP YOURSELF."

Then I pull on my tank top and run.

I HAD NO IDEA I WAS PRACTICALLY IN BALTIMORE CITY—A GOOD forty minutes from my apartment—until I run into a diner. A waitress looks up at me, notices I don't have a coat, and immediately ushers me to a booth. She pours me a cup of coffee and grabs a jacket from the coat hanger.

All I do is cry. I can't say where I've been, because I don't know. I just tell her that I need to go home. I don't even think about calling Jess, or a friend, or even my parents. I just want home.

She calls for a taxi and hands me a twenty. "I think you need this more than I do," she says. "Your little face. Did someone hit you?"

I nod. I want to tell her—this stranger who has given me free coffee and a free taxi ride—but I can't. And the taxi arrives as she's called back to serve other patrons.

I get in and tell the driver my address. Then I close my eyes and sleep the entire way home.

When I put the key into the lock, I know that I'm not safe. I know I better not stay long, or that, if I do stay, I should call the police.

But when I enter, I don't expect the mess and the missing items.

My stereo has been tossed on the carpet. My TV is gone. Half my furniture is missing. Luckily, my cat—Marley—is still there, and as big as he is, I still pick him up and sob into his fur. Then, I feed him. He must be starving, poor thing.

How had I fallen for this?

My clothing is all there, as is my makeup. My books, journals, and photos are untouched. I grab what I can and shove it into backpacks and grocery bags, and I load everything into my car. Thank God my car is there at the apartment. Rick had picked me up for work the day that Ryan had taken me to his Baltimore apartment, and I think about how lucky I am.

My answering machine is still there, too, and it shows that I have tons of messages. But I leave it. I throw clothing and books into the car, wondering if my work will allow me back and if the church will still let me work there. I think about Jess and if he's missed me, or if he just thinks I'm working too much. I think about how Marley and I are going to survive.

I briefly clean up the apartment so that it looks as though I live there. It's not safe to stay, but it presents a very nice illusion. I put out tons of food for Marley, and I promise him I'll come back every few days. Then, after one last look, I lock the door behind me and go.

It takes several hours, but on the first night, I see Jess, and even though I'm crying, I tell him I've been so busy with work and the church that I hadn't even answered the phone. Plus, I say, the medications make me sleep too much. He understands and holds me. I'm forgiven.

I call work and the church and tell them both that I had been in the hospital, and could I please have my jobs back? Both places tell me that I hadn't been fired, and I can show up as scheduled. Everything is in place. The only thing that isn't is college, but I hadn't been attending classes, anyhow. I hate that local college. Let me flunk out, I think. It's just one semester.

The voice makes a triumphant return. "We handled that well," she says. "Now take your meds and go buy some water. And a blanket. It's going to be cold."

She's right. The first night that I sleep in my car is almost unbearable. I don't have enough money to keep it running, and the car is so old that sleeping with the heat on could kill it—or, potentially, me. I put on as many layers as I can, huddle up in the backseat, and sleep against my backpack. In the morning, I shower in the gym at the college—I may not be showing up for classes, but I still have a student ID—and go into work.

But I'm always watching out. Ryan could return. Even after a week of sleeping in my car, moving it to various locations every night so that no one catches on, I'm terrified to go back to the apartment. I'm paying four hundred fifty dollars for my cat to live there. But he's safe when I run in, hug him, and put out more food. I'm just doing what I need to do.

I am so cold, and so depressed, that I stop going to my waitressing job. I still go to the church so that I can play and sing, but otherwise, I spend my afternoons with Jess. I have no idea how to pay rent for the month of March. I have no idea how to be safe.

I break down. After a random trip to buy Jess a PlayStation for his eighteenth birthday—a purchase that leaves me with only twenty dollars to my name—and a bizarre stop at a car dealer to test drive a BMW (which I can lease for four hundred a month until I mention that I don't have a job), I call my parents. I don't tell them I'm living in my car, but I do tell them I need to come home.

"There will be rules," they say.

Anything is better than living in my car and wondering if I'll be murdered. "Whatever you want. I just need to go back."

My dad meets me at the apartment, and we load up the rest of the belongings. Marley will stay with me; he'll just have to adapt to being an outdoor cat. Out of kindness, or relief—maybe both—my dad settles the rent issue with my landlord and tells him I'm not coming back.

And then, with the few possessions I own, I go back to living with my parents again.

———————

THE SITUATION IS IMMEDIATELY AWFUL. MY MOM READS MY JOURNAL —luckily, I'd been smart enough to not write much about Ryan and what he did, as well as all my psych ward details—and berates me for having sex with Jess in my apartment. What she doesn't know is that I hadn't had sex with him. Since he was a virgin, and inexperienced, all I had to do was hold him tightly in between my legs and moan. It didn't take long. People are easy to fool.

But the invasion of my privacy is something I can't overlook. I sleep all day, refuse to listen to my parents when they tell me to go find a job other than the "church gig," and hide. It's better to hide. It's always safer to be locked away when you're the one holding the lock and key.

Eventually, I get a job as an assistant at a senior living center, and I enjoy it. My Doo-Da had spent some of his sicker days here, and the nurses and I talk about my beloved grandfather.

One night, I go to Jess's after work. His mom, irritated that I've returned home to my parents, doesn't want me in the house. Jess and I sit on the porch swing and try to figure out what to do.

"There's a music college in York," I tell Jess. "I think I want to move there."

"Actually, there's a school near there I was looking at, too," he says. "An art institute."

"Maybe we could move in together."

"Maybe we should just get married."

I look at him, stunned. "What? You just turned eighteen. I don't think we can."

"Well, we can. Why don't we just get married at the church you work for? No one has to be there. Our parents don't have to know. We can plan it, get married, and then go to York."

"You want to marry me?"

"With every inch of my soul," Jess says. "I love you. This will help us."

I work extra shifts so that I can save money. Jess finds a job at night so that he can save up, too. By the Fourth of July, we have enough to get an apartment. But first, he proposes. Under the fireworks in Baltimore, he gets down on one knee, holds out an engagement ring, and tells me he'd be honored if I would say yes and spend the rest of my days with him.

I run into his arms, knocking us both over, and say yes. All the people nearby cheer.

This is happening. I'm leaving home, I'm going to a different state, and I'll finally be happy.

Two weeks later, as wedding plans are in full swing—kept secret from everyone except for the members of my church—my parents ask me to go to the Outer Banks with them for a week. Since I know this will be my last trip down there with them, I accept. But it's miserable. They watch me constantly, not trusting me to be out of sight.

On the ride home, my parents tell me that I am spoiled. I'm awful. I am a waste, and when we return, they will find the appropriate way to deal with me.

"Well, that won't be your problem," I say. "Because I'm getting married in six weeks."

My dad pulls the van to the side of the road, and my mom asks me to get out.

But it's not the bloodbath I expect. She's sad, but she says that she'd rather me be in York, going to college, than living in some shitty apartment and not eating. She doesn't like Jess, but it's my life to ruin. She just wants to be at the wedding of her only daughter. I say yes.

Things don't get any better. I ask my friend Allen to be in the wedding, and he refuses, giving me a lecture about how far I've strayed from my musical path. My parents invite their friends, and suddenly, the tiny, twenty-person wedding now involves people I don't know.

Jess and I drive up to York—about an hour away from our home-town—and fall in love with the first apartment we see. It's in a quaint, safe neighborhood, only five minutes by foot from a grocery store and a strip mall, and only ten minutes from the colleges we want to attend. We pay the five hundred dollar deposit and marvel at the space in our two-bedroom home.

I can be an adult. I have this. I can be a responsible, married woman. I will focus on Jess, on our home, and on college. I will drive to the church and continue to work there. And I'll find a part-time job in York. None of those plans can fail, especially since Jess already has a job in York. His current store transfers him to a store in the strip mall, so he doesn't even need a car. Everything is working in our favor.

Our wedding day is on a warm September morning. I push thoughts of getting married too young out of my head as Ann and my mom help me into my new gown. I put on makeup and look in the mirror. I look like something out of a magazine. I am the perfect bride. This is what I'm supposed to look like, I think. This is what those guests expect.

Jess cries when he sees me. Our pastor says some brief words, I sing my vows to Jess, and within twenty minutes, we go from two teenagers who had been dating to a married couple.

The pictures tell the true story, however. No one is happy. I am wearing my fake smile, and my parents don't smile at all. At the tiny reception in the church basement, people clap, but they look like statues.

We can't even drink real liquor here. This is a joke. I shouldn't be doing this.

After the reception, I drive us to a hotel in Baltimore, where we'll be spending our three-day honeymoon. It's the only thing we can afford: to be tourists in what is practically our own city.

But I don't want to leave the room. And I don't. I don't leave the bed until the last day of our honeymoon. I order room service and watch the end of the Summer Olympics. When Jess suggests we go out, I tell him no. My life feels like it's ending, not beginning.

Back in York, Jess begins his job at the strip mall, and I spend most of my days in bed. A new psychiatrist I've been seeing has given me a fifth medication, so it's easier to crash and burn than try to give a damn about my life. Jess seems worried, but does little. He works, brings home food, and watches movies with me. I forget about college plans and just sit there, eating.

Two days later, my car dies, and we don't have the money to fix or replace it. We're stuck in York. I call the church and resign. I've resigned to the notion that this is my life. What's the difference? And I've resigned myself to the fact that starvation no longer works. In only four months, I've gained thirty pounds, and I don't care. Maybe people won't rape me now.

When I eventually find the energy to pull myself off the couch, it's in time for the 2000 Election. I spend two days on the floor, glued to the TV, talking about hanging chads and voter fraud. And that's when I realize I miss human interaction. I dress in my nicest clothes and walk to the strip mall. I'll take a job at whatever place happens to be hiring.

The Bon-Ton hires me on the spot. I'll start within the week. My hours are flexible, which means that, when I do want to go to college, I can. And now we'll be able to afford a car, too.

But working at a clothing store is mindless. I was happy working at the church. Now? I fold shirts. All those years of people telling me I was so intelligent and talented seem to be wasted on this job. And the more I think about my life, the more I hear the voice.

"End it," she says. "You know how. You've had enough. It's time."

On New Year's Eve, Jess finds me in our kitchen with a knife up against my wrist. I cut, but only slightly, and then I collapse to the floor, too exhausted to finish what I'd started.

"You can't die and leave me," Jess cries. "I love you."

"Oh, child," the voice says as I stare at him. "Love doesn't save anyone."

And from my nineteen years of experience, I know that she is right.

2001

My life is not worth living, I think as I grab discarded clothing from the men's section of Bon-Ton. I'm nineteen, married, not studying music at a college I want to go to, and no one understands why I think about dying. My parents hate me. I have nightmares about Thomas, and Stone, and Ryan. Everything I do seems to be wrong. I even weigh too much now. I'm the worst.

Lorna, a fellow employee at the Bon-Ton, notices that I'm often talking to myself.

"What's wrong, honey?" she asks. She's sixty, working here as a retired woman to get out of the house, and she's one of the only friends I have in York.

"My head is just—foggy," I say. "I can't explain it to you. I'm sorry."

Lorna looks around the store, and we both notice that it's empty. It's 2:00 p.m. on a weekday. Of course it's empty. "Come here," she says. "I want to tell you something."

She pulls me into a dressing room and we sit on the bench together.

"Look," she says, taking my hands into hers. "I'm old. Much older than you. I could be your grandmother. But that doesn't mean I don't get it. That doesn't mean I don't have issues."

"I never assumed that my life was worse," I say. "I'm sorry. I didn't mean that."

Lorna shakes her head. "No. What I'm trying to say—poorly, but trying—is that I have a disorder. My husband noticed it about ten years ago, and he took me to a hospital."

"What's it called? Are you going to be okay?"

Lorna smiles softly. "I'm okay," she says. "It's bipolar disorder. I hear voices. I see things that don't exist sometimes. I've tried to harm myself. Yes—at the age of fifty, my husband found me in the kitchen with a knife pressed to my throat. I didn't feel like I could control it."

I break down into sobs as she hugs me. Finally, I think. Someone gets this.

"What do I do?" I ask. "I'm not the girl everyone thought I would be. I've let everyone down."

"You've let yourself down," she says. "And it's not too late. You're nineteen. Live your life. Go back to college. Go sing. Take healthy risks. Don't do the things that could hurt you. If you love something, do it. You're still so pretty, and young, and healthy. Why not live?"

And for the first time in ages, I wonder if she's right. Why not live?

The next day, I tell Jess that we need a car. It's February, walking to work is a freezing proposition, and my boss just so happens to have a husband who sells used vehicles.

"Can we afford it?" he asks.

I look around at the gaming systems Jess has bought, at the DVDs he's collected, and I nod.

"Yeah," I say. "It's a top priority. Not all this shit. We're getting a car tonight."

"But we can walk to work."

"Not to school," I tell him. "I'm going back. I'm applying for the fall semester."

That night, we haggle with my boss's husband, who wants to sell us a death trap for six thousand dollars. But instead, we find a safer car for less money. It's only one hundred eighty dollars a month. We can afford it.

Jess takes me to dinner at a chain restaurant that night to celebrate. And as I complain about working at a clothing store, our server overhears our conversation.

"You know, the boss is hiring," she says. "I think you'd like it here."

"Serving food? Probably not."

"It's flexible. Nights and weekends work well for college students."

She must assume I'm in school. And while I'm not yet, that's still the goal. I ask her to bring me an application, and at the table, I fill it out. If I get this job, I'll have to drive, as it's about ten minutes away from the apartment, but Jess can still walk to work. We'll make do.

But making it doesn't seem good enough. I need more. I need to be better.

So I stop taking my medication.

"You're falling apart," Jess says one evening. "Please, just take your meds."

As much as I don't want to admit it, Jess is right. I'm in withdrawal. I spend days in bed, sweating, vomiting, coming down hard from the impact. I can't eat or sleep, and I scream constantly. I'm sure Jess is going to leave me. I wanted to be a wife, but I'm just insane.

Eventually, the haze passes, and when it does, I find out that I've been hired by the restaurant I'd applied to the previous week. Thanks to my former serving experience and a surprisingly good recommendation from that establishment, I can begin training in three days. I'll be on weekend shifts to start and will then end up working four full nights until midnight.

I'm thrilled, but I don't know how to show it. I'm too worn out. And on top of everything else, it's Valentine's Day. I'd been too sick to think about it, but now, I realize that my first Valentine's Day as someone's wife isn't going to occur in a romantic manner.

Because money is so tight—the car payments are hard to make since I haven't been working—Jess and I eat in. Tuna sandwiches and pickles. And then we hit up the one-dollar movie theatre to see a movie we've already watched ten times. But at least it's something.

When Jess is at work the next day, I take the kitchen knife to the inside of my thigh, in the usual spot—where Thomas scarred me in 1996. I can't get over it.

"You need me," the voice says. "Don't medicate me away."

"I know I need you."

But I silence her as I put on my black pants and red shirt for work. The training is ridiculous and a total waste of my time: I'm given one table each night for two weeks. As a person who served ten tables at once only a year prior, I feel personally insulted. But by the end of the two weeks, the manager is impressed with my skills, and I'm given a decent rotation—Saturday nights, Sunday afternoon through closing, and two weeknights. Most servers with that schedule clear a hundred dollars in tips per night.

Things seem to be looking up.

Spring arrives, and with it comes my typical mood—carefree, overly confident in my abilities, and with a massive need to spend money. I decide to put it all to good use. I go to York College, pick up the applications I need, and apply to the music program. I go out and have my hair cut in a style suitable for my rounder face—on stage, I have to look pretty again. That's half of what counts, and I know this. I buy a few outfits that flatter my body so that I'm ready for the academic interview and the performance I'll have to give the department if they accept me. I'm working, and making my own money, so why not splurge on my future?

It doesn't take long for the mail to get to me. I've been accepted into the college, and pending a "stellar performance" for the music department, I will be part of the program in the fall. I run around the apartment, screaming. My life is happening!

And the audition goes better than I had hoped. The choral director, as well as three voice coaches, sit in the theatre seats as I sing two arias from well-known operas and a song from *Jekyll and Hyde*. When the director stands up and says, "Very nice. Excellent breath control. You have a clear and strong sound," I know that I'm in.

When that official letter arrives the following week, I run around the apartment some more. Finally, I'm going to be a vocal performance major. I'm going to sing in operas. I'm going to study what I love and will make a career out of it. I just had to do it in my own time.

My parents are thrilled. They are thrilled that I'm working so hard and will be going back to college. My focus is now on more than just suicide and Jess—it's on my future.

I spend the entire summer working, saving up as much money as I can so that I can try to cut my hours from forty a week down to twenty-five. With performances, I'm going to need nights and weekends. At first, the manager protests. I'm one of his best servers, he says as we close down the restaurant. I bring in a lot of cash from the bar. Losing me at night would cost them.

"Then compromise," I say. "Make a deal with me. What am I worth?"

He takes me over to the bar where Patrick, the bartender, is still cleaning up.

"Do you know how to mix drinks?" the manager says.

I laugh. "I've been mixing drinks for two years. I learned well at seventeen."

Patrick smiles. "You know, our other bartender isn't here on weekends right now. Maybe we can just bring you on and tell people you're twenty-one, not nineteen."

The night manager nods his head. "I was thinking that as well. Here's the plan: you work regular shifts twice a week and tend bar Friday and Saturday nights, unless you tell me you have a performance. Otherwise, as long as you're here by five p.m., I don't care. Deal?"

He extends his hand, and I look at all the sparkling bottles behind the bar. I smile, and take a sip of the drink Patrick has placed in front of me.

"Deal." I shake the night manager's hand. "Most definitely a goddamn deal."

I'VE SIGNED UP FOR FIVE CLASSES AND TWO PRIVATE MUSIC LESSONS for my Fall 2001 semester. My advisor, Dr. Anders, thinks I may be overloading, but I smile at him.

"I took twenty-one credits at my last college, and despite being hospitalized for septicemia, still received a 4.0 GPA—and I performed while septic. I can do this."

And I believe I can. I go to campus, explore how beautiful it is, marvel at the music building, groan a bit as I buy my books, and prepare for this new life.

On my way home from buying books and turning in a scholarship form, the car dies.

I have no way to get to college now.

I don't want to do it—I know the emotional ramifications, the stipulations, the fact that I'll have to sacrifice some semblance of freedom —but I call my parents. I tell them that the car has died, and while Jess can still walk to work, I can no longer get to work or college.

And they help. The next day, they take me to a car dealership, and I find a small, used, reliable Dodge Neon. My parents make the down payment, but the monthly payments are mine. The title is in their name, but they don't place any stipulations on the transaction.

"We know you want to go to college," my mom says. "And you did that on your own. You applied. You got in. You got the aid and scholarships. We're proud of you."

She hugs me, and this time, I hug her back. Maybe the worst has passed. Maybe now, as a college student, living the life they had hoped for me, I can be their daughter again.

As long as I don't talk about being bipolar. We don't talk about that.

In their world, that doesn't exist.

I BEGIN MY SOPHOMORE YEAR AT YORK COLLEGE AT THE END OF August and immediately immerse myself in the music program. It's a true time commitment. We have Friday afternoon concerts every week. We perform four or five shows a semester. We are juried often.

Music Theory, Composition, Music History, Choir, Women's Choir —whatever the music program has offered that fall, I'm taking it. I spend my days in the music building, making friends with fellow singers and instrumentalists. And I don't feel out of place. I feel a little old sometimes—I'm almost twenty, and some of the students have just turned eighteen—but the age difference isn't drastic. And I have more experience. I know how to use that to my advantage.

But I'd forgotten how intense college could be, especially with regular performances. And a husband. And work. And, on occasion, sleep.

Something has to give. But I don't let it. I attend classes. I sing everything asked of me. I show up on time for every shift at the restaurant and make excellent money. I'm flourishing.

But then the world falls apart, and the entire country falls with it.

I SEE ABSOLUTELY NOTHING OF THE EVENTS THAT OCCUR ON September 11, 2001. The news is on in the bedroom while I get ready for my 9:00 a.m. class, but Jess and I barely pay attention. As I prepare to leave, I hear something about New York City on the TV, but I think nothing of it. NYC is always discussed on the Today Show. That's where they film it.

My class is in the music building's basement, and it's followed by a 10:30 a.m. workshop. Those of us in the 9:00 a.m. class are all in the same workshop, so we just hop from one room to the next and spend three hours inside.

When we exit the music building at noon, the campus is empty. Most of the cars are gone. The sky is clear, and there's a slight breeze, but the calm nature of the campus is eerie.

"Aliens," a friend jokes. I smack him on the arm and we head over to the student union.

Inside, hundreds of students are crowded around the large TV. No one is moving. Some of them are on their cell phones, but the calls don't seem to go through, so they cry in frustration.

On the screen, I watch as a tower is blown up. And then another. There are screams. People are jumping out of windows thirty stories from the ground.

"Are you guys watching *Independence Day?*" I ask a fellow college student.

He shakes his head. "Honey, where have you been? This isn't a movie. It's real."

"What?"

He tells me the details: hijacked planes, bombings, crashes, attacks on the Pentagon, and the collapse of the Twin Towers in NYC. As I stand there in shock, he puts his arm around me.

"We're in danger, too," he says quietly. "We're only twenty miles from a nuclear power plant. The entire county has been asked to evacuate."

I run out of the student union to call Jess, but I can't get through. So many people are making calls—no one can find out if their loved ones are safe.

I start to panic. I go home, where I find Jess. We hug each other and then load up the car. We'll head back to check on our families. We shouldn't stay this close to a nuclear facility.

But we have no concept of what is safe. As tornado sirens and emergency alerts sound throughout the county, we're paralyzed. We don't go anywhere. Instead, Jess heads back to work and I call a few college friends. We hide out in a basement, talking about the apocalypse, and how we should have known this was going to happen.

We spend several hours in that basement, and nothing occurs. Finally, I go home. Jess is back by then, watching the news. Matt Lauer is still on—he's been on the air for twelve hours now, I think—and he's crying. Matt Lauer is as exhausted as everyone else in America.

"Let's go to the mall," I say. "I need new shoes."

"Right now?" Jess says. "In the middle of a worldwide crisis?"

"Well, what the hell else are we going to do? Drive to DC? We don't have anywhere to go. We don't have anywhere to be. We have to just be—normal people."

He nods, and we get into my car. The mall is mostly closed, but there are enough people that we feel safe. We're able to get my shoes and some coffee. We're okay.

Our college holds a vigil the next day. I go, but only because I'm required to sing one song. Then, as people hold candles and cry, I leave and sit in my car.

I have about ten Xanax left over from last year's prescription. They're probably expired.

I take five of them. And I fall asleep in my car, blissfully unaware of the world around me that is slowly tearing itself apart.

LIFE RESUMES TO SOME SEMBLANCE OF NORMALCY BY MID-OCTOBER, and at this point, my days begin at 7:00 a.m. and end at 1:00 a.m. I stop sleeping, because I always need to be somewhere: in class, at an opera rehearsal, doing homework, or at the restaurant. Money is good and my grades are fine, but my health is slipping. I find myself losing chunks of time, but when I wake up, I see that my homework is finished. I have no idea what's happening to me.

I star in an opera, but remember little about it. It's good, I'm told. And when I sing Mozart's Requiem in D Minor, I sound like I'm part of the music, my choir director says.

Then he, along with my private voice instructor, tap me for a national competition at an Ivy League school three hours away. I'm to perform three opera pieces in front of a jury, and then perform one on stage in front of the select group that has been chosen for this honor. All that's required of me is a car and my voice. The hotel room is paid for, and we'll receive free meals. I just have to drive up on Friday, sing on Saturday, and come home on Sunday.

I tell work that I cannot come in two weeks from now. I prepare my pieces, and do little else, until the day arrives and I make the three-hour drive.

The competition begins at 9:00 a.m. Saturday, so by 7:30 a.m., I am dressed in a formal gown, my hair is curled, and I am ready. As I walk into the prestigious university, I study the room. I'm up against twenty other female vocalists. But this is not a challenge. I can win.

But when I walk into the jury room, I see that my voice coach is one of the jurors.

I try to brush off the feeling that he shouldn't be grading me—he's the one who helped me learn this music, after all. But I feel awkward, and as I sing, I hear it in my voice. I strain when I shouldn't. I don't hit the highest note in my aria correctly. I'm not going to win.

I'm handed my evaluation sheet at the end of the day Saturday. And, much to my surprise, I am a finalist. I'll sing in front of the group. Besides, most of the words on the sheet are kind. "Clear voice." "Beautiful appearance." "Fantastic breath control."

The only negative words come from my own voice instructor. "Didn't sing with passion," he writes. "Doesn't understand how to sing in Spanish."

Motherfucker. I'm fluent in Spanish. Are you fluent in asshole?

The next day, I don another dress and perform for everyone. But I don't win. I place, but I don't win. Another girl, who chooses a song from a highly overrated music, wins instead.

I go home jaded. Jess is at work, and I slam through the glass doors, telling him that this is bullshit. I should have won. I'd been set up.

"You were not," he says. "Maybe you just didn't sound that great."

Infuriated, I shove the evaluation at him. "According to this, everything I did was great! The only criticisms came from my vocal instructor. This is bullshit!"

Jess ignores me and returns to work as I drive home in my gown, sobbing. I'd come here to succeed. And I just failed in a major competition. I knew I was worthless.

I take a handful of pills, drink a bottle of cheap champagne from the strip mall's liquor store, and fall onto the bed. Maybe I'll die, I think as I begin to fade. Maybe no one will notice.

With only a week until finals and winter break, I find something that lifts my spirits. The theatre department is putting on a production of Jason Robert Brown's *Songs For a New World*. I don't know much about it, but there are only four parts—two males, two females—and I decide, without telling anyone, that I'm going to audition for the female lead.

Auditions close at 6:00 p.m. At 5:45, I walk through the door and meet the directors, Jodie and Brennan. I hand my sheet music to Ed, the pianist for the show, and I perform.

"We were about to give up hope," Brennan tells me. "We had one girl in mind to sing this role, but you—you nailed it."

The cast list is posted the next day. I get the lead—female #1. I am vindicated.

Rehearsals don't start until after the holidays, so I take my finals, sing in my juries, perform at several Christmas concerts, and still work at the bar. I'm doing just fine.

On my first free day before Jess and I leave to visit his parents for Christmas, I fall asleep on the couch. I don't wake up for thirty-six hours.

And I don't care. My grades are in—a 3.8 GPA, and I'm angry, because I think I deserved the 4.0—and I have no desire to spend Christmas with Jess and his parents. But we do. We smile, unwrap gifts, sing carols, and eat. Jess and I sleep on a fold-out couch, celebrating our second Christmas as a married couple.

"This feels weird," I say to him. "I don't—I don't feel anything."

"You're still tired." Jess kisses me. "I love you. And I know you love me."

But deep down, I know the truth: Things have changed. I don't love him at all.

2002

Our first rehearsal for *Songs For a New World* is held during a blizzard at the beginning of January. But that doesn't deter our four-person cast, our pianist, and our two directors. We meet up, we all get to know one another, and within the hour, we're hitting it off like long-lost family members. Everyone there is talented and dedicated. Within days, we have the music down, and the music director and I often drive around in her car, singing the songs.

"Belt out this note," she tells me. "You have the power to do it. Don't sing it like it's opera—sing it like it's your life."

The line she refers to mentions being afraid but pretending not to be. This character can hide fear and pain like a champion. Does her family love her? Maybe. Does her boyfriend love her? Potentially. Is she going to build up walls in case they get to her before she can get to them? Absolutely. And the more I think about it, the more I relate. That night, in the car, the note comes out, strong and powerful. We pull over to the side of the road, hug, and cry.

I find my family with this cast. In the seven weeks we have to prepare everything, we spend almost all our waking hours together. Even when spring semester begins at the end of January, we go to class, go to work, and rehearse. Then we go get Chinese food or Dunkin'

Donuts. We sing for patrons in fast food joints, and they cheer. Everything is perfect.

Except Jess is angry with me. I'm never home. If I'm not at school, I'm at rehearsal. Or I'm in a concert. Or I'm at work. When I mention to him that a professor has told me about transferring to an elite music school to study opera, he rolls his eyes and tell me I'll never make it. Plus, we're not moving four hours away just for me.

In four years, I've gone from being his beautiful, talented angel to someone who just pisses him off. But the sad thing is that I no longer care. I'm only married to him now because it's easier than getting a divorce. And we both know it.

My mom calls one night—a bizarre night when I don't have to be at rehearsal or at work—and asks how things are. I want to tell her that my life is wonderful. But thoughts of Jess race through my mind, and I ask her if I can meet her and my dad.

She agrees, and I drive the hour to my hometown to meet them at an upscale restaurant. And there, I tell my parents that I had been foolish. I shouldn't have married Jess. I did so to escape, but then I learned that I could have done all of this on my own. I didn't need him. I didn't love him. I wanted to go wherever my career choices took me, and he was holding me back.

"He has always held you back," my dad says. "If you leave him, we will support you."

"I think you're really starting to make wiser choices," my mom says.

We discuss the fine details—I'd stay in York until the end of the semester, come home to them for the summer, and then get an apartment on campus with fellow students. I'd be a junior, living a normal college life. I'd still work, go to class, and perform. I'd just be divorced.

They agree, and that night, I contemplate how to tell Jess.

But I don't tell him right away, because Hell Week is upon us in the theatre. We're there almost sixteen hours a day. The restaurant is fed up with my schedule, and they ask me what's more important—school or money? When I say school, I also tell them I quit. I can do better than what they provide. I refuse to denounce my education for bartending.

Jess, who's been working two jobs, is angry at my impulsive decision. He doesn't seem to understand that college—musical aside—is a full-time job. And York isn't lacking places that need servers or other workers. When the musical is over, I'll slide into another job. Simple.

The night before *Songs* opens, Jess and I have an argument while trying to go to sleep. He is tired of working and getting nothing in return. He wants to go to college, too. When I tell him to go, he says he can't work and go to school.

"Well, what the fuck do you think I was doing?" I ask. "I worked fifty hours a week while taking twenty-one credits. And I was in operas!"

"And you didn't give a damn about us," he says.

"No," I say, and without meaning to, I start to cry. Out of instinct—or maybe some remaining love, I'm not sure—Jess pulls me to him.

"You don't love me," he says. "Not in the way you used to."

And I shake my head. "No. I think that, at the end of this semester, I need to move out. I want a divorce."

He cries, and I cry with him. Despite the lack of love I feel, I do care about his wellbeing. And I'm grateful we did leave to come to York. That created a new life for me.

"Okay," he says. "I understand. It hurts, and I do love you, but that's what we'll do."

"Then you can do anything," I tell him. "You can live on campus. You can focus on school instead of work. You'll have so many opportunities. We're limiting each other."

"Really?" he says. "I just thought we'd been in love."

My heart aches. But I know I'm doing the right thing. I'm setting both of us free.

ALL FIVE PERFORMANCES OF THE MUSICAL DO EXTREMELY WELL, AND on closing night, I'm greeted with kind words, flowers, visits from friends I hadn't seen in years (including Carrie, who is now dating Bo—and while he stares at me and doesn't say much, I'm glad that they connected and that he's finally moved on), and a few newspaper interviews. One of the reporters is from our tiny school newspaper, and when he catches me before the after-party, he lavishes me with praise. I sing like an angel, he says. He wants to write the entire article about me. But I say no.

I drink at least a dozen bottles of beer at the after-party. Carrie and Bo attend to spend time with me, but I'm a mess—drunk, still high on praise, and a nightmare to be around. When they leave, I feel badly, but then a bunch of us pile on the floor to cuddle up and go to sleep, and I don't care about anything else in the moment. I'm with my new family.

"You know that in a few weeks, you'll have no one," the voice says in the middle of the night. She startles me, and I sit up. I'd been laying with the male lead, but at some point, he'd made his way over to another girl, and they are making out.

"Maybe it's already over. Maybe this whole 'we'll always stay in touch' thing is bullshit."

"Now you're catching on," she says.

I leave the party, completely hung over, and drive home. Jess isn't expecting me, so I crash on the couch. The musical is over, and the next opera isn't for another eight weeks. All I have are classes and a pending divorce, and the definite need to get another job.

The depression kicks in again. I miss a few weeks of class, and do nothing but stare at the TV. I know I'm falling apart. And it's more than just post-show blues. I'm not needed. The cast has already started to break apart—we don't email and talk as much now. We go see a musical together, but things already feel strained. Our bond, while there, is starting to unravel.

To pay rent and put gas in my car, I take a job at Subway. The pay is awful, and the work is demeaning. The benefit is the free food, but every night, I come home smelling like processed meat, and I find myself eating far too many subs and cookies.

I look at myself in the mirror after work one night. And the difference from early 2000 to April 2002 is astonishing. I am at least twenty-five pounds overweight. I've given up.

The next night, I take some pills—pills I hadn't touched in six months. Lithium, Zyprexa, all the ones doctors keep prescribing without much thought. But they make me sick.

There's an upside to this. If I want to lose twenty-five pounds, I can vomit them away.

This semester, I take a public speaking class. It's an easy A, especially as a performer, and I bond with the professor. He uses me as an example of what to do while speaking for others. But one day, after class, he asks me to stay.

"Did I do something wrong?" I ask. "I thought things were going well."

"They are," he says. "And in a month, you'll be out of here, on summer break, probably having the time of your life. But something is wrong right now, isn't it?"

All I can do is nod.

"There's a counselor here at school," he says. "Her name is Julie. I hope you don't mind, but I've made an appointment for you to see her."

I'm so tired, strung out from old pills and vomiting and lying. I agree.

After all, I keep breaking my life. I blow it all apart. Now, I need help to rebuild.

I MOVE INTO THE SECOND BEDROOM OF THE APARTMENT JESS AND I share. It doesn't make sense to sleep in the same bed during the last month of our time together, and plus, I'm rarely home. I think he knows why, but keeps silent. We pay bills and the rent. We work, and I go to school. He's going out more with people I dislike, but what do I care now?

I'd be a hypocrite to say anything, since I've taken to sleeping around with other men.

In the middle of a very busy musical month—I'm in an opera, a musical, and prepping for May juries—I meet with Julie. She takes one look at me, shuts her office door, and says, "Okay. What happened? It doesn't take much to know that you've been through trauma."

How can she tell?

"It's not that bad," I tell her. "I sing. I have a job. Things are good."

"You can lie to yourself all you'd like. But I can see through it."

During that first session, I spill my past to her. And it's all too much. I have, without thinking, given her my complete trust.

Julie asks me to try to focus. "You can't handle all that trauma at once," she says. "You have to start somewhere. And you know you can live what you call a 'good' life now and still feel rooted in the past. Let's pick a place to start, and try to get your brain out of trauma."

"Thomas," I tell her. "I need to forget Thomas. If I forget him, I can be happy. I can be thin and pretty again. I can perform better. I can have the life I want."

"We can start there," Julie says. "But it's not about forgetting. It's about learning to deal with the horrible things he did to you."

And I listen. Something about Julie's demeanor calms me. I am her attentive audience.

I pack and prepare to move my life back to my parent's house. I work, I go to rehearsals, and I try not to piss off a very aggravated, emotional Jess.

But Jess is easy to aggravate, and one night, after he forces me to have sex with him, I know how much I need to get out. It's as though I'm leaving my parent's house in 1999 all over again: as long as I have the important things, like my books, photos, and clothing, I don't care about the rest. It's all shit. I just want out. Retraction: I need out.

But I stick around through the final musical, juries, and academic finals. I stay on campus most of the time, practicing my vocal techniques, and talking to the head of the music department, who thinks that I might want to consider "more advanced" colleges for music.

"Actual institutions," he says. I cringe when I hear the word "institution," but know he's on a different wavelength. "I think performance schools should be your focus. You have a 3.8 GPA through the school and a 4.0 GPA in the music program. You've performed in almost every major concert and opera this year. You'd have tons of recommendation letters. I don't doubt you could handle the audition. As much as I'd hate to lose you, you have the qualifications to get in. Why not choose a school that focuses on opera?"

I debate it for about two nights. Am I well enough to start over, as a junior, at a prestigious music college? Or am I just some twenty-year-old who is going to wash out, and the degree won't mean anything?

I make my decision when my jury results come back. I did well: my performances were solid, heartfelt, passionate, and beautiful to listen to. My interpretation of the recitatives in Handel's *Messiah* were very well performed. But I only score what amounts to a 92 percent.

And that's not good enough for me. It's probably my appearance, I think. Weighing 150 pounds is a bad thing. They're not just judging my voice. I know better.

I tell the head of the music department that I won't be leaving York. I'll be staying, and taking voice classes, but that I will likely be switching my major for the Fall 2002 semester.

He's stunned. "We're losing you anyhow? Why? What's more important than music?"

Nothing, to be honest. Music is my life. I promised music to Doo-Da, too. But I don't feel as though I'm cutting it. I tell him that I'll be turning toward two new majors—English and History. "I'm going to study International Relations and go to law school," I say. And this makes sense. I've been raised by an attorney. I've worked for him. Why not go into law to help other people?

I drive away from campus, the semester finally over. Julie, my therapist, says she'll keep in touch via email during the summer, and that, in the fall, I should find a proper psychiatrist to monitor my medication. I load up my car with everything I own, and before heading the hour away, leaving York to move back home, Jess and I share a long hug, some tears, and a brief kiss. There are papers being filed. This is the end. And endings have the right to be emotional.

As I head home, the windows down, I smoke. I can't do this around my parents—I'll get kicked out—but I have plans to be out, go out, and work. Everything will be fine.

Incubus's "Drive" comes on the radio as I near home. It's fitting, and I smile.

Maybe, after all the heartache, I will have a second chance.

THE SUMMER ISN'T AWFUL, AND MY PARENTS, THRILLED WITH MY homecoming and the notion that I now want to study law in college, grant me more freedom than I'd expected. And, much to my surprise, the voice doesn't command me to go out and get drunk. I work at my dad's law firm, and I make good money. I put dating on hold and start walking every night to lose weight. I check in with Julie once a week, and tell her that I'm starting over. September 2002 will produce a better version of who I am: dedicated, focused, a twenty-year-old with an actual mission.

I have time to contemplate my choices as I drive alone to the Outer Banks. The seven-hour drive only takes five hours as I speed to my destination. Once I'm by the water, I'll have my answers. I know I will. The ocean is my home, and in my heart, I know that she will provide.

The ocean provides for certain. At night, alone, on the pier, I sing, and the ocean sings back. We are in harmony. One night, I go to the edge of the water and let the waves lap at my toes. I feel beckoned. "Take that kayak your dad still has and come join me," the ocean says. But I don't. Maybe I should, I think. But I can't. I can't be that kid any longer.

Two weeks is a long time to spend in a small beach house with my parents, my thirteen-year-old brother, and four family friends. While I'm lucky enough to have my own room, I know leaving it means I must interact with everyone else. And when my mom is around people, she is in overdrive. Sometimes, this is a good thing: everyone is happy and entertained. But sometimes, it's damning. Things must be her way, according to her schedule, and I don't want a scheduled vacation. I'm here to write, to think about my future, and to plan.

But it's rare that I'm left alone, and the two weeks drag. And I'm consumed, without reason, by morose thoughts. As I write them down, the voice comes out to reprimand me.

"You already gave up music. Give up this emotional bullshit. Be normal."

Normal? I have a voice inside of my bipolar brain telling me to be normal?

When the vacation ends, I'm relieved. I'll miss the ocean, as always, as well as the local coffee shop and the pier, but I'm ready to go back to work and to prepare for the fall semester. In about a month, I'll be living back in York in an on-campus apartment with two roommates. And I think about how incredibly normal this will be for a twenty-year-old college junior.

I check my email after returning home. A former high school friend has messaged me—someone who knows about Thomas and all the things he did to me between 1996 and 1997.

"I hate to tell you this, but you should know," he says. "Thomas and his wife? They had a baby girl three days ago. It was in the paper."

My dad hadn't mentioned Jen's pregnancy. But she'd left the law firm about six months ago.

I get up, run downstairs, and search through two weeks of newspapers. And then I see it. There's the birth announcement. Thomas and Jen are parents to a beautiful baby girl.

I go back upstairs, shut myself in my bedroom, and take out my fingernail scissors. As I cut my stomach—a place I know no one will see—I pray. I'm still not sure where I really stand on the God thing, but I take a chance.

"God," I say. "Please, please don't let Thomas hurt that baby. Please. If he's angry, let him come back and find me. But please don't let him hurt that little girl."

The fact Thomas has a daughter sends me spiraling out of control. I head back to the one thing I know will comfort me: alcohol.

———

THE APARTMENT AT YORK IS FANTASTIC, AND MY ROOMMATES, Christa and Terri, are exceptionally sweet. They're only nineteen, and I'm about to turn twenty-one. I feel a bit out of place. But as we set up the apartment and then go out to dinner, we connect. Living with them will be easy, as long as I don't let on to the fact that I drink profusely and allow the voice to lash out at people.

I attend a party, a drunken orgy, only a few days later. I hook up with three guys. I can't remember any of them, and I have no idea how I make it back, two days later, to my apartment.

I'm so drunk that I cannot fall into a college routine. Julie refers me to a wonderful psychiatrist, and he prescribes me more Lithium and Adderall. I'm pleased—Adderall causes weight loss, and my friends have already noticed that I dropped fifteen pounds over the summer. Fifteen or twenty pounds to go, and I'll be a size two again.

But when Terri confronts me about my drinking and calls me an alcoholic, I stop talking to her. I stare at my face, blurry and pale, in the bathroom mirror.

"You've had enough," the voice says. "Just do what you're planning to do."

I open a bottle of Motrin, take two handfuls, and lay down on the bed.

I hope they find me like this. I hope for the absolute worst.

ONE OF MY ROOMMATES CALLS MY PARENTS, BECAUSE WHEN I GET UP to answer a knock at the door—not dead, much to my dissatisfaction —they have a new computer in their hands, and they have incredibly shocked looks on their faces.

"We thought you could use a better computer," my dad says. "But something's wrong."

"I'm busy," I tell them. "Classes. Life. Studying law—you know."

I've been to six classes in two weeks. I'm shocked no one has kicked me out yet.

"You look so pale," my mom says. "Can you come home tomorrow night to talk?"

I tell her yes, and when they leave, I fall back down on my bed and go to sleep.

Before going home the next day, I see my psychiatrist and ask him to write an absence note for me. I lie and say, "I've been too sick on the meds you prescribed for me and can't go to class. I don't want to get kicked out. Can you just write something for me?"

He excuses me from classes for the entire month of September. Surprised, I take the note to my advisor. He tells me that as long as I can do the work online and come in for exams—and drop the gym class I'm taking—my absence will be fine. I agree to his terms.

Back at home, my mom sits with me by the pool and asks me what's wrong. I don't want to tell her. But eventually, I do. I hear voices, I say. Someone used me, and my body hurts because of it. I tried to take too many pills the day before. I drink too much.

"I think you have two options," my mom says, and I wait for a harsh ultimatum. But it doesn't come. "One, you live on campus but commit to seeing a psychologist and psychiatrist down here twice a week—and obviously, you stop drinking. Or two, you can move back home, and you can come and go for school, work, and friends, as long as you aren't drunk."

Despite how much I'd wanted to run away, I go with the latter option. I'll move home, live in my old bedroom, commute to York, and be able to see my local friends.

Christa and Terri are infuriated. We were supposed to have fun together, they say as I pack up my belongings. Why did I turn into a pill-popping drunk? I don't answer. All I say is, "Keep my furniture. I don't want that old shit, anyway," and I head out the door.

But the depression doesn't stop at home. Despite the Lithium and losing more weight—and spending time with my brother, whom I'd missed so deeply—I'm not seeing my friends or drinking, and I desperately crave both.

I take to the Internet. One night, I go onto a chatroom for single people in their thirties. I just want to screw with them. Chatrooms are for losers, and I have never had a problem hooking up.

A guy begins to chat with me. Our conversation grows intense and private, so we leave the chatroom and talk one on one. He tells me that he's only twenty-eight, and when I say that I'm only twenty, we both laugh at the fact we'd met in the thirties chatroom. We both have been to Spain, we both love bacon burgers, we both love going to baseball games, and we both have similar career paths—I want to be a lawyer, and he works for the government.

"But where do you live?" I finally ask this stranger.

"In Maryland," he says. My heart jumps. He lives forty minutes from my house.

"We should meet." I tell him where I live. "I'm in York a lot for college, but we could meet somewhere. Maybe in Baltimore for a day?"

"I work Saturday through Wednesday," he tells me. "If you're available on Thursdays and Fridays, well, it's definitely a date."

I tell him my name, and finally, I learn his. It's Alexander. A name I have always loved.

"This Thursday," Alexander tells me. "We'll meet in Owings Mills, and then I'll drive you into Baltimore for the day. How does that sound?"

My heart is pounding from too much excitement. How is this happening? But I say yes.

We talk on the phone every night and send pictures to one another. He's handsome—tall, with dark hair and glasses. He reminds me of a slightly less buff Clark Kent, and the notion of him being some sort of superhero to me sinks in. He did, after all, save me from suicide. I had planned to drink myself to death that night, but going online and meeting him stopped me.

I skip class that Thursday and spend three hours getting ready. And I think I look cute. I'm thinner—not thin, but getting there—my blondish-red hair is wavy, and my red tank top and jeans flatter my figure. I throw on a pair of heels and head out the door to meet Alexander.

We spot each other at the Metro station immediately, and we hug without thinking.

"Finally," I say. "But I feel like I already know you."

"I know. But you look different from your photos. Did you change them?"

"Why? Is there something wrong with me?"

Alexander smiles. "You're gorgeous. I'm a very lucky man."

The age difference doesn't bother us, and we drive into the city, holding hands and talking. And after only three hours of walking around, getting dinner, and standing by the water at the harbor, he tells me that he can't imagine being without me. Back in his car, we kiss. It's soft and slow, but I trust it, and when we pull away, he says, "I want to do that forever."

"I do, too," I say. "Forever."

He meets my parents that night—they disapprove of the age difference, but like Alexander's accomplishments—and two weeks later, I
meet his grandparents. They ask me to sing for them, and I do. His
grandmother hugs me and says that I'm Alexander's angel. He
needs me.

I don't know what that means, but I soak up her affection. Apparently, I need a grandparent.

That night, Alexander and I skip a lecture on foreign relations that
I'm supposed to attend and end up in his bed. I'm not ready to have
sex, I tell him, and he honors that. But everything else is on the table,
and everything else is performed. I don't talk to him about BDSM
when he smacks me once—I just moan, hoping he'll catch on.

After laying in his bed for an hour, cuddled up and talking, he says,
"I hope this isn't too soon, but—I'm in love with you. I love you. I
can't imagine a life without you."

"Alexander," I say, looking into his eyes. They shift color, almost as
much as my hazel-green eyes do. We are perfectly matched. "I love
you, too. So completely."

But it doesn't take long for me to learn that "completely" comes
with a very extreme catch.

I begin working at a music store in my hometown three
nights a week when Alexander is away in DC at his job. But on the
nights he's home, I stay with him. And his passion and love for me
ignites my desire to do better. I start attending classes and catch up
within two weeks. My International Relations professor and I have
great debates about world politics. My Latin America class sends me to
the library so frequently that Alexander takes me to a large bookstore
one afternoon and buys me every book I need. I marvel at him—
twenty-eight, with a house and an apartment, a government job, and
clearly, money.

I don't deserve him.

But I'm happy. I work, attend class, take my medications, and see

Alexander. I tell him about my disorders, and some of my past, and he holds me. He promises never to let me go.

We spend two nights at his apartment in DC, and while he does work, I do homework. We often glance up at each other and smile, kiss, and go back to what we're doing. It's like we're married but without the paperwork. Eventually, he keeps poking me in the ribs enough that I can't stop giggling, and we end up in his bedroom where we spend hours finally making love.

The next night, though, he has a breakdown. "I saw what you were looking at on my computer! What the fuck is wrong with you?"

I am honestly confused. I don't know what he's talking about.

He drags me by the arm to his desktop. "All of this music college bullshit! I thought you said you wanted to be a lawyer! If so, quit fucking around!"

I'm terrified by how angry he sounds. "I do," I tell him. "I just—I studied opera for many years. Sometimes, I think about going back to perform while working on my law studies. I just wanted to look into my options. I'm sorry."

He slaps me. "Go into the bathroom," he says. "Get in there. You fucking child."

I go into the bathroom, completely numb. I'm two weeks away from turning twenty-one, and I don't know what to say to stand up for myself. I can't rationalize his anger.

Alexander hands me a razor blade. "I've seen your scars," he says. "Sit down and cut until you bleed."

"What the fuck? You want me to..."

I lose my thought as he sharply kicks my knee. I wince and fall to the floor.

"Do it," he says.

And I do. Tears roll down my face as I slice into my leg. He walks out of the bathroom, but I hear him by the door. I can't leave or run away.

It's more disturbing that I hear him masturbating while he listens to me cry.

When he finally checks on me—the wound in my leg bleeding

enough for him to be satisfied—he picks me up, carries me to bed, and holds me. "I'm so sorry," he says. "I love you."

Do you? Is this your way to show me how you love me?

He's at work the next weekend when I go to our state Renaissance Festival with Carrie. She asks to meet Alexander, but I quickly say no. He always works. She stares at me, her eyes saying everything.

But I still drive from York to his house—almost ninety minutes away—to be with him three days a week. We celebrate my twenty-first birthday at a club, and since it's right around Halloween, he buys expensive costumes so we can go in style. But he's dressed me as a hooker.

"You're mine," Alexander says, "and I want people to be jealous."

But when I go out on the floor to dance, he doesn't join me. He tells me to go have fun. Thirty minutes later, sweaty and ready for another drink—legal now, finally, though the appeal is wearing off after four years of illegal drinking—he's furious. Why did I dance with that other guy? Just because I look like a hooker doesn't mean I should act like one. I'm a stupid bitch.

At his house, he takes my pill vials. "You don't need these," he says. "You need me."

I can't tell anybody about this. I love him—I really do. I can't imagine losing him.

I'm just worried he's going to destroy me.

BY MID-NOVEMBER, ALEXANDER AND I HAVE BROKEN UP TWICE. The first time was my call, as I'd grown tired of his antics. But the second time was a bloodbath, and I'd ended up bruised and drunk in a random hotel room. The voice urged me to call Alexander to tell him I was dying.

"I'm so sorry," he cried, arriving at the room shortly after. "I do love you. I'm just scared. I don't know who I am. But I promise you this—I want to be with you. I will always love you. That will never change. Stay with me."

I stayed.

But staying didn't make things better. He stops calling me every night, and after a week of me crying in bed, missing more classes—certain I've flunked out of York by now—I decide to give up. He's a liar. He claims to love me but then asks me to cut myself weekly. Sure, we've had sex, but he isn't present—something about him isn't all there. I don't know what to do.

On a random, late-November night, Alexander takes me to DC. We stop at a popular restaurant for dinner, and our conversation is normal. It's as though things are back to the way they were in September when we fell in love. We are happy. We're normal. We'll be just fine.

Halfway through dinner, he takes a phone call, and while I mentally tally up my purchases from the day—I had to buy yet another dress for an upcoming government dinner, and some early Christmas shopping got added to the list—I realize that I've maxed out almost all my twelve credit cards. I can't tell Alexander—he has a lot of money, but he'll berate me. Why does he do this back and forth routine? Tonight is fine. Even taking a call during dinner is fine—I understand that his job is important. But why does he love, then hate, everything about me?

As I sit there, I remember something his grandmother had told me a few weeks earlier during one of our regular visits. "Darling," she had said, holding one of my hands while flipping through a photo album with the other. "Alexander needs you. He's been through a lot. He was in the military—he saw some things that scarred him. He had to have a major surgery—I know you know about the surgery, but it was because his heart stopped. He still thinks he's running on borrowed time, though his doctors say he's perfectly normal. He lives in fear. And when we met you, we knew you were his angel in disguise. But I know all this may be hard to understand."

No, I had told her. I knew all too well about living in fear.

"Just love him," she had said softly. "Give him a chance to prove he is a good man."

Alexander walks in from his phone call, and he smiles. We finish dinner, and back at his apartment, he tells me that he may be getting a promotion. We make love to celebrate.

I can do this. This is okay. And when we both leave the next morning, I kiss him furiously. "I love you," I say. "I will always believe in you."

"I love you so much," he says, holding me to him. "I'll never betray you."

I don't hear from him for three days. On the night before Thanksgiving, I call his neighbor, panicked—Alexander hasn't been answering his phone—and his neighbor tells me Alexander is at a strip club. He gives me the name, and I drive up there. But no one is there. The club is closed. And Alexander isn't at home. His car isn't in the driveway. He's alive, but not home.

I spend the night crying, and on Thanksgiving, Alexander calls me.

"You idiot," he says. "I don't go to strip clubs. We were just playing a joke on you. You need to get over yourself. You aren't perfect, you know."

"I'm tired of this," I say. "I can't do this anymore."

"You can't love me? Well, fine. Because I was never really in love with you. I mean, I love you as a person, but I am not in love with you. You don't mean anything to anyone."

"Are you dumping me?"

"You've never been dumped?"

"Not really, no," I say, shaking. "I usually—get to that part first."

"Well, princess, live and learn. I never want to see you again. Don't call me. Goodbye."

I'm stunned. I know it's over this time. And when I tell my mom, who is recovering from a surgery, she says that he's an ass. I'm better off without him.

I want to believe her, but I can't. He said he loved me. I gave everything up for him—mental health visits to my counselor, medication, money in gas and clothing for events we never attended, even my entire college semester—and this was the return. What had I done wrong?

I'd been a fool. I cry myself to sleep that night, and the night after, and pray I can forget.

ALEXANDER HAUNTS ME. AFTER HIS NEIGHBOR CALLS ME TO TELL ME that Alexander hadn't been up for a promotion, but had been fired, I understand his anger. But it doesn't excuse his behavior. Why did he want me to cut myself or keep discarding me whenever he felt like it?

I start to act like the fool I'd been made out to be. I max out the remainder of my credit cards on things I don't need. I go to the club Alexander and I went to for my birthday and get drunk, grinding up on random guys, hooking up with them in their cars. I stop at the 7-11 near my house and smoke, often grabbing numbers from guys looking for a quick fix. I stop eating entirely. I talk to Bo, and he tells me that he still likes me as much as he did in high school, even though he's with Carrie. I tell him to figure it out because he cannot win me back.

A few days before Christmas, I arrive home from work and prepare to go out to have my hair dyed. Joe, one of the guys who has been remodeling my parents' house for almost a year now, flirts with me, and I joke back. But when I leave my bedroom after getting ready, he pulls me into my parents' bedroom.

"Girl," he says. "I've been seeing you for like, six months. I would fuck you so hard. Look at those titties. I would just—eat that pussy until you screamed. And I know you'd like it."

I walk out of the room, leave the house, and don't tell my parents a thing. Instead, I get my hair dyed, go to a local bar, get wasted, and throw up in my car. I fall asleep in the parking lot.

The next morning, I call Alexander. I don't feel well. I need help. But he hangs up on me. I go home, climb into bed, vomit again, and spend a sick Christmas with my parents and brother.

But Christmas gives me a renewed sense of self. I'm euphoric. After a basketball game of my brother's, I drive over to Target, shoplift a leather jacket I'd been wanting, and then buy something small so as to not get caught. And that night, in nothing but a tube top, tiny skirt, and the jacket, I go to the club to drink and dance. I take hits of ecstasy. E makes everything feel perfect. It makes me feel perfect.

But I get sick again. Something is definitely wrong. But this time, I call Bo.

"Do you think it's the flu?" he asks.

"I think it's my life," I say. "I've been sick like this for weeks—since

Alexander left. Even before that, actually. Maybe it's mono. I mean, I think I've thrown up for two months now."

"Um—you guys were together, right?"

"As in, had sex? Yes. A lot. Why?"

Bo picks me up and takes me to buy a pregnancy test. Back at my house, he waits outside the bathroom door while I stare at the little white stick, wondering what will happen. I can't be pregnant. I had my period. Didn't I?

But on that test, I see two little pink lines. I panic and do the math. I'm almost eleven weeks pregnant, but because I've been starving myself and vomiting, I haven't gained a pound. I'd been too drunk and too stupid—and too heartbroken—to pay attention to my body.

"Well, congrats," Bo says. "Maybe Alexander will want to be with you now?"

I just stare at the test in shock. I'm twenty-one, single, and pregnant.

And I have no idea what to do.

2003

It's obvious that I've flunked out of York College, even though I hide this from my parents. But they know I haven't been going to class. The only things they don't know about are the way Alexander treated me and the things I did—still do—in clubs.

And they don't know about the pregnancy. They are unaware that their daughter is a mother.

But to stay on my parent's insurance, I need to be in college. Despite taking a major step backward, I enroll in four classes at our local community college. It's just for the insurance. My parents are footing the bill, and besides, I should see an OBGYN soon.

During the day, I attend simple, boring classes. At night, I go to work. On the weekends, however, I can't stop myself from going to bars and clubs with friends. The baby must be fine, as it's been exposed to alcohol and tobacco from the start. I dance and drink and don't say a word. The only person who knows is Bo, and he won't tell a soul—not even Carrie.

And that poses a problem. Bo is living back with his dad, and I'm living with my parents. We're both twenty-one, and can drive to see one another within minutes. We start hanging out. I don't cross the line with him—I love Carrie and refuse to betray her—but one night,

Bo asks me to go get some coffee. He's upset. And despite my ever-raging nausea, I get dressed at 10:00 p.m. and head out the door to meet him at Dunkin' Donuts.

After I down far too much caffeine, Bo asks if we can drive around for a while. I agree and put on some music. We sing, and when we eventually arrive back at his house, the snow has started to fall. We stand in it, and some child-like part in me begins to laugh. It's beautiful. It's perfect. And I need to find something good in this life.

"You can't tell Carrie," Bo says. "But I'm still in love with you. I haven't stopped loving you since you dumped me. I thought I was over it, but I'm not. I love her, too, but you—you're the one who is always on my mind. And you always look so sad and alone now. I know what's wrong. But watching your eyes change to that bright green—that means you're sad."

He remembers. After all those years, he remembers how to accurately judge my moods.

"I don't know what to tell you," I say, letting the snow pile on top of me. "If you're with Carrie, then—I can't. You know I can't."

"I know," he says. "I just wish things were different. You weren't supposed to be single."

"I wasn't? Why?"

"Because you never have been."

That statement depresses me so much that I spend several days in bed, still vomiting constantly, and calling off work for almost a week. I'm granted my right to mourn.

I'm just not sure what it is I'm mourning.

I GO WITH MY PARENTS AND BROTHER TO DISNEY WORLD IN LATE January—ready for some warmer temperatures and a brief escape from reality—but when we arrive, the weather isn't that much different from what we'd been experiencing in Maryland. Schools close because they don't have heat. We go to water parks—mostly deserted in the forty-degree weather—and laugh during the rides, but we shiver tremendously and buy ponchos and sweatshirts.

At night, I share a room with the family. Hiding a pregnancy while staying in the same, four-hundred-foot space as my parents feels impossible. But at night, while they sleep, I go into the bathroom, turn on the light, vomit, and feel my stomach. I'm noticing that it is getting bigger. But luckily, it's winter. Sweatshirts will hide me until I'm able to reveal the truth.

I write a lot of poetry in that bathroom. When we arrive home a week later, I've filled a composition book with my words and thoughts —some about Alexander, some about the baby, and some about my mental health. Around one of the poems, there is handwriting—mine, of course, it has to be—that looks strange. It's all in capital letters, and I've never written that way. When had I started taking notes like that?

After an absolutely insane weekend with Bo constantly messaging me about how to break up with Carrie, I tell him not to. If their relationship works, let it work. I'm not interfering. Eventually, he says fine —I don't want him back, and now he knows. He'll leave me alone. But I should tell Alexander about the baby. Doesn't he have the right to know?

I've attended a piano training at the music store where I work, and since Alexander's grandparents own a beautiful baby grand, I decide to call him under the guise of being helpful. When I do call, he answers, and I feel like getting sick again.

"Oh my God," Alexander says. "You're still alive."

"Did you think I wouldn't be?"

"Well, with you, it was always hard to know. Your moods were the worst."

Hypocrite.

"Well, I hope everything's been good," I tell him. "I was just calling because I'm selling pianos at the music store now, and one of the models is an updated version of what your grandparents have. I don't want them to buy a new one, but I wanted to pass along some maintenance info that could help them."

"Sure, of course," Alexander says. "They still ask about you, you know. They miss you."

"I miss them," I say honestly. "I miss those Thursday dinners where I'd sing for them."

"Me, too." I can hear the smile in Alexander's voice. Maybe, I think —maybe now is the time to tell him. Maybe we can reconcile and become an actual family?

"I do have another reason for calling," I tell him. "But I don't want you to be angry or upset, and if you don't want to talk about what I need to tell you, I respect that."

"That sounds ominous," he says, but his tone is still light. "Just tell me."

"I'm pregnant. With your child."

There's a moment of silence. Then, Alexander says, "How far along are you?"

"I don't really know," I say, embarrassed. "I just found out at the end of last year. I'm probably sixteen or seventeen weeks along? It's getting hard to hide it. I can feel it—her, I think. I think it's a her."

"You don't know shit. You haven't even been to a doctor yet?"

"I don't know where to go. I'm back on my parents' insurance. What happens when they get that bill? They'll kick me out. I can't do anything. I've spoken to someone at Planned Parenthood, but that's about it."

"You are a fucking joke," Alexander says. "First of all, Planned Parenthood caters to, you know—abortion freaks and gays who don't want to give up secrets. And secondly, you tell me you're pregnant but you don't know all the details? You're lying."

I shouldn't have called. I should have just kept the secret.

"I'm not lying. If you want me to drive up there and show you, and if you want to take me to the hospital for an ultrasound, you'll have your proof."

"I don't need your proof, and I don't need you! How dare you lie to me? I am not a father. You can't trick me into getting me back. Plus, it's too late—I'm seeing someone else."

I don't mean to, but I break down into sobs.

"What? When did that start?"

"About a week after Thanksgiving. A week after I dumped you. I met someone closer to my age—a teacher. Someone mature. She lives with me. We got a dog. Stay away from me."

"You want nothing to do with this baby? Our baby?"

"What baby?"

He slams down the phone, and I sob along with the dial tone.

Why had I tried? Things had been fine. I'd been pretending to have my period, rolling up empty pads and throwing them into trash cans. I'd been wearing large sweatshirts to cover my stomach. A little weight gain on my face didn't really catch anyone's attention.

I rub my abdomen. I haven't felt many kicks—a few light flutters here and there, which makes me think that everything is just fine—but when I touch my stomach, I swear that I can feel the baby. Or her. Convinced the baby is a girl, I've named her Sophie—a name Alexander and I had agreed upon in our better days, when we talked about marriage and children.

"Sophie," I say. "I've treated this body like crap. I hope you're okay."

I go to Target and buy a few tiny newborn outfits. I hide them in the trunk of my car. One of the outfits is a little green and pink dress, perfect for the summer when she'll be born.

Now, I just have to figure out the logistics. I spend most of my time in my college classes ignoring the professors, trying to calculate if I can save enough money for my own apartment. But who would watch her? How could I work and finish college if I can't take her with me? The music store is pretty forgiving, though. If she's sleeping in one of the offices, she might be able to come with me, at least at first. I'm treated like family there. That plan might be viable.

On March 10, I'm asked by a fellow writer to be a featured poet at a reading at our local coffee house. I'm honored, and I accept. I can't wait to share my words with everyone in about a month. Maybe I'll write something about Sophie—I can tell the world that way.

A week later, as I'm about to head to a class, I feel a tremendous cramp in my stomach. I wince, bend down, and talk to my abdomen. "What are you doing, Sophie? What's up?" The cramps continue all day—like menstruation cramps, but far more powerful—and I take Motrin, trying to ignore what I'm certain is just normal pregnancy pain.

But I come home before my 1:00 p.m. class, screaming in agony. No one is there. I'm alone.

And I don't even make it to the bathroom before the blood starts to rush down my legs.

SOPHIE DIES IN MY ARMS ON THE BATHROOM FLOOR OF MY PARENTS' house. The labor is excruciating, and I think about calling Carrie, or even Bo, but decide against it. I grab towels, mop up blood, and push. If women had been doing this for eons, I could do this, too.

When Sophie arrives—my intuition had been right, I do have a little girl—she doesn't look like a baby. She is bigger than the palm of my hand, but not by much, and she is a mottled, distorted red and blue color. Her eyes aren't completely on the front of her face. I don't see her open her mouth. Parts of her haven't even developed yet.

But as I hold her, forgetting about needing to push out the placenta, I see her move her amazingly tiny hand. Her head shifts toward the sound of my crying. But she makes no noise.

And then the movements stop. She hadn't even taken a breath.

Sophie, at twenty-one weeks, is dead.

I clutch her tiny, blood-soaked body to my chest and sob. I've never sobbed like this before—not after Thomas or Stone raped me, not after being kidnapped, not after Alexander's treatment of me, or any of the other events I'd experienced. This pain guts me so deeply that the sobs carry like screams. Luckily, no one is home. If they were, they'd see a screaming girl, holding a deceased baby, with an entire bathroom covered in blood. I'm still bleeding. I don't know how to get it to stop.

Maybe this is how I'll die, I think. I'll die holding Sophie. I was the one who killed her, after all. She might have had a chance if I'd received care. I'm a murderer. I should bleed out and die.

But I don't even pass out.

The house is still empty as I look around the bathroom. I have no idea how to clean this up. I have no idea what to do with my daughter. I need help but refuse to ask for it.

Despite the pain and the blood, I take off my clothes and pile them on the floor. I rest Sophie on top of them and then shower. The water runs red, and I sob, but at least there's nothing on me. I wrap myself in a towel that's on the back of the door, hobble to my bedroom, and put three pads on inside my underwear. I put on two pairs of pants, just in case. The pain is sickening, but what choice do I have? I have to move.

I scrub the blood off the carpet. I scour the bathroom with cleaning solution and wipe up every blood stain. The only things left are my blood-soaked clothes, the towels, the placenta, and Sophie. Otherwise—everything looks ordinary.

But everything is far from it. Everything is hell.

"Sophie," I cry. "I'm so sorry. I don't know what to do."

I find a small shoebox and line it with pieces of my clothing. I know she's dead, but maybe she'll be comforted, wherever she is, by something that's mine? I wrap her in those rags, kiss her tiny head, and tell her how much I love her.

I throw towels into the washer and start the cycle. I toss the remainder of the clothes and the placenta into a garbage bag. And then, bag and shoebox in hand, I go out into the mid-March air.

I'm shaking, and I can feel blood seeping out of me. But I bury the garbage bag at the bottom of the can and look around. I don't know what to do with my daughter. Maybe I should take her to the hospital. Maybe now is the point where I have no choice but to go.

But I have a different plan. Instead, I go back inside, change my already bloody pants, grab my car keys, and leave. Sophie rests in her box on the passenger seat beside me—a place she'd sit in eight or nine years had she lived. If I had been a good mother and had let her live.

I stop at a hardware store and buy a cheap shovel. From there, I go to a private location—a place I've always loved, but that few people ever visit. It's my secret spot in this county. And that is where I should bury my daughter.

I shake and sob and I dig. I think about taking her picture, but I don't. Instead, I bleed, cry, and prepare a space for her.

When it's ready, I look at her body again. Despite how disfigured it is, she is still beautiful.

"My Sophie," I cry. "I will love you forever. I'll never forget you."

I place her shoebox in the ground, cover it up, and then leave. I can't stay and look at where she is and what has happened. I can't do it. I should have been better for her. I'm a monster.

222 • A.E. HAYES

I throw the shovel into a dumpster behind a grocery store and then head home. My parents and brother are back, but no one says anything. I quickly make my way upstairs, grab a new outfit, and change in the bathroom. The blood still seeps out of me, and the cramping is intense, but what else can I do? I can't go to the hospital. I'll just claim that I have the flu, stay in bed for a while, and let it pass.

And that is exactly what I do. When I come downstairs, clad in flannel pants and a sweatshirt, I'm hunched over. My dad touches my forehead and says I feel clammy. Maybe I should go to bed. I nod, and knowing that he thinks I'm simply ill, head into my room.

Underneath my bedspread are three towels—spares I had kept in my car after leaving Jess. I unfold them, put on another pad, and lay down. I swallow a handful of Motrin that I've left on my nightstand. I'm going to get through this, I think. People have babies all the time and don't receive help after. That's how it was done so long ago. I can survive it, too.

"But you can't survive what you've done," the voice says, and I drift in and out of consciousness. "You need to forget this. You have to forget her."

"Forget her?" I say. "I can't forget about Sophie."

"Yes, you can. Trust me."

I fall asleep, and when I wake up, I'm startled to find that I'm lying in a pool of blood. I call for my mom, and when she sees, she tells me that I must be having my period—and a hell of a period at that. We clean up, I take some Motrin for the pain, and then, I climb back into bed.

I didn't know it, but my daughter died yesterday.

Somehow, I'm given the ability to bury the memory—just like I had buried her.

FOR REASONS THAT I CANNOT SEEM TO UNDERSTAND, I'M TOO depressed to drag myself out of the house and go to community college. It's just too easy there. I need a challenge. The semester will be over in two months, anyhow. I apply once again to the local four-year college, and after I meet with an admissions officer who wants to know why I didn't finish my fall 2002 semester at York, I'm accepted. I haven't chosen a major yet, but anything is better than community college.

When I'm not in bed, I'm at work, or at the coffee house. There are so many music and poetry events that I feel at home there, surrounded by other artists who like to sing and write just as I do. Every so often, Bo accompanies me—but only as a friend, he swears. Nothing else.

My poetry reading at the local coffee house goes extremely well, and I'm flattered by the large crowd. I share my words—poems about loss, heartache, rape, and betrayal—and am mystified by one I find tucked into the back of my portfolio. It's about a woman who wants a baby but can't carry one. I read it, and many people are in tears.

But I don't recall writing it. My name is on it, and the words and flow of the piece sound like something I would have written, but I just don't remember doing so.

Why can't I remember so many things about my own life?

Despite a very busy work schedule—taking on piano and voice students during the day, and the music store at night and on the week-ends—I still manage to escape to the Outer Banks with my family and my former roommate, Ann, for a week.

During the vacation, Bo calls me almost every day. He and Carrie are having issues. She's leaving him to go to Colorado. And that means they're breaking up.

"You guys are ending it?" I ask. "I'm sorry."

"She wants to go. She wants to leave me in our apartment. So—yeah. I'm alone."

"Can I—help somehow? I don't know what you want me to do."

"Can you visit me when you get back?" he asks. "Please. I miss you."

This is a trap, and I know it. But I agree. If he and Carrie have broken up, then visiting him isn't an issue. Plus, I don't have to sleep with him. He's just a former boyfriend.

At night on the Outer Banks, I stand by the water, and I ask for help. I tell the ocean that I can't be with another man. I need to be free. Bo would hold me back.

The waves crash around me. One almost knocks me over. I don't know if that's a sign that I can't hold myself up on my own or that I'm strong enough to keep standing.

But when I return home, I realize that I hadn't been given a sign.

Instead, I spend the rest of the summer messing up everything for everyone.

I VISIT BO AT HIS DC APARTMENT SEVERAL TIMES A WEEK, AND before I know it, he's calling me his girlfriend. He feels so lucky, he tells me, that after five years, we can get back together again.

Glancing around the apartment tells me what I need to know: Carrie doesn't live there any longer. Some of her older clothing remains, but that's it. Bo had told the truth. It's over.

"I'm not looking to be someone's girlfriend," I tell him. And a few nights later, I hook up with our friend Dan at a party just to prove my point. But Bo isn't deterred. In his eyes, I can do no wrong. He hates how much I drink and smoke, but one night, he joins me on his balcony and has his first sip of wine. It makes him wince, and I laugh. He's still such an innocent, I think. Like the kid I dated so long ago.

We sing together in my car, and he praises me. I wear low-cut halter tops, and he tells me that he's missed my style. But his phone rings a lot, and despite the fact he isn't working—and yet, somehow still affording this apartment—he tells me he's taking calls from work and steps out onto the balcony for privacy.

At first, I have no idea who is calling him. And then, like a shot, it hits me: Carrie is calling him. This secrecy isn't about some job. It's about her.

I confront him. But he denies that they are still together. "She thinks we are, but we broke up when she left," he says. "I swear. I've only ever loved and wanted you. She knows that."

"Are you telling me the truth?"

"Yes. Plus, when I told her that you were here with me so often, she told me that you're a psychotic bitch, and she can't believe she ever trusted you. She hates both of us. Let's move on."

But I'm heartbroken and angry. My best friend hates me?

In my anger, I turn to Bo. "Fine," I tell him. "I'll date you, and you alone."

I'm not good at monogamy, though. One night, I meet a guy in Hot Topic, and we hook up in his car. On another night, I attend a pool party thrown by my boss at the music store, and I begin to date his son. We make out in the hot tub well after the party has ended, and my newly dyed bluish-black hair is, to him, a turn-on. He likes my punk-rock style, he says. He can't stop touching me. We keep making out until my boss grows angry.

"You're a good girl," he says. "You're too young for my son. You've changed."

"Fuck you," I say. "I don't need your money. I quit."

The fact of the matter is that I do have a lot of piano and voice students. At forty dollars an hour per student, I don't need to work at the music store. I like teaching kids how to love music. But that store was a home for me. I was treated well. Why did things always end so drastically?

Carrie returns from Colorado, and Bo tells me she's housesitting for a friend. I want to visit her, and he says we can stop by—on our way to the Vans Warped Tour. When Carrie finds out, she asks to come along, but Bo tells me to tell her no. We have our tickets. She can't go.

Everything is wrong about this. When I see her, she is so angry with me that I know our friendship is ruined. But when she looks at Bo, it's as though she's spitting fire.

"We've shared your bed for weeks now," I say to Bo the next morning. "We've done practically everything in there. Is it possible that Carrie still lives here? Is that what's going on?"

"Well, technically," he says. "I mean, she's housesitting, so no, she's not here now."

"Cut the bullshit. Are you still with her or not?"

"I am, kind of. But I'm in love with you."

"I knew it." I uncork a wine bottle. "I knew you were full of shit."

"But I just wanted you back. You're everything she's not."

"And you're a total asshole for staying with someone if you're going to talk about her like that." I drink straight from the bottle. "If you want me, then leave her. If you want her, tell me. But at this point? I'm not fucking staying around for this. You ruined a friendship!"

"We can still be friends."

"Not the two of us," I say. "Me and Carrie. And she'll never know what a dick you are."

"I never wanted to hurt you. I love you."

"I'm out." I collect my backpack and purse, and with the wine bottle still in hand, I slam the door behind me and drive home.

I shouldn't be driving. I'm drunk.

"Maybe you *are* a drunk," the voice says.

I begin to cry and toss the bottle out the window. "Fuck yourself," I say out loud. "Fuck this whole summer. I can't do this anymore."

"Slice your wrists open when you get home."

"What?"

"Just do it. Do it before college starts. Then you don't have to attend that bullshit school."

She has a point. On the way home, I stop at a liquor store, buy a few bottles to stash in my closet, and begin to gather the energy for a September suicide.

MY PLANS ARE SLIGHTLY DERAILED WHEN I'M ASKED TO PERFORM AT a local jazz club. I can put death on hold for that, I think. Death can wait.

I sing well. An operatic version of "Summertime" from *Porgy and Bess* surprisingly wins over the crowd, and the lead guitarist wants to keep me on as their head vocalist. I agree but tell him I may not be available too much in the near future.

A week later, I'm hired as a staff writer at a music magazine. My friend Mark—a fellow music lover and singer—works for the publication and had dropped my name. When the publisher requests a music review from me, I write a piece about the Warped Tour and am hired only days later.

I'd stepped back from music, but now, it's the center of my life again. I'm singing it, teaching it, and writing about it. Maybe that's the sign. Maybe music is here to knock me over.

Right around this time, I discover an amazing indie prog-rock band called Coheed and Cambria. They are relatively unknown, and their music appeals to me right away. One song in particular, "Delirium Trigger," seems to scream my name. The story in the song feels like mine. And when I learn the band's history, and discover that every album is part of a great, sweeping sci-fi narrative, I'm hooked. This will be my favorite band for the rest of my life.

My first published piece is about their music, and it receives great praise. And even though I'm a week away from starting a seemingly pointless education program—something I don't want to do, though I have massive respect for teachers and the bullshit they put up with—something about Coheed and Cambria keeps me alive. I'm part of something bigger now.

I decide not to attend classes, but my parents keep an eye on my schedule and, in a way, force me out the door. I'm almost twenty-two. I can suck it up and deal.

But the classes are awful. The students are young and eager, from rich families and wearing expensive outfits to show their wealth, and they eye my dyed hair and band shirts with disdain. I give it a week before simply leaving the house every day to write articles in local cafes.

One night, in late September, I'm watching Jay Leno. I start to hallucinate. It looks like the guests on the show are coming out of my TV and into my bedroom. I cover my eyes, but I can still hear them. I hear the whispers in my head. There's a party going on in there, and I can't get it to stop raging. I take about five of my Lithium—far too strong a dose—and pull out a knife I'd stolen a month ago from my parents' kitchen drawer.

"Do it," the voice says. "You're ready."

I fall to my knees on the green carpet and cut. But the blade is dull, and I hadn't noticed. I toss it into my closet, grab a bottle, and take a swig of rum. Then, I begin digging at my wrists with my fingernails. I bleed on the carpet, and I press my face into the mess as I dig. The pain is tremendous—almost pleasurably so. But when it fades, I won't be alive.

I pass out on my carpet, lying in puddles of my blood.

No one wakes me the next morning, and I'm startled to wake up with my face on the floor. What if my parents had walked in? Or my brother? I listen, and it doesn't sound like anyone is home. I look at my alarm clock—and it's 2:00 p.m. I'd been on the ground for hours.

But I'm still alive. How am I still alive?

As October approaches and my desire to teach piano and voice wanes, I know that something is wrong. I can't recall what it is, but I feel it. This depression is more than chemical.

I desperately hope that I don't live to see my twenty-second birthday.

ANN INVITES ME TO A HALLOWEEN PARTY UP IN PA, THROWN BY A friend of hers who is attending the same law school she attends. I agree and start prepping my costume. This year, I don't have to buy anything—thanks to all the clothing I've purchased to go to concerts for my writing job, I have everything I need to dress as Trinity from *The Matrix*.

The party is set for Saturday, November 1, and even though I'm hungover the next day from too much alcohol I'd had in a club I'd visited in Baltimore, I drive to Ann's to prepare. It's clear that there's a dress code for this law school Halloween gathering, and I somehow missed the memo. Princesses are in; girls in black leather are out. As Ann puts on her pink princess dress and I line my eyes in deep black, she says, "I think you're going to stand out."

"In a bad way?"

"In a 'I don't go to law school here' kind of way."

She's right. When we arrive, every single female is in a very feminine costume. The guys, who have varied costumes, talk to me, but the girls do not. I'm some kind of misfit among them, despite the fact that I had planned to go to law school. At this stage, since I had worked in a law office for several summers, I probably had more legal knowledge than the entire group combined. But I just smile, down some shots, and meander through the crowd.

"Dude," Ann says to me a while later. "It looks like one of your kind has shown up."

"The fuck you talking about?" I say. "My kind? Like I'm a different breed than you?"

"There's a guy in the basement wearing a dog collar. Go get that one."

I roll my eyes and walk down to the basement. There's a keg there, so I can just check him out while I get another drink.

And there, sitting alone on a couch, is an extremely tall, dark-haired, incredibly handsome man, wearing black leather and a spiked collar.

My heart jumps, but I tell it no. I'll get my drink, I'll flirt, and I'll go back to Ann. I'm finished with relationships. All I want now are simple hook-ups. I'm not falling for this again.

I take my drink over to the couch, and the guy stares at me.

"Trinity," he says.

I smile. "Someone not dressed like a princess."

He laughs, and his tone immediately puts me at ease.

"Do you go to law school with these guys?" he asks.

"Nope. I came here with a friend—a former roommate from college."

The guy in leather nods. "I know one of these girls from online. I'm not dating her—I just had a free weekend and decided I'd come visit. I don't go to law school, either."

He seems sober, and he's not acting like a pushy asshole, so I flirt a bit. "I'm sitting down," I tell him. "We're almost the same height when I stand and you sit, and that's weird for me. I should sit next to you." He laughs again as I sit beside him.

This guy in leather tells me his name. "It's Toby," he says. We shake hands.

"I've never met a Toby before."

"How many guys have you met?"

We fall into a very natural rhythm. Within the hour, we're talking about politics, the state of the world in late 2003, religion, music, and how to raise children. When I tell him that I'm a singer who teaches kids and writes for a music magazine, he's intrigued.

"I work as a temp right now," he says. "But I host karaoke, too. I like to sing. I'm not trained, but it's fun for me."

"Maybe we can do a duet some time. Where do you live?"

"Michigan."

So much for that.

"But I drove here," he adds. "It's an eight-hour drive. Four or five roads. It's not impossible if we ever want to hang out some time. I don't live in another country."

"I'm in Maryland," I tell him.

"Then I'll tack on another hour. It's not that far."

Don't do this, I tell myself. Do not fall in love with Toby.

An hour later, we find an empty bedroom, and he asks to kiss me. It's not forced—it's a welcome reprieve. I nod, and we kiss. I connect with him, and while I want to have sex with him, there's something else there—some sort of comfort. It's as though we'd kissed before, and I'd forgotten about it. It doesn't bore me nor upset me. It riles me up and yet calms my soul.

There's something special about this beautiful, leather-clad guy with his shy grin.

"Are you sure you're okay with doing this?" he asks me as he pulls out a condom.

"Yes," I tell him. "This seems different. It's okay."

"Yeah," he says. "This is definitely different."

We make love several times, and I ignore my phone—probably Ann, wondering where I am. When I eventually look at the clock, it's one in the morning, and she's most likely irritated that I'm not ready to go.

But I lay there with Toby, wrapped in his arms. He's six-four to my five-two, and I feel tiny in his embrace. I feel safe.

"Do you feel something for me?" I ask.

"Yes," he says. "I want to see you again. Can you stay tonight? I'll take you home tomorrow."

I shake my head. "I don't want to do that," I say. "Not with you. I want to be with you, but—the right way. Whatever that is. I'm trying to figure that out. It's been a rough year."

"I understand." He kisses me, and we get dressed.

Back at the party, people whistle and clap as we come into the room. But I'm smiling. Toby is kind and giving, and I feel a bond with him. He's not too old for me—he's almost twenty-six, and I just turned twenty-two—and he's the right mix of experienced but not overly so. He isn't commanding or intimidating. He isn't looking for a quick lay, and I'd felt no need to put on a performance for him during sex. He wants somebody to love.

We go outside to find Ann, and she tells me that she wants to leave. I ask her for ten more minutes, and she agrees, staring at Toby. Then Toby and I light up cigarettes and, holding hands, stand together by the road.

"Maybe we can see one another around Thanksgiving," he says to me. "That's almost a month away, but—I'll have a few free days then."

"I wish I could see you sooner," I say. "But that works. Let's not rush it."

We exchange phone numbers and email addresses, and then we kiss goodbye. I get into Ann's car, and she says, "So, I guess the guy with the dog collar turned out to be a good one?"

I send Toby a quick text. And then I say, "Actually? I think he's the best I've ever met."

ANN AND I DECIDE TO MOVE IN TOGETHER BACK IN EMMITSBURG, MD—only a few minutes away from our former school, Mount St. Mary's College. Being near the school makes me feel a little nauseated, but it's been four years. And Ann doesn't like her law school. The plan is that we'll get an apartment and then get our degrees here—she'll finish a Masters, and I'll finish my Bachelors, probably in History. We find a place downtown and pay the deposit.

I don't tell my parents about moving or about Toby. Despite that fact that he and I talk every night and message each other constantly, all I say is that I've become good friends with a guy I met at a law school gathering. And that seems pleasant enough.

The more Toby and I talk, the more we realize that we can't wait until Thanksgiving to see one another. He has booked plane tickets already—he admits to me that he did so the moment he arrived home in Michigan the day after the party—but he really wishes he could visit now.

But I teach piano and voice. I can move my schedule around. After a few phone calls, I clear my Thursday through Sunday schedule and tell him I'm coming up that weekend. I'll see him in two days. And we're both elated.

I pack and tell my parents I'm visiting friends in Ocean City, and then, early Thursday morning, I stock up on cigarettes and coffee, and make the drive from Maryland to Michigan.

Toby is waiting for me outside of his apartment. When he sees me, he rushes over to my car and gathers me in his arms. "I feel like it's been—well, far too long," he says. And we kiss.

The weekend is a whirlwind. I meet his parents and brother, and they are amazing people who bond with me instantly. Toby and I sing karaoke, and my voice impresses his friends—as well as him. And back at his apartment, he looks me in the eye and says, "It's only been two weeks. This is too soon, I know. But—I love you. I really and honestly do."

"I love you," I say. "I've just been—really burned in the past."

"I'm not going to hurt you." And his blue eyes reflect the truth: he won't.

We only leave his apartment to eat and sing. Otherwise, we make love, watch movies, and spend hours in bed, talking. And I know—this is the man I'm going to marry.

But I felt that with Alexander. How do I know Toby won't be insane?

When I leave that Sunday afternoon, we're both in tears. But I'll see him for Thanksgiving. We can do two weeks. And then, we'll figure it out from there. We are in love.

Ann understands the extent of my feelings, and when I ask her if Toby can move in with us in Emmitsburg, she hesitates for only a moment before saying, "Well, we have three bedrooms, and that would make rent cheaper. So, sure. If he's a good guy, why not?"

I call Toby, and after his Thanksgiving visit, we make plans for his move from Michigan to Maryland. We're going to be together every day! Sure, he'll have to find a new job down here, but I have some money saved. We'll be okay.

I sing at the jazz club again that winter, and when I come home, I get sick. Odd, I think. I hadn't been drinking. I'd actually backed off a bit—I drank a little around Toby, and at bars with friends, but never alone. And never to the point of complete nausea. But I let it pass.

The next night, I attend a party thrown by one of the music magazine's staff writers, and, while there, he hands me a beer and a purple straw. I take a small swig of the beer and then look at the straw.

"Um, I'm not five," I say to him. "I don't need a straw for my beer. But thanks."

"The straw isn't for drinking," he says to me. Then he leads me over to a table.

Four or five guys are sitting there, snorting coke.

I've seen this before, I think. When was that? I recall being young, sitting on a man's lap.

A friend pulls out a chair for me, and I sit down.

"One time," the voice says. "He used you for this when you were a kid. Have your fun."

I watch myself as I snort. I cough. I have no idea what I'm doing. But I try again.

"I'm out," I hear a voice say. It's coming from me, but doesn't sound like mine. "Fuck all of you. I know what you're setting me up to do."

I go to my car, but before I climb in, my friend slams his hands against the car on both sides of me. "You were supposed to come here to fuck me."

"I was? I didn't get that memo."

"It's not that hard to snort a little coke and get drunk," he says. "Some musician."

"No. I actually *am* a musician. I pride myself on my work. But this is a lifestyle. This is a choice. And I'm not having it. Get the fuck away from me."

He tries to grab my throat, but I twist away and open the car door into him. He falls back, and I speed off.

I arrive home far earlier than planned. Bars and restaurants are still open. It's not too late to call Toby, or to keep packing for Emmitsburg. But instead, I pull over and vomit again.

That's from coke, I think. And beer. And deception.

But then I start doing the math. I last had my period in mid-October—that's what I can recall. Toby and I made love on November 1. It's now mid-December. I'd been so distracted by Toby, and by my writing and music, that I hadn't thought about it.

I rush over to WalMart and buy several boxes of pregnancy tests. In their bathroom, minutes before the store prepares to close, I shut my eyes and take the test.

How? How did this happen? That's my only thought as I exit the store. I'm holding the test: there are two pink lines. I'm pregnant.

But how? I have been on birth control. We used a condom. And I'd miscarried before, so I can't just get pregnant this easily—right?

But apparently, I can.

I go home and immediately hide my medication. If I'm pregnant, I'm going to do this correctly. No meds. I'll call for an OBGYN after week twelve, as I should. No more drinking. I wish I hadn't gone to that party, but I hadn't put much in my system.

Toby and I have only known each other for six weeks, though. There's no way he's going to want to become a father. He'll stop loving me, I think. I don't know how I know, but he won't believe me. He'll hate me and leave.

When I call him that night to tell him, he's quiet, and asks me to take another test. I do, and I get the same result: two pink lines.

He starts to cry, and I know it's over.

But he surprises me. "It's soon," he says. "Probably way too soon. But we're going to have a baby. I'm having a baby with the woman I love. I do love you. I'm glad I'll be there soon."

I cry in response. He could have hung up and blocked my number. He could have said no. He could have said goodbye. And instead, he offered love and support.

But we agree not to tell anyone until I hit my twelfth week. At this point, I'm only at week eight and so much can happen.

I have a recital for my piano and voice students that Sunday, but I decide to drive up to Michigan. The downtown streets of his city, Rochester, are strung with lights and the poles are topped with bows. A snowstorm is brewing, and electricity is in the air. Everything is beautiful and serene, and for a second, I feel at peace.

At his house—Toby has moved back with his parents for a few weeks to save up money for the move to Maryland—I let the secret slip to his mom: I'm pregnant. I'm eight weeks along. She's understandably shocked, but then she hugs me.

"You are loved and welcomed here," she says. And I cry. I've never had such full acceptance from a family before—not like this. If I told my parents, all hell would break loose, despite the fact I'm twenty-two. But here? I'm safe.

But the fact that I can't take my medications makes me hallucinate. I have odd flashbacks to events: my birth father. Thomas's rape. How my mom treated me when I was eighteen. How I hear a voice. As Toby holds me, the memories spill out. In one night, he learns everything—my past is a nightmare. I hear a voice. I have disorders. I'm psychotic.

He clutches on to me. "I love you," he says. "We'll get through it. You're not alone."

I leave one day before the snowstorm is supposed to slam down upon us, but as I near PA, the snow is so thick that I can't see where I'm driving. On the PA Turnpike, I slide and my car almost goes through a guardrail and off the side of a very steep cliff. In terror, fighting through sobs, I call Toby, and he talks to me as I try to find the nearest exit that has a hotel. I won't make it home that night.

The closest hotel is a rundown little disaster, but for thirty-nine dollars, I can afford it, and I don't have to drive. I happily hand over the cash and go to my room. There's no food, but I'll survive. The fast food place next door will open in the morning.

The storm persists, and I cancel my recital for my kids. In Maryland, the storm rages on as well, so it's understandable. But I'm sick, pregnant, off my meds, and feel like a failure. Eventually, I call every parent and say that, as of January 1, I won't be teaching any longer.

They're sad, but they understand. I try not to sob. I need the money, but I know I need to protect this baby—and my sanity—even more.

I pay for a second night at the hotel, go to the fast food place, and pick up enough for the day. Back in the room, I eat, get sick, and eat some more. On CNN, people are swearing that Saddam Hussein is dead. Or is that happening? I can't differentiate fiction from reality. Everything is like a dream. I go to the bathroom to get sick again, and when I look at my face, something shocks me: my eyes, normally a greenish color, are jet black. I've never seen anything like this before.

I call Toby, tell him I'm going to kill myself in this hotel, and that I love him.

I dig at my wrists, pull out my hair, throw myself into furniture. I try to find sharp objects with which to cut myself, but I don't have any. I simply tear at my skin, hoping I'll eventually just bleed enough that something will get infected and I'll die.

Toby tries to call me, and I pick up once, in a daze.

But five hours later, he's there. He drove through a two-foot blizzard to save me.

"You can't do this," he says, holding me to him. "Your life is going to be better now. I promise. We'll be together, and we'll have our baby. You'll go back to school, and I'll work to support us. This is a good life, love. You are a good, beautiful person. I love you."

I want to believe him. Maybe everything will be okay—maybe I'll be a good mother, and maybe we'll be fine. But it's so hard to trust people. I can't even trust myself.

"You're the Coheed to my Cambria," I tell him, talking about my favorite band—a band he's now come to love. Toby smiles and kisses me.

"I promise that, no matter what we go through, I'll never leave you," he says.

Dear God, I think as I rub my abdomen where our baby rests. I hope he's right.

2004

Toby, Ann, and I move into the Emmitsburg apartment to find weeds growing out of the toilet and mold in the third bedroom. Good thing we are just going to use that for storage: clearly, Toby and I are sharing a room. Ann tells us that we can take the bigger bedroom if we're willing to pay four hundred of the five-hundred-fifty-dollar rent, and we agree. She's basically paying nothing, but it's a good deal. In this state, four hundred a month for rent is incredibly cheap. Toby can clear that even if he found work at a fast food joint, and he has enough qualifications to go into something better.

A few nights later, while Toby is back in Michigan to pick up the rest of his belongings, I start to bleed a little. I panic and rush to my computer. The Internet has been hooked up in the apartment, and I search signs of miscarriage. Bleeding is one of them, Google tells me, but even a healthy pregnancy can have some spotting. Unless it becomes heavy, I don't need to worry.

Ann tells me she's going to her parents for the weekend, and as I say goodbye, I'm hit with a horrible cramp. I look down, and see thick, dark blood on my pants.

This is not normal spotting.

I call Toby. He's out with some friends and is a bit intoxicated, but he hears what I'm saying: I'm bleeding. I may be miscarrying the baby. He tells me to keep him posted, but the people he's with distract him. I throw my phone across the room and go into the bathroom.

It takes all night and part of the next morning. I sit there, singing to myself, sobbing in short bursts, and then, at almost eleven weeks exactly, I miscarry the baby.

My body is clearly not meant to carry life.

I don't remember the first miscarriage—I'd been in college and had been sick. And I think that was the only time that had happened before. I don't know what to do, but I look at the sticky blob that was supposed to be my baby, and I cry. I knew I was going to have a boy—I felt strong with that conviction, and Toby and I chose the name Dante—but now, we have nothing.

I flush the mess down the toilet and finish bleeding. Then I slowly clean up and call Toby.

"He's gone," I cry. "The baby's dead. I did something wrong. I couldn't carry him."

"I'll be back in a few days," Toby says. I hear him crying on the other end. "We'll be okay. I promise. We have so many years to have tons of babies together."

But I can't wait a few more days.

I make a brief stop at a local hospital—I walk in, tell them I miscarried a baby at eleven weeks, and am examined, but they don't need to do too much to me other than some routine "cleaning," as they call it. They ask if I've miscarried recently, but I say that I don't remember—something had happened in 1999, but I didn't have the specific details.

I'm told I'll be billed for the visit. Then, I'm handed a prescription for antibiotics and another for more birth control, and I get those filled before returning to the apartment, packing a few items, and hitting the road. Toby may not be able to come to me yet, but come what may, I'm going up to him.

I drive through the night. On his parents' porch, Toby rushes out to greet me, and I sob in his arms.

"I'm a failure. I couldn't get it right. I'm sorry."

But he doesn't blame me. He says we'll wait until we're settled, and until we have more time together, and then, we'll try again. The fact I'd gotten pregnant despite pills and a condom must mean that we can conceive.

He's right, and I stay with him for a few days while he finishes packing. Ann calls, irritated that I left without telling her, but I'm paying for the apartment, too. I don't need someone to check in on me. Toby's friend, Lisa, tells him that I'm just using him for sex and money, and that my "suicide attempts" are all lies. He tells me people like her are the reason he's leaving.

We're both sad to be leaving his family, though. They've been so kind to me, and they really seem to love and trust Toby. His mom—who knows about the baby—hugs both of us, tells us she loves us, and asks us to visit again soon. We make plans for May, and then Toby hops into his overloaded car, and I climb gently into mine. I'm still so sore. But we drive back to Maryland and are home that evening.

Carrie messages me, and we talk. We make amends for the past, neither of us knowing how much Bo had lied. "I'm so sorry," I tell her. "I wish I had just trusted you, not him."

"He manipulated me for a long time," she says. "But I'm sorry, too. Things are better now, though. I've met someone. His name is Steve. I really want you to meet him, and I want to meet Toby. He sounds amazing, and I'm really happy for you."

We make plans to go clubbing downtown—back at the place I'd gone to for Halloween last year—and since it's a goth club, Toby and I show in our black leather and eyeliner. Carrie is dressed up, too, but the cute, brown-haired guy she's dancing with just has on a black shirt and a pair of jeans.

Carrie meets Toby, and I meet Steve. We dance together, shouting conversations back and forth. We want to have a couples' dinner in a few weeks. We want to make plans to hang out more. And as we dance, and drink, everything feels right with the world.

Within the hour, though, right dies, and everything wrong comes into play.

TOBY AND I LEAVE THE CLUB BEFORE CARRIE AND STEVE, AND WHEN we get to my car, we stop short, stunned into silence.

The windows have been broken. And while the actual vehicle is still there, nothing else is. The coat I'd left in the car has been stolen. Groceries from the trunk have been taken. Toby's cell phone and glasses are gone. Frantically, I search for my purse—which contains credit cards, cash, concert tickets, and my passport—and find nothing. And since we'd still been unpacking, even basic items, such as my hair dryer and clothes were in the car.

Almost everything has been stolen.

We run inside the club, call 911, tell Carrie and Steve, and run back outside and stand there, shivering. The police tell me there's nothing I can do. My car is in working order except for the two busted windows, but unless someone uses one of my credit cards, it's just another random theft in Baltimore. The officer is flippant about it. And yes, compared to rape and murder, this isn't a big deal. But everything I own is gone. I'll have to pay at least five hundred dollars to fix the windows. We'll have to get new phones, new licenses, and now, we don't have any money. If the thief used my debit card, my bank account is probably drained, too.

Both Toby and I are too depressed to even be angry. Instead, we help the police clear the glass from the car, and they help us tape trash bags to the two broken windows so we can drive home. I have to file a report, but otherwise, there's nothing left for us to do.

I drive straight to my parents' house, and when I show them the car and tell them what happened, I burst into tears. Of all things, I'm devastated that my passport has been taken. Not only am I worried that someone will use it, but it also contained all my amazing travel stamps—all the proof of my trips to Spain, Portugal, and Morocco. How could someone do that?

My parents kindly front me the money to have the windows fixed, and they give me fifty dollars to buy some essentials in case the bank can't refund any purchases that "those assholes" may have made. I'm so grateful. I thought they'd blame me, but instead, they just want to help.

Back at home, the police contact me, and say that my gas credit card was used to fill up cars.

"Cars?" I ask.

"Two hundred dollars worth of gas," the officer says. "Someone hooked up some friends."

I cancel everything immediately. Luckily, no one had touched my checking account, but I call to have the number changed and to ask for a new debit card. Within twenty-four hours, everything is secure again. We can't get back the three thousand dollars-worth of stuff stolen from the car, and we can't get back the feeling of not being violated, but no further damage can be done.

We visit my parents the next day to let them know that we've done all we can, and while there, my fifteen-year-old brother hands me a box. "I bought this for you with my own money," he says. "I hope it makes you feel a little better."

I open the box and, inside, is a brand-new hair dryer—one of the objects stolen from the car.

I can't stop crying. I hug him and tell him he's the most thoughtful human on the planet.

In order for us to make ends meet, Toby looks for work. But no one seems to be hiring. Frustrated, he finds a job at Best Buy, and while the money isn't great, it will allow us to get by.

But on Valentine's Day, as we sit in our bedroom and watch movies, the depression kicks in. I have another dead child. My property was destroyed. I feel ruined.

"Where are you going?" Toby asks as I head into the bathroom with my CD player.

I turn up Coheed and Cambria, grab a razor blade, and slowly start on my wrists. It's hard to get the blood flowing, but this is routine by now. I need this pain. I have nothing left, and eventually, without a job or college, Toby's going to leave me as well. I'm a burden.

The bathroom door is locked, but it's flimsy, and Toby breaks in. He finds me on the floor, bleeding, and grabs the razor.

"Why?" he says. "Why do you keep doing this? What do you need? I want to help."

"I don't know," I mumble. "I just—need to die."

Startled, Toby calls my parents and asks if I'm on their insurance. I need some sort of help. They ask to meet with us the next day, and when we do, I assume it's to work out some sort of plan—if I give them money, they'll add me to one of their policies. My parents have money as it is. It wouldn't be a burden. I just know that I need to see a psychiatrist again.

But we don't have a meeting. Instead, both Toby and I are berated. I'm irrational, and he should leave me and allow my parents to "take custody" of me—as though I'm fourteen, not twenty-two. I've given up, they say, and no, they won't add me to their insurance.

I thought things had improved, but I'd been wrong. Toby and I drive home in quiet shock, and as we make our way through the mountains back to our apartment, I try to figure out how to get the help I need so that I can make my family love me again.

———

AFTER TWO MONTHS OF SUICIDE ATTEMPTS AND DEPRESSION, THE warm April weather lifts me up. I feel as though I could be useful if I just found a local job that provides insurance. Then, we'd have money, and I could see doctors.

But it doesn't seem as though anyone is hiring.

Finally, I stop by a little restaurant close to the college. There's no "Help Wanted" sign in the window, but I straighten my clothing, fix my hair, and decide I'm going to get a job.

The owner, Frank, and his wife, Beth, are stunned when I say, "I'm here to be a server. I can work every night and every weekend. I've managed fifteen tables at once, don't mind cleaning up after everyone, and I've never had one customer complain about me."

"Of course you haven't," Frank says. "You're adorable."

I think he's mocking me, but by the way he's leering at my pigtails and tank top, he's not.

"Does that mean I have a job?" I ask.

"We have two servers," Frank tells me. "We don't have a lot of traffic here Monday through Wednesday, but if you're willing to come in and be flexible—I think we can make some room for you. That would help us on the weekends. Do you know how to properly pour beer?"

I step behind the front counter without permission, grab a pint glass, tilt it at the right angle, and pour. My hands are shaking, but when I finish, it's perfect.

"Hired," he says. "Let's get some paperwork."

"What about a uniform?" I ask.

"No one wears those here," he says. "You can wear whatever you want. What you have on is fine—whatever attracts customers, honey. Just take orders, drop them off, and bring in some cash. We keep it simple here."

When I get home, I'm elated. I tell Toby I'll be serving again, and while that's not my dream job, I should make good money. And after a month, I'll have insurance. We're elated, and despite our limited budget, we go out to dinner to celebrate.

Despite my elation, Ann asks me if I'm ever going back to college.

"Yes," I tell her. "But not here. I'm looking at other places."

"You can't just be a waitress forever, you know. That's kind of low-class."

I try to ignore her, but her attitude has turned from friendly to high-and-mighty. She believes herself to be better than I am because she is working on a Masters—and yet, I'm only a junior in college. This, apparently, makes me stupid.

Toby and I discuss it, and I tell him that I want to move to Frederick. There's a college there—Hood College—and it has a decent music program. It also has an excellent English program, and since I've been so busy with music reviews, maybe I should consider that option. He agrees, and I drive there to tour the beautiful campus and pick up my application materials.

When I'm not at work or filling out college paperwork, I go see my new psychiatrist, Dr. C. He believes my bipolar has been severely mismanaged by too many doctors over the years.

"You did the right thing by coming to me," he says. "I'll get you hooked up with a therapist, too. But for now, I think you need to be off Lithium. Permanently. I'd like to try some other medications, but slowly. And first, I want to address the insomnia and the ADD. Are you opposed to taking sleeping pills? And Ritalin? Ritalin for the day, sleeping pills at night?"

I'd admitted to Dr. C that I only was able to sleep about four hours a night. Otherwise, I was writing, spending time on the Internet, listening to music, or working. I tell him that any sleeping aid he offered would be something I'd try.

Luckily, I submit my application to Hood before beginning the sleeping pills. They're called Ambien, and supposedly, they allow people a good night's sleep.

But the combination of Ritalin and Ambien is not a good one for me. Ritalin makes me shake, obsessively clean the apartment, constantly rearrange furniture, walk to work because I have the energy to get there on foot, and not eat. I'm losing weight again, which makes me happy, but a heart rate of 130 beats per minute terrifies me.

The Ambien, however, is a different story.

The Ambien is how I went away for a month and let the voice take over my entire life.

AT FIRST, THINGS SEEM NORMAL. I WALK THE THREE MILES TO WORK, ignoring cat calls because people think they have the right to stare at me in a tank top and shorts. I make good money, and I see my new therapist, Michelle, who doesn't understand "the scope of my issues," but tries to deal with rape, abuse, trauma, and attempted murder. I'm fine.

One night, after taking the Ambien, I see the room slip away from me.

"Go," the voice says. "This is your chance."

And a series of events occur that I don't remember. I eat glass. I burn plastic to get high off the fumes. I drive while asleep. I wake up in the middle of the night, screaming that I'm falling from a tall building. Toby holds me and tells me we're not on a building, but I don't believe him.

And I don't act as I should one afternoon when Frank pulls out a gun he's kept hidden behind the counter of the restaurant, cocks it, and points it at a customer's forehead. I get in front of the customer and dare Frank to shoot me instead.

Frank puts the gun down and the customer and I both leave. I never return.

Other things must have occurred during that mid-May to mid-June period of time. But I didn't know about them. It's only when Toby finds me trying to take ten Ambien at once on the kitchen floor that he tells me he's seen enough. I come off it cold turkey, and then, I'm back.

And two major things have happened in that time: one, I've been accepted into Hood College for the Fall 2004 semester, and two, Toby and I are moving to an apartment in Frederick, only five minutes from Hood and ten minutes from his new job as a manager at a craft store.

Wondering what's happened to my life, I visit Dr. C. I throw the vial of Ambien at him.

"You piece of shit!" I say. "You didn't tell me I'd lose a month of my life on these!"

"How many did you take?"

"One a night, like you said. And I fucking lost track of time. I ate glass, for the love of God. I stood in front of a loaded gun. I don't remember choosing an apartment to live in. I even got into college and didn't know. What is this shit?"

"Well, it helps some people, but it's not for you," he says. "Let's try Lamictal. It won't help with sleep, but it will help with mood changes. Take it with the Ritalin. You'll be fine."

I don't trust him, but I accept the sample pack and tell him I'll start it once I move.

Ann decides to move on campus, and we part on civil—but not friendly—terms. Toby and I fit everything into, or on top of, our cars, and we head out toward our new home.

The new apartment is in the basement of a townhouse. The owner lives on the main floor, and she has a tenant living above her. In our small section, we have a tiny closet, a living room/bedroom, a small kitchen, an area for two desks, and a bathroom. There's also a sliding patio door, garage access, and a fenced-in backyard in a safe community. I could almost walk to college from here. And for six hundred dollars a month, it's worth it. We'll save a ton on gas, and Toby's new job means that he'll be making an actual living wage.

And my parents make a triumphant return into my life. When they hear that I have a proper psychologist and therapist, have been accepted into a private college, and am living in a better neighborhood? I'm their daughter again. My mom tells me how proud she is of me—despite the small apartment, it's a step up. And when they find out that Hood will be giving me tons of scholarships and financial aid, they are even more excited and offer to put me back on their insurance. I accept, but I feel nervous about it. As long as I act normal and seem normal, I'm their daughter. But if I don't comply, I'm a waste.

When I find out that Lamictal gives me a horrible rash and causes my throat to swell, Dr. C prescribes two medications to take its place: Depakote and Risperdal. Taken separately, they may have been fine. Taken together? I lose my hearing and cannot get out of bed. Toby worries about me, but since college doesn't start for several weeks and I'm currently unemployed—except for the here-and-there articles I write for the music magazine—he leaves me alone.

Eventually, the hearing loss is so horrible that I can't take it. I give up. I decide that I don't need the pills, and I don't need Dr. C. He's only steered me in the wrong direction, and refuses to take the blame for overmedicating me. I flush the Depakote and Risperdal down the toilet, and within a week, I feel like myself again.

Except that I'm twenty pounds heavier.

"When the hell did that happen?" I yell at Toby. "Why didn't you tell me? I can't go to college looking like this! Everyone's going to think I'm just some old loser."

"I hadn't noticed," he says. "You look the same to me."

Bullshit. I haven't weighed this much in my entire life.

"It's the pills," I tell him. "If all I did was take pills and sleep, and I didn't eat or move, well, there we have it. But they're gone. I flushed them. I'm doing this on my own."

"Doing what?"

"Handling these disorders. If pills don't work, then fuck it. I'll go to therapy, but I'm done putting this shit into my system."

Before school starts, Toby and I go see Coheed and Cambria

perform. And the experience is astounding. I meet the guitarist, who winks at me and smiles. I stand on a balcony and sing my heart out to all the songs that have kept me going in my hours of need. I cry when they play "The Light and the Glass." This night makes up for all the lost time.

Things are going to be okay.

But on the night before my classes begin, Toby and I lose everything.

I'M AWAKE, STARING AT THE CEILING AS ALWAYS WHILE TOBY SLEEPS next to me. I'm anxious—is my first-day outfit right? Is this a good hair color for me? Do I have everything I need?

The landlady's dog starts to bark. He doesn't bark much, but this time, he goes crazy. He doesn't stop. I get up to go pound on our ceiling, hoping that will quiet him.

But something's wrong. I can feel it.

That's when the smoke detector goes off.

"Get up," I say to Toby. "Something's really wrong. Get up!"

He's still in a haze of sleep and confusion, but he pulls on some pants and puts his wallet and car keys in his pocket.

We both hear sirens.

I grab my new backpack and my purse and head for the sliding glass door. That seems like the best way to get out of here if the house is, indeed, on fire.

But when I pull back the curtain, I'm met with a wall of flames. For a moment, I stare at the fire. It licks at the wood around the deck above us as it climbs, and despite the destruction, there's something amazing about this strange, orange creature that has taken over.

"Come on!" Toby yells. "We have to get out!"

But the garage door is locked, too. We're trapped. And no one has ever been able to hear us down in this apartment.

Through some miracle, the upstairs tenant unlocks the garage door, and as Toby and I exit with nothing but his wallet, my backpack, my purse, and the clothing on our backs, we run to the other side of the road, pavement and glass sinking into the soles of our feet.

I slowly turn around to look up. The entire townhouse is engulfed in flames. Our cars are only twenty feet away. If the house falls, we'll lose them, too.

I see the landlady and the upstairs tenant, and both are crying. Firefighters are struggling to put out the unstoppable flames. Neighbors are screaming.

And something comes over me for a moment. I calmly call my mom and tell her that our house is burning down, and then I walk over to a firefighter.

"I live in that house," I say, my voice sweet and light. "How can I help?"

"You can help right now by praying we do our jobs. If not, you're about to lose everything."

Something in his voice snaps me out of my state. I look up at the townhouse again, and realize that two of the most important things I own—my photos and my pen drives with ten years of writing contained on them—are still inside.

I rush toward the house, but when I get to the lawn, I'm shoved back. A reporter comes up to me and asks me how I feel.

"I feel like you should fuck off!" I say. "And quote that!" Then I turn back to Toby, tell him that my writing is inside—as well as my pictures of Doo-Da—and start to vomit.

It takes an hour, but just as my parents arrive, the fire is quenched. But the house is barely standing. A fire chief asks to talk with me, and that's when I learn the cause of the fire: the landlady had been smoking on her deck. She put the lit cigarette into a dead plant, situated right next to a propane tank for the grill. It didn't take much to cause a fire of this magnitude.

I want to kill her. In that moment, I feel nothing but rage. But then, I'm overcome by that strange shock of gentleness again. "What can I do?" I ask. "Can I go in to get some belongings? Can I fill out some paperwork?"

"We're going to get everyone some info from the Red Cross," he says. "But I do want a statement from you regarding what you saw. As for going in, we're waiting for the all-clear. There's a chance you can since you were on the bottom floor. The top two floors? Doubtful."

We wait, covered in ash, smelling like fire, until the sun rises. The fire chief approaches and says, "You have ten minutes to go in with my crew and gather whatever you can. Be careful. If they tell you to get out, you get out, no questions asked. Understand?"

Toby and I nod, and with the crew, we walk back into the basement apartment.

We're knee-deep in water and broken bits of wood. Our clothing is a loss. Most of the electronics have been damaged. We had our wallets, so we didn't have to worry about that, but all our things have been damaged by smoke and fire.

But tucked away in the corner where Toby and I have set up our desks is salvation. The fire never reached that corner near the bathroom. Everything on our desks is safe—including my pen drives, photo albums, and some of my books.

I sob in relief, and we carry out all we can before the fire crew tells us to evacuate. The house sounds like a ship about to break: it groans as though its bones cannot handle anything further. We run back to our cars and realize I have my first class in two hours.

And we realize that we're homeless.

"Come back to our house for now, and we'll figure it out," my mom says. "As for class, well, I think what they read in the paper will explain why you're missing your first day."

In my car, I notice that my face is dark with ash. My arms and legs are covered in blood and debris, and I'm soaking wet. The smell is awful, too—I smell like I'm on fire.

I take four showers that day. But the smell never leaves me alone.

I don't think it ever will.

I CALL THE COLLEGE AND LET THEM KNOW THAT I'LL BE MISSING MY first two days of class. When I tell my advisor why, he says to take all the time I need. But I'm fine. I want to go to school.

My parents have offered to let Toby and me live in their basement until we find a suitable apartment, but staying there comes with a price. My dad thinks Toby should move out and find an apartment on his own—we shouldn't live together if we aren't married. He even offers to buy me a car if I agree. But I say no. I'm grateful for a place to stay, but I won't leave Toby for a car.

Toby and I spend most of our time in Frederick. He goes to work, I attend classes at Hood, and we fall into a routine, usually meeting right around dinnertime.

And I love Hood College. My classes are interesting, my professors are engaging and intelligent, and the other students usually act as though they want to be there. I've missed this about college. I haven't had this since York. It's like a homecoming for the homeless.

But while I attend this first semester, I'm not working, so Toby is the only one making money for us to find a place to live. We look around for something near campus, but it's almost impossible. Housing has been taken since it's late September, and while the offer to stay at my parents' house is a standing offer—rife with terms—we know we need to leave.

After a journalism class one afternoon, I search through the want ads in Frederick's paper. And finally, I find something. It's a basement apartment, but it's in a house, so it's large. Rent is nine hundred dollars a month, but that includes all utilities and cable. I call the number right away, and the landlady tells me that we can come see it that night.

The apartment is huge. It's ten minutes from college, but it's tucked back into the country, so everything is quiet.

"What's the catch?" I ask the landlady. Nothing this nice happens for nine hundred dollars.

"Nothing," she says. "You do have neighbors living above you, but they're older, so you'll probably only hear them every so often. I need eighteen hundred for you to move in."

The next day, the deal is done. We hand her a check and she hands us the keys.

My parents are strangely sad that we are leaving, but I ignore them. I cannot tolerate this back-and-forth bullshit. We move out, and thank them for letting us stay.

But when we're gone, we're gone. We won't go back. We move in, set up the huge apartment, and celebrate with a bottle of wine and sex on the living room floor.

Suddenly, everything is coming together. I find a part-time job at a local bookstore, and while it won't cover the rent, it will cover food and gas. I do my homework, go to class, and meet new people. We're saving money again. We've beginning to thrive.

But I have night terrors. Every night, I dream about the house burning down, but when I wake up, I can't move. I stare at the ceiling and don't know how to break free. And the voice is there. For some reason, she's always there now, and she's relentless.

I finish my first semester at Hood College with a 3.7 GPA, the friendship of a wonderful advisor, and the faith in my decision to major in English. I am focused and dedicated.

On New Year's Eve, Toby and I throw a party at our new apartment. Twenty of our friends arrive, and a few of them crash on the couches or the floor.

And I think 2005 is going to be amazing. We have this house, I have college and work, and Toby is steadily employed. There is nothing that can get in our way.

This is finally how life should be.

2005–2007

My hometown is about forty minutes away from the apartment, and therefore, my therapist is now too far away for me to reliably meet with her. I start searching the Internet for psychologists and psychiatrists who specialize in bipolar, depression, anxiety, suicide, trauma, and eating disorders within the Frederick area.

Very few doctors match my search, but within the same practice, I find two who do: Dr. Levy, a psychiatrist, and Dr. Palmisano, a psychologist. I call the office and find out that visits will be my standard co-pay of twenty dollars. Considering that to be reasonable, I book appointments for the quickest openings, which are in February.

Before the Spring 2005 semester begins at Hood, I also take on a new job: I work for a private tutoring company that helps kids pass the SAT to get into college. And when I take this job, and complete the rigorous training, I realize two things: I am not meant to be a teacher because I hate the system's bureaucracy, and I am *absolutely* meant to be a teacher because I am able to teach kids how to rebel against that very system without getting in trouble. Teaching high school students how to find tricks that the SAT plays on them is like giving them cheat codes in a video game: the codes are there to use, and they are there to improve your skills. If I have been instructed to teach them these cheats, then I will happily do so.

My first class only has three students, but within one week, their scores all improve by 100 points. At least I know that I'm doing my job correctly. And since this job pays twenty-five an hour, I leave the bookstore behind and focus on the ten hours a week I do have to work.

When my own classes begin, I'm thrilled to be in actual literature courses with like-minded students. Dr. C, my new advisor, takes me under her wing, and we discuss modernism well after class has ended. She shows me different sides of Eliot and Woolf that I've never seen before, and suddenly, the world is infinite. I may be a singer, and I may be a teacher, but literature—reading it, writing about it, and then writing my own works—is my calling.

Before February arrives, however, I receive a phone call from my dad.

"I know the semester just started," he says to me, "but if I were to ask you to come with me to Mexico in a few weeks for a lawyer's conference—you know, to explore, and help me with my Spanish a bit —could you take off a few days?"

"What? Hell yes! I mean, yes. It's early in the semester. What do I need to do?"

I'm so delighted by this prospect—my dad wants me to spend five days with him in Mexico—that I brush up on my Spanish immediately. I buy some new outfits, though I refuse to wear shorts because my legs are now too fat to look cute in them. I'm gaining too much weight, and while I want to blame some of the meds I've been on, I also know that eating at IHOP four times a week probably isn't helping. The morning trips to Sheetz probably don't help, either.

On a snowy February morning, my dad picks me up to take us to the airport. Toby is sad to see me go, especially since I won't be able to call him every night, but we kiss goodbye and I head out the door.

And I realize that I've never been alone with my dad for five days. Will he be as stern and strict as he is when he's at home? Will he boss me around and tell me what to do the entire trip?

As we board the plane and prepare for the long flight, I'm anxious.

Maybe it's just the caffeine from the airport Starbucks. Or maybe it's me, with my black hair, my blue nail polish, and my dark eyeliner. I don't fit in with the lawyers on this plane. I don't look like someone who should be seated next to my dad unless I am one of his clients. I am sorely out of place.

But we're in the air. It's too late for me to turn back.

I DON'T TURN BACK, AND THANK GOD FOR THAT. HAD I WASTED MY time worrying about the assumptions that had consumed me in the airport, I wouldn't have had one of the most memorable experiences in my lifetime.

My dad and I bond during this trip. While he does need my help with some Spanish, he picks it up quickly, and when he's not in meetings, we spend our time swimming and drinking in the pool. He loosens up then, and we gossip: which lawyer is having an affair, which lawyer is about to be disbarred, those sorts of things. It's like talking to Carrie, only I'm talking to a fifty-year-old man.

Not that we don't have serious conversations. At dinner, we discuss politics. During a tour of the town, when I ask our guide about economic policies in Mexico and how Mexico views America in terms of capitalistic idealism, my dad lights up. He's proud of me. He engages in these discussions. Our common ground has always been academia— anything dealing with literature, the law, economics, or policy.

We also go whale-watching—a spectacular adventure that leaves me soaked in ocean waves and tears—and drink in Cabo San Lucas. We eat actual tacos. We ask locals for restaurant recommendations. He steps out of lawyer mode, out of sternness, and during those times, he's just—my dad. And I like him so much better that way. I'm twenty-three and he's fifty, but we feel like teammates, like intellectual peers, during this trip. There are no limitations.

On the last day of the trip, we spot a young woman walking along the shoreline. She's holding something in her hands, but we can't determine what it is. We sit up and look, more determined than ever, and then she spots us and waves for us to come closer.

She's not allowed on resort property, she tells us in Spanish. But she is allowed by the shore. She braids hair for the tourists as a way to feed her children. And I have long hair. Would I like it braided? She can do it for twenty dollars.

I tell her yes, and she sets her belongings by the water. She unfolds a blanket, pulls out rubber bands and beads, and sits behind me. She says my hair is beautiful, and begins to work.

It takes her two hours, and it's almost completely dark out by the time she finishes. But we converse in Spanish. She has five children, and a husband who works on a boat. They live nearby, in a small house with her parents that has a leaky roof and only one bathroom. She makes her money off tourists. They pay her well, and twenty dollars American is more than some people make in a week.

I shake my head, feeling the tiny braids and the beads at the end slap against me. This is such a tourist thing to have done, I think. But I did it for her as much as I did for me.

"What is your name?" I ask her. "I should have asked you that two hours ago!"

"Carmen," she says. "I'm so glad I could make your beautiful hair even more beautiful."

Before I can go back to get my purse, my dad pulls out his wallet and gives her forty dollars.

I don't think I've ever loved him more than I do in that moment.

The morning of my departure, my dad takes my picture in the garden outside of our room. I'm sitting at our breakfast table, staring into space, and he captures the moment: a brooding girl with a hundred tiny braids in her hair, thinking about the universe. It's a picture he keeps.

As I get on the shuttle, he thanks me for the help with his Spanish, and for the company. I hug him and tell him that I have had a genuinely amazing time. I thank him for the experience.

There are tears in his eyes as I leave. He doesn't want me to go.

My dad loves me. This trip is worth everything, I think, just so I could see it for myself.

It's hard to get back into the subzero temperatures at home, but I go to class the next day—everyone asking about my hair and about the experience I'd had—and prepare for my upcoming sessions with Dr. Levy and Dr. Palmisano, who are both going to see me on the first day. They'll do an hour-long evaluation together, and then, will meet with me separately as needed.

The doctors are both nice, but I'm particularly taken with Dr. Palmisano, simply because he looks like Captain Picard from *Star Trek*. He rolls his eyes, but he smiles when I say it.

The evaluation leaves me dizzy. I've been raped? How many times? By how many people? Have I ever been sexually abused otherwise? Yes? How old was I? Where was I? Do I have fits? Suicidal tendencies? Weird stories about my childhood? Do I hear voices?

I can't keep up, and I notice that I start to fade out.

"That's a trauma-based response," Dr. Palmisano says.

"Fading out? Fine. What does that mean I have?"

"It means you can distance yourself from your trauma, and that's intriguing. We're going to definitely be talking about that."

"Look," I say to him. "What happened to me just happened. I can't go back and change it. It's easier to just talk about it like it's—a story. Like it's someone else's story."

Both Dr. Palmisano and Dr. Levy write down every word I say.

Then I take a test to see if I actually do have ADD. It's on Dr. Levy's computer, and I'm supposed to hit a button whenever I see an "X" pop on the screen. But after a few minutes, the test is ridiculously boring, so I talk about my trip to Mexico with him, and I forget about the "X."

More notes are taken. More questions are asked. When the hour is over, Dr. Palmisano asks for me to schedule an appointment for next week, and Dr. Levy echoes his sentiments. And then I go home, miss my classes that afternoon, and sleep. It only took an hour, but those two doctors broke my already-broken brain a bit more than I had anticipated.

After a normal week of classes and SAT tutoring, I go back to the doctors.

I see Dr. Levy first. "Okay," he says. "So, I think your former doctors were all onto something when they talked about bipolar and ADD. I won't deny that you have those, and I do want you on something low-dose for the ADD component. But there's something else going on, and I don't think it's something I can medicate."

"You're a psychiatrist. Isn't that what you're supposed to do?"

Dr. Levy shakes his head. "Trauma-based disorders are usually only treated with anti-anxiety medication," he says. "And I'm not going to load you up on tranquilizers until Dr. Palmisano has a better understanding of what your disorders really are."

"What do I do?"

"I do want you to take Valium three times a day, but at a low dose. That will help the anxiety. I also want to put you on a medication called Seroquel. It's an anti-psychotic."

I sit forward. "You think I'm psychotic? You're not telling me everything."

"I am," Dr. Levy says. "It's not uncommon nor unusual to give a patient with bipolar disorder a medication like Seroquel. Just because we call it an anti-psychotic doesn't mean that you *are* psychotic. You may have psychotic tendencies, but you can't define yourself by all these terms and labels. We just need them so that insurance approves your medication and your therapy. That's all."

"That's all?"

"Yes. Take the Adderall, the Valium, and the Seroquel, and let's see how you do." Then he writes the prescriptions, asks me to come back in a month, and sends me next door.

Dr. Palmisano is waiting for me. I pick a spot on the couch across from his desk and say, "Okay, so, I'm psychotic. What other news do you have for me?"

He laughs. "Don't give yourself such high praise yet. This is just our first session. But you did mention a lot during the evaluation. Is it hard for you to comprehend the scope of the trauma you've been through?"

"Are you going to ask me questions like that thinking I have the answers?"

"Do you?"

"Do I?"

Dr. Palmisano laughs again. "Well, the tests are right. You're quite far from dumb. Intellectually, it's clear that you could talk us all out of the room. But emotionally—something holds you back. You said your life felt like someone else's story, and not real, right?"

"Sometimes, sure."

"Do you ever hear voices that tell you to do things?"

"I answered this last week. Yes, but it's usually a voice. One. She just talks to me."

"But she's pushed you toward suicide."

"Only when I'd been considering it myself."

"Does she tell you to starve yourself?"

I look down at my body. Five years ago, I weighed 98 pounds. Now, I weigh 170. And while part of me is appalled, another part of me is relieved. No one has raped me recently. No one has tried to get me into their bed in a while. There is safety hidden in this fat. As long as Toby loves me, despite how I feel regarding my own looks, then I'm staying this way.

"Where did you go just now?" Dr. Palmisano asks.

"I'm here," I tell him. "I heard you. I just don't have the answers."

At the end of the session, he asks to see me once a week and gives me his cell number in case I have an emergency. When I ask what he means, he says I'll know it when I need to call that number. I leave, make my appointments, and go home, once again drained.

How is it that I can breeze through my classes, maintain enthusiasm with my SAT students, but feel this useless after therapy? There's a disconnect.

I just don't know how big that disconnect really is. Not yet.

SPRING SEMESTER FLIES BY IN A WHIRLWIND OF PAPERS AND TESTS. SAT classes come and go, and anxious kids and parents email me on a regular basis. I maintain my focus, receive A's on all my work, and help every one of my students.

But alone, I am struggling.

The Valium is a damn blessing. It takes the little things and it makes them tolerable again. But the Seroquel renders me a zombie. So even though I go to class, and I teach my students, I can't remember much of my life.

Toby is worried. "You sleep all the time," he says.

"This is supposed to make me less psychotic," I say. And in a way, it's working. I don't hear any voices—or, more specifically, her voice.

"Do you even know what month it is? Or what we did last night?"

"It's April. We went to Chipotle."

He shakes his head. "It's May. Your finals are in a week. And we went to a movie last night, and you fell asleep halfway through it. You've been out to see friends. We've gone to a few poetry readings. You hosted one. Remember that?"

"Sure," I say. "Now let me sleep."

"This isn't normal. You're not supposed to forget your life."

"Maybe my life won't bother me if I forget all about it."

"But then you'd forget me."

I pull myself up and rest my head against Toby's shoulder. "There's nothing in this galaxy that could make me forget about you."

But in reality, it's just a beautiful lie. I can seemingly forget about everything.

During my next session with Dr. Palmisano, he asks me to talk about Thomas. "I know that the rapes—the horrible things he did to you in your own home—really bother you," he says. "But what I keep wondering about is why you talk about those events so calmly."

"Because I can't be—un-raped?" I say. "Because I can't trust my own brain. If my mom walked in and saw Thomas and I together, but she walked back out because she said I looked 'content?' Well, how do I know I wasn't?"

"Did you want him to shove his fingers inside you?"

I wince at the words. "Fuck no."

"Well, there's your answer. Maybe you should tell your mom what actually happened."

I laugh. "That will never, ever occur."

"Consider it. At least tell her that you know what she saw. Just be delicate about it. Talk to her as an adult. You're not fourteen now. You're twenty-three. You can do this."

When I leave his office, I see Dr. Levy. He reduces the dose of my

Seroquel but asks me to stay on it. "It's rough during the first few months," he says. "But you're doing great."

I call my mom, and when she arrives at the Frederick apartment, she brings a vacuum. "You don't have one," she says. "You don't vacuum. I thought this would be a good gift."

"Thanks," I tell her. "But I just really wanted to have dinner with you."

As we drive to Chipotle, I can tell she's nervous. But we talk about my schoolwork and my tutoring, and she mentions how proud she is that I'm accomplishing so much.

"And on my own terms," I tell her. "That's a big thing I've been working on in therapy—that the decision to return to college, to get this job, were decisions I had to make for myself. They weren't based in fear or negativity. They were just things I wanted to do."

She's quiet as we order our food. When we're eating, we look at one another, and she says, "So, I guess you talk about me in therapy, don't you?"

"Yes," I say. "You're a big part of my life. Of course I do."

"Is it all negative?"

"No. Some of it's not pleasant, but it's not all bad."

"What do you say?"

"Well, I was just talking to Dr. P about that." I feel sick, but I know I have to have this conversation. "Why did you walk away from me that day when you found Thomas holding me in the kitchen? Why didn't you seem to believe me when you found the letter I wrote about how he raped me?"

"Because I didn't think he actually raped you. You looked okay. I didn't know what to do. My kid was being hurt. I'd been in that position myself before. I was shocked."

"So, you shut down and let me handle it?"

"What do you want me to tell you? I screwed up? Is that what you want?"

"No," I tell her. "I just want to know why you didn't help me."

"Because I didn't believe you! Not about most of it. Not at the time."

The drive home is pretty quiet, but in the apartment, when she hugs me goodbye, she says, "I'm sorry." I nod. And then, smiling for Toby's benefit, she adds, "Enjoy the vacuum!"

When she leaves, I stare at the present. As though a vacuum can solve the real problems, I think. As though a vacuum can make me less dirty. As though it can eliminate everything.

DURING MY FINALS AT HOOD—WHICH ARE SELF-SCHEDULED DUE TO an amazing honor code the school adheres to—I find myself doing something strange.

I start driving to Alexander's house, which is only about ten miles away from campus.

Sometimes, this happens before an exam, and I'm shocked to find myself on the street in front of his house. Sometimes, this happens after I leave college, and as I'm singing to music, it's as though the car steers itself down his road.

But Alexander doesn't live there. He's married now. I know he's moved.

One morning, after I end up at Alexander's house again, I park in a church parking lot. The church is right across the road, and I don't feel safe driving. If I don't even know how I'm ending up here, why am I driving a car? I turn up the radio, sing along, and cry. I don't know what's happening to me.

Luckily, I do make it through my finals, and receive A's. A perfect 4.0 semester.

But I don't remember much about it.

Carrie and I have been hanging out a lot recently, though, and we talk about renting a house together. She and Steve would share a room, Toby and I would share a room, and we'd have common spaces for dinners and parties. We could sing, she tells me. And it sounds like a plan. As much as I love my apartment, our neighbors have started to breed dogs, and the incessant barking and whining wakes me up even through my Seroquel haze. I've asked the landlady to speak to the neighbors, but she just sighs and says, "Family. I won't stop them."

The perfect opportunity to move comes when fleas enter our

apartment. I call her and tell her we'll be out in a month, and I want my security deposit back in full since I have to pay for flea removal and have to put up with another thirty days of nonstop dog noise. She agrees, and July 1 is the move-out date.

Carrie and I begin looking for houses right away, and after a week, we find a place in a quiet, lakeside community. It's fifteen minutes from school, but it's forty minutes from her job, so she's the one making the larger sacrifice. Still, when we see it, we know it's right, and for fourteen hundred dollars, it's a steal. Carrie, Steve, Toby, and I sign the lease, and the landlord hands us the keys. We can do whatever we want but paint. He's flexible. He doesn't plan to be around very often.

The summer flies by as Toby and I pack, move into the beautiful townhouse, go to the beach, and work. Summer is SAT hell time, as kids prepare for the fall exam, so we have money. And we have most of our evenings free together to go out for dinner and enjoy ourselves.

But in August, I start blanking out again. I've grown accustomed to the Seroquel and Valium—I can't imagine life without those medications now—but I often drive without knowing where I'm going or how I get to a certain location. I still end up at Alexander's. Something is calling me there. And I don't know what it is.

Memories of Thomas and Stone hit me, too. Both had raped me in August. And the house fire happened in late August as well. This is not a month I want to recall.

"Anniversary syndrome is very common for people who have been through significant trauma," Dr. Palmisano tells me during one hot summer session. "And you had three major events occur within the same month. You were harmed as a child. You were harmed at college. No one ever believed you, so you were betrayed. And then, you lost your home. Of course you're going to—disconnect."

"You're not telling me something," I say to him. "I can see it on your face."

"I want you to do something for me," he says. "As long as you can trust me."

I don't trust easily, but he hasn't hurt me yet. I tell him that I'll be okay.

"I want you to lean back on the couch," Dr. Palmisano says. "I want you to close your eyes and start talking about one of the memories that is really bothering you. Don't think about which one—just let the words come out. Let me hear what you have to say. But when you talk about it, keep your eyes closed. I don't want you to engage with me. I just want you to talk."

I lean back and take a few deep breaths.

What I am not prepared for is a hostile takeover of my brain.

"This bitch right here," I hear the voice say. "She can't handle any of this on her own."

Can Dr. Palmisano hear the voice? Am I even talking?

But he can. "I wouldn't call her a bitch," he says, talking to me as though I'm not in the room. "Who are you?"

"I'm the one who controls everything. When she was hurt as a little kid? She wasn't there."

Inside, I'm screaming. I can hear this voice. But I can't seem to respond.

"And you were there?"

"Someone had to be. Who do you think handles this? Who handles rape and trauma and abuse and the loss of a child or two—or even three? She doesn't. She can't."

"Maybe you haven't given her a chance," Dr. Palmisano says. "You should."

I gasp for air and sit up. When I do, I'm dizzy and I'm crying—something I never allow to happen in therapy.

Dr. Palmisano stares at me for a moment and then sits beside me. "How much of that do you remember?"

I wipe my eyes. "I could hear you. And I could hear her. I thought I was the only one who could hear her. But—you can, too?"

"The voice is yours. It's just a little altered. Look. I need to do a little more work with you on this, but I'm not surprised in the slightest by what we've uncovered today."

"Which is?"

"I think you have a fractured brain. It's been shattered, so to speak. When you were harmed as a child, you didn't know how to cope—and when children are creative and smart, like you, they create fragments of themselves to deal with the trauma they are afraid to confront."

"The voice—she takes on trauma for me?"

"You were there, too. It's your body. It's your life. But if you don't remember all the fine details, it's because she's been there."

"That can't be possible," I tell him. "This isn't a soap opera."

"No, it isn't," Dr. Palmisano says, shaking his head. "It's your life. And in your life, you have something called Multiple Personality Disorder—or, as we tend to call it now, Dissociative Identity Disorder."

I stare at him. "You're telling me that something is so beyond fucked up in my brain that there are—two of me?"

"Actually, for patients with DID, there are usually more than two different personalities. Discovering one today doesn't mean two don't exist. Sometimes, three do. There have been cases where a patient has presented more than one hundred different fragments, or alters. And with the symptoms you have—blanking out, not knowing how you drive to certain locations but waking up there, comorbid disorders such as Borderline Personality Disorder and anxiety—this all fits."

"I don't want to do this anymore," I tell him.

"We should stop for today. I'm glad to have received confirmation about something I suspected, but this is going to be a process. And I want you to process it."

I walk out of the building in a fog. Back at the townhouse, I sit on the staircase and cry.

"You've known me for twenty years," the voice says. "What changes now?"

"You aren't real!" I scream. "This isn't real!"

But I know it is. And I know that if I tell anyone anything, other than the fact that I sometimes disconnect from reality due to medication or an overload of traumatic memories, I'll be shunned.

I never say a word. No one knows that, on that August day, I've been diagnosed with DID.

———

MY FALL 2005 SEMESTER BEGINS IN A FOG OF DEPRESSION. I CAN'T care about anything. I don't have it within me.

There is happiness in a weekend where Toby, his brother, his best friend, and I all drive up to Pittsburgh to see Coheed and Cambria perform songs from their new album. The club is huge, and we score a great place to stand. And that night of the concert, as Claudio Sanchez pours out his story of writing, heartbreak, wanting to find home, and wanting to forget betrayal, I sob. Everyone else moshes or dances, but I lean against a railing and absolutely break down. My fellow musicians get it. I wish I could go up to Claudio, hug him, and simply tell him that his words change me. I can exist in their comfort.

But once I'm back home, I find myself seeing Dr. Palmisano twice a week, and dissociating far more frequently than that. I attend my friend Paul's birthday party, laced up in a tight black corset, and remember very little of it. Toby and I start meeting up with friends every Saturday to have dinner and watch our favorite geeky shows, and while I can recall the music I sang during the drive, I can't always recall the actual event. I start to get tattoos as reminders of things I love and places I've been, but I don't remember sitting in the chair.

Do I even exist if I fail to see that I exist?

And I stop attending classes. I do work at home, turn it in, but cannot pull myself off the futon in my office to show up. I no longer care. I don't want to flunk out of college, but I don't want to show up and be—someone else.

I speak to my advisor, and she tells me to take incompletes for the semester. I can focus on my mental health for now, she says, and then, between January and March, make up the rest of the work. It will be daunting, but if I take six weeks now, I will have a better focus for 2006.

Documents are filed with disability services at Hood College, and when the service coordinator meets with me and asks why I need to take the leave, I tell her that my advisor and psychologist want me to. I'm not myself these days.

I stay awake all night and work on a novel. I sleep all day, sometimes scratching off the skin on my wrists during terrible night terrors. I don't remember Thanksgiving, and I barely recall Christmas. Nothing seems to connect any longer.

Toby is worried about me, but he doesn't know I have DID, either.

All I've said is that, due to past trauma, I sometimes act like another person and the real me goes into hiding. I give him a quainter Jekyll and Hyde scenario than the actual war that is being waged inside my head.

But now, I understand why I've always connected to that story and musical.

I only hope I can find a way to rid myself of however many Hydes I have in 2006.

I START TO TAKE ON PRIVATE TUTORING STUDENTS FOR THE SAT IN the new year, and I sign up for Spring 2006 classes—all English courses this time. It looks like I'm still on track to graduate in the winter of 2006. I get to work on the four incomplete classes I must make up. There are twelve papers to write, four exams, and several other assignments, but if I do one a day, I'll easily hit the March deadline. I'm lucky to have received the time.

When classes begin, I'm immersed back in the world of modern literature and Shakespeare. I have an escape. DID doesn't exist when I recite Eliot's poetry.

Carrie and Steve get engaged, and Toby and I are thrilled. We all set out to do preliminary wedding planning, and Carrie asks me to sing during her ceremony. I'll be in the wedding as well, and of course I say yes. She's been my best friend since 1995. We're roommates, more like sisters than anything. I'll be there.

The voice is always there. I talk to Dr. Palmisano about this, but he says she is a part of who I am. She's not just "the voice." She's a repressed, created part of the person I am. And she probably has memories that I don't. If I can get her to communicate with me to determine if other alter personalities are there within what he calls "my system," then I'll learn more.

But she doesn't cooperate. In fact, despite her never-ending presence, she's quieter than ever. She doesn't let me forget about her, as I can sense her hovering in the background, but she's not actively talking. I'm not sure if that's a blessing or a curse.

However, it does lead to a remarkably easy semester. There's just one hitch: I'm not going to graduate in December of 2006. I'll be two classes shy of being able to graduate. Instead, the date has been pushed to May of 2007.

I storm into my advisor's office. "What the hell?" I ask her. "I was told 2006!"

"There are two classes offered here that didn't transfer over from your other two colleges," she tells me. "And they are Hood requirements. Even if you max out your Fall 2006 semester and we allow you to take eighteen credits instead of twelve—something I don't recommend with your mental health issues—you still may not get into the classes. Plus, Senior Seminar is only offered in the spring. You'll have to stay on through May of 2007."

"Then you lied to me," I tell her. And she asks me to sit down.

"I don't know your medical condition," she says, her voice soft. She's an older woman, and stern, but her eyes reveal compassion. "And you don't have to tell me. I just know it's there. If we map out your schedule together for the remainder of your career here—only two more semesters once this one ends, and we don't have far to go now—we can figure it out. We can find what works for you and what won't overload you. I think twelve credits in the fall and fifteen credits in the spring is a good plan. Spring is your better time. How does that sound?"

I'm so startled by her compassion that I begin to cry.

"I'm not going easy on you," Dr. C tells me. "But I know this road you're walking down. Some of the best writers do. Plath walked it. Eliot walked it. Woolf most certainly walked it. Immerse yourself in them. When you're alone, make yourself read their words and their diaries. Find comfort in the fact that other good writers, such as yourself, are not an anomaly."

The semester ends with another 4.0 GPA, a celebratory dinner at one of Frederick's finest restaurants, my newfound love of modernist literature, and an incredibly deep respect for my advisor. She gets it. She's not giving me a free pass, but she wants to help.

I don't even know how to thank her for that.

THE SUMMER IS MUCH OF THE SAME: GO OUT ON SATURDAY AND HAVE dinner and drinks with friends, tutor for the SAT, and go to the Outer Banks. But three things occur that make this summer a bit different.

Wedding plans are in full swing for Carrie and Steve, and our living room suddenly becomes an arts and crafts store. I understand; my OCD doesn't. But I simply take more Valium, talk to Dr. Palmisano about how to control my need to clean it all up, and as I belt songs by Coheed and Cambria, as well as Green Day, from my car, I feel just fine. Music calms me.

During our trip to the Outer Banks, Toby takes me to the Corolla Lighthouse for a picnic. I know what's coming: I knew it the entire time we'd been away. But he waits until close to the end of the vacation before getting down on one knee in front of the lighthouse, holding a beautiful opal ring that once belonged to my Grandmama, and asks me if I will do him the honor of becoming his wife. I say yes, and run into his arms. We kiss, and I know that this marriage is destined to work. It won't fail. I've been so good—only a few guys have caught my attention, but I've pushed them away. Toby knows I'm a flirt, and he accepts that, but I can be a married woman. The only stipulation, I tell him, is that the wedding has to be after I graduate from Hood next year. He agrees, and when we go back to the beach house to tell our family and friends, as well as to send texts to everyone we know, happiness greets us. We're going to pick a date in 2008—after I've had time to get into a job and maybe grad school, I say. My mom cries. But unlike my marriage to Jess in 2000, this is a different response. This is the response a mom would have when she hears that her daughter is graduating college, wants to go to grad school, and will get married when she's twenty-six—not when she's eighteen and an alcoholic.

The third event is a bit more damning. When we return home from the Outer Banks, I meet with Dr. Palmisano. Our session is going well as we talk about further trauma and DID, and I realize that I've never been with a psychologist for as long as I have been with him.

"Now you have to leave him," the voice says. "Dump him before he dumps you."

I ignore her until Dr. Palmisano makes a joke about my engagement ring. "You'd think guys these days could afford diamonds," he says. "You don't want a knock-off."

Fueled by the voice, and irritated at him for disparaging a three thousand-dollar ring of my beloved Grandmama's, I tell him I won't be coming back. I thank him for his help, and I go.

I never see him again.

Maybe that wasn't the wisest of choices, but I'm on the verge of becoming a college senior. My life will be devoted to school, as well as to my work, Carrie's wedding, Toby, and trying to find a house in 2007. I don't have time for more psychobabble bullshit, I reason. I still have Dr. Levy, and I can handle this DID thing.

But as it turns out, I can't.

DR. C HELPS ME SET UP A RELATIVELY EASY FALL SEMESTER, understanding that my darkest times fall between August and January. I'm only on campus three days a week, and one of my classes is a gym requirement. Two are literature based, and another is fiction writing. I can do this.

During the first week of class, I meet a girl who is in both my Brit Lit and Fiction Writing classes. Her name is Catie, and despite the fact that I'm twenty-four and she's nineteen, we bond. We find commonalities about past hurts and enter into deep discussions about the art of writing and how Marvell was a bit of a hack. We have lunch together frequently, and soon, she's training to become an SAT tutor to make money on the side as well. It's late in my college game, and while I've made several friends, Catie is the first friend I've made whom I actually care about seeing once I leave in May.

Dr. G, my Fiction Writing professor, is impressed with part of a novel I've presented to her. When it's shared with other members of the class, they tell me it should be made into a movie. I soak in the praise. Music has always been my first love, but I like this path. Plus, I'd been awarded a writing scholarship for this semester. Dr. C must have put me up for the award.

But the voice tells me that I'm caged up. I need to go out more. Why aren't we drinking? It's Senior year.

"I don't know how old you are," I say to myself. "But I can't. I have to work."

"Yeah, because that's always so much fun. Learn how to live!"

But this is one of the first times I've had a normal life. It's September 2006, and it's taken me twenty-four years to be able to say the words "normal" and "life" in the same sentence. I don't want that to slip away.

A father of one of my SAT students, however, helps it slip away within moments.

I'm finishing a fall tutoring session at the home of yet another upper-class family and am tucked away in one of their three offices with their sixteen-year-old son. I had asked to work with him in the kitchen, believing that visibility was always a good thing when it came tutoring minors, but his father had winked and said, "No. Take this office. It's a spare."

The father has deemed this my space for the ten weeks I work with this son. During the final tutoring session, my sixteen-year-old student is eager to find out if his score has improved. It has, and drastically so, which causes my student to jump around in excitement. He can go to Duke now, he tells me. I'm the best teacher he's ever had. Then, he quickly hugs me before running off to find his dad to tell him the good news.

The father walks in and shuts the door.

"You've been a blessing," he says to me and hands me a check. I'm not supposed to take money—the parents pay the company, and the company pays me—but when I refuse, he reaches for me and puts it into the pocket of my jeans. "You've more than earned it," the father says. "How else would my son be able to learn so much so quickly? Your company is smart: hire pretty, young college girls to teach high school kids how to pass the SAT. It's a good tactic."

"They hire anyone who is competent enough to do the job," I tell him.

"Just let him," the voice says. I smirk, and then, I slip away.

I watch as the father of my student starts to brush his fingers through my hair. The voice—this personality, I suppose—lets him.

"You are so beautiful," he says. "And that one day, when you were grading a test? I heard you humming. I'm a singer, too. Maybe we could do a really great duet together."

"I'm a trained opera singer," I hear myself say.

"No, you don't get it," the father says. "We'd perform a good duet. You know."

He pulls me against him and begins to rub my back. In my head, I'm screaming—I want to leave. I don't have any reason to be here, and my work with this student is over. I want to go home. But I'm stuck there. I'm trapped in a scene that I cannot control.

"Could you come around one afternoon—maybe at, say, 1:00 p.m.?" the father asks. "We'd have a few hours together."

When he starts to kiss the side of my neck, I snap out of it and push him away. "No!" I yell. "What in the hell is wrong with you?"

"Twenty seconds ago, you were lapping up every word I said. What is this bullshit? Are you just some whore? Get out."

I grab my belongings, say goodbye to my student, and run to my car. On the drive home, I'm sobbing. What had happened? I hadn't wanted to be with that man. Why hadn't I pushed him away from the start? Was I that terrified—or was some other part of me in control?

Once home, I call my tutoring company and tell them that I'll no longer be working with private students at their houses. I'll meet them at Hood, or I'll take on classes with more than one student, but no more home assignments. I refuse.

I stop eating again, make it through Carrie and Steve's beautiful wedding with the last bit of sanity I have remaining, write as though my life depends on it, and spend most of my time fading in and out of being present. I know it's called dissociating. I just can't call it that when it applies to myself.

Toby is worried again. He sees me come and go. He watches my eye color change.

"What's happening to you?" he asks. "Do you need another doctor?"

But I ignore him and push on. I write several hours a day. Dr. G tells me that she expects to see my books published one day, and I pray that she's right.

I finish my second-to-last semester at Hood with a 3.8 GPA—I've been given a slightly lower grade in gym because I wasn't there often, but I hardly care—and I celebrate the end of the year with our Saturday night dinner friends. We joke, we flirt, and I reconnect with so many people I once knew in high school. Everything is well, and I can't believe that I'm going into my graduating year of college.

I think that now, I'll be okay.

DR. C HELPS ME SET UP MY FINAL SEMESTER OF CLASSES, AND MUCH to my surprise, I need eighteen credits, not fifteen—we'd forgotten about a technology class that is a Hood requirement.

"Do you think you can handle six classes? One of them is Evolutionary Biology, one is your Senior Seminar, and one is Advanced Fiction Writing. But the other three should be pretty simple for you."

"I can do it," I tell her. "I'm graduating this May."

She smiles at me. "I like seeing you this way. It's good to see you confident."

The beginning of the year is mindless. All I do is tutor and go to my classes. Two days a week, I practically live on campus—I'm there from 8:00 a.m. until 8:00 p.m.—but I know that it's worth it. I'm about to have my Bachelor's degree, and the best part is that I did it on my own.

Catie and I hang out at the bookstore where Toby works, drinking coffee and talking about how to solve the world's problems. When I'm not with her, I'm with Carrie, and we talk about how we're going to have to find new places to live. We don't want to stop being roommates, but she and Steve are looking to buy a home. Toby and I return to my hometown, and, as fate would have it, an apartment that my former college roommate, Ann, is renting will be vacant come June 1. She speaks highly of me to the landlady, and the deal is done. It's only March, and Toby and I have our next place to live.

Dr. G calls me one night before our Advanced Fiction Writing class. "I have a family emergency," she says to me. "Do you think you could teach the class? Just focus on the book we were reading about how to become better writers."

I'm sure my peers are going to mock me—teacher's pet and all that. But instead, the class is amazing. We laugh and have a good time, and I actually teach them something about writing.

Maybe I should teach English, I think. Maybe I should go to grad school and then come back to a place like this to teach students what I know and love.

"You will hate that," the voice says. "You've strayed off your path, anyhow."

"Shut the fuck up. You're just me. How are you even protecting me?"

"Trust me. I am."

I hate these conversations, and I hate that people have seen them in public. I can't imagine how crazy they make me look. And yet, no one has shunned me. I fly through my classes, become friendly with everyone, and with the exception of DID messing up my head, I'm doing well, all things considered.

As I start to pack up the townhouse, years of memories—most of them good—flood me. I hadn't been extremely suicidal here. I hadn't been in a mental institution. I had received help, had several different diagnoses, was on meds, and got through college. I was at the finish line.

I have four days to take five finals and turn in a thirty-page paper about Eliot. As usual, I wait until the last minute, and I know Dr. C will hate the paper. I'll get a B in Senior Seminar. But since I was one of only two people who ever spoke up when it came to literature, maybe I have a fighting chance for an A. I can only wait and see, and that won't happen until after I cross the stage and am handed the diploma.

Even though I don't know my grades, I'm told that yes, I will be walking in the Spring 2007 graduation. I've also won a writing award— five hundred in cash—from the college, which is the highlight of my career there. On top of that, my poetry is being published. Everything I could have ever wanted from my college experience is happening.

Graduation is bittersweet, and I hold back tears most of the time. As my name is called and I get up to receive my diploma, two of my friends squeeze my hand. I hear Toby, my brother, and my parents cheer as I shake the hand of our college's president. In my pictures, I'm smiling.

But I'm also crying, because I don't want this to end.

Dr. G spots me as all the graduates exit the outdoor ceremony, and she stops me. "I am so, so proud of you," she says, and pulls a card out of her robe to hand to me. Then, she hugs me. I cry against her. I feel as though I'm losing part of my family.

I take one last walk around campus as the graduates depart. My family, Toby, and I have plans for lunch, but I have just enough time to buy a cheesy "I graduated" shirt from the bookstore and to walk up into the English department offices to see if anyone is there.

And everyone, with the exception of Dr. G, is there. All my favorite professors from my three years at Hood see me, and they offer congrats, handshakes, and hugs. Dr. C puts down a glass of champagne, goes into her office, and hands me a folder.

"What's this?" I ask her.

"Open it and see," she says, smiling.

Inside is my Senior Seminar paper—the one I'd struggled to write, because I never thought I'd find the words to properly discuss Eliot and his poetry. But on the front cover, there's a big letter "A", and under it, in Dr. C's classic chicken-scratch writing, the text reads, "This is a beautiful, intellectual, and well-developed paper. Tremendous work."

I can't help but hug her. "Thank you for believing that I could get through this," I say.

When I look at her, she has tears in her eyes. "You've been the brightest student I've had in years," she says. "I wasn't going to watch you fail."

I carry those words—and the words in Dr. G's card to me, that echo similar, emotional sentiments—with me to lunch. It's finished, I think. I had found home, and now, I'm gone.

So then, where do I go from here?

AFTER ANOTHER EMOTIONAL GOODBYE—LIVING WITH CARRIE AND
Steve for two years had been an amazing experience for all of us—Toby
and I pack up and head to the new apartment, forty minutes away in
my hometown.

It's a rundown little thing, but it's cheap, and it's temporary. For
now, until I find a steady job, it's all we need.

It takes a month, but finally, I find a job. It's not one that I want,
though: I'll be doing background checks for potential employees by
going through their personal histories and then writing reports on if
the employees should be hired. It's a mind-numbing nine-to-five job,
and every day that I go in is another day that I find myself sinking
deeper into depression.

Our spirits are a bit lifted, however, when Toby finds a job only
minutes from mine—at a local airport. He'll be making good money,
and he'll have benefits. I have them now, too, which is a good thing—I
seem to be getting sick often. And I know I need to see a psychologist
again. The voice won't stop, and my thoughts are getting darker. I can't
fight off my depression.

In August, my mom calls me at work, frantic. "Your Grandmama,"
she tells me. "She's not breathing. I don't think she'll make it." I've
already had a rough morning—I'd been so exhausted from insomnia
the night before that I'd accidentally come into work in flip-flops and
had been sent right back home to change after a twenty-five-minute
lecture—and now, I am panicked. My Grandmama has been stable in
her nursing home since her stroke almost twenty years ago. But now,
she is dying. I hang up, grab my purse, and rush into my boss's office.

"My grandmother is dying," I tell her. "I have to go."

"You're out of paid time off," she says to me. "You took it all
already. Every time you take an extra minute for lunch, I dock your
time. If you're a minute late coming into the building, I dock your
time. You don't have any time left. You can't leave."

"I can't?" I say. "Watch me."

I head out the door. I'm sure they won't want me back, but I don't
care. Clearly, I'm not meant to do nine-to-five work.

When I get to the nursing home, my mom shakes her head. "Her lungs are filled with fluid," she says. "It's probably a matter of time. She has a DNR. We're just waiting."

I sit out in the lobby, and while I'm there, I receive a text from a friend of mine. "Hey," it says. "You were looking for a kitten, right? Any chance you want one tonight?"

I call him. As it turns out, his cat had given birth four weeks ago, but she has since abandoned the babies. One is still unspoken for. I tell him to hold up—I'm driving the two hours to his house to come and get her.

My brother goes with me, and when we meet up with my friend, he hands us a tiny box. In it is a kitten, no bigger than my palm.

"Oh my God," I say. "So little."

"This one's a girl," he says. "No name yet. And she's going to need to be bottle-fed and bathed—so I hope you have some time on your hands."

Considering I'm probably out of a day job for a while, I have time.

My brother holds her as we drive home, and she cries the entire way. "What are you going to name her?" he asks.

"I don't know yet. I haven't figured it out."

Toby, who has been working, meets up with us and takes the kitten into his palm. He falls in love with her immediately.

After checking in with my mom—my grandmother is stable, but she may not make it through the night—Toby and I head home.

"I want to name her Ritty," I say.

"Ritty? Why?"

"That's my grandmother's nickname. Her name's Harriett, so, people called her Ritty." My eyes well up with tears. She's been in a nursing home since 1988, I think, and despite holiday visits and occasional times I've popped over, I haven't seen her much. And this woman helped raise me. The very least I can do is name a kitten after her.

The next day, I see Grandmama. "I have a kitten," I tell her. "I named it Ritty. For you."

She wakes up that evening, and she lives.

That night, I also take my security card, enter into my office building, gather the rest of my personal belongings, and show myself out. I'm not going to work in an office again.

I'm still tutoring, and now I'm qualified to teach the GRE and the LSAT, so I'm making good money. But it's not a career. I'm still searching.

A long-term substitute position opens at a high school in late September—the woman going on leave will be gone for eight weeks, so I'd be employed through Thanksgiving. The pay is fourteen dollars an hour, and I can tutor on the side.

I don't want to wake up at six in the morning, but I'll be taking over an AP Literature class, as well as a Brit Lit class. If I'm going to teach, I should teach what I know. I shake hands with the principal, and while it's not a career, at least I'll be making money.

The job is simple, as every single day has been outlined by the original teacher. My job basically consists of babysitting high school kids and grading essays about Chaucer and Twain. During my planning period, I work on my novel. I call Catie and tell her that I'm miserable.

"Do you ever feel like you don't fit in anywhere?" I ask her. "I hate this job. I like what I teach, but I am not a teacher, even if I'm good at it. This isn't a career. It's a shitty pit stop."

"Do you mean that you're there but you don't feel like you're there?" she asks.

"Yeah. All the time. As though my brain is somewhere else."

"I don't feel that," Catie says. "But I'm ready to graduate college."

Don't leave, I think to myself. It is so much better there.

My tutoring company asks me if I can teach the GRE on the Eastern Shore for four weekends—with a company-paid car and hotel room. I accept, knowing that Toby and I could use the extra money.

What I don't know is that I'm accepting another attempt on my life.

TOBY COMES WITH ME DURING ONE OF THE WEEKENDS, AND CATIE joins me on another. But on the first and last weekends, I'm alone.

And that is a very dangerous place to be.

During the first weekend, depressed that I don't have a job, haven't sold a short story, and can't seem to hack it in what people love to call the "real world," I buy bottles of alcohol and get drunk in my hotel room. I am sober when I teach, but other than that, I sit and drink.

The last weekend is the worst. I get just as drunk, but this time, I break an empty bottle and jam it into my leg. I scream, almost shocked at what I've done, and then I hear the voice.

"You're going to die in a shitty hotel?" she says. "Like a rock star? When you aren't one?"

"This won't kill me. Stop talking!"

"If I'm just you, then *you* should stop talking."

I pull the glass out of my leg and hobble to the vending machine for ice. While there, a guy sees me, smiles, and then looks at my leg.

"Jesus Christ!" he says. "What happened?"

As he pulls out his phone to call someone, I grab his hands. "Don't," I tell him. "It was an accident. Please. I'll be okay."

"Someone did this to you?"

"I guess you could say that."

Back in the hotel room, I wrap my leg, sob, and wonder why I can't stop my urges to die.

My long-term teaching position ends at Thanksgiving, and I have no job lined up. We can't live off Toby's salary alone, and we're as poor as we've ever been.

I take to the newspaper. After two days of searching, I see what I'm looking for: the paper itself is hiring. They need an editor. As long as I have a Bachelor's in Journalism or English, and some editorial experience, I can apply.

I'm called in for a four-hour interview the next week. It goes well, and then the day after the interview, Carrie is taken into the hospital to have her first baby.

I'm there for every minute of it—from 7:00 a.m. until almost midnight. Everything looks painful, but when her child is born, it's amazing. We cry. This is something that few people ever get to share, I think. This experience is life-altering.

Toby and I go to another Saturday night dinner with our friends Paul, Richard, Faith, John, Sadie, and a handful of others, but despite the bountiful food and the never-ending supply of liquor, I'm empty. I want to smile, but I don't know how. I should be working and having a baby. I should have bought a house by now. I've just turned twenty-six, and while there are eight months to go until the wedding, I feel as though I can't keep up.

But that Monday, as I'm getting out of the shower after having spent an hour sobbing inside of it, I receive a phone call. It's from the paper. They want to hire me, and if I'm available to begin working January 2, that's my start date. I'll be on the crappy shifts for a few weeks—Tuesday through Saturday from 1:30 to 10:00 p.m.—but will quickly move up to the normal 4:00 p.m. to 2:00 a.m. schedule.

Journalism is a career. The salary they offer is meager, but it's money, and it's needed. I tell them yes. They tell me to dress semi-casually and that they'll email over the formal paperwork.

No more teaching, I think. Unless I want to teach voice or piano again, I don't have to teach. No more searching for bullshit jobs. Soon, we'll have enough money to leave the apartment and buy a place of our own. Finally, all the hard works seems as though it's paying off.

OUR FRIEND PAUL THROWS A CHRISTMAS PARTY TO CELEBRATE THE end of what is a tumultuous 2007. It's going to be a small gathering, he tells me via text, which I read on my cell phone I can barely afford. My new job at the paper doesn't start for another two weeks. We're a one-income household, and that income is barely paying the rent as it is. But still, Toby and I decide to go to this party. It's just Paul, and our friend Richard, and the two of us.

"Oh," Paul adds. "Someone from our high school days will be here. He remembers you. He helped you when you sprained your ankle during your senior year—apparently, you guys had a Humanities class

together. He carried your books. Well, we're still close, and he'll
be here."

I have no idea who Paul is talking about, but I'm fine with more
people. I love people. People are not a problem in my life at the
current moment.

But after we dress—I wear black velvet pants and a very low-cut
red top, because my friends are male and I feel some inclination to
show off what I have—and begin to make the drive to Paul's, my
stomach starts to ache. Something is weird about this night, I think.
My intuition tells me as much. And so does the voice. I am to pay
attention to "this one."

Forty-five minutes later, we walk into Paul's. Richard greets me
with an enormous hug, and behind him, I make out the sounds of
some sort of racing game.

"Nothing says 'Merry Christmas' like Grand Theft Auto," I joke,
pulling away from Richard. He laughs and agrees.

Toby and I head over toward to living room and see Paul, situated
in a gaming chair, controller in hand. He nods at me. I know better
than to break his concentration.

On the couch near Paul is a boy. A boy from high school who once
carried my books.

He is beautiful.

I don't know if he's conventionally beautiful, but something about
him strikes me. Had it struck me in high school? I doubted it. Life had
been too hectic then for me to be concerned with this one, particular
boy. Besides, he isn't my normal type—there's no danger in his stare,
no tattoos adorning his body, and he's dressed as though he's about to
pop by an office holiday party. But it doesn't matter. Something within
his quiet presence, within his dark hair and equally dark eyes, draws
me toward him.

"We know each other, don't we?" I say as the boy stares at me.

He nods. "We do. From high school. And before that, we played
soccer together as kids."

I have known this beautiful boy for probably twenty years and had
no idea. What had I been missing? And why am I feeling this way
when my wedding is only eight months from now?

Something inside me crashes. This boy—his dark eyes reflecting the lights above him like stars—has my full attention. And I can tell I have his. We all make small talk while Paul finishes the game, and once he does, he embraces me, thanks me and Toby for coming, and heads into the kitchen to prepare dinner. The party is underway.

But right before the meal, I duck into the hall bathroom. My long hair is dark and dramatic. My clothing fits my body well. I suck in my stomach, lower my eyes and then raise them in a seductive stare, and part my lips. I've trained for this. I've been training for this for decades.

"It's time," the voice tells me. "This is it. Now go and change your life."

THE NIGHT IS FESTIVE AND LIVELY AS WE FEAST ON CORNISH GAME Hens. There is wine and laughter, and both warm me as we talk. This is the kind of talk I love - it's reciprocal, and there is give and take within the banter. No one tries to outshine anyone else to share a better story. There isn't chaos. It's a comforting calm.

I cannot help but stare at this boy from my past—the one with perpetual stars in his dark eyes. I deem him Starlight Boy, and from that moment forward, call him nothing else. And Starlight Boy and I can't help but to remark about our similar pasts—our parents were friends, we played sports together as children, we were in the same high school classes, and almost attended the same college. We'd missed a lot of time together, he says. I nod, my heart beating heavily. But how is this right? My fiancé is right beside me. We're in the home of one of my best friends. Do I have the right to feel something—whatever this may be, this hint of attraction or chemistry or connection—when I'm about to get married?

After the meal, Toby and Paul head to the living room to play a video game. The victor, Paul states, is the one who gets to "keep me forever." Toby argues, his voice raised in mock protest, but we all laugh. Toby knows that Paul and I dated in the past. It never worked out.

Richard, Starlight Boy, and I head toward a rec room down the hall to listen to music. Starlight Boy and I sit next to each other on the couch, our legs almost touching. We stare at one another. We talk about my upcoming job and his applications to graduate school.

"And I have this amazing girlfriend," Starlight Boy says. "She's on vacation right now."

Part of me feels jealous, and while I know that the feeling is irrational, I can't help but allow it to surge through me. I'm grateful to be the only girl at the party, but the selfish part of me wants to be the only girl in Starlight Boy's life. But I smile and nod and say nothing further.

Richard plays a duet that both Starlight Boy and I know. As I begin to sing, both stare at me, and Richard says to Starlight Boy, "Remember now? From high school. She's still really good." I'm flattered, and I turn the simple song into a full-out performance.

Starlight Boy joins in, his voice an untrained, albeit smooth, tenor. Within moments, our voices connect, and we fuse together. We match tone and mood. I see the colors of the music swirl around us, binding us together, creating an unbreakable connection. I think Richard sees it happening, too, as he watches us with a look that conveys more than just awe at our sound.

When Starlight Boy and I sing the final note, I am a changed person.

"Hey!" Paul exclaims from the living room. "I beat Toby! I get his fiancée forever now!"

"I guess I better pack up and move in," I yell down the hall. Starlight Boy laughs but then looks at me seriously. I stare back, trying to discern what he's pondering. But instead, we both break into a smile. Then, I put my hand on his leg for just a second, and I push off the couch and go into the living room where my fiancé and Paul are mock-fighting over my new arrangements.

I want to kiss the hand that touched Starlight Boy's leg. I want to hug him, without reason, and feel his arms around me. I want to absorb him in a way I haven't felt about anyone in ages. But I don't do anything. Even at the end of the night, Starlight Boy and I only hug briefly, in a way that seems as though we are both afraid of what a longer embrace might imply.

"This was great," I say to Paul. "Thanks for having us."

"Thanks for letting me win your love." As Paul hugs me, I look at Starlight Boy. And when I do go to say goodbye, to give him that brief hug, we promise to stay in touch this time. Social media will keep us together, as will Paul. Years will not pass; we refuse to let them.

On the way home, I ask Toby if he had a good time. He says yes and then compliments my singing, which he had heard while playing the video game with Paul.

"I felt really good in that moment," I say truthfully. My body is tingling in ways I can't explain. But connection is connection, and Starlight Boy and I have it. We have similar pasts, experiences, and future goals. We're musicians. We're wise. And we're in far over our heads.

As Toby and I drive home in the darkness, days away from the start of a new year—a year that will bring a new job, a new home, and a new marriage—all I can think to do is to lean over, turn up the radio, and sing. My soul parts my lips; my emotions are in every lyric.

Otherwise, I dare not say a word.

2008–FEBRUARY 14, 2009

Despite my new job, Toby and I are poor. And when the oil tank in our rundown apartment bursts, we lose half our possessions. Then, in a perfect storm of events, I get so sick that I miss two weeks of work, and Toby is fired from his job because he has to stay home to care for me. Wedding plans are on hold. Our lives are in limbo.

Paul takes pity on Toby and me and invites us to come live with him until after the wedding. I accept, in tears, and we cart a few truckloads of stuff into his spare bedroom. And then, we start counting the dollars we're saving, minus the gas for my new forty-five-minute commute and the insane amount of cash I blow on coffee.

Living with Paul isn't horrible. People are often hanging out, and suddenly, it's perfectly acceptable to get drunk on a random Tuesday night while playing Guitar Hero on the Xbox. And while Paul and I work, Toby searches for jobs and ponders going back to college. At night, we sit around with glasses of wine and debate everything from county recycling policies to how I can score concert tickets from our entertainment reporter.

And there, in the midst of Guitar Hero, wine, wedding planning, and work, is Starlight Boy.

He stays at Paul's a few times a month. Our connection is clear, but I try not to think too much about the might-have-been factor of our past.

"Think about it," the voice says. "He'll be yours within a year."

But I don't do anything outrageous. What can I do? On the days when Paul is at work, when Toby is out searching for a job, and I'm waiting for the late afternoon so I can leave to go to the paper, I hang out with Starlight Boy. We sit on the sofa bed, listening to Disturbed, Coheed and Cambria, and Incubus. He dares me to apply to a top-notch graduate program at Johns Hopkins University. I bounce on the squeaky sofa bed, an adult in her not-so-adult pigtails, belting songs so that Starlight Boy notices. Sure, I'll apply, I tell him. I'll apply right now.

"Apply right now" turns into "I only have two weeks to get this right, what the hell was I thinking?" But I do it anyhow. My undergraduate grades are good. I've won writing awards. And I am an expert at cover-letter bullshit. As long as my writing sample—a chapter from a novel I've been working on for years—is good enough, I think I have a chance. Starlight Boy says he knows I have a chance. I mail the application and tell Starlight Boy that I'm going to graduate well before he does. It becomes a flirtatious, charged competition. It ignites me.

Seeing Starlight Boy sleeping as I walk through the door of Paul's house at three in the morning—arms burdened with papers, notebooks, coffee, and the type of dinner that only McDonald's can provide at such an hour—ignites me as well. But I try to ignore this as I sit in the kitchen, working on my novel, listening to this beautiful boy turn and talk in his sleep.

Toward the beginning of May 2008, Hopkins is pleased to inform me that I will be joining their writing program, and I have been invited to take a summer course to accelerate my MA.

A few weeks later, Toby accepts a job with an IT company in Baltimore and begins a new undergraduate program on the very same day.

Things are overwhelming, but not shitty. Despite my confusion, I know it's time to carry on.

THERE IS A NEW PROBLEM.

About a month before the wedding, I begin passing out. I also find myself in possession of a bizarre capability: I can watch myself type, witness my fingers hitting the keyboard, even though I know I must be the one doing the actual work. I can't feel the action of my fingers on the keys, but I see it happening. I'm shaky and nervous. Is this just the DID? Do I need to tell someone?

But I keep my mouth closed, don't talk too often about the passing out problem, and prepare to become a bride. The wedding is a five-day event: greeting family, a rehearsal with an informal dinner, a formal rehearsal dinner, the wedding day itself, and finally, a poolside brunch. There is no downtime. Passing out isn't an option. I stay alert.

Knowing that we are to be husband and wife in a matter of weeks, Toby and I begin searching for a place to live. In what can only be called fate, we drive by the duplex I lived in as a child. The side I hadn't lived in is for rent, and we immediately call the number. A tour is scheduled for the next day, and a few days later, we learn that the place is ours. Come September 1, Toby and I will have our own home. It's conflicting to visit that spot, but we need a home.

Part of me aches, however. We won't have the constant company up at Paul's, with Paul, Richard, and Starlight Boy continuously making life enjoyable. I don't know how to say goodbye. But I tell myself that this is for the best. A married couple needs their own space, I'll only be five minutes from work, and besides, I shouldn't be around Starlight Boy. All we do is stare at one another. I didn't invite him to the wedding; I couldn't do it.

This is the life I choose.

And I'm proud to say that, during the week of the wedding—as contracts for the house are being signed, as hair and makeup are being applied, and as I prepare for my new role in life—I only pass out three times. And no one knows.

THE DAYS OF EVENTS LEADING UP TO THE WEDDING ARE BEAUTIFUL and contain little drama. There's wine, flirting with random patrons in a bar, gifts being exchanged, packing, last-minute seating chart rearranging, and other typical occurrences. Friends and family help, and I smile.

"You're going to fucking hate this," the voice says. "But I'll fix it."

"Fuck yourself," I whisper inside my head as I blow-dry my hair for the formal rehearsal dinner Toby's parents are hosting. "I choose this. There's nothing to fix."

"Just you wait."

The rehearsal dinner is romantic and emotional, and copious amounts of alcohol quiet the voice. From my seat at the head of the table, I glance around in wonder. These people are here because they love us. Despite everything, they love us. They have busted ass and spent money to be here, and for the first time in a long time, I start to cry. I can't stop.

Back in the hotel room that night, only twenty hours before the wedding, Toby and I stare at one another.

"Is everything going to change?" I ask.

Toby laces his fingers through mine and kisses my forehead. "Only that you'll be my wife," he says. "But we're still the same people."

We cling to each other in nervousness and exhaustion. And there is love. I can feel it, body to body, soul to soul. Despite the chaos, there is calm.

But then, there is the storm.

And the storm is literal. On Saturday, August 2, a hurricane blows through Maryland. We wake to a bizarrely still morning, but as the day progresses and the hour draws closer, the rain begins. The hail follows. The winds pick up, and I cover my long hair, which took the stylist two hours to perfect. And while I'm not superstitious, I grow wary. I tell Toby that no one will show up. Plus, what does he care? I've been running errands while he's been playing video games with his groomsmen all afternoon. Why should he care about the weather? I yell at my mom, telling her that my head hurts, that everything is too loud, and that we were stupid to host a wedding during hurricane season. But she puts up with me and tells me to sit down and eat. The ceremony is in the same building as the reception, she says. Everyone will come, and have fun, and be just fine.

They'll all stay until midnight, the magical Cinderella hour when we must start paying by the minute if our wedding party hasn't cleared out yet.

I love my mom so much in those hours. Her calm tempers the tempest.

Two hours before the wedding, the skies clear. As I'm getting dressed, laughing with the photographer, I look out the large window next to the spiral staircase. The sky is a mesh of tangerine and robin's egg blue. It's all okay now, I think. The worst is over. There will not be anything that could ruin this wedding—or, more importantly, this marriage.

Toby's vows to me make people cry. I'm moved beyond words, wondering how my graduate school writing pales in comparison to these words that have so easily flown from his heart and straight into his mouth. But I'm proud, and my guard is down. I'm ready to let go of the past now. Whatever I have been feeling for Starlight Boy, whatever has happened to me before this very evening—that is to be erased. Life begins now.

And then, just like that, I am somebody's wife.

DAY FIVE IS POOLSIDE BRUNCH DAY, BUT IT IS ALSO THE DAY TOBY and I leave for our Hilton Head honeymoon. I'm so exhausted that I cannot keep track of time and barely recall much of the party, but I feel happiness. Somewhere within me, I trust that everything is fine.

About an hour before we're supposed to leave for South Carolina, I rush to the bathroom and throw up blood. Clearly, things aren't as fine as I'd hoped. The dizziness is there, and now, my mouth is caked in blood. And I know this: I can't tell anyone. I can't even tell Toby. I've only been his wife for half a day. He doesn't need to know. I wash out my mouth, fluff up my still-curly hair, and smile as I return to greet my guests. I am an actress. This is what I do.

The drive down to Hilton Head is insanely hot, and with gas at a record four dollars per gallon, I'm constantly nauseated. But I don't say a word. Toby and I make the best of it, and when we get to the resort, everything is wonderful. There's a waterslide for adults. This is time for fun.

Then I grow too sick to leave the room.

I'm in bed as Toby sleeps, and I count. My life as Toby's spouse began August 2. His life as my caregiver began August 6. That seems unfair. I stand up and stagger around in dizziness, my heart pounding, my stomach churning, feeling as though I'm on a balcony with no railings to keep me from falling. This will pass, I tell myself. This has to pass.

"Keep dreaming," the voice says. "I warned you."

"I'll take care of you no matter what," Toby says when I get back into bed. "Whatever's wrong, we'll figure it out. Once we're home, we'll get you to the doctor right away."

He's lying to me, and I know it. He probably knows it, too. And he doesn't deserve this.

When we return home and move into the duplex, I think that maybe things will be okay. The dizziness is there, but we have a home. Three bedrooms, two bathrooms, a huge deck for the parties I plan to throw—what's there to be sick about? And even though Toby has a thirty-minute commute to work, I only have to drive for five minutes.

This ends up being an unexpected blessing, because the day after we move in, I'm hooked to a portable heart monitor as a doctor attempts to figure out why I always keep fainting.

Driving has become next to impossible. I start to forget things like the names of my friends. I legitimately hope—and assume—that I'm having panic attacks. I know I have anxiety. The doctors told me that a long time ago. That's all this is. I'm a wife, an editor, a grad student who has to graduate by the end of 2009. I'm not letting that slip away.

It slips away entirely on September 11, 2008.

I climb the stairs to get some documents before going to work, but as I climb, I grow dizzy. I hear the voice.

"Stop," she says. "Sit down now. You're going to kill us."

I begin to walk back down the stairs, but it's too late. I pass out, and when I come to, I'm on the bottom stair, having fallen about four or five feet. My mom is the one who finds me and rushes me to the emergency room, where I'm taken to the oncology wing.

But I don't have cancer. The doctors rule that out immediately after rounds of CTs, MRIs, ultrasounds, and other scans. They take twenty vials of blood. I pass out, barely coherent, and when people are in the room, I try to joke with them, but I'm just too tired. I can't do this.

There is an answer: low blood pressure. But the doctors don't think that explains everything, and so, they run more tests and take more blood. Then, they tack on the diagnosis of hypothyroidism, as well as a syncopal disorder in which my body and brain cannot seem to communicate properly and therefore keep me in a perpetual state of dizziness.

And I have Multiple Sclerosis.

I'm told this as I'm standing up—against hospital policy, but who am I to suddenly follow the rules? —to use the bathroom. I step around the multiple IV lines hooked into my hands and arms, and I carry the heart monitor and EEG pack against my chest. But before I can enter the restroom, a doctor walks in and tells me to sit down.

"No," I say.

The look on his face is serious. "Your symptoms match up to textbook Multiple Sclerosis," he says. "You have lesions on your brain. They aren't big, but they shouldn't be there. We're going to need to find a good neurologist for you before anything happens—more passing out, an inability to walk, even some hallucinations. But we'll help you."

And it clicks. The voice. Her voice. I'm not crazy, or bipolar, or anything that doctors have diagnosed me with. Dr. Palmisano messed up, too, saying I have DID. I have MS. A medical condition. I'm hallucinating. The voice isn't real—and it never was.

I start to cry, simply because I am relieved that I'm not as crazy as I think I am. But then, I realize what the doctor said, and it hits me. I stand there, holding my medical equipment, streams of fluids and medications dripping into my system, and I begin to sob.

I have ruined Toby's life. I have ruined my friendships with everyone I love. People will start to pull away, and soon, I will have nothing except for work and grad school. Sure, people will feel sorry for me at first, but once this progresses? They'll leave. I know it.

Back at home, I'm forced to fill out paperwork that puts me on permanent leave from my job. I'm too sick to work, they tell me. But maybe one day. The same thing happens with graduate school: I won't be finishing the entire program on campus. I can't drive there, and I'm too sick to pay attention. I fill out the forms, fax them, watch as my car keys are taken from me, and fall back on the couch.

I have ruined everything—every dream I had for myself, and every goal I had for my future. I feel so guilty that I stop sleeping, and I start something else: I lose track of place and time every day. I watch my life, but I don't live it. I dissociate because I simply don't want to be there.

And that is okay by me.

DESPITE THE MEDICAL MADNESS, I TRY TO REMAIN THE SAME PARTY girl that everyone wants me to be. Yes, I can admit to illness now, but as long as I throw a party to cover up the sadness, no one will pity me. And I don't want pity. I want camaraderie.

And despite Toby and I no longer living at Paul's, we remain best friends—even with Starlight Boy, who is hundreds of miles away at his own graduate school. But he misses me and is miserable there, he tells me during our four-in-the-morning conversations, and he visits Paul often. He is lonely, and I am sick, and our vulnerabilities push us together.

"I grew up with a mother who was sick," Starlight Boy says to me. "I'm here for you."

Suddenly, I've found solace in someone whom I haven't seen in months, and through our early morning words, my bizarre crush reignites. I'm a new, sick wife, with a childish crush on her closest ally.

"Fan-fucking-tastic," the voice says. But now, I know the voice is just me. It's just MS.

I throw a Halloween party to show I am that same party girl, and considering that I could be dead by the end of the year, it's going to be a big party. "Go big or go home," I say to Toby. He worries that this will tax my health and our already empty bank accounts, but the party plans continue. We buy enough alcohol to inebriate the entire state.

Forty people will be attending. We're ready for the party to end all parties—which this may well be for me.

Paul and Richard arrive early to play Guitar Hero—just like old times, and I take comfort in that. I can still sing along, even if I have to do so sitting down. We play until guests start coming through the door, and then we just leave the door open, ignoring the October chill.

Starlight Boy arrives late. And, by some odd coincidence, he's dressed exactly like Toby.

"Well, two hardcore rockers," I say to Starlight Boy. "However shall I choose?" He stares at my costume—a tight black corset, tight boy shorts, and a wand. I'm Glinda from *The Wizard of Oz*, but in dark leather, BDSM-style. And I want him to stare. This is what I want. He's awkward and unassuming, and he stays with me throughout most of the party. I'm sick, but I am his guide.

But there are single girls at this party—healthy girls in sexy costumes, pretty girls who are still working and getting their educations. Why me? What is my appeal?

The crowd doesn't thin after midnight, and despite my exhaustion, I rage on. But my brain starts to overload, and so, I step outside to take a walk. Starlight Boy is right behind me.

"I thought I could keep up," I say, stopping against a car. "And I can't. I get so dizzy."

"I wish I knew what caused this," he says. "Why you?"

"All I know is that it's something in me. I'm broken, love. I can't be mended."

The wind swirls around us and I shiver. Starlight Boy reaches out to hug me, and I allow myself to fall against him. He's only a few inches taller than I am, so our faces are almost touching. I feel his warmth. I feel something inside of him telling me I'm still fine.

This is not a big deal, I tell myself. I start to hum a lullaby as we hold onto one another and find that I can't stop. If I'm humming, it can't be a big deal. Nothing is happening. I hug people all the time. I'm a flirt. He's my friend. This is all normal, especially given the circumstances.

"I want to mend you," he says.

And my heart sinks.

Despite what we both want—despite the myriad things we both want—that can never be.

THERE ARE PILLS. THERE ARE SO MANY VIALS OF PILLS—PILLS FOR staying awake during the day, for sleeping at night, for halting the headaches, for stopping the flares. There are pills with names I cannot pronounce. They line up on my end table like soldiers, promising me that they'll fight.

They fail and are defeated.

"I wish we could catch more of your seizures on the EEG," my neurologist tells me. She's a kind woman, and she tears up as she watches me shake. But she needs more clinical proof. Until then, there's nothing else she can do but medicate me.

On the day our country shows a slight bit of progress and elects a young, smart, African-American to lead our nation to greatness, I find out that, despite the fact I had been allowed to take some graduate classes online, I haven't been keeping up. And therefore, my advisor says I must withdrawal entirely and reapply when I'm "better."

I will not be completing my Master's degree. Outraged at the disappointment I've become, I leave the house with nothing but my keys and walk up the sidewalk of my neighborhood. I veer off into the road and realize something I've never noticed before—I can't differentiate between right and left. I've somehow lost my ability to understand a concept that most five-year-old children can grasp. I stand there, wondering if a car would see me if it were to come racing around the corner. Maybe it wouldn't. Maybe that would be best.

No cars drive down the street. I place my head into my hands and scream. No one notices.

I head home, because I can't even find the proper way to die.

CHRISTMAS BRINGS ABOUT A FEW GOOD PARTIES AND A FUN shopping trip to my favorite bookstore near Hood College. I'm dizzy and sick during the ride, but I don't let on, and as Toby and I share a meal with my parents and brother, I plaster a fake smile on my face. The holiday has been fine; my body, however, is reeling from that ride.

But in the bookstore, I am set free. There is always solace in literature—other places, other people, other times. People who know the true nature of suffering. People who will make me laugh and cry and nod my head in agreement. But leaving the store with two large bags of books makes me think about my own writing. Ever since the MS diagnosis, I've struggled with my ability to write. The dizziness makes it nearly impossible.

On the way home, my body slumped against the car seat in exhaustion, I put my iPod on shuffle. Randomly, it plays five songs from one of my favorite bands, Disturbed. And as the iPod keeps making the selections, Toby and I keep laughing.

"Not a very intuitive shuffle," he says, chuckling.

But I sing and I listen. And by the time I'm through the last song, I know what's happened.

I've been given a sign. Those five songs, in that specific order, make an incredible rock opera. It's a story about lust, adultery, desire, murder, politics, and deception. And while I can't share it with the world because the music isn't mine, I yearn to tell the story.

The depression lifts, and that night, I type out a nine-page synopsis and figure out the Disturbed songs I want to use. And I title my opera "Stricken." After all, Madeleine—my main female character, whose name comes to me in a flash—is stricken with love by a man she cannot have. Her father, Parker, is a corrupt politician who wants to destroy their state in the name of the Almighty Dollar. Madeleine's love interest, Jim, is a journalist who loves her but cannot be with her. The world is cruel and love is unkind. And that makes the opera perfect.

Starlight Boy keeps sending me messages as I write, but I ignore them. I want to talk to him, but telling this story is paramount. He'll see. I know I'll share it with him.

I guess I just don't think that he may already understand it.

A MONTH LATER, TOWARD THE END OF JANUARY 2009, PAUL THROWS a huge party. About thirty people are set to attend, so I dye my hair blue, find a seductive dress, and say we'll be there.

As usual, I'm asked to sing as we play Guitar Hero. Everyone stares at me when I do, but I notice Starlight Boy holds his stare long after everyone else turns away.

It doesn't take long before I need a break. I take a handful of pills that allow me to keep enjoying the evening, and then, step outside onto Paul's front porch.

It's beautiful out in the frigid air, among the stars and the silence. The skies are illuminated, and I study the constellations, grateful for this serene moment. As I hear Paul singing from inside, butchering a classic, I laugh to myself and begin to shiver. It's twenty degrees outside, and I'm in a sleeveless black dress with no shoes on. Par for the course, though, I think. I've always hated shoes and long sleeves. I may be ill, but I'm not a completely different person.

Starlight Boy joins me, wrapped in his thick jacket. He wears shoes like a responsible adult.

"It's way too loud in there," he says, and I laugh.

"That's a mild way to put it," I say. "Hence my escape. Hence my obvious lack of wardrobe planning." I point down at my bare feet and shiver. Starlight Boy stands a little closer to me. His dark jacket brushes up against my pale shoulder. I shiver again, but this time, I'm not cold.

"What are you doing besides escaping?" he asks.

"Stargazing. Finding the constellations. Searching for peace."

"I can help." Starlight Boy rattles off a list of constellations, ones I've missed that night—as though he knows what I've been looking for —and I point them out with him and smile. Why is this moment the best I've had in weeks?

Starlight Boy and I look at each other. For a moment, a second of enchantment, I know we are going to kiss. His eyes light up, and we move toward one another.

But I can't. "I should go in," I say. "It's cold out here. I don't want to get sicker." Starlight Boy stares at me and then nods in agreement. But before either of us move, we continue to stare at one another. It's the same look we'd just shared a moment ago. I know that look. I feel it.

Stricken.

I smile at him, at my Starlight Boy, rub his jacketed arm with my ice-hold hand, and step inside. I escape into chaos, because the thoughts inside my head scare me.

As the night continues and the crowd thins out, only myself and six other guys remain. We decide to get hammered to intentionally butcher songs on Guitar Hero that we know well. We rap to the Beastie Boys with made-up lyrics. We toss the mic back and forth between verses, letting everyone sing. And then, when the guys pick a metal song I don't know, I decide to sing the ridiculous lyrics in my best coloratura soprano voice.

At first, they all start laughing—we're looking to fail, and this will do it. But then, they all stop playing. I'm not failing. For whatever reason, I'm succeeding. I'm soaring. My voice is rich and colorful, as clear as it was when I trained professionally. Despite the horrid lyrics, I'm belting them out as though I'm performing at the Met.

When the song ends, I laugh hysterically. But no one else joins in.

"Well, fuck me," Richard says.

Toby smiles. "See? It doesn't matter if you're sick. You still have it. You're still you."

Starlight Boy just stares.

After some down time to sober up, Toby and I call it a night. Starlight Boy has planned to spend the night at Paul's, but Toby and I have a guest room, not just a fold-out sofa. It's easier for Starlight Boy to stay with us, and he's eager to come over. As I pack up and prepare to say my goodbyes, I hum to myself, content with how things are going.

"I knew you were a trained singer," Starlight Boy says, watching me pull on my boots. "I remember that from when we were younger. But that? That was—you're incredible."

I feel myself blush. Don't blush, I think. You're not that type of girl.

"That?" I say. "I was honestly fucking around. It was fun to just—burst out like that."

"It doesn't matter. It was really good."

I drive home with Toby, high on Starlight Boy's praise. Every so often, I turn my head to make sure he's still following us back to the house.

Something is happening. Something has happened. I'm living out the plot to my musical, and while the guilt sets in, the longing does as well. I look up at the stars and ask for forgiveness. I'm not sure what I'm asking to be forgiven for yet, but I know that I better begin now.

ABSOLUTELY NOTHING HAPPENS THAT SATURDAY NIGHT WHEN Starlight Boy sleeps over. We look at some pictures, laugh about the party, and then go to bed. He heads back to Paul's the next afternoon while Toby and I prepare to attend a post-season football party.

"You're disappointed," the voice says. The hallucination. Fucking Multiple Sclerosis.

"I'm not," I say to myself. "There's no reason to be. What would have happened? I wasn't looking to sleep with him. We just had a good time. Let it go."

"He's coming back tonight," the voice says. "Maybe things will go your way. Just wait."

My hair is a brilliant blue against the green of my football jersey. I'm hung over, and I know the doctors have told me to slow down, but screw it. I'm twenty-seven. If they're telling me I'm going to die, anyhow, why not die doing some of the things I love? Most of my dreams have already been dashed—I won't get better, I won't finish grad school, I'm unable to have children, I'm supposed to file for disability—and I want to rebel against the world. But how can I rebel against the truth? So, I dye my hair blue, drink a bit too much, party a little too hard. It's nothing serious, but I take it seriously. I'm dying inside. My life better look fun before I go.

Toward the end of the football party—an event that about fifteen of us have been enjoying despite some horrendous hometown losses— something goes wrong. My twenty-year-old brother has been screaming at the TV, just like all of us have been. My mom is in a bad

298 • A.E. HAYES

mood, and as I watch her glance over at him, my stomach drops. The tone in the room shifts and grows cacophonous. I feel my head spin, and suddenly, I start to view the room from outside myself.

I'm there, but not fully, when my brother yells, "Goddammit, you shithead!" at the TV. I'm there, but not fully, when my mom turns around, grabs him by the collar, screams in his face, and shoves him out of the room and into an upstairs bedroom as punishment.

He's twenty, not ten. Did this just happen? It couldn't have. He had been yelling the same things as the rest of us. But Toby confirms it occurred. Catie, who joins us for the party, provides a second confirmation. Later, my own brother provides the ultimate confirmation.

I go home that Sunday night, outraged and sick.

"Why didn't I do anything?" I ask Catie a few hours later. Starlight Boy hasn't returned to the house yet, and I'm glad. I'm still shaking. I promised to defend my brother, and I hadn't.

"What were you going to do?" she says. "It happened so fast. But now I get it. I understand your teenage years now. I know why you are —well, the way you are. Christ."

Starlight Boy returns to the house around midnight. I'm the only one awake, still pondering what happened. I don't tell him, however, though he can tell I'm upset. Luckily, he doesn't say anything and proposes a quiet game of Guitar Hero. If I don't stare at the TV for too long, I can play bass, so I agree, and for an hour, we let music consume us.

"You look pale," Starlight Boy eventually says. "What's going on? Are you okay?"

But I am pale by nature now. I've noticed that, as the months have passed, I've gown paler. And I must look horrible. I'm a mess of confusion, of tangled blue hair and fear. I can't speak.

I stare at my end table, where the vials of pills reside. "I'm okay." I sit on the couch. He sits a few feet away from me.

"Do you want to go to bed?" he says. "It's two in the morning."

"No. I'm not tired. Plus, we have all day tomorrow to hang out. Let's make plans."

But we don't make plans. Instead, after flipping through channels to find a TV movie, I lean against Starlight Boy's shoulder. And without hesitation, he puts his arm around me. Then, we pull a blanket over ourselves.

And I instinctively reach for his hand. But he pulls away, and I know I've crossed a line. I'm a jerk, I'm destined for Hell, and I am an awful person for wanting what I wanted.

Maybe all those things remain true, but Starlight Boy merely readjusts his hand so that our fingers are intertwined. He wasn't pulling away; he was weaving us together.

Neither of us moves for hours. We watch the movie, lean against one another, and feed off the comfort. But at six in the morning, I look at him and say, "We should probably go to bed." I don't want to, but Toby will wonder why he doesn't see me when he wakes up.

"I don't really want to move," Starlight Boy says. "This is comfortable to me."

"Same here."

"What are we going to do?"

The voice tells me. I don't care if she is an MS-related hallucination, because somehow, she always has a plan, and I trust her. After all, I've known her forever.

"How about this," I say. "When I wake up in a few hours, I'll come into the guest room to get you, and we'll just, you know, resume this. This is okay, right?"

He nods. "It's more than okay." I smile, and we both stand up. We hug, the blanket still wrapped around us, and then he heads up to bed. But I stay downstairs, staring out the window, and wonder what is existing in both my head and my heart.

TOBY LEAVES FOR WORK AT EIGHT. BY NINE, I'M SICK. I'M SO SICK that I cannot stay out of the bathroom. I try to vomit silently, hoping I don't wake up Starlight Boy who is still asleep across the hall. I am a damn mess, and annoyed with myself and my illnesses, so I wet a washcloth, open my bedroom door in case I need to call out for help, and climb back into bed. I won't wake Starlight Boy now. I need to put the cold washcloth on my face and sleep. I guess it's a sign.

But the sign changes when Starlight Boy walks into my room only a few minutes later. He sits on the edge of the bed, and I tell him that I'm sick—it might be the MS, or the meds, or just a virus. But I'm sick, and I'm sorry. And then, as though this was our unspoken plan, as though we have a set of unspoken rules that seamlessly fit into our friendship, he climbs into my bed.

This—whatever this is—is happening. And from the way Starlight Boy stares at me, I can see that it's genuine. He takes my head, rests it against his shoulder, wraps his arms around me, and we fall asleep together, slightly propped up against the pillows.

And we sleep until four in the afternoon. Any plans that we could have made are gone now, because I know he has to leave by five. But we're okay with that, we say, and spend that last hour—my stomach finally allowing me to feel human again—in bed. We lace our fingers together, we tell inside jokes, and we recite song lyrics and poetry. We talk about politics, religion, and how to make the world a better place. He's my intellectual soulmate, and my best friend, and why can't best friends be just like this? There's no rule that says they can't.

"Oh, little girl," the voice says. "Oh, you've been trained so well."

If there is a line, though, I'm certain it's being crossed. And even though we laugh and talk, it's clear that any notion of a normal friendship is over. This is our new, uncharted territory.

"As a former journalist, I just want to go on the record and say that this has been one of the best days I can remember," I say to Starlight Boy. "And I wouldn't take it back for anything. But we kind of have to address the white elephant in the room here, don't we?"

He rubs my back. "Yeah, I know. But we are very good friends."

"We are. But it's just that—you and I know that this is more than that."

He looks at me, strokes my arm, but doesn't reply. I know he believes in my words, but maybe he doesn't want to admit to them just yet.

Real life begins to kick in. I'm sweaty from not taking my medication on time. His stomach rumbles from not eating all day. It's getting late and dark, and while we have lived for every moment, today is coming to an end for us. Slowly, we both get up. We talk as we get dressed, and we try to crack a few jokes, but neither of us is laughing. If what's racing through my mind is racing through his, nothing could possibly be funny right now.

I walk Starlight Boy to his car, and after he starts the vehicle, he turns to me and reaches out. I bury my head in his shoulder, and we hold each other in the middle of the road, illuminated by the street-lights and the cars that pull into driveways. It's cliché, but time stops. We are given a sense of forever in that moment. I can't imagine myself anywhere else. Not now.

When he says goodbye and drives away, I walk back to the house. As I reach the front door, I wipe my face, and I'm shocked by this. I'm shocked to realize I'm sobbing.

"Don't cry yet," the voice whispers. "It's over, but not in the way you think."

Fucking voice.

⸻

"IT'S OVER," STARLIGHT BOY SAYS VIA TEXT THE NEXT DAY. "WE crossed a line. I mean, I wanted all that to happen, but I think we should have just stayed on the couch—not in bed."

"Then why didn't you say so?" I ask. "Why did you climb into my bed?"

"You're my best friend. I want to be with you. I always want that."

"Liar. I know what this is." And before I can put my thoughts into rational, adult words, the voice fills my head, and she speaks for me. "You were thinking about your ex, weren't you? You miss her and were imagining I was her stand-in. It wasn't about me or us. It was about her."

Text messages don't sigh, but if they could, I imagine that's what Starlight Boy is doing. I don't understand this message, or his sudden guilt, but only a day later, he's changed everything. And yet, he still wants to be with me, but only on his terms? I feel jaded and used.

"You're wrong," he says. "It was never about her. I just don't know, okay?"

"Then I need time," I say, and the dizziness takes hold. My hands start shaking. "I need time away from you. If it's over, then it has to be over for a while."

"Don't leave me. Please don't. I need you."

"Too late," I say. "Goodbye, Starlight Boy."

I knew we had been doing the wrong thing, but part of me honestly believed he was trying to save me. He wanted to help me feel better. But I am wrong, and I am a fool. He won't admit to his feelings, and that makes those seemingly perfect hours a lie, wrapped in guilt and shame.

But by the end of the month, the emotional drama is over. Starlight Boy and I decide that we need some space, but we still talk almost daily. I begin to focus my remaining energy on Toby, on my marriage, and things feel a bit better. Even though thoughts of that day in bed with Starlight Boy threaten to occupy my mind, I shut them out. Plus, I'm working again. My grandmother has fallen and broken part of her spine, so three days a week, I'm her caregiver. It's an easy job, and it's helping family, so despite my dizziness, I drive to her and learn more about my dad's side of the family. I feel included—accepted, even.

I clearly don't do well with the notion of calm, however. Despite how much better I feel, at least on an emotional level, I plan two events: a poetry reading and a Valentine's Day party. The timing couldn't be more perfect. The owner of an art gallery wants me to come read my work the night before Valentine's Day, so people can come, listen to my words, and then stay over and get the party going the next day. I'm excited. And then, I grow so excited that I throw up. What if I pass out that night and can't go? What if I'm unable to speak for forty-five minutes?

"Fuck the what-ifs," the voice says. She's right. Or I'm right. Whatever we are, we're right.

Nothing is going to stand in the way of those two days. It's time for something brilliant, for something bright and fun. I'm going to make it happen. We're all due for something good.

FRIDAY THE THIRTEENTH IS A WONDERFUL NIGHT, COMPLETE WITH

friends, praise regarding my poetry, and deep conversations about the freedom that poetry provides the mind and soul.

Starlight Boy is supposed to be there, but during the reading, he texts to say that he is caught in traffic, so he'll catch us at dinner later. When he arrives at the run-down little diner our large group chooses, I run outside to meet him. He tells me how nice I look, and I hug him.

"Well, hello to you, too," he laughs, holding me against him.

Later that night, after the crowd disperses and the dinner conversations that have moved from the diner to my living room break up, Starlight Boy and I find ourselves alone again at two in the morning. We both change into pajamas and meet up in the living room, and without saying a word, we sit down next to each other on the couch. Our arms immediately lace, and then our fingers intertwine. It's as though we must be connected as tightly as possible to one another, since for so many weeks, our connection had been severed.

I'm back in a headspace I can't describe: I'm watching this happen. I'm in the moment but somehow filming it within my mind. This is both absolutely right and completely wrong. I have full control and no control. So, as though in a dream state, I continue to watch.

But I can feel, too. I feel my head reposition against his chest. I feel him wrap his arms around me and hold me, and then we slide down on the couch so we are lying down. We're not in bed, but given the position, we might as well be.

Hypocrite? Who cares? I inhale him, take in the familiar scent, feel his chest rise, and fall asleep as his fingers skim my skin. I drift in and out for hours. The night sky is infinitely brighter as the stars burn, die, and are reborn, and without a sound, we are seamless, multitudinous, and infinite.

TOBY, STARLIGHT BOY, AND I SLEEP IN LATE THE NEXT DAY, BUT soon after waking, we set to work preparing the house for the massive party. The forecast that predicts a certain snowstorm worries me, but both Toby and Starlight Boy tell me not to worry. People will come for me.

Am I nothing more than some flirtatious socialite, more interested in attention and drinking than stability? If so, why am I not being called out as the worst girl to walk the planet? Is it because I offer comfort in the form of affection, food, a warm house, and a drink? Or am I misreading the entire situation?

These thoughts plague me as Starlight Boy and I take a brief trip to the liquor store. We link arms as we walk through the aisles of alcohol, and the cashier assumes we're a couple. We laugh but don't correct him.

Back in the car, we sing a song called "Lazy Eye." Suddenly, it's our song. It's not a life-altering proclamation, but the chemistry between us is intense, and we shoot pheromones back and forth like Cupid's arrows on this odd Valentine's Day.

Once home, we all shower and dress. I put far too much effort into how I look. I want Starlight Boy to notice. My hand shakes as I hold the curling iron, and my arm feels like dead weight. I know sickness wants to knock me down. But I refuse.

And he notices.

"Do I look okay?" I ask.

He nods. "Yes. Yeah, you absolutely do. You look... it's better than just okay."

As people begin to arrive, Starlight Boy and I step out onto the large deck to check the weather. The snow is beginning to fall. We both hold out our hands at the wonder of it, and then look at each other until a friend of ours comes out and breaks the moment by gathering a handful of snow and shoving it onto my bare neck. I scream, throw snow back, and the party begins.

The music plays. I sing, I flirt, and I allow alcohol to squander my sensibilities. I make drinks for everyone, especially Starlight Boy, and he and I drink champagne out of my wedding flutes, linking arms as we down glass after glass. The irony of the moment isn't lost on me.

Toby is neglected, and I know it. I feel horrible, and I don't know why I'm doing this to him. It's not right, and I should be better. I know better. I have been a complete asshole to him and have flirted with every human at the party except my own husband. I sit on the floor with him, and we sing. Starlight Boy watches from the couch, a look of jealousy taking the starlight from his eyes. When I eventually get up to sit with Richard, Starlight Boy looks even more jealous, but I do nothing. Let him be jealous, I think. We're not married or anything.

The party is a hit, and when people filter out around one in the morning, I begin to feel ill. I try to calculate how much alcohol I've consumed, and it amounts to several bottles of champagne. But I can't think about it. Toby goes upstairs, drunk and exhausted, and Starlight Boy and I fall onto the couch. He puts his arms around me and we don't move. We're both fighting off the intoxication.

"We always find ourselves like this," he says. "We say we won't, but here we are."

"Here we are," I say. "And I saw your jealousy earlier. Don't think I didn't."

"Can you blame me? You're everything to everyone. I want you to be everything to me."

I begin to fall asleep in his embrace, but I keep some semblance of sense about me. I force myself to head upstairs after giving him a long hug goodnight. He watches as I depart. He must know that I don't want to leave. He must know that I can always tell he's watching me.

He must know that I can't admit to anyone that we're in love.

FEBRUARY 15, 2009–AUGUST 24, 2010

The Final Before

My grandmother grows very ill, though she has far more mental clarity than I do. However, she cannot live on her own. After some debating, she moves into an assisted-living facility only five minutes from my house, and my part-time work with her turns into an almost full-time caregiving assignment. But I don't mind. I'm learning amazing things about this woman—a trail-blazer in her time, who didn't want to do what her friends did and stay home to raise children. She went to college, found a job, and waited to have children until she was thirty—which was mostly taboo back in her day. And during the dinners I share with her, she brags about me. Her friends tell us we share a similar face shape and spirit. The former compliment isn't biologically possible, but the latter praise always makes me smile. I wish to emulate her.

As we share those meals, however, something starts happening within my body. I cannot eat without getting sick. I try to have a sand-wich with her, but I immediately feel dizzy and stumble to the bath-room to become ill. When I make her lunch, my hands are itchy.

Both my mom and my therapist agree that I need to see my doctor about this new concern. I do so, but with hesitation. Seeing a doctor these days never brings about good news.

There isn't good news, but there is clarity. I have Celiac disease, combined with a gluten allergy and ataxia. Not only does my digestive system reject gluten—hence why I'd been so ill for so long—but it also alters my mental state and cognitive functioning. Furthermore, the simple act of touching it makes me break out into hives. The tests are damning, but they add up. I have to stop eating almost all the food I always eat, and I now must shell out more money for safer options. But my doctors are optimistic. This change could reduce my seizures, stop my hallucinations, and make me feel less shaky.

The changes only alter the food I put into my body. Nothing else is different. The grocery bills increase, but the time Toby and I spend in the kitchen together helps us bond. Cooking together works for us, and it's a good step to bring us closer. As we spend more time cooking and adjusting to this lifestyle, thoughts of Starlight Boy leave my mind. Mostly.

Sickness is never a good thing, but in this case, it's a welcome relationship panacea.

I DON'T SEE STARLIGHT BOY FOR MONTHS UNTIL A RANDOM DAY IN May, when he stops by on his way to Paul's. And when I see him, I remember how much I've missed him. The texts we've exchanged haven't been enough.

But things feel different, despite what I still feel. He's more of a friend now, and while we do sit together on the couch, nothing occurs. But then, I start to talk about going to the beach, as I have made plans to do so that summer. I feel at home listening to the waves, I tell him. I like to sit on the pier in the dark, with the moon glowing over the ocean and the wind whipping up a gentle chorus on the shoreline. Nighttime on the beach is where I am allowed to be myself, I say. That is where I am whole, and where I can recover and heal.

Starlight Boy touches my arm. "I wish I could see you down there," he says. "I'd like to see the ocean through your eyes—to witness it the way you do. I've never felt that strongly about too much in my life. But I think I understand it now."

When he departs, our hug is brief, and we don't make future plans. I feel sad, but there's nothing else I can or should do. It's over now, but I know it will never be truly finished.

We both know, and secretly feel, far too much.

Before my trip to the beach, however, there is a weekend-long camping trip, and a group of about twelve of us head up near Camp David to hike, swim, and drink in the woods. I can't do the first two things, but I'm interested in the latter, and I want to spend time with the people I love. Toby and I buy a huge tent, some gluten-free beer, and load up to join our friends.

But the group of people in attendance is a cast that even the best soap opera cannot rival. Drama will go down. I can feel it. And when, much to my surprise, Starlight Boy shows up and parks on our campsite, I pray that things will remain calm.

They don't. Starlight Boy is in a horrible mood, and though I spend an hour with him in his car, trying to talk him out of his depression, all I've managed to do is to get him to admit that he wants to spend more time with me. Two of our other friends are fighting so frequently that I think they're heading for a divorce. The mood is awkward, and it only gets worse when Richard's girlfriend Vanessa, my good friend Faith, and I head to the bathroom to wash up.

Vanessa points to Starlight Boy. "What's going on between the two of you?"

"Nothing! Seriously. He's just one of my best friends. That's all."

"He's in love with you," Vanessa says, and Faith nods. I know Faith is on my side, but I also know that she can't deny what she's seen. At least she's in my corner, though.

"Please let it go," I say. "You have to leave me alone about this."

Unfortunately, "let it go" is not the motto of the wayward camping trip, and by the end of the two days—with only one brief, beautiful afternoon of peace as I take a small, solo hike through some of the flatter terrain—everyone is mad at someone about something. Toby and I return home, depressed, and a few days later, I fall down some stairs and injure my knee.

Luckily, an MRI reveals that I've only slightly torn the meniscus in my knee and that I don't require surgery—just a brace, some crutches, and limited walking. But I still toss the crutches to the side to pack for the beach, and I fight through the pain. If I can do so with my other illnesses, why not this? This will heal. The MS won't ever go away.

Two days before we leave for the beach, Paul invites us to a party. It's last minute, but he tells me to please come. "I miss you," he says. "And all of your people will be there."

I know he means Starlight Boy. And Starlight Boy knows I've hurt my knee and am not supposed to be driving. Since the party is set to begin while Toby is still at work, Starlight Boy says he'll take me to Paul's. I agree, and Toby seems on edge about my decision, but I blow off his nervous attitude. Starlight Boy and I are only friends. Nothing will happen.

When Starlight Boy arrives to pick me up, he compliments my hair and outfit, and then helps me into his car. It's the first time I've been in his vehicle. As I hand him a CD I've made for the drive, something hits me. It's a combination of new-car smell, Starlight Boy's scent, and the summer air. It's a perfect moment. I want someone to come and record how I feel, because words cannot do it justice. I want to crawl into the sheets of this moment and wrap myself in it while it's still so cool.

But I can't say any of that, so Starlight Boy drives, and we sing along to our bands—Silversun Pickups, Disturbed, Queens of the Stone Age, R.E.M. I harmonize effortlessly above his sweet tenor, and we're connected again. I look at him, and then, as he stares at me, I look down at his leg. I need to rest my head on it. I have to do it; the impulse is too strong not to. I easily could have done so six months ago. Why not now?

I go to lean my head down, but I stop. I've given up on you, I say to him silently. We'll just live through music. That's how I live through everything, anyhow.

Maybe I want a bit. Maybe I ache. Maybe I am an asshole for feeling that way.

But as I watch Starlight Boy, I know I'm not the only one holding back.

TOBY AND I RETURN HOME FROM A ROMANTIC, BONDING TRIP TO the Outer Banks, more connected and secure in our relationship than ever before. Our first anniversary has passed, I haven't spoken to Starlight Boy in weeks, and we begin to make plans to have a baby.

But I don't want to have sex with Toby. August is here, and anniversary syndrome is hitting me head-on. Thomas raped me this month. So did Stone. I'm haunted.

And this is the ten-year anniversary of my beloved Doo-Da's death.

"Fuck this entire month," says the voice. "Do whatever you want to feel better."

I ignore her. Nothing will make me feel better right now. Why does everything horrible happen in August? Why have so many people died or been injured? What causes increases in cancer and rape during this month? That cannot be statistically possible.

One night, when the pain is too much, I sneak into the kitchen, grab a small knife, and make a semi-deep gash into my inner thigh, where Thomas had once scarred me so terribly.

Blood stains my hands, and I laugh.

If there's a God, he hates me. He could take me right now, delete the pain of my past—but he doesn't. I'm supposed to believe that God wants me to cut myself and suffer?

I don't believe in anything anymore except for gluten-free alcohol, Toby's love, and the amazing remake of *Battlestar Galactica* I'm watching with Catie and Toby. Those things help.

But I especially stop believing when, on September 1, I see a new rheumatologist who tells me that, in addition to MS, hypothyroidism, a syncopal disorder, Celiac disease, and my other disorders, I have Lupus. My lab work is highly abnormal, she says. No wonder I'm in pain and can barely move half the time.

"I'm referring you down to Johns Hopkins Hospital for a full work-up," she says. "I want you to see your neurologist first, though. Those lesions in your brain? I'm not quite so sure they are MS. I think you may have Vasculitis. You need to get to the hospital soon."

"My husband and I are trying to have a baby," I say. But all she does is shake her head. No.

After the appointment and phone calls to my neurologist and the hospital, I rush into the nearby Burger King and throw up in the bathroom. My life is nothing but one incurable illness. I don't know what to do. I throw up again, and then stand, go to the sink, and splash water on my face. To the people coming and going from the bathroom, I'm just some random girl.

They don't know that my brain and body are both being eaten alive.

———

THE FIVE-DAY HOPKINS VISIT IS A FAILURE. AN INTERN incorrectly performs a lumbar puncture, leaving me with nerve damage in my leg. The results are inconclusive. We know nothing more coming out than we did when we went in, except now I cannot walk.

I sleep all day and stay up all night. I take thirty-one pills a day, go to physical therapy I can barely afford to learn to walk again, and have panic attacks every hour.

I'm living a half-life. My real life is over. And I know it won't return.

I file for disability. It's taken me a year to accept the severity of my conditions, but I file. When the attorney tells me that his office is an hour away, I panic, so he offers to come to me—on the afternoon of my twenty-eighth birthday. But I accept, and he is kind. He believes that, within a year, we'll win my case without any problems. And I place my trust in him.

Friends come and go, and even Starlight Boy visits, shocked to see me so exhausted and pale. I know I mean nothing to him now. My days and nights become a monotonous blur. During the month of November, I write an eighty-thousand-word novel in six days because I have nothing better to do. But performing that act—writing an entire book—gives me a small sense of hope. Maybe there's something good left within me after all.

Paul hosts a small party toward the end of November, and I desperately want to go. I'm able to walk a bit, and I can sing, so I tell him I'll
attend. Starlight Boy texts me and asks if he can spend the night that
Friday so that he, Toby, and I can all go to Paul's together the next day,
and I agree—forgetting that Toby has class Friday and won't be home
until 11:00 p.m. But it's not a big deal. I just want to go to the party
and be a normal person again.

On the same Friday Starlight Boy comes to my house, my rheumatologist decides to put me on a new medication to mitigate some of my
worsening Lupus and arthritis symptoms. It's called Methotrexate, or
MTX, and is a form of chemotherapy. It will probably make me sick,
she says, and I may have thinning hair, if not total hair loss. I tell her
that I'll start the treatment in a few days, after I enjoy this weekend,
and while she isn't happy about the delay, she understands.

As I'm researching the side effects of MTX, Starlight Boy arrives.
He gathers me into a huge hug, and tells me that he's missed me. I tell
him the same. He notices that my hair is a different color and makes a
point of saying that I look pretty. I desperately hope that's not lip
service, but Starlight Boy isn't one to use words like "pretty" unless he
actually means it. After all, he still hasn't said how he feels about me,
even though we both know the unspoken answer.

We decide to watch a movie, and end up choosing *Stranger Than
Fiction*—in honor of the novel I wrote, Starlight Boy tells me. We laugh
about how the movie seems so relevant to us. As we continue to watch,
he puts his arm around me, and just like that, we're back to where we
once were. I curl up against him, safe in his arms.

Neither of us is ready for Dustin Hoffman to deliver a powerful
speech to the main character:

"Harold, you will die, someday, sometime.... Even if you avoid this
death, another will find you. And I guarantee that it won't be nearly as
poetic or as meaningful as what she's written. I'm sorry, but it's...it's
the nature of all tragedies, Harold. The hero dies, and the story goes
on forever."

I have just told Starlight Boy the details about my own novel and
the characters in it, and how it is based on our own story, in a way. And

when this quote is delivered, I feel Starlight Boy sigh, and when he does, I begin to sob. I turn and bury my face into his chest.

"Shh," he whispers. "Your story will go on forever. Nothing could ever change that."

"But everything has changed," I say, sitting up and wiping my face. At least I didn't ugly-cry in front of him, I think. There's no mascara on his shirt, and my face isn't puffy and weird. It's a fine line between the pretty cry and the full-on, snot-inducing ugly cry, but at least I stopped myself before the latter.

"Things are different," he says. "But you're still yourself. You still sing and write and are an intellectual. You still love people. It's just the physical—it's not who you actually are."

"I'm letting everyone down," I say. "Toby, my family, my friends—hell, even you."

"You're worth more than you think. Who else writes a novel in a week? Who else sings like you? No one. Don't sell yourself short."

And while he's talking to me, I feel the change. I hear the voice, and she tells me to let go. I do, and I start to view the scene as though we are the movie. But I can't break the fourth wall. I'm stuck, and the moment is timeless.

"Look," Starlight Boy says. "You know how I feel. I know you know. And believe me when I tell you this: if I could go back to school for another eight years, I would. I'd do it."

"Why?"

He takes my hands and gives me a soft smile. "So that I could fix you," he says. And I cry.

I don't make it to Paul's party the next day, despite my best efforts and an outfit that causes both Toby and Starlight Boy to drop their jaws. I try, but I'm too dizzy. I can't be there for the two most important men in my life, no matter how much I want to be.

The *two* most important men in my life? Where, I think, did that come from?

I thought I'd moved on. But I'm a fool. I'm too in love to let go.

THE GREAT FALL BEGINS A FEW WEEKS BEFORE THE END OF 2009.

Methotrexate hurts me—a cure worse than the disease. When I start it, I throw up daily. After only two weeks, my hair thins. My mom takes me to her hair stylist to see if we can cover up the bald spots, but not much can be done. A few days later, I ask Toby to buy an electric razor. When he brings it home, I plug it in, clench my teeth, and regain control. I won't let the medicine take the rest of my hair. If it's going to go, I'll get rid of it myself.

"I look like a female Fidel Castro," I say, putting on my hat that Catie jokingly refers to as my Ernest Hemingway cap. But now, it's for warmth, not just for show.

"Yeah, if Castro were hot," Toby jokes. I love him for saying that, but I don't think he means it.

Throughout the medical hell, Starlight Boy graduates with his Master's degree at the end of the year, and we decide that we must throw a "Good Riddance 2009" party. Plans are made, and my in-laws decide to come to town for the party as well. As December 31 approaches, about thirty people say they will be in attendance. And that makes me feel better. That makes me feel normal. Normal people throw parties, even if they have to wear wigs.

It takes me forever to decide what to wear, especially since I have three new wigs and really want to show off my black and blue one, but I settle on a low-cut black top and velvet black pants. Starlight Boy shows up, stares at me, looks at his own ensemble—a red shirt and jeans—and then, as we're talking, changes. He's now all in black, too. We match. We're a couple.

When 2009 turns into 2010, everyone raises a glass and kisses someone. Toby and I kiss for a moment, but when we disengage, I'm dizzy. I'm in a haze of too-much-party and not-enough-sleep, mixed with thirty different types of medication. I'm popping pills every twenty minutes just to keep functioning. In a way, I'm addicted to the control. I regulate my own Valium usage now, and my doctors never seem to mind writing new prescriptions if I run out. I'm up to thirty mg a day, but hey—it's a new year now. If 2010 is less stressful, I can cut back. The anxiety won't be as bad this year, I think. Things can start over. It's a brand-new world.

Starlight Boy is standing near me. I smile as we approach one another.

"To our year," I say. I lean up and kiss his cheek. It seems risky, but I don't care.

"To our better lives together," he says, smiling. Someone notices how happy we look and takes a picture. Starlight Boy's arm is around my waist, clutching me protectively. I'm dizzy, I'm sick, and all I want to do is lie down, but I can't help but smile. So much is going to change.

But as much as I want everyone to be happy, it isn't meant to be. On New Year's Day, Starlight Boy, Paul, and Richard come back for Guitar Hero and dinner, and Toby is less than pleased at how much attention I'm receiving. There's a brief argument, and it's made clear to me that Toby and Starlight Boy don't want to hang out. I worry, but I know this will pass. I can sort it out. I won't upset my husband or my best friend. I can fix everything but myself.

Besides, I still really want to have a baby with Toby. But there's a fatal flaw in this plan: I'm still on MTX. It's a Class X drug, designed to create miscarriages. I can't get pregnant now, just as I couldn't before. But the stress wears on me. Every time I manage to get out of the house to go to Target, I pass by the baby section and swear I hear a little girl giggle at me. I just don't know why. Who is this little girl? It's not the MS voice. This is something entirely different.

Maybe I am hallucinating. Maybe I am still crazy. Why would anyone want to love me?

IN FEBRUARY, I NOTICE THAT I'M LOSING WEIGHT AT A RAPID PACE. I was overweight back in 2009, but now, my clothing is falling off my body. My wedding dress is several sizes too large. When I step on the scale, I'm startled to see that I've lost almost twenty-five pounds since December—a combo of chemo meds, physical therapy, and sleeping most of the time, I'm certain. And then, the obsession hits: if I can lose a bit more weight, I'll weigh what I did when I was in high school and college, when everyone seemed to love me. Maybe being attractive would help my mood.

I stop eating entirely. I think about how to look decent despite illness. I forget that not eating is an illness unto itself. And I think about Starlight Boy. He's not tiny, but he's not built, either. He's a thin to average weight, and since he's not very tall—well, wouldn't it be nice if I were on the smaller side so that we could look perfect in pictures together?

This selfish thought consumes me as I try to walk faster on the treadmill at physical therapy. Brian, my therapist, who has been trying to help the neuropathy in my hip after the botched lumbar puncture, tells me to slow down before I have a heart attack. But I don't. I can't.

I need to be everything for everyone. No one understands this but me. And the voice. She gets it, too, even if she's just a hallucination caused by my lesion-laden brain.

Starlight Boy and I talk every night via text. Sometimes, I don't even realize I'm texting him until I scroll through the messages. Where have I been? But the conversations are deep and intimate. He feels every hurt I feel. I cannot emotionally distance myself from him.

I'm in love with two men, and I have to make a choice.

But before I do, Starlight Boy visits on a Friday night while Toby is taking his final class before obtaining his Associate's degree. And he's brought a gift with him.

"We talk all the time about science and geology and the universe," Starlight Boy says. "And no one can ignore your beautiful voice. I want you to have this. It was mine once."

He opens his hand, and nestled in his palm is a deep blue, heart-shaped stone.

"It's Lapis Lazuli," he says. "As brilliant as our night sky, on all those nights we've shared the stars together." I pick it up gently from his palm. The stone is smooth, except for one, jagged edge that I run my finger over constantly. It is glowing, brilliant, and perfect.

"Are you sure you want to give this to me?" I ask. "I don't deserve this."

"You know I don't believe in alternative healing stuff," Starlight Boy says. "But I want you to keep this. It's supposed to help with sleep. It's connected to the throat, and since you're an opera singer and you have thyroid issues, this is supposed to help your voice. And it's a stone for creative people. You should have it. It's yours."

I close my eyes. He's right—I don't believe in alternative healing, either, but my thyroid issues have grown worse recently, and I've just been diagnosed with an autoimmune thyroid disease called Hashimoto's. I have nodules on my thyroid, and they sometimes change my voice. This stone can't heal me, but maybe the love behind it can.

When I open my eyes, Starlight Boy is staring at me. I rub my thumb against the jagged edge of the stone, and then throw myself into his arms. He holds me tightly.

But I still have a choice to make, gift or not. And the next day, when my endocrinologist calls to tell me that he is worried about the nodules on my thyroid, he mentions a biopsy. Then, he dismisses the notion. Thyroid conditions grow slowly, he says. We'll just monitor it, because it's unlikely to be cancerous. Plus, there's a bigger issue, which is why he is calling. Due to years of endometriosis and other issues within my body, it doesn't seem I'll ever be able to have kids.

"Ever?" I ask.

"You need to talk to your OBGYN and a fertility specialist," he says. "But in reality, since you aren't menstruating regularly, haven't been able to get or stay pregnant, and have a serious history of health issues, it may be best to do a partial hysterectomy. I know you're only twenty-eight, and that may sound radical, but—talk to your doctor. Okay?"

I clutch the stone, letting the jagged edge scrape against my palm. I'm not thinking about Starlight Boy, and I'm not thinking about Toby. I'm thinking about infertility.

"What if I stop taking the MTX and start IVF or something?" I ask. "Could that help?"

"It may be risky, given your health," my doctor says. "I don't know. I'm sorry."

When the call ends, I think about what might never happen. I stare at the phone, and then, as I begin to sob, I throw the phone against the wall, and watch it shatter into uselessness.

I STOP TAKING THE MTX AND TELL MY PHYSICAL THERAPIST THAT I need a break. When Starlight Boy keeps texting me, asking me when he can come over, I tell him to back off. Toby and I want to have a baby, and that is my priority now. He's hurt, but he leaves me alone.

In the waiting room of my OBGYN's office, a young father waits with his daughter while his wife is in the back, having a routine exam to make sure her second child is healthy.

"Am I horrible for hating these people?" I ask Toby. He shakes his head no, and I stick my hands into my coat pockets. I'm shocked when I feel the stone in one of them. I could have sworn I'd left it on my end table at home. But I pull it out and clutch onto it.

My ultrasounds all reveal that I have large ovarian cysts and endometrial tissue. My body is frail, and carrying a baby will put me at risk—so much so that my kidneys could fail and I could die before a potential baby is even born.

"I want to do a partial hysterectomy," my OBGYN says. "But first, I want to do a surgery to remove the cysts and tissue. If I can do that for now, maybe we can avoid more drastic measures. However, I want your permission that, if things look worse than your scans reveal, I can go ahead with the partial. You wouldn't be thrown into full menopause, but you wouldn't be able to have children. I don't suspect you will, but this would mean you absolutely cannot."

"Do what's best for her," Toby finally says. I'm unable to speak for myself.

I know now that I'm never going to be a mother.

Back in the car, after signing a lot of documents, I stare out the window. Starlight Boy texts me, asking how I am, and I reply, "I can't have children. I need surgery soon. More later."

"I'm not ready to lose you," he texts. "Never. But this is awful. I'm sorry."

I don't respond. What's the point? After all, it's not like he can fix me.

After several weeks of moping around my house and trying to decide what to do with my life, I send Starlight Boy a final message. I need to focus on Toby and my health, I tell him. There's too much chemistry between us, and while I know that we have genuine feelings, we're not meant to be. We both need to let go. We can chat online, but that's it. No other contact.

I must make him hate me, I think, just as I've had to make other people hate me so that they don't get hurt in the long run. It's what's best. He'll understand. He has no choice.

But I still hold the beautiful blue stone he gave me, and I cry.

Toward the end of March, I'm sitting in my mom's living room, helping her work on a website, when an email comes through on my laptop. It's from Starlight Boy. I tell my mom I need a moment, and then I quickly read the message.

It's simple. He's been unable to eat or sleep without me. He's been reading and rereading the novel I wrote, and now he has to tell me the truth.

"I love you so much," he says. "I know I've never said those words, but there they are. Nothing could ever change that. I should have told you that night under the stars at Paul's, or the other month when I gave you the stone. I should have told you when we watched that movie. You complement my life. I know you don't want to talk in person, but I couldn't spend the rest of my days with you not knowing how I honestly feel. Despite the emotional oceans that divide us, I love you, and not having you in my life doesn't feel right at all."

Starlight Boy loves me. He loves me. I have proof. He's said it, and now, there's no doubt.

I read the email several times before shutting my laptop. Then, I run into the bathroom. The sobbing begins almost as quickly as the vomiting does.

When I can finally leave the bathroom, I tell my mom that I'm sick and need to go home. Once there, I email Starlight Boy, and I tell him yes, we should talk in person. I love him, too.

More than two years since we were reintroduced at Paul's house, the truth is out in the open. There is love. And there always has been.

We'll see each other in a week. And I know that will change everything.

STARLIGHT BOY ARRIVES IN THE MIDDLE OF THE AFTERNOON, AND AS I open the door, he smiles, and I start to cry. He tosses his duffel bag onto the floor of my foyer, and within seconds, we're wrapped up in one another, both of us crying. Neither of us lets go.

"I am so sorry," I whisper. "But I know now. I know what our story is."

"I'm sorry, too," he says. "I wish I had said everything I'd been feeling for you."

"You can't fix me," I say, and as we're still holding onto one another, I tell him every medical thing that's wrong with me. He hugs me as tightly as possible, as though he can absorb me. I wish he could. I wish he could make me disappear.

"This won't be easy," he says. "I don't know where to go from here."

"No one said it would be easy," I say. "Things worth fighting for never are."

Then I risk it. I take Starlight Boy's face gently into the palms of my hands, and he looks at me. I press my lips against his over and over again, simple flutters of kisses to hold his attention, and nothing stronger. He doesn't pull away.

I bury my head into his chest again. "I don't want to pretend anymore," I say. "Not now. I don't want to have to hide or pretend."

"We don't have to."

When Starlight Boy departs hours later, and I watch him drive away, I'm punched by guilt. Starlight Boy and I may not have to hide from one another, but from the rest of the world? From Toby? That's a given.

But the weeks pass and no one catches on. Sometimes, even I don't catch on. I feel as though I'm living in a dream as I watch myself interact with Starlight Boy on the days he's able to come over, and I can't alter the scene. It's as though someone pre-planned these encounters for us, and even though it feels right, I'm stuck as a witness behind a glass pane. My screams of happiness, confusion, guilt—I'm the only one who hears them.

Two days before my surgery, Starlight Boy makes plans to sleep at

Paul's and to visit me during the day. He also will be there in the hospital with me. Toby is confused, but I tell him that I want both my husband and my best friend there. I'm scared, and that is not a lie at all. He quietly relinquishes control, and only an hour after he leaves for work, Starlight Boy comes over.

"That kiss from that one time?" he says. "That was unfinished business. It feels like it was."

"It was," I say.

And then, as though neither of us has ever kissed someone before, our lips connect. We are unable to let go. For hours, we kiss with fury, hidden from the world in my small home where my whole life has changed. And somehow, without making a big deal out of it, we end up in my bedroom. My carefully planned outfit ends up on the floor, and I end up on top of Starlight Boy. He sticks his fingers into my bra and gently strokes my nipple, and I stifle screams by biting his neck. My hands make their way down to his pants. I can feel how hard he is against me, and as much as I want to make love to him, I can't. It's not just the upcoming surgery: somehow, for me, that is the new "crossing the line." So, I gently slide my hand into his pants and stroke him. He groans and bucks with pleasure, and as he touches me, we kiss and orgasm together.

What am I doing? Who am I? But isn't this love? I know this is love. I can tell by the way he looks at me, talks about me, converses with me about music and literature and life. This love isn't just physical —it wasn't for several years. It's real, and we're making up for lost time.

We say "I love you" frequently. Sometimes, it's after we've had an orgasm at the same time, but usually, it's during random moments. That same afternoon, as we're in bed together, his phone rings. It's a potential employer, and he has to take the call. He stands up and paces in my humid bedroom, wearing nothing but boxers and socks. The image is endearing, and I smile, hop up, and put my arms around his neck. "I love you," I whisper, and he loses his train of thought on the phone call. But he doesn't say anything. He does, however, lean down at one point and traces something on my bare stomach with his fingers: the letter "I," a heart, and the letter "U."

Twenty minutes before Toby is supposed to arrive home for a presurgery Guitar Hero party with our closest friends, I get up to get dressed. I pull on my black dress—the one I wore in 2009, back when Starlight Boy and I stood out under the stars and had our first honest moment together. The dress is far too big now, but it means something to me, and it still fits in the bust area. And with my tall black heels and makeup, I feel as though I look pretty good for someone who is about to have her fertility taken away.

Starlight Boy watches me get ready, and then he wraps his arms around my waist. With my shoes on, I'm almost as tall as he is. And there, as sunlight streams through the bedroom window, we press together in a dramatic, beyond-perfect kiss that I know can never be recreated. Everything is just right—the temperature, the sunlight, the moment, the passion, and the love.

It's hard to hide this from Toby, Paul, and Richard, but I do, and Starlight Boy follows my lead. However, we sneak into the kitchen during the Guitar Hero party, and I press him up against a wall and kiss his neck. I'm both reckless and cautious, listening to make sure no one interrupts us but not truly caring. I'm intrigued by my actions: they are wrong, they are impulsive, and I feel as though I can't control them. But I persist. I feel driven to do so.

Toby is acting strangely, and I know I have to pull double duty. It's only fair, because I have betrayed him. So, I make sure that he knows I love him, too. We take pictures together. I still want him, and I am still grateful for his love. I just can't talk about Starlight Boy.

But I can't help but guess that, on the day of my surgery, he is going to find out.

On the sign in front of the hospital, there is a big, black crow. I tell Toby and Starlight Boy that this is an omen. Something is going to go wrong. But they both tell me I'll be fine.

They're both wrong. After I'd been admitted, prepped, and medicated, the anesthesiologist comes in. I'm so strung out on drugs that it's hard to understand what he's saying, but then, the words become clear: I am a surgical risk. My neurologist hadn't told him about my seizures.

"Chances are that, if I put you under, you won't be waking up," he says. Toby squeezes my hand. Starlight Boy puts his hand on my leg. Both demand to know why these matters hadn't been settled before I was prepped for the OR, but there are no answers. So, drugged up, the world spinning around me, I get dressed, and we all head home.

And I'm angry. The voice yells at me, telling me that I'm a failure. I need to run away, leave all of this behind, start over, and I can't help but wonder why MS is such an asshole to me. Is it because I've been such a horrible person to Toby? I never meant to be the villain in our lives, but I am. So maybe this confusion and pain is something I deserve.

At the front door of my house, I hear myself screaming. I take off my shoes and hurl them against the living room wall. I yell at Toby and Starlight Boy, telling them that all doctors are horrible people and that they should let me die. Both listen to me rant, and then, in an odd moment of calm, I ask Toby to go get a Frosty from Wendy's for me. I want this Frosty, goddammit, and even though it might cause some Celiac-related issues, I don't care.

What I want is to be alone with Starlight Boy. And when Toby leaves, unwilling to deny my request despite the sadness on his face, I collapse into a sobbing heap in Starlight Boy's arms.

"I don't want this life!" I say. "I can't do this. I want to be okay. Please make me okay."

"Shh. I know," he says, rubbing my back, trying to calm my panic. "I love you. I know."

I look up at him and see actual sorrow in his eyes, and it angers something within me. I don't want his sorrow. I don't want any fucking pity. I just want his love.

And I want to feel something, anything other than what I'm feeling right now.

I kiss him roughly, and he reciprocates. I grab his hands and place them against my breasts. I have to feel this. I need pain. And luckily, Starlight Boy catches on. The anger subsides as he digs his nails into my flesh, scrapes my back, and bites me. I bite him back. I shove him against the staircase and pin his arms down. We're both so caught up in the moment that the sound of the front door shocks us, and quickly, after a brief kiss, Starlight Boy heads to the bathroom, leaving me alone by the stairs. I can tell my wig isn't on correctly, so I straighten it as quickly as I can, hoping Toby won't notice. And as he brings in the food, I look at myself in the hallway mirror—my pale face smeared with lipstick and mascara, my ribs jutting out, my wig in total disarray.

Who, exactly, is this person? I swear I don't know her anymore.

NOT KNOWING WHO I AM DOESN'T SEEM TO STOP ME, HOWEVER. Only a week later, Starlight Boy receives news that he has a new career waiting for him, and his training will begin soon. He has to fly to California for it, and knowing we'll be apart for several weeks cements our decision. We both nod and climb upstairs to my bedroom.

"Are you sure you want to be with me like this?" I ask him. I've already started to undress, but I'm stumbling, drained from being in the moment and slipping out of it. I can't keep up.

"First, I love you," he says and kisses me. "None of this is wrong if I love you. And second, you're asking me this while taking off your clothes?"

I laugh, and once again, he remarks that I'm getting too thin. I know he wants me thinner, but now, he says it's too much. He threatens to tie me to the bed and feed me. When I taunt him and tell him that he should tie me up, he pins me down, bites me, and tickles me. I'm laughing beyond control, and I'm turned on. I know we're seconds away from making love. But how do I tell him that I want him to keep making me laugh so hard that I feel sick? How do I say that I want bruises on my body and blood on my skin? How do I tell someone who knows I've been brutally raped and tortured that pain is pleasure now, and that it allows for control?

I say nothing, and as he begins to slide into me, I'm watching the scene. I can't do this, I think. I can't. When I tell him, he reluctantly agrees that we should wait, though he's already come. I look at the sheets and begin to have a panic attack. This is the bed I share with my husband, I think—the first rational thought I've had all day. I can't look at where Toby sleeps and do this.

"It doesn't matter," Starlight Boy says as we lay together. He kisses my forehead and strokes my arm. "We love each other. We have so much time. Every moment matters."

"I can't believe you'll be in California soon. I love you, my Starlight Boy."

He smiles at the nickname, and then he gives me one of my own. "I love you, too, my Siren. I'll come back home for you. I could never leave you behind here."

"I know. Nothing will ever keep us apart. I promise."

But as Starlight Boy is gone for several weeks, that promise is harder to keep. I'm angry, and I feel sicker than normal. The voice won't stop talking.

And then, there is a rush of blood. I cramp, I vomit, and I spend all day in the bathroom.

The baby—this baby that somehow came to be—is only five weeks old when I miscarry. I originally think I'm just having an awful period, since I haven't had one in months, but that's not it. I know this feeling. I am miscarrying, and I can't call anyone. Who can I call? Toby? We haven't had sex in ages. And Starlight Boy is in meetings. There is no one.

Did Starlight Boy and I actually have sex after all, and I somehow blocked it out? Or was this the result of that day where we decided against it, but on his part, it was already too late? I didn't know how to tell. My brain isn't reliable, I say to myself, and bleed copiously in the bathroom.

When I finally do get in touch with Starlight Boy, he asks if I'm okay. And I tell him no—I've just miscarried our baby. I wanted a baby, and somehow, we had one together, but I lost it. The chance is gone. And he says he's sorry, but that he's glad I miscarried. What if the baby had been sick? What if Toby and our families found out?

I hang up. He tries to text me, but I shut him out. If he cannot love this child, then he could never really love me.

A potential child—my last hope to be a mother—is dead. And now I feel dead, too.

THREE DAYS BEFORE MY NEW SURGERY DATE, I LISTEN THROUGH ALL of Coheed and Cambria's newest album, *The Year of the Black Rainbow*. I am in shock. Somehow, all the songs fit my life perfectly—track one is January, track two is February, and so forth. They all make sense. This always happens with Coheed's music, though. There's a strange connection, and part of me wishes my life was chaotic enough for them to be spying on me to write their amazing lyrics.

Track eight tells me that, come August, there's a chance I'll die. But I figure that's an error.

Starlight Boy messages me constantly, telling me he's back from California and desperately needs to see me. We plan to meet after my surgery, but then I tell him not to come. I still don't want to see him, especially since he keeps saying he's glad I miscarried the baby. The love hasn't faded—I still know it's there. But my trust has. My heart is too empty for him to fill it.

This is when Toby notices that everything is wrong. But I think he's always known.

He presses me that night while we are in bed. "I know something has been happening," he says. "Tell me what it is. I have a right to know!"

"Well, it's clear you already fucking do!" I scream. But it's not me. I'm not in control. I just listen to myself and wonder what the hell is happening.

"I do?"

"I've been with Starlight Boy," I say. "Okay? Is that what you wanted to hear? Well, now you know. He's been here while you've been at work, and we're in love, and I know I'm a horrible person, but there you have it."

"How long have you been together?"

"Long enough."

"You don't love me anymore?"

My heart is breaking. "Of course I love you. I love you so much, more than I could ever explain. That didn't stop or change. I just—I love him, too. I love both of you."

"You can't. That's not possible."

"It is! I do love you both. You hate me, and I don't blame you. I don't know what to do."

"I don't want you to see or talk to him ever again," Toby says blankly. It's not even an order as much as it is a flat, emotionless plea on his behalf. "If you want this marriage to work, you will end it."

I sob on the edge of the bed. He's right—if I see Starlight Boy again, I will end up divorced. And I don't want Toby to leave me. I do love him, despite how I feel for Starlight Boy.

"Okay," I say. "I won't see him again. We won't go to Paul's when he's there. And I'm about to have surgery and will be on bed rest for six weeks. You can trust me."

"I can't trust you right now," Toby says. "But I'm going to have to learn to try."

I don't deserve him. And even as we say goodnight and he crashes into a hard, emotion-laden slumber, the voice tells me to betray him. I send a brief text to Starlight Boy:

"He knows. Stay away. But I do love you."

"Okay," Starlight Boy replies. "Let me know what's next. I love you always."

Part of me thinks that Toby won't come with me to the hospital for my surgery now, but when the day arrives after my final pre-op to make sure I'm properly medicated for my seizures, he proves me wrong—he proves he is a better person than I deserve. He's right there with me, and he kisses my forehead and tells me he loves me as I'm wheeled into the OR.

When I wake up and am coherent, the news is mixed.

My OBGYN didn't have to perform a hysterectomy after all, which means that, with help from medications and fertility experts, I might be able to have a child. However, he had to remove a very large ovarian cyst and a lot of endometrial tissue. My insides are a mess, he says, and staying pregnant will be a serious challenge. And I could still die if I did go into labor.

Toby and I are both relieved and devastated. And the next day back at home, as he helps me onto the mattress that he's pulled down onto the living room floor, two thoughts cross my mind: one, that we could still have a baby, even if that causes my death, and two, that Toby has had my phone for more than a day now, and I never told Starlight Boy not to text me.

But I'm coherent enough to keep my mouth shut. And I'm still not sure what to say to Starlight Boy, since he disregarded losing the child we'd conceived together. In time, I'll tell him the surgery went well, but nothing else. My love for him mixes with the hatred that he wanted me to lose our baby. I can't talk to him. Not after knowing what I now know.

I spend more time with Toby, and on the days he's at work or school, I sleep, take pills, watch movies, and cry. I down a lot of Valium. I schedule a consult with a fertility specialist. And I sleep some more after all that.

I'm haunted by dreams of Starlight Boy kissing me. I'm haunted by his voice, his scent, by the way he somehow commands me to love him.

My surgical wounds ache, but I give up the painkillers. I'm a monster. And I deserve this.

ONCE I'M ABLE TO MOVE COMFORTABLY POST-SURGERY, I FIND A NEW sense of empowerment. It starts off innocently, but then, I move into the role and inhabit it completely.

I begin modeling.

Catie comes over one night, and we try on clothing and take pictures. I'm in some pain, but I can pose, and I'm stunned to see that we both look so good in these photos.

We do another photoshoot and share our pictures online. Hundreds of comments come in, so I decide to risk sending some pictures to a modeling site. Photographers message me immediately, asking if I'll work with them. I schedule dates for late August and September, when I know I'll be fully healed, and I'm sent locations and contracts.

I have a new obsession. And as we experience an earthquake in Maryland—the state's biggest in decades—I experience trembling along my own fault lines. The world, I think, is going to move for me because I am going to make it move. With my hair growing back in, my body thinner, and limitless time to put on makeup and take pictures, I'm going to invest in myself.

Starlight Boy and I begin to text one another again, and by August, I've forgiven him. Perhaps he was right, I think. We couldn't have had a baby then. Besides, he tells me that he misses me, and that I look so beautiful in the pictures he sees of me. He's jealous of Toby, and he really wants to come over. He's the one who loves me the most. I agree to his wishes, and we choose a date in mid-August.

"Toby cannot know I'm doing this," the voice says. "Don't say a word."

"That *we're* doing this?" I ask in reply. "Who is this *I*? Is it me?"

But I only receive silence.

Starlight Boy is granted a personal day from work on the date we selected, and he comes over. Immediately, we fall back into our old habits: he holds me, we kiss, and we end up in bed (even though, this time, that bed is the mattress on my living room floor). We spend the day there, kissing and talking about what can become of our relationship. And the more we discuss a potential future together, the more I start to lose control over what I'm saying. I still can't explain it, but I say things to him and then don't realize I've said them.

I need to call the neurologist, I think. It must be MS. Or Lupus. Or something.

At one point, I tell Starlight Boy that I'm calling all the shots now. I love Toby, but I won't deny this love right here and now, either. I can —and will—love two people at once. I am powerful, and I am in charge. Being sick doesn't mean I can't have complete control.

Starlight Boy stares at me, surprised by my declarations. And then, in defiance, he pushes me onto the mattress, straddles me, and kisses my neck. I reach up and take off his shirt. He takes off my bra and pinches my nipples, causing so much pain that I scream in pleasure.

"I have trained him so well," the voice says to me. "We are so very lucky."

I start to undo his jeans, and realize that, when we first got together, he'd had such limited experience. The voice is right: he's been trained. But he wanted that. And now, we could have everything together. I am feeling exactly what I want to feel, and the fact that I can make him orgasm six times in a row? I may be the one squirming on the bed right now, but I am, ultimately, in control.

Starlight Boy pulls out a condom. I nod and tell him that yes, we're going to make love. It's a statement. My surgical wounds still ache, but I want this. I'm going to change his life.

Once the condom is on, he slides inside me. Both of us moan, and I hold his hips, showing him what I like. We go on for what must be hours—I float in and out of the room, out of my head, losing track of time—while kissing, touching, and saying how much we love one another. When we orgasm together, I smile. I'm his first. I'm the only one.

"I love you," he says. "I've never connected with any other person like this before."

"I know," I reply. "I love you, too. And no one will ever destroy us again."

MUSE'S SONG "UPRISING" IS POPULAR RIGHT NOW, AND DURING A photoshoot that involves corsets, gothic gowns, several wigs, the Lapis Lazuli stone I've had turned into a necklace so that Starlight Boy is always with me, and a red fan from Spain, a theme is decided. I strip naked, wrap myself in red duct tape, and hold a sign in my hands. The camera captures my smirk:

"They will not control us."

This is my warning to the world. I am not to be controlled. And Starlight Boy is pleased with the photos, though he worries about my safety. Am I really okay right now?

"I have this," I tell him. Power surges through me. I have everything I want at the moment. For someone who is sick with MS, Lupus, Hashimoto's, Celiac, depression, anxiety, and a host of other illnesses, my life is on fire. I'm singing, writing, and modeling. I'm thin again.

Starving myself gives me power. Toby loves me, and we want to have a baby. Starlight Boy and I are strong together, too, and we will fight to live our lives together and share our love.

Everything is going my way.

And just like that, everything stops, and I cease to exist.

THE AFTER

September 1, 2012-Present

The fingernail scissors sat on the bathroom counter. It was September now. I could get away with long-sleeved shirts. No one would see. No one would find out.

And who would care? I was a horrible person. I'd lived an appalling life. The blame ran through my veins, and I needed to rid the world of my villainy.

Slowly, I opened the scissors and sliced a thin line into my left bicep. I watched the blood drain out of me, and I smiled.

I did it again. Ninety-nine more times.

The blood from each cut dripped out and mixed with the other cuts into one beautiful, darkish-red pool. When I finished, I washed my arm, but it ached, so instead, I squeezed the cuts and allowed more blood to come out. It felt so good—to open up like this, to let the pain ebb and flow without having to say a word.

Ruby had contacted Starlight Boy. I found out that they had been chatting on and off, but he swore he had "moved on and away from me." However, Ruby knew better. She taunted me by telling me that he didn't live far away now. He could be mine again if I wanted him. All I'd have to do would be to show up.

"He's just some lonely loser," she said. "But you love him. So do I. Go get what we want."

I looked at the scissors. I thought about the past that was returning to me in fragments—the memories that my brain injury hadn't washed away. The newest alters to come forth, Pandora and Green, knew about miscarriages, other rapes, death, and torture. When Pandora first announced herself, she slept under the dining room table, afraid of an unknown "he" who would come find her. Green was blind and claimed she was trapped in thick piles of snow far too heavy for her to move. She had been bound, my therapist said. Green must have been forced to do something while tied up that she hadn't wanted to see—hence the blindness and the thick snow.

I couldn't live like this. I decided to cut one hundred more gashes into my other arm, and then, after an hour, I bandaged both arms and climbed into bed next to Toby.

I already knew too much. Nobody else needed to know.

THE CUTS ON MY ARMS BECAME INFECTED, BUT NO MORE SO THAN MY mind. Ruby had memories of Starlight Boy that left me heartbroken. Shilo told Toby a terrible story—through her tears, she said that the last time Ruby had seen Starlight Boy, she had grown tired of his "pathetic attempt at sex" and had pushed Shilo out to deal with him. She'd said no and had been completely ignored. Toby knew about some of the details, but was shocked to hear the entire version.

Before Shilo could finish her story, a new alter emerged, let out a scream, and crawled on the floor to hide behind a living room chair. When Toby approached this alter—a growling, primal personality who said very little—it stuck its head through an electrical cord and tried to die via strangulation.

I needed help—more help than my therapist knew how to provide. No one knew what was happening besides Toby and me, but we were too overwhelmed to live like this. I had scars, bruises, and burns covering a majority of my body. My stomach was puffy and bloated— between my horrendous thyroid issue and Ruby's love of drinking dish soap, I looked more pregnant than I did when James resided within my body. Everything was wrong.

But I didn't speak up, and so, the cutting continued as Toby and I tried to push forward.

Things became worse that October when my parents wanted to have James baptized at their church. Toby and I—who felt no connection to their choice or religion—objected, but we still attended a somewhat-forced meeting with the head of the church. He was a nice man, but the decision did not feel like ours. And suddenly, godparents were chosen and invitations were sent out without our knowledge. When one of the godparents contacted me to say he received the invitation—something Toby and I had never seen—I called my parents in a rage. They claimed I had approved everything. Toby, not one to create dissension, spoke up and objected as much as I did. After all, he wasn't crazy—I was. His voice carried more weight. He never lied.

And just like that, things were strained between my family and me, just as they had been before I'd become pregnant with James, and just as they had been when I was a teenager. James had allowed me to reconnect with my family, but now we were back to fighting minor wars that soon escalated into international conflicts.

When my mom called me to tell me that I was selfish and for the most part unloving, I gave up. I told Toby I was ready to die, and I showed him my infected arms. Then, I drank dish soap and took several handfuls of Valium.

Toby had me temporarily and involuntarily committed in the county psych ward until he got through to someone at the trauma unit in Baltimore. While I was locked away, scratching the skin off my wrists and letting Carmen beat every single patient at card games, he made the arrangements. My parents, stunned by the crisis, backed away from the baptism plans and arranged for James to attend a steady, loving daycare three days a week so that I had fewer burdens at home.

I had tried to be a good mother. I had hoped my love would be enough. But I was no longer myself. I no longer wanted the life that I had to share with so many other fragmented minds.

The trauma unit coordinator said that I would be able to come back to the hospital within two weeks. The stay would be long; I knew that, and I warned my closest friends, who rallied around me.

Ruby notified Starlight Boy. In his messages, he didn't understand what happened to me—to the girl he used to know two years prior, before the traumatic brain injury had occurred. He wanted her back, he said. He wanted the girl who loved him and wanted to be with him, not the girl who spent hours carving up her arms with scissors. Selfishly, he only wanted the past. He had no consideration that I, as myself, didn't have a real past any longer.

I grew addicted to the sadness associated with the word "past." Everything that had meant something—James aside—had been in the past. The sadness felt real and tangible, like the frozen oranges I was supposed to hold in order to remain in the present. But the present kept slipping away. Starlight Boy was Ruby's sadness, and her past. Being homeless and used for sex was Pandora's sadness, and her past. We all had our addictions and sorrows, and together they caused a commingling of intense pain.

I placed a lot of my hope in the idea of a second trauma unit stay. It hadn't gone well during my pregnancy, but nothing could stop them now from using every method they had to help me. James was in good hands with Toby and daycare. I didn't work. My health, while poor, could still be managed in the live-in trauma unit that already had a history of my illnesses on file.

I had to go. I had to learn, once again, who I was—and if I could become someone I would actually like. I might even have the chance to become the person I used to know. Maybe that girl still existed. And if that girl had been worth something, then I desperately wanted her back.

THE SECOND STAY AT THE LIVE-IN TRAUMA UNIT WAS A HORRIFIC blur of medication, switching, and being told that I was a bad person for having DID. The hospital was understaffed, and that took a considerable toll on those who were trying to keep watch over twenty PTSD/DID patients. But that also meant harsher rules, people trying to break those rules, more medications to keep us sedated and compliant, and very anxious patients.

In my private room, I stared at the wall. I had been allowed to hang pictures of James, Toby, and my friends on the concrete, but other than that, everything was sterile. I couldn't keep track of time or place, of how old James would be that next day, or if I would see him for Christmas. The psychologist told me no—this trauma unit wouldn't let me out on Christmas, or let James in to see me. He was still a baby, she said. He didn't need to see me.

"Show them rage," Ruby yelled into my head. "Stop eating. Show them who we are."

And then I heard a man's voice on top of hers—an odd layer of seductive feminine and country-western masculine:

"I *am* rage," the male voice said. "Stand up to them."

I stole a Sharpie from the nurse's station and started to write manifestos on the walls of my room. Ruby wanted to post a letter telling people to stay out, and in big, capital letters, it hung from the wall: GET THE FUCK AWAY FROM US. The male voice wrote out one long, strung-together sentence about who he was and how he was going to keep "the little ones" safe. In his writing, he said his name was Johnny. He liked to drink, smoke, gamble, curse, and play music. But he wouldn't ever hurt a kid, especially, "Those ones in this here head house."

Johnny was my birth father, minus the hurting children factor. He had been the rage Ruby mentioned. He had been the one to keep the child alters quiet within me.

One morning, I woke in horror. There was black—almost like dried blood—covering my pillowcase and sheets. When I stood, I saw it on my clothing.

Johnny had run out of paper that night. My bed, my clothing, and my skin had been his Sharpie-laden novel. The word "rage" was written in bold letters on both hands. Everything else was a terrifying testimony about my past.

And I couldn't wash it off me.

Since the trauma unit was so short-staffed, I knew that asking for help would be pointless. I had to learn to handle Johnny on my own.

So, I played a song that Starlight Boy and Ruby used to listen to together, and I purposefully triggered her to become co-conscious with me.

"I need your help," I said to her. "I need to control Johnny. Please help me."

I must have been a terrible sight. There I was, sitting alone in my room, covered in black ink. The walls were a disaster zone, and my face and arms were more disastrous. And I was, to any observer, talking to myself. If a passerby wanted to define insane, I would have fit the definition better than anything the dictionary could have described.

And yet, I wasn't insane at all. I was asking Ruby—my strongest alter—to help me. I was doing as I had been taught: I was communicating with an alter to find common ground.

It took a few days, but eventually, Ruby stopped Johnny from writing on my body. However, once a staff member finally caught onto the fact that I'd been hiding a Sharpie—a forbidden object in a psychiatric facility—the writing stopped, and my body was scrubbed clean.

Except for the tops of my hands. Those, in their bold, thick lettering, still read "rage."

And they stayed that way, those subtle reminders of my past and present, for days.

ONE NIGHT, I WAS ATTENDING A SMALL GROUP MEETING WHEN I heard a horrific scream from down the hall. The two staff members who were in the room with us told us to stay put. They left and locked the door behind them.

"Did they just trap us?" N, a fellow patient and one of the only people I could trust, asked.

I tried the door handle. "Yes," I said, my heart racing. "We can't get out."

While, intellectually, I could rationalize the staff's need to contain ten DID/PTSD patients while dealing with an emergency, I absolutely couldn't rationalize it emotionally. I was triggered by the other patients who began to panic, and in turn, I ran out of breath. I switched, terrified about being locked in a room, and Carmen came out.

"Let's play a game," she suggested. "Kids play all kinds of games!"

But this wasn't a fun game. Between her and about five other patients who had switched into a child personality state, the game wasn't a simple hand of poker or a round of Candyland. It was, "How do we scare the staff members so that they start paying attention to us?"

K, a tiny twenty-three-year-old who had been triggered and switched, giggled and crammed her body into the fireplace. The only way anyone could see her was if they were standing at a particular angle. To those of us who were children in that moment, ranging in age between five and fifteen, it was hilarious. The staff would have to pay attention now. K had gone missing!

The rest of us hid behind couches and chairs and waited.

It took quite a while, but when the two staff members returned, they were perplexed as to where we could have gone. Some of us were easy to find—Carmen was behind a chair, for instance—but no one could find K. And none of us were going to rat her out.

Her giggling gave it away. And the staff members, so overwhelmed by what we later learned was a patient's attempted suicide in an isolation room, told us that we were going to be kicked out of the hospital and sent home. The child alters mostly vanished then, and we, as adults, had to explain what had happened. But in truth, we didn't know. We knew we'd been locked in a room and had switched, but we didn't feel right trying to explain that the staff's actions had triggered us to commit the immature act of hiding. Why didn't the staff in a trauma unit for patients with DID understand that confining us might cause a switch?

I started to doubt if this stay was the right choice for me. And the next day, when I refused to eat—knowing that the food would poison me since it was sitting right next to a gluten-laden piece of toast—I was forced into a nurse's station, and I quickly learned the answer.

"You're not supposed to lose weight while here," the nurse said to me. She handed me a bottle of Ensure. "Drink this in front of me. And drink three a day. You have to have enough calories to survive."

I looked at the drink and pulled back. I wasn't drinking that. No one could force me to do so.

"I can't," I said. "I'm sorry. I have Celiac. I don't know what's in that drink. If you let me bring in my own food, maybe I'll eat, but I won't drink that."

"Yes, you will." The nurse's tone caused an immediate switch, and Ruby came forward to argue.

She lost.

According to a very angry journal entry that she wrote, and that Johnny later finished, we were force-fed the Ensure—to the point of choking. It was dumped down my throat continuously, not allowing me time to swallow, and when I started to choke, I was told that if I spit it out, I'd have to start all over again. I, as Ruby, choked my way through the entire bottle in about three minutes. After, when she started to throw up, she was told that if she did get sick, she'd be force-fed more Ensure. She went back to the room, vomited silently into an old shirt, and threw it in the hallway trash can.

I was fucking furious. How was anyone supposed to get better if they were going to be treated like this? How had this expensive, prestigious trauma unit become a jail? I'd even been in an isolation room after a mostly benign switch, trapped in a small space with a mat on the floor, forced to wear a blue shirt and a weighted vest to calm me down. The vest did the trick; the shirt that said "This patient is non-compliant and is being punished by staying in a windowless room" did not. I received no medication during that isolation, and no water was offered to me.

The final straw was during a snowy day around Christmas. I'd been force-fed the Ensure that morning and was trying—unsuccessfully—to ask my psychiatrist for an early release. However, she didn't feel comfortable granting that request, even when I broke down into tears and said that my retrograde amnesia wouldn't allow me to fit in. I didn't understand TV programs like Law & Order yet; they struck me as real, and scary. I didn't know most popular music artists or actors.

My motor skills made art therapy nearly impossible. I didn't fit in, and so, I wanted out.

But during our discussion, the fire alarm went off. And because of the house fire I'd been in when I was twenty-two, I couldn't handle the sound or the thought of twenty patients and ten staff members rushing to get out of the trauma unit. I switched, and Madeleine presented herself.

"I can help," she said calmly to the psychiatrist. "Please. Let me help."

Madeline got up, left the office, and collected blankets. She stepped outside and handed them to the shivering patients, smiling and offering comfort. It would be okay, she said. She could handle a fire. Then, she walked back into the evacuated building to get fruit.

She was grabbed by both arms and shoved outside. And when I came to, standing in the cold, barely able to remember why all of us were outside in the first place, my psychiatrist walked over to me and said, "You're right. You don't belong here. You are nothing but trouble. When you're ready to leave, you just say the word, and you can go back to your regular doctors to deal with your—bizarre habits."

What had Madeleine done wrong by trying to help people? What had I done wrong by not having a good enough memory to make it?

I hung on a bit longer, just to see if the trauma unit psychiatrist and psychologist could help me. But that evening, when another patient switched, turned violent, threatened my life, and slammed me into a wall, I called Toby and told him I was leaving. No one wanted me there. I was going to come home. I already had permission. This visit, this stay we had yearned for, spent our savings on, hoping for some sort of relief after so many weeks? It was worthless.

"You'll never return here," Ruby said to me the next day as Toby and I drove away from the unit. "No matter what you do, you will not come back. I will not let you."

She didn't always live up to her promises. But in that case, I knew she would.

As usual, it took a while for me to grow accustomed to being back home. It was 2013 now, and James had had a fantastic Christmas. He'd grown so tall. How had he grown so tall that quickly? And that smart? Even though it was sometimes difficult to understand him, he was incredibly intuitive to the world around him and would discuss music and cars with us.

But everything was too loud and too bright, and I spent more time as Ruby, Carmen, or Madeleine than as myself. Luckily, certain people knew how to get me to emerge: Toby could put on a piece of music that I liked, and I'd come back. Carrie, determined to rid me of my fear regarding public movie theatres, took me to see a showing of *Les Misérables*. And James kept me grounded because he needed me. If I was needed, or felt wanted, I could stay. The second that sensation slipped? I was gone, lost into darkness, only emerging with vague memories and the terrifying sense that I would never have a good life or be a good mother.

Despite two additional psych ward stays that helped me overcome the trauma that had occurred during my visit to the prestigious private trauma unit, I decided to throw a party in honor of one of my favorite books—*The Great Gatsby*. The movie was just about to be released, and I was in the mood for decadence. On days when Toby worked and James was in daycare, I made the arrangements. Sure, the party would cost about two thousand dollars, but that was nothing in the long run. Making sure everyone was happy was what mattered.

And the party was a great success. My handmade Daisy Buchanan gown gathered a lot of compliments, the gluten-free food Carrie had made was amazing, and we had enough alcohol to make 1920s party-goers jealous. I danced, flirted, and sang my way through what felt like a normal night.

Normal only lasted for so long, however. Ruby, who loved my new short, blond 1920s hairstyle, thought that we were attractive enough again to contact Starlight Boy. Without my knowledge, they messaged one another, and decided to meet—simply to talk, the email stated.

And they did meet, in a grocery store parking lot. They hugged, and Ruby told him that she was happy as she pretended to be me. Life was successful. James was flourishing. Toby was making a lot of money.

Friends came and went constantly. When Starlight Boy admitted jealousy and loneliness, Ruby comforted him, and that was when I finally came back out.

"No," I said, shoving him away. I got out of his car and saw that I was in the parking lot of a shopping center ten minutes from home.

Starlight Boy followed me to my car. "I thought we were just talking."

"You loved me once," I said, shaking. "But you hurt me. Was it all an illusion?"

"You don't understand that I wanted to be with you. I would have done anything."

"And you did. You used me! You made me believe that you were the only man I was supposed to love. You promised to give me back my life!"

"That's not true. Plus, we're not together now." He paused and stared at me. "You made your choice when you stayed with Toby."

"I don't know where you came from, but go," I said. "Please, just go."

He drove off, and I sat in my car, sobbing.

Nothing was in my control. Not even love. I wasn't over it—not quite yet.

DURING THE SUMMER, AND DESPITE THE PAIN IN MY BODY FROM constant Lupus flares and a biopsy of some nodules my endocrinologist had found on my thyroid, my family, Toby, and I took James to the Outer Banks for his first big beach trip. I hadn't been since 2009, and while the drive terrified me, I was immediately soothed by the ocean.

"I'd forgotten about you," I said as I walked to the shoreline. I dipped my toe in the water and let the wind swirl around me. "I'm home now."

James ran through the sand, and I chased after him. We took pictures together, smiling and carefree. Toby and I held each other at night, listening to the ocean from the pier near my parent's beach house. I decided that I didn't want to leave—I felt less pain by the water.

But James became outrageously ill the next day with a stomach virus, and it took four adults to keep him calm and clean. No one knew what had happened, but as we wearily packed for what was certain to be a messy ride home the next day, it was clear that the fun was over.

On the way home, I sat in the front seat as my mom drove. The sky was beautiful, a pristine blue with minimal cloud cover. I sang along to the radio, checked in on James—sleeping, and luckily not sick to his stomach—and tried to relax.

Two hours from home, however, as I stared at the clouds, a memory hit me: I'd had a baby before James. A baby girl named Sophie. She'd died in my arms, and I'd buried her in a shoebox. I'd only been twenty-one, and she'd died at twenty-one weeks. Alexander, my abusive boyfriend, was the one who got me pregnant.

The memory hit me with such force that I asked my mom to pull over at the upcoming rest stop. I rushed into the bathroom before she could ask what was wrong, shut myself in a stall, and sobbed quietly. Where had that memory come from?

"You were there for all of it," I heard Madeleine say. "But I helped. Just like I helped with the house fire."

How much of my life had I forgotten? And why was I remembering it in a rest stop bathroom?

I needed to cut. I needed to hurt myself. But there was nothing. And my mom wouldn't leave the bathroom until I was ready, so I couldn't even scream. Instead, I allowed Madeleine to come out, and, smiling, she washed her hands and climbed back into the car.

Back at home, after putting James into his bed, I told Toby what I had remembered. He recalled the house fire, as he'd been in it as well, but had never heard about the stillbirth.

I tore through old journals and computer diaries, determined to find proof. And I did: in one entry, I mentioned that I was pregnant and that I'd lost a daughter because I'd been a drunk. She died in my arms March 17, 2003.

And then, in the bottom of a chest I'd kept of special memories, I found a little green and pink dress, wrapped tightly in a Target bag. It must have been something I'd been saving for her.

"I can't do this," I said to Toby. "I can't keep reliving my life like this. I don't have a life. I have fragments of a story. I can't be a good parent or a good wife. I'm sorry."

I ran to the bathroom, locked the door, swallowed whatever pills I could find, and started cutting my wrists. Toby broke the door, dragged me out into the living room, and, after calling my mom to watch James, took me back to the local psych ward.

Perfect place for a baby-killer, I thought. Where else should I be?

MY STAY ONLY LASTED THREE DAYS—JUST LONG ENOUGH FOR ME TO quiet most of the alters. Some new memories surfaced, but my psychiatrist, Dr. L, told me that the hospital wasn't equipped to handle DID.

"You have to learn to control them on your own, with therapy," she told me.

"But when the memories come back, they destroy me."

"Don't you have more to live for than just the past?"

I did. And so, by the third day—after Pandora had had her fun hiding under tables and Carmen had beaten every patient at Rummy—Toby came to pick me up.

On the way to my parents' house to get James, he looked concerned. When I asked what was wrong, he said, "Your endocrinologist called a few hours ago. He told me to tell you to call his cell as soon as you could."

I didn't think anything about it. "I had that biopsy a few weeks ago," I reminded him. "If it had been bad, I would have known by now."

"Yeah, but didn't your mom have one, too? And hers was clean, and she got the results."

That was true. She had her results in hand a good week before I'd received the call.

Back at my parents' house, after hugging James and playing with him for a bit, I called my endocrinologist.

"I'll cut to the chase, since it's late," he said. "But every single one of the nodules on your thyroid came back cancerous."

"What?"

"They're malignant. You have follicular thyroid cancer and will need to have surgery to remove your entire thyroid before it spreads. Unless it already has. I'll contact a surgeon tomorrow and get you down to him for a pre-op immediately."

Numbed by his words, I hung up the phone.

"Well?" Toby asked.

"I have cancer. Thyroid cancer."

My parents and Toby just stared at me.

"Don't worry. I won't start doing walks or any crazy shit. I just have to have my thyroid removed so that it doesn't spread. Unless it already has. The doctor doesn't know. But I'll be seeing a surgeon soon."

No one said anything. And as the voices rattled the inside of my head, I realized that maybe there was nothing else to say.

Earlier that afternoon, the hospital had triggered Ruby to come out and sign a contract stating that she wouldn't cut or poison the body. She signed it in her typical capital-letter, block handwriting. But she had also said that it was pointless.

Maybe she had known, I thought. Maybe she sensed my body had already poisoned itself.

SEPTEMBER 2, 2013–JUNE 30, 2014

September and October were a whirlwind of medical and personal drama. I met with a surgeon who told me that he wanted to take out my entire thyroid on November 4. When Toby asked if I could wait that long, the surgeon said, "Thyroid cancer grows slowly. It won't get much worse between now and then." But I didn't like the sound of "much worse," and we both felt uneasy.

"I'm a trained opera singer," I told him. "What if something happens to my voice?"

"I'll take really good care of you. I'll even write, 'Opera singer: Please don't cut' on your neck."

I laughed. Maybe it would be okay. I didn't feel differently, after all. I'd just gone from being sick to being sick with cancer. I wouldn't make a big deal out of it.

But when people started to ask how I was doing, I'd tell them: I have cancer. The words fell out, and my friends rallied around me in support. When I told my psychologist, Dr. M, she told me that I should lean on others—cancer, no matter the type, wouldn't be an easy challenge. And the alters would have something to say. Carmen came out during therapy and told Dr. M that she was scared, but otherwise, the space in my head was silent. No Ruby. No Johnny. No one.

Toby decided to throw a thirty-second birthday party for me, since my birthday happened to be exactly one week before "cancer surgery." Six of our closest friends were invited, and my parents said they would watch James for the night. They'd also promised to watch him the night before and of my surgery as well, and I was grateful for their help. I thanked them several times.

But when they came to pick him up that evening—my friends already there, and Carrie preparing the food for us to enjoy—my mom asked to speak with me privately in the office.

We went inside, and there, she lashed out. "I saw your Facebook post about how we don't support you!" she said. "How dare you accuse us of not supporting you when you're sick?"

That was the problem with Facebook: first, people read too much into it and reported back the incorrect information. And second, the post hadn't been about her. It had been about a friend of mine who had told me my cancer was "easy," so she wasn't going to concern herself with it. I'd simply written that if I was a burden to anyone, they could walk away. If friends or family didn't want to support me, I would be fine on my own. But it had never been a direct stab at her. By now, if I had wanted a direct stab, I would have just told her to her face.

"That post wasn't about you," I said calmly. "It was about someone else."

"Bullshit. Your brother read it and replied. He knew it was about us."

"He was wrong."

"He's not an idiot!"

"I didn't say he was. I don't think he's an idiot at all. He's my brother."

"Well, one thing is clear," she said. "With the exception of James, the only person you love is yourself. You don't love or trust anyone else. Do you know how disappointing it is to have to deal with your selfishness?"

I was thirty-two, standing in my own home, and being yelled at by my mom—who had made plenty of her own errors. I had every right to kick her out. But part of me held back—the part that wanted her to say that she was wrong, that she was scared, that she loved me.

Instead, she said, "Happy birthday," grabbed James, and took off with him and my dad.

Needless to say, the party was ruined, despite how hard Toby had tried. And the week leading up to my surgery was much the same. It wasn't until the day before we left for the hospital in Baltimore that my parents hugged me and said they'd be praying for me. All was suddenly forgotten when my life was about to be on the line.

I woke up on the morning of my surgery feeling like I was going to vomit. What if the surgeon cut my vocal cords? What if the cancer spread? What if everything? But Toby, who remained calm as we packed and then drove to the hospital, told me I'd be fine. Thyroidectomies were routine, and I'd been under the care of good doctors for five years now.

The surgeon greeted us back in pre-op, and told me that he was going to get the nurse to give me the IV containing anti-nausea medication and a light sedative. The only surgery I could actively remember was when I had James, when the light sedative had been an almost lethal dose of Versed. I started to panic, but when the nurse came over, she told me it was just ten mgs of Valium—far less than I took daily.

Toby walked alongside my stretcher until we got to the operating room, and then he kissed me. "See you when you wake. I love you."

"I love you, too," I said.

And those were the last words I remember saying, because between the IV Valium and the anesthesia mask that was quickly placed over my mouth and nose, I passed out.

———————————

When I woke up, I was in post-op. The nurse saw me, checked my vital signs, and told me I'd done very well. The surgery had taken a little longer than expected, but I was okay. When I pointed at my throat, she said, "Don't try to talk yet. You'll hurt yourself."

But I was in pain, and I wanted to know if my vocal cords had been cut. I moaned, which not only let me know I still had some sort of voice, but also earned me a steady Morphine drip.

Toby came back into the room and held my hand. "The surgeon said they removed your thyroid. It was a good surgery. You'll stay overnight so they can monitor your calcium levels and thyroid hormones, but otherwise, we can go home tomorrow."

I nodded. But as I was wheeled up to my room for the night, the Morphine kicked in. Everything from my neck to my toes hurt tremendously, but I could not have cared less. I sat up in bed, still hooked to an IV and a heart monitor, and started to sing.

"Stop!" Toby said. "You'll hurt yourself."

I sounded awful, but I had a voice. The surgeon had kept his promise: my vocal cords hadn't been sliced in half.

The night was a blur of visitors, doctors, and medications, but the next day, as we were set to go home, I whispered to the doctor that my fingers and toes felt numb.

"That's normal," he said. "It will take a few days for all of the hormones in your body to balance out. Stay on your thyroid meds and take a lot of calcium pills. I know it's hard to swallow right now, but if you can do that, and just keep resting, you'll be fine."

The drive home was painful, and I desperately wanted to see James. But he was two now and was starting to pick up on things. He'd uttered the words "Mommy has cancer" several times, and while he didn't know what that meant, he'd grown a solemn look in his eye when he said them. He'd always been intuitive, and all I wanted was to protect him from this.

My parents kept James on my first night home as well to give me more time to recover. And it was lucky that they did, because I woke up in agony multiple times. The bones in my hands and feet felt calcified. I couldn't flex my toes. And the next morning, when Toby came in to bring me some ginger ale, I said, "I can't feel my mouth."

"What do you mean?"

"My lips are numb."

"They look really blue," Toby said. He immediately called my endocrinologist, and when he hung up the phone, he said, "Let's get you to the car. Right now."

"Where are we going?"

"Back to the hospital."

I have no memory of the ride there or of what happened when I was admitted to the ICU. But I woke up the next day and learned that I'd been unconscious. My TSH was extremely pathetic—it was two hundred, when a normal value should have been one, and I had hypoparathyroidism and hypocalcemia. I needed a calcium drip and a Vitamin D drip, or I wouldn't live.

My friend Lee, whom I'd met at Starbucks about a year earlier—who had understood about my memory loss and didn't mind when I cried as he showed me the International Space Station flying above our heads one night—came for a visit.

"I'm just here for the cute nurses," he joked.

"What if I die in here?"

"You? You're not going to. Not yet."

I got sick in front of him. I cried. I asked him if it was too late for God to forgive me for what I'd done in my life. But he stayed by my side and never wavered with his friendship.

Two days later, I was stable enough to leave the ICU and to be transferred to a critical unit. I had to continue wearing a heart monitor and needed several IV infusions, but if they could get my TSH to at least fifty and bring my calcium levels into the normal range, I could go home.

Ten days later, I did. I hadn't seen James, and I wondered if he'd forgotten about me. But he hadn't, and I spent days holding him and feeling like the worst mother ever. It wasn't DID now that was making me a terrible mother. It was cancer.

I floated in and out of consciousness a lot that winter, barely remembering a visit from my in-laws for Thanksgiving and having no memory of Christmas whatsoever. All I could remember was that Toby and I decided that we needed to move to Baltimore to be closer to the hospitals. I'd been readmitted three times since my surgery, and the drive was taking a toll on all of us. We contacted a wonderful realtor and a fantastic mortgage lender and got down to work. But we still hadn't found a house we liked or could afford yet.

The day after Christmas, I told Toby that I didn't feel alive—I could see the world around me, but it didn't make sense. I was asleep, but awake.

"Are you dissociating?" he asked.

"No. I'm me. But I'm not here with you."

But we were out looking at houses to buy. And we found one—a cute, three-bedroom rancher with a large backyard, only minutes from schools, shopping, and two major highways. In a haze, I called for a tour, discussed financing, and then slumped down into the car.

"Are you with me? Honey, are you with me?"

But once again, I was gone.

It took me another two days in the ICU to wake up again, and when I did, the head doctor of endocrinology came in to see me.

"We can't seem to regulate your TSH," he said. "It should eventually be between zero point four and four point zero. But yours likes to hover around three hundred. People don't function at that number."

"I functioned yesterday. I walked. I saw a house."

"That was almost three days ago, honey," he said. "You're in the ICU again. We can't get this under control."

In the meantime, the surgeon had contacted the hospital. After a thorough examination of my removed thyroid gland, it was noted that the thyroid had been littered with papillary thyroid cancer—little grains of rice embedded in the gland itself. I had had two forms of cancer raging inside me, and God only knew how long they'd been there.

"Am I going to die?" I asked the endocrinologist.

"You keep going into and coming out of something we call a myxedema state. Your temperature gets very low—almost like hypothermia. With that, your TSH fluctuating, and your anemia reaching new lows, well, we're going to have to give it some time. I just hope the Synthroid pills are kicking in for you."

He had avoided the dying question. I automatically knew what that meant. "What if they don't because of the Celiac or Crohn's?"

"What do you mean?"

"I don't absorb food well. I take liquid forms of most medications. I can only digest about four things. Maybe the pills aren't working?"

"They'll work. We just need to give it time."

He had listened, but not fully, and as 2013 turned into 2014, I watched the fireworks from my hospital room window, shivering from another bout of hair loss, and wondering if I was ever going to make it out there alive to see James again.

THE FAULT IN OUR STARS WAS A VERY POPULAR MOVIE—BASED ON the teen/young adult novel by a wonderful writer named John Green—and in the movie, the female lead is dealing with progressive thyroid cancer. She's fifteen years younger than I am, and in the movie, she lives.

Well-meaning friends—and even strangers—started bringing me copies of this book. They sat with me to watch the movie. They kept using the movie's catchphrase of "Okay? Okay" with me. And while I was grateful for the company, I couldn't help but think that I wasn't fifteen. I was thirty-two and buying a new house with my husband and child. My life was not this drama. It wasn't a movie. It wasn't here to make people upset and to give them something to talk about.

But that was what happened. People took to Facebook—sometimes with good intentions, and other times, simply for attention—to talk about me. Before I knew it, my story was all over the Internet. And I had never wanted that.

I didn't have time to concern myself with the Internet, however. Instead, I had to have RAI—radioactive iodine—to try to kill off the remaining thyroid tissue in my body.

And the process was complicated. The dose was high, which meant that I was radioactive once the treatment was inside of me. No one could come to visit me for forty-eight hours, and doctors had to enter the room in biohazard suits. Anything I touched would be contaminated. I had very little contact with the outside world.

On the plus side, I peed green for a while, so that was a nice source of entertainment.

I went home for about a month—just long enough to tour the new house a second time, sign some more papers, and get the financials settled for a March move to Baltimore—before I went into another coma state. My lips turned blue, my body temperature dropped, and my TSH reached an astonishing level—three hundred ten.

But I was awake when my dear friend Catie, who had been visiting me, drove me to the hospital. "How are you talking to me?" she asked, fear in her eyes.

"I'm not," I told her. "This kind of coma is funny. I'll be awake, and then, I'll leave you."

This time, the ICU stay was shorter, but my overall stay was entirely too long. I thanked God for daycare and for the fact that Toby's work was flexible. And while I wasn't fully coherent, I finished up the final papers for the Baltimore house while hooked up to machines in my hospital room.

What I was not prepared for, however, was for a doctor of psychology to come visit.

"I've heard you aren't doing well," she said to me, shutting the door and pulling a chair to my bedside. "About six stays in four months. That must be scary—to have uncontrolled cancer."

I nodded and relaxed a bit. It made sense, I thought, to send in a psychologist. If a cancer patient is struggling to live, seeing a psychologist would be reasonable.

"Well, have you ever considering that maybe something—you know, *within you*—isn't medically compliant?"

"What in the hell are you talking about?"

"We know that you have DID," she said. "A system to protect you. Have you ever considered that maybe your system wants you to die?"

"Obviously, you don't know how DID works," I told her. "If you're here to tell me that I'm purposefully putting myself in the hospital, spending time away from my child whom I love, and driving us into debt while trying to buy a house? I'm not the delusional one in the room."

"You're lashing out at the wrong person," she said. "I think you aren't taking your medication and you're causing your cancer to get worse. And your regular endocrinologist believes that is true as well. We'd like you to take a large dose of oral Synthroid—about twelve hundred mcgs—to see if we're right."

By that point, I'd learned enough about thyroid conditions and medication to know that dose of Synthroid could be potentially deadly. It could cause heart failure.

"No," I said. "If you don't believe me, and if my own doctor doesn't believe me, then send me home. This is bullshit. You've just blacklisted me from getting care at a good hospital!"

"You're doing this to yourself. Your alters are doing this. And because you're lashing out, I'm asking that you stay another twenty-four hours, with a person from our psych department in the room with you, to make sure you don't kill yourself."

"I never said I was going to! I'm saying you're ridiculous. I have every right to leave here if my doctors tell me I can. Go get the hospitalist."

"No," she said. "You're staying. I want to see which alter isn't taking the medication."

I called Toby, sobbing uncontrollably. "This isn't about DID! Why are they trying to lump this thyroid disease, and this cancer, with a mental illness? Lab work doesn't lie. Why are they?"

"They're crazy, and you're right—you've been blacklisted," he said. "You need to go."

I stayed the night as a psych student watched me. She watched me take my pills and looked into my mouth to see that I'd swallowed them. And when the lab ran my next round of tests, my TSH was exactly the same. The pills had been taken, I had been compliant, and nothing changed.

"I told you," I said to my endocrinologist, who had come to check on me. "Now, get me out. And you're done. You can go fuck yourself if you think I'm trying to die from cancer."

Toby took me home—to our new house, only twenty minutes away now—and as we stared at the piles of snow in the driveway, we hugged one another.

"At least it's ours," he said. "We'll be safe. We'll be inside with James. We'll be okay."

I desperately wanted to believe him, but I knew that I could not.

LATER THAT MONTH, I WAS GREETED WITH AN ENORMOUS SURPRISE:

I was pregnant.

I hadn't been on chemo—not yet, as my team of doctors was still trying to figure out how to help me—and the few times Toby and I had been together must have done it. I was pregnant again, just as we were settling into our new house and our new routine.

But I didn't want to tell him, or tell anyone. I'd been pregnant in September 2012, too, but that hadn't lasted past five weeks. I was only around the five-week mark now, I guessed. At ten weeks—maybe twelve, given my history—I would say something.

I was so sick that I started losing weight, and as I began to lose some of the thyroid blubber that typically accumulates after a surgery changes the body's hormones so rapidly, my mom and I decided to join Weight Watchers. I didn't say anything about the pregnancy or the vomiting, and going to the meetings wasn't helpful. I couldn't eat, and most of the people there were overeaters. My problem was medical. There was nothing I could eliminate from my diet.

But between the vomiting and the daily walks I took around our new, quiet neighborhood every day, I did start to lose weight. I lost ten pounds in three weeks and started to feel better about my body. I wasn't cancer-free—the word "remission" hadn't come close to anyone's lips yet, as my medical team couldn't verify if they'd really been able to remove all the thyroid tissue—but I was doing what I could to try to live longer.

I even signed up to do Relay For Life. I had promised myself not to give in to cancer hype, but I wanted to be part of an event that gave back. And since the American Cancer Society did, I signed up, and despite my exhaustion, I walked the track that night, holding the survivor banner. I didn't feel like a survivor yet, but I was still breathing, so I was surviving something.

I did end up in the hospital one more time before the summer after going numb. My TSH, I had said to Toby, was probably at about two hundred fifty. I told him to wait until the next day to take me to the hospital, when it would probably be two hundred ninety. I knew the numbers by now. I could feel every change in my body.

And I had been close. My TSH was two hundred ninety-nine when I was admitted again. But this time, the doctors rushed me to the ICU for a different reason.

"You're so anemic that your heart is about to fail," one doctor told me. "We're doing blood transfusions."

"When?"

"Right now."

Toby sat with me as several bags of A+ blood flowed into my system. I didn't react poorly to the transfusions. But my heart rate was still dangerously low, so I was kept in the ICU for four days—right before Toby's graduation from college. Somehow, he'd kept up with all his undergrad classes online and was graduating with honors at the end of June. I was tremendously proud of him. He'd kept going—and had kept our family going—while I floated in and out of various states of being alive.

When I came home, my heart rate was still low, and I had trouble breathing. My new endocrinologist—a kind woman who didn't think DID hindered my ability to take care of myself when it came to cancer—told me I might need to go on oxygen, and she started to petition my insurance company, which hadn't been very cooperative when it came to my treatment and hospitalizations, for my right to breathe.

That night, I died.

It was brief—only for a few minutes until I was able to be resuscitated—and I don't recall the actual event.

What I could recall was seeing Doo-Da.

We were in a bowling alley—something he and I had liked to do when I was younger—and I was warm, so warm after having been freezing cold for ages. I was wearing a black tank top with an orange and blue bird on it, and had on jeans. My hair was long and dark, like it was when I was sixteen, and I was thinner.

Seated at the counter by the shoe rentals was my friend, Jon, who had died as well.

"Oh my God," I said, and I hugged Doo-Da. "You're here! Jon's here!"

"Look around," Doo-Da said.

There were tons of people talking, bowling, and drinking—not drunk, but just having a drink. The music was lively. Everyone was friendly. I didn't recognize anyone else, though.

"Where is this?" I asked him.

"Not your place, honey," he said. "Not yet."

"I don't believe this. I know this is a trick—no oxygen, my medications, all of that. What this is—it's just a dream, right?"

"No," he said. "But when you start breathing again, you'll understand. I can't wait to be with you—my beautiful granddaughter. But not now. When it's time."

I woke up, gasping for air, startling the techs and Toby. He cried, but all I could do was stare at the ceiling, unable to talk.

Had I seen where I'd end up? Had my grandfather actually held me?

It couldn't have been real. But I honestly wasn't that certain.

———

TOBY'S PARENTS FLEW INTO TOWN TWO DAYS BEFORE HIS graduation—just as my car died and my credit card was hacked. While I spent most of my time on the phone, dealing with fraudulent charges (I wish I was in St. Thomas, I said to Chase) and trying to figure out what part could repair my fifteen-year-old Dodge, Toby prepared to walk down the aisle to receive his hard-earned degree. We were all so proud—and he'd been accepted into a Master's program, too.

Luckily, we had a second car—a brand-new Kia we'd purchased a year earlier—so Toby could get to rehearsals. And my father-in-law was an expert with cars, so he had mine up and running. "She won't last long," he said. "But she'll hold for now." And that was good enough.

On the night before graduation, I was pleased to see that I could slip into a size eight dress. But my stomach wasn't getting bigger. I knew that I was twelve weeks pregnant, but at twelve weeks with James, and with Sophie, I'd been bloated. But every pregnancy was different, right?

And then, after everyone had gone to bed, I started bleeding profusely.

I hid the fear and pain from Toby and his family, and I went to bed wrapped in towels, praying for a miracle to save this secret child.

JULY 1, 2014–JUNE 15, 2015

In all of Toby's graduation pictures, he and I are smiling as we hold onto one another. His mom is crying—this is her first child to have graduated college, and she's proud. The pictures taken at dinner with both families and James are testimonies that the day had been perfect.

But photographs lie. Despite the smile on my face, I was miscarrying during graduation.

The blood and pain had not let up, but I wasn't going to ruin Toby's day. Instead, I wished him well and hugged him as he left for the ceremony site. As I kept running for the bathroom to grab towels, I dressed, put on my best wig—my hair still too short and brittle to let it be seen in public, though it was growing in pretty well—and put a pack of pads in my large purse.

I'm sure I seemed crazy, excusing myself to go to the bathroom every twenty minutes during graduation. But I had to. Blood was seeping down my legs, and the thirty-six pads I had brought wasn't containing it. I was dizzy and ready to collapse. But I couldn't. I stood and cheered as Toby received his diploma and accolades, and I smiled for the pictures after.

But after dinner, when we went to get ice cream, I felt a terrible cramp. My body was telling me that something major was happening. Without a word—and without my purse—I ran into the bathroom of the ice cream store, pushed down, screamed a little, and then looked.

I had miscarried. It had taken twenty-four hours, but there was the baby—at just about twelve weeks.

I didn't care how gross it was. I reached into the toilet, picked up the insanely tiny bundle that I had hoped would be our second child, and sobbed. Then, without anything in my purse to help me, I cleaned up with paper towels, placed the miscarriage back into the toilet, and said goodbye. What else could I have done? I'd been eating well, never smoking, never drinking, and trying to work out. I should have sought care, but that only worked once, for James.

And I knew that I was finished. James wouldn't have a sibling. My body wasn't meant to carry life. I would make certain this would never happen again.

Back outside, I couldn't stop sobbing. My mom walked me over to the curb, and I told her everything. Blood rushed down my legs, and she asked what I needed. All I could say was that I wanted to go home.

Toby didn't even know yet as we all drove back to Baltimore. Inside, once James was tucked into bed, I asked Toby's parents to please give us a moment alone. And still cramping, still bleeding, I told him.

"I was pregnant," I said. "I miscarried in the bathroom at the ice cream store. I should have told you. I'm so sorry."

"Why didn't you tell me?" he said, holding me. "We could have gotten you to a doctor."

I kept sobbing and bleeding. "Because with the exception of James, I can't have children," I said. "I was worried I'd lose this one, too. I lost all the others. And I..."

But my words stopped as another unbearable cramp hit me.

"We need to get you to the hospital," Toby said. "You're as pale as you get when you go into comas. It's the blood loss. Let's go."

"I can't," I said and ran into the bathroom. He followed me as I clenched my jaw.

And I miscarried the other baby—the one I didn't know about.

We were going to have twins. I'd lost them both.

Toby saw this one—not much more than a mass of cells and tissue, surrounded by blood—and we both cried.

"I know it's over," I said. "I just want to go to bed, okay? Can you tell your parents?"

He nodded, helped me clean up, and then, swaddled in towels, I climbed into our bed.

"I'm sorry," I said. "This is my fault. I just wanted us to have another child."

"It's not your fault," Toby said. "It happens. Your body isn't well."

"I know. It shouldn't have happened on your graduation day, though."

"You couldn't help that. Go to sleep, love. I'll be here."

Toby's mom hugged me for a long time the next day. "We love you," she said as Toby and James prepared to take her and my father-in-law back to the airport.

"I know you do. I'm sorry."

I felt as though I'd ruined the weekend.

But that was only the beginning of the ruining.

A FEW NIGHTS LATER, AS TOBY AND JAMES SLEPT, I WAS ON THE couch, writing on my laptop. The bleeding had mostly stopped, but the noise inside my head hadn't. Carmen cried a lot—she'd never have children, she came out to tell Toby. And Ruby was angry.

Ruby's anger triggered a switch—but instead of allowing me to be co-conscious with her, she shut me out. I had no idea what she was there to do.

When I came to as myself, Toby found me in the living room. Ruby had consumed a few glasses of dish soap and water, and had then taken a lighter to my left arm. She burned six major wounds into my bicep and burned off most of my remaining hair.

I looked at my oozing arm, at the hair on the floor, and then shook my head.

"I don't remember a thing," I told him. "Why is she doing this?"

"You know Ruby," he said. "She never wanted your body to be pregnant, even with James."

"But we had an agreement. She wasn't supposed to harm me. She broke that."

"I don't think she ever planned to live up to it."

After an incident where Johnny came out and punched someone in the face for shooting off fireworks after midnight— "can't wake up the goddamn kids," he had said before getting in the car and speeding off —I told Toby that I needed help. I needed to find a new psychologist who could deal with this. Dr. Housel was still a wonderful psychiatrist, and after five years, I refused to leave her care, but finding a DID/PTSD/trauma psychologist was almost impossible.

But it didn't matter, because a few days later, I ended up back in the hospital.

"You're so anemic that you'll need more transfusions," the doctor said. "You have infected wounds on your arm. And on top of that, there's still cancer. Your scans are—they aren't what we want. Plus, your TSH is back to two hundred eighty. Are you taking all your pills?"

"Of course I am," I told him. "I don't want to die."

But he put me on oxygen and told me that I'd probably have to do chemotherapy and radiation in the near future if I wanted to live.

The next morning, a social worker named Nick walked into my large, private room. I'd joked, my breathing labored, with Toby and Catie the night before that we could throw a party in here. They agreed. I wondered if I should—if it would be a last party.

When Nick closed the door behind him, I knew things were serious.

"We've had five different doctors petition your insurance company for oxygen and IV Synthroid infusions," he said to me, sitting down in a chair next to my bed. "Insurance is denying all coverage."

"Why? I don't understand. We pay every month. We pay a *lot* every month."

Nick pulled his chair closer to me. "I've spoken to your doctors here." I saw tears fill his eyes. "Your heart isn't stable—the fluctuations in your TSH, along with the comas and the instance of cardiac arrest, have made your body weak. One or two more coma states, and..."

"Just say it. Say what you've come here to say so that I know."

"You're terminal. You're going to die in a year."

He held my hand for a few minutes while I stared out the window. James was going to be three in only a few months. We'd just bought a house. I was only thirty-two.

"I don't accept that," I said. "I want to fight back."

"Insurance companies don't tend to bend much."

"They'll bend. Or they'll be all over the news. I'll make them suffer."

"You should get this story to every news outlet you can," he said. "Your insurance company is deplorable—letting a young mother die."

When I finally left the hospital days later—not any better, but knowing they had no reason to keep me there if I was actively dying—I started making calls. I called my insurance company daily and told every representative my story. I wasn't going to die.

My new psychologist, Dr. E, told me to make a "bucket list."

"Whatever you want to do between now and, say, summer of 2015," she said, "you might want to write it down and try to do it."

I automatically disliked her. She came highly recommended and absolutely believed in DID and PTSD, but I wasn't going to accept death as quickly as she was.

Instead, I started to embrace the business of living.

I'D BEEN VERY BEHIND WHEN IT CAME TO CULTURAL PHENOMENA. Between amnesia, DID, and what was now considered incurable thyroid cancer, I hadn't much time to catch up in four years. But I finally got around to watching Disney's *Frozen* with James, and as I watched—and as James danced, sang, and marveled at a girl who could shoot ice from her hands—I cried.

I connected to this movie. This movie that people were so tired of was something that I understood. Elsa is an outcast from birth—her parents had told her she was different. Elsa tries to leave, but someone finds her. And when someone tells her she can be okay, Elsa is triggered into a state, similar to dissociation, which causes her to lash out in rage without meaning to.

Between that and constantly feeling shrouded in ice, I'd never related to an animated character more than I did to Elsa.

"Let it Go" was an annoying song by that summer. But to me, it was an anthem. I was finally regaining my vocal strength almost eight months after surgery, and I belted the song with every ounce of strength I had. I vowed that, if I lived—and lost the fifty pounds of thyroid and steroid weight I had accumulated due to cancer—I would make Elsa's costume and perform for other kids. And at least Ritty, my seven-year-old cat, didn't mind when I sang it. She'd climb on my lap, knead, and purr, as though asking for more. I sang to her all the time.

By the fall, I had perfected shooting ice from my hands, which was a trick James found mesmerizing. I wasn't going to dress as Elsa for Halloween—my doctors all told me it was best to stay inside if the weather dropped below fifty degrees—but it was one of the best things in the world to fill my sweatshirt sleeves with ice cubes, start singing "Let it Go," and shoot ice around the room toward James as I twirled. It became a daily routine. He told all his friends at daycare—local now, and only a five-minute drive so that I could pick him up when I was awake enough to do so—that his mommy was Elsa without long blond hair.

That winter, I landed in the hospital again in another coma state. I was taken to the local hospital in my hometown—I'd passed out in my doctor's office, too cold to move and too shaky to stay focused—and had no choice but to be transported to a hospital I didn't trust. But being in a coma made them pay attention. I spent days in the ICU, in and out of consciousness, seeing my Doo-Da again in the bowling alley. He told me to hold on. He wasn't ready for me.

But my body was so tired. I was ready for him and to be with his warmth.

I woke up briefly, looked at Toby, and told him I loved him and James so much. I had documents for both of them on my computer. Everything would be OK now.

And then I flat-lined.

According to Toby, it took almost ten doctors to revive me. I was a

DNR by this point—I'd specified as much in my will and Advanced Directives—but that was ignored as one doctor had said, "She's too young, so we're going to try."

I was brought back after seeing Doo-Da briefly, and instead of gratitude, I was filled with exhausted outrage. "You can't play God! Why keep me miserable when I had the chance to go in peace?"

"Because we don't want you to die," one of the techs said. "You're just too young."

When we returned home, my dad called to let me know my grandmother—his mother—was in the same hospital I'd just been. She had a bad case of pneumonia, and since she was ninety-four, they were certain she wouldn't make it through Christmas. I came back down to visit her, dressed in scrubs, gloves, and a mask, and brought her a teddy bear. In her delirious state, she'd been "knitting"—pulling on the blanket as though creating patterns. I'd done that, too—it was a grounding technique. I knew it all too well. But when I placed the bear in her arms, she settled, and rubbed the stuffed animal instead.

Soon after, my mom called to let me know my other grandmother was in the hospital as well. It was also questionable if she'd live through Christmas.

There was a church only five minutes from our house—a Catholic church, and I wasn't Catholic—but I went inside of the little chapel one night, and I prayed. With my walker, and in my ski cap because I'd started chemo and had no hair, eyebrows, or the ability to stay warm, I dropped to my knees and prayed for peace.

Toby and I ended up meeting with one of the sisters at the church, and we found out that James would be eligible to attend private Pre-K there in the fall of 2015 if we were members.

"But we aren't Catholic," I said. "And I don't want to lie to you. My doctors have told me I have terminal cancer. I don't have the time or the energy to study."

"But do you believe in God?" she asked me.

"I know what I've seen," I told her truthfully. "I know that there's a place bigger and greater than this. I think you can call the force behind it whatever you'd like, but I believe in something much greater when we die."

"That's good enough for me," she said. "Meet with me on Saturday mornings once the new year begins, and we'll have you and Toby as members within a few months."

It seemed like a solid plan: James would be able to attend a good, safe school only a few minutes from the house in the fall, we could meet new people at church, and maybe I could find answers for my questions. Plus, they had a choir. The sister had told me that they could use a trained singer, and if I needed my walker, so what? They accepted everyone.

Christmas and the New Year came and went with too much worry. James was the only one who could celebrate, because the rest of us were on edge. If I went outside, I'd get sick and end up in a coma. Both of my grandmothers were in the hospital, and it was only a matter of time. There was too much sadness to be celebratory.

On January 2, 2015, my dad's mom passed away.

On January 7, 2015, my mom's mom passed away.

My lab work the day after my Grandmama's passing showed that my TSH was back at three hundred, and I needed to be readmitted to the hospital. But I refused to go. I'd missed the small funeral for my grandmother. I was going to be there for Grandmama.

But instead, I scared the hell out of people. I was puffy and bloated from the steroids that were keeping my heart pumping and my body moving. I needed a walker to stand upright. People hugged me and cried, but when they cried, they didn't mention my seventy-seven-year-old Grandmama, except to tell me that she had loved me so much and that I'd be with her in God's good hands soon. I wondered if they thought that would be the last time they saw me, too.

I had no memory of the funeral or the reception after. I missed the burial. Instead, I went home, took my medication, and fell into two straight weeks of sleep. I had told Toby before I climbed into bed not to wake me. I wasn't going to the hospital. I'd get up to take my pills and use the bathroom, but otherwise? We weren't dragging this out. James could see what was happening, and he was becoming anxious. No matter how much we shielded him, he'd cling to me whenever he saw me. It wasn't fair, and I didn't want him to worry any longer.

"Mommy loves you," I said to him one day in bed. "I swear I always will."

"I love you for all the days," he replied. "Every single day. All of them."

I cried, because I knew he wasn't lying. He'd love me. For all the days.

MY ENDOCRINOLOGIST, WHOM TOBY HAD CALLED AS I SHIVERED under five blankets in our bed, upped my oral Synthroid dose from three hundred mcg a day to six hundred. A normal dose for someone my size and with my condition, she had said, would be two hundred mcg. But it was clear I wasn't absorbing it. I needed infusions—despite the fact insurance was continuously denying coverage. However, she was going to keep fighting on my behalf.

The six hundred mcg of Synthroid, along with sixty mg a day of Prednisone, gave me enough energy to get out of bed. If I only absorbed half of it, at least something was getting into my system. I was walking and able to attend Saturday classes at the church with Toby so that we could become members. Not much was happening, but for now, we had that.

A few weeks later, after yet another hospital trip to pump me full of IV Synthroid and steroids, Toby and I met with a priest at the church and were welcomed. Once James was baptized—something we had arranged for that spring—he could attend the private Pre-K in the fall at a reduced rate. It was something we could afford—barely, but it was doable—and so, with every ounce of strength I had, I started to try to do more again. I signed up and created a team for a second year of Relay For Life. I went to baptism classes so James would be ready. I spent more time figuring out home improvements, realizing that our kitchen and bathroom were so outdated that they were going to collapse on us at any moment and that we needed to renovate. And I wrote. I wrote a few short stories and finished a book I'd started in 2009. I wasn't well, but I was productive. I felt as though I was going to live.

One week before James' baptism, I was in my endocrinologist's office, and she had good news—I would be able to have injections of Synthroid for fifty dollars a month. Now, I wouldn't have to worry about a pill getting into my system. A shot would deliver the medication straight to me.

But there was a complication. The pharmacy refused to mix the solution, so my endocrinologist and I, along with Toby, sat there and measured our how much saline should be mixed in with the Synthroid powder. Then, grabbing the correct needle, she asked if I was ready. I said yes. By this point, needles didn't bother me at all, and I knew daily injections would give me a fighting chance to live. She gave me the injection, showed me how to dispose of the needle, and told me to stick around for a few minutes to make sure I felt okay.

Toby and I sat in the waiting room, staring at the walls. I was fine. We needed to go home.

And then, I turned to him and said, "I can't breathe."

I collapsed on the floor, had a seizure, and was taken via ambulance to the hospital.

I WOKE UP IN THE ICU THAT NIGHT AS A NURSE WAS PUTTING something into my IV. "What's that?" I whispered.

"Steroids. To help your heart." She patted my arm and walked out. I heard her talking to someone, and I looked over to see Toby sitting on the couch nearby.

"What happened?" I asked.

"Something about the injection—your body didn't handle it. You had a nosebleed and went into shock."

"Then I guess I have to go back to pills."

We were both dismayed, and since it was late and Toby needed to get James, he kissed me and left. I stared at the ceiling and wondered if this time, this was it. I'd now run out of options.

A man dressed in purple scrubs entered the room. "I'm Dr. Richardson," he said. "And you are one sick girl."

He sat on the side of my bed and told me everything that was wrong. I nodded—everything he said was correct—and then, Dr. Richardson asked if I had been able to get insurance approval for a port or a PICC line to get IV Synthroid directly into my body.

"We tried," I said. "Insurance denied it. They caved on the injections, but—here I am."

"But the only option is a port or PICC," Dr. Richardson said. "Your heart—I don't know what to say, but your body can't take more of this. Your TSH is so abysmal that it's shutting down everything in your body. Your bloodwork is terrifying. One more incident and I'm afraid you won't wake up—or, if you do, you'll be catatonic."

"Tell that to insurance."

Ten minutes later, he walked back into the room. "You know," he said. "I'm the one in charge around here tonight. And I'm calling the shots. I don't give a *damn* what your insurance company says right now. Tomorrow morning at eleven, a team is coming to put a PICC line into your arm. Then we'll set you up with home health care, and you'll have a daily injection of Synthroid right into the line. You'll feel alive again within weeks."

I took Dr. Richardson's hand and cried. "How can you do this?"

"Because I'm not letting a company decide if you get to live or die," he said. "Now, get some sleep. We have some work to do in the morning."

True to his word, two nurses came in at 11:00 a.m. with two machines, a huge box of supplies and smiles on their faces. "Today is the day you get to live," one of the nurses said.

"I almost don't believe it."

She leaned down to hug me. "Believe it," she said. "Sometimes, miracles do happen."

The PICC insertion was slightly painful, but nothing I couldn't handle. Using an ultrasound, they inserted two thin tubes through my right arm into my veins near my heart. Thirty-six inches of tubing was used, all wrapped around a tiny machine that was strapped to me. When I looked down, I saw that it said "POWER PICC." It was purple, and the ends of the tubes were capped.

"OK, Elsa," one nurse said—her nickname for me since I'd been given a small plastic Elsa doll to hold. "We're going to show you how to do the injections, and even though home health care will likely do most of them, you need to know. They're also going to clean the site once a week, and that's going to feel very strange. We'll show you."

And they did. The pre-mixed syringes were a breeze to use and toss. The cleaning felt awkward, but otherwise? This little device was going to save my life.

That afternoon, I saw Dr. Richardson again. "When do I get to go home?" I asked him, holding out my arm that sported the PICC.

He smiled. "When your TSH isn't two hundred sixty," he said. "With the injections straight into the line, it will still take a week or two for your numbers to get better. But they will. I just want to see them at one hundred before I let you go."

The days were getting closer to James' baptism. I could call the caterer, I could make sure people were coming, but otherwise, I was stuck in a hospital twenty miles from home.

Finally, when my TSH was near one hundred—two days before the baptism—I was allowed to go home. I felt better when I walked around. My appetite was back to normal. And, as several doctors pointed out, I wasn't deathly pale. My TSH had improved. The only visible signs of my cancer were the thyroidectomy scar, the PICC line, and the permanent staining on the outer corners of my lips. They were a dark blue. "That's from the hypothermia," one of the doctors said. "It may fade in time, but it will never go away."

James had his baptism, and despite my puffiness and exhaustion, I was present for every moment of the celebration. And the same was true for Relay For Life—I was able to lead my team of nine people to triumph, my hair dyed the colors representing thyroid cancer to show that I was still a total badass at kicking this thing down.

But on June 1, Toby's company switched insurance carriers. On June 2, I received a phone call that, to cover my PICC, medication, and home health care, it would cost me two hundred ninety thousand dollars per year. That was how much it would take to stay alive.

"I can't afford that," I sobbed into the phone. "I'm doing much better. I'm alive. I'm able to focus on things. My TSH is down to forty, and it hasn't been that decent since 2011. Please."

"No," they said. "Try pills like everyone else."

I went through the next few weeks in a total daze, ranting to anyone who would listen about our shitty health care coverage. I petitioned, my doctors petitioned, and nothing happened. A date was set: the line would be pulled on June 16, 2015.

"Fuck this," Ruby said. I switched, and she tried to pull the line. Luckily, Toby stopped her. If she had succeeded, I could have become septic.

The alters came out during therapy to scream. But I remained silent. I had nothing to say any longer. I'd been given about three months of extra time, and now, I would lose it. I was going to fail out of life.

And all I could do was wait to be taken back to my worst nightmare once again.

JUNE 16, 2015–DECEMBER 31, 2015

Toby and I sang along to Coheed and Cambria as we made our way to the hospital to have the PICC line removed. He was trying to distract me, and I knew it, but I felt tremendous guilt: from the start of our relationship, especially the last five amnesia years, he'd been my caretaker. Husbands and wives were, perhaps, supposed to stick it out through sickness and health, but this had gone beyond that. Every day, he had to wake up wondering if I'd live or die. He had to wonder if he'd be a single parent. He had to bet on my life just as much as I did.

I took his hand. "I'm sorry I turned out this way," I said. "All of it—just, I want you to know. In case I get worse again. I want you to know that I'm sorry."

"You have nothing to be sorry about," Toby said. "The stuff that happened right before the amnesia—I know you weren't fully in control. And you're not in control of cancer at all."

"I did love him—emotionally—before Ruby took over," I said. "You know that."

"Yes. And you've apologized enough for it."

"I can't apologize enough for it. But I wouldn't have let it go as far as Ruby did."

"I know," he said. "I trust you."

We didn't wait long inside the hospital. A nurse took us back to a room, and within minutes, she had the PICC line out—all thirty-six inches of tubing that had been keeping me alive.

I felt like crying but was too numb.

"The spot will be sore for a while," she said to me. "That's normal. But it will heal, and you won't even remember that you had it."

"Yes, I will," I said. "It saved my life. And now, it's gone."

"I hope your medical team has a good plan of action," the nurse said. "I'm sure they do."

"Not yet," I said. "But I'm counting on it."

Back at home, I sank into a deep depression for weeks. Alters came in and out, covering for me on days when I was unable to walk. My TSH was getting worse again—despite the pills Toby watched me take, he could see that I was unwell, and the lab work showed a rise from forty to one hundred. But Madeleine took Toby aside one night and said she would help.

The morning after Madeleine's arrival, I noticed something odd within my head.

I couldn't sense Shilo any longer.

She was always there, as she was one of the alters with whom I was co-conscious. I could hear Ruby, Madeleine, and Carmen, as per usual, but Shilo was absent. I didn't hear her voice. And as odd as it was to explain to both Toby and my therapist, I could feel that she'd left.

"What happened to her?" I asked my psychologist at my next session. "Why did she go?"

"Alters integrate sometimes," Dr. E said. "When you no longer need them, they—disappear. They aren't gone forever, but they are no longer at the forefront of your consciousness. Perhaps Shilo, who had handled all your medical trauma for you before you even knew about DID, realized that you could handle medical trauma by yourself."

"I don't know if this is trauma," I said. "Plus, I'm not handling anything well. Am I?"

"Having incurable cancer is most certainly a form of trauma," Dr. E said. "And given the circumstances? You're handling it better than most. You have to give yourself some credit. Why not do something fun for yourself right now, or good for you and your family?"

When I arrived back at the house, I looked around. If this was going to be our home—whether I lived in it with Toby and James for forty years or four months—then it needed to feel more like our home.

My grandmother had left me some money when she died—not a lot, but enough to take care of James' education for a few years and to do some other, minor things. I called a contractor.

"What do you want done?" he asked.

"The entire kitchen and bathroom," I said. "I need a wall knocked down. Our bathroom hasn't been updated since the house was built in the 1950s. It all has to go. It needs to be new."

Matt, the contractor, came over and gave us a reasonable price. I shook hands, and we signed the paperwork. Within two weeks, we'd have a modern kitchen that opened up into the living room, as well as a bigger, updated bathroom.

The only thing left to do with the house was some landscaping and finishing the large basement, but that could wait. We needed the kitchen and bathroom more.

The summer was a mess of dust, noise, and pipes flying out of our bathroom window. We lived in a hotel for a week while some of the major work took place. But when it was finished, we came home to a different house. The old green kitchen floor had been ripped up and replaced with white Pergo. Everything was blue and white—a beach theme, to remind me of the ocean, and how connected I felt to it. The bathroom was done in marble with bronze fixtures. It was beautiful, bigger, and functional. I wanted to cry, but instead, I wrote a large check, thanked Matt and his crew for giving us a beautiful home, and realized that my grandmother would have been happy. She would have wanted us to have felt at home. And now, we could.

With only a few weeks until James was to start private Pre-K at the church, we had a lot to do. Despite the fact he was three, he had to be tested, and he tested at an incredibly high level—he would fit in better with six or seven-year-old kids, the principal told me. But socially, he was shy. Daycare hadn't taken that out of him. He was in love with life, adored animals and nature, and wanted to build and solve math problems, but people under the age of eighteen were annoyances. Considering that a lot of kids annoyed me, too, I laughed and enrolled James in his first year of Pre-K. And then, I spent two hundred dollars on uniforms—complete with white polo shirts for three-year-olds. Did they think we owned stock in stain removal spray?

Right before school started, I received a call from my endocrinologist. "So, your last ultrasound of your neck showed something a bit—abnormal," she said. "I think we need to talk about it."

"You have my attention," I said. "Tell me."

"Maybe you should come in."

"No. You can tell me now."

"The lymph nodes in your neck are growing. Their size is twice what it was last year at this time. And when I combine that with your lab work, it doesn't look good."

"The cancer has spread, hasn't it?"

"I think so. I mean, the radiation didn't get all of that tiny piece of remaining thyroid tissue," she said. "I think more radiation, at a clinic, may help you."

"Will insurance cover it?"

"That's what I'm going to find out. I just needed your approval."

I said yes, and she made the calls. When I told Toby, he was surprised, but I told him not to worry yet. I was functional—more so than I'd been last summer, or even a few months ago—and despite the absence of the PICC line, my TSH was hovering around one hundred. I hadn't gone into a coma state recently.

But I still felt the PICC in my arm sometimes—a phantom pain. I'd wake up in the middle of the night to readjust some of the tubing, and realize it wasn't there. And in a way, it hurt. The absence of the device hurt. But I couldn't explain why.

Insurance approved ten radiation treatments, and my endocrinologist scheduled me to go to a clinic once a week for ten weeks, starting in September, to have them performed. I said I'd go.

I was alone in the house, and for the first time since June, I cried.

I was terrified once again that I was going to die. No one could save me from this.

ON THE NIGHTS WHEN INSOMNIA HIT ME THE WORST—WHICH happened almost every night—I'd walk to the local Rite-Aid, buy something I didn't need, and walk home. Then I'd fall asleep on the couch. I could have walked around the corner to the bedroom, but I didn't want to. I wanted to watch reruns of sitcoms, laugh at something stupid, and feel connected to a world that was a lot better than my own.

James began school, and loved it. And at nights, after I told Toby that I felt lost and needed something to entertain me, we started watching *Battlestar Galactica*.

"We watched this with Catie in 2009," he said. "But I'm guessing you don't remember it."

"Not a thing," I said.

But I was intrigued. A space drama—remade from a 1970s version that had somewhat flopped after the first season—that dealt with fifty thousand people having to relocate their lives aboard spacecraft due to a hostile takeover? With political intrigue, emotional drama, some definite dissociation, and a very good team of actors, writers, directors, and musicians? I was immersed in every episode. I identified with the wayward rogue, Starbuck, a smart-ass pilot with a traumatic past and an even more intriguing present. And I identified with Six—a Cylon model sent to corrupt and seduce a man to save her species. But she had a human side, too, and her ability to love as well as feel rage, pain, hatred, and confusion captivated me. This beautiful, sly blond woman was everything I wanted to be.

It took us weeks to get through the show, but when we did, I sobbed at the finale. "I'm Six," I told Toby. "And not in some DID way. I just—am."

I had a little bit of hair—enough so I didn't have to wear wigs. Radiation was making it brittle, but the treatments weren't as horrid as I'd expected, so I found the nearest salon, showed them a picture of Six's hair, and said, "I really want you to do that. Whatever it takes."

My hair was a light brown and roughly to my ears. It wouldn't be long and curly, down to my shoulders, but the stylist bleached it and curled it, and suddenly, I felt better about how I looked. I felt motivated. Despite the dizziness from treatment and my constantly changing thyroid hormones, I didn't feel as ugly.

I met some people online who were as into the series as I was, and I connected with them. When I wasn't with James, doing homework (Pre-K homework baffled me, as it seemed unnecessary), or spending time with Toby, I was talking *Battlestar*. Nothing had connected with me in the way that show did, with the exception of Coheed and Cambria's music.

Just as things—even with the radiation—seemed to be okay, and as fall started to turn into the colder, harsher winter that always threatened my existence, I received an odd message.

It was from Starlight Boy. He had heard through friends that I was dealing with cancer, and he wanted to know how I was.

The smarter person in me told me not to reply. The person who still felt some odd, manipulated connection to him told me to message him back.

And Ruby made the final call. "Do it," she said. "He was an asshole, but he loved me. You should know how much."

"Don't talk to me as though you aren't me!" I yelled. "Stop! You've been doing this my whole life! Why don't you ever go away?"

"Because you need me. I'm stronger than you are."

"Give me time. I'll prove you wrong."

But the message was sent to Starlight Boy. It was a simple hello and a wish that he was well.

Nothing ever ends that easily, though. And I'd been a fool to think it could.

"YOU HAVE TO SHUT HIM DOWN," DR. E SAID TO ME AS I READ HER the messages from Starlight Boy. "Stop engaging in this."

"But Ruby wants to know if he ever loved her. And he won't answer."

"Then she'll have to live with her doubts."

"You know she won't. She'll keep doing this, and then she'll block it from me. I don't want to lose co-consciousness with her. I feel like we can—kind of trust one another this way."

"But Ruby *is* you," Dr. E said. "Granted, she's her own identity, but you made her. Have you ever considered saying *we?*"

"We? As in, 'My fucked up alters and I made a decision. We've decided to contact him.'"

"You aren't just you. You are part of something greater—this system that you created, and that you need."

"I can't say we. I'm me. My own person."

"And to the alters, they're their own people, too. Why do you think they're sometimes confused when they come out and aren't wearing their clothing? Or don't have the hair they're used to? Or freak out when you change something about yourself—like another tattoo?"

Madeleine hated my tattoos. I had twelve by now, all signifying memories that I didn't want to forget. But she hated them. They all did have their preferences, and catering my closet to at least ten alters who regularly presented themselves wasn't an easy task. Nor did I want it to be. I didn't want them to own my life.

"What do I do about Starlight Boy?" I said. "That's the big issue."

"I already told you," Dr. E said. "Shut it down."

It wasn't that easy. But one night, I knew what I had to do: I knew Ruby had to end it.

I played a song that was something Starlight Boy and I had intimately shared. And it triggered me. It sent me spiraling into a depression so deep that Ruby came out, and she completely took over.

While I didn't know it at the time, the plan had worked perfectly. I knew what my triggers were. I just hadn't expected to use them against myself.

"I can't let it go," she said in her email to Starlight Boy. "You loved me so much during those three years. And now, you won't admit to it. Why?'

"Because it was wrong," Starlight Boy replied. "You treated Toby like crap."

"I did?" Ruby wrote. "Aren't you the one who claimed to be my husband? Aren't you the one who called him a monster and wanted to take me away? You manipulated me!"

"I may have been wrong, but you caused it. You caused everything."

"You didn't love me because it was wrong?"

"No, I..."

"Say it," Ruby wrote.

"I loved you until I knew you were crazy!"

Ruby left, and I sat there, dizzy, with my typical post-switch headache. And I read everything. Starlight Boy had loved me—until I was "crazy." I was fine when I was physically ill with MS, Lupus, and Hashimoto's, and I was fine with bipolar disorder, depression, and anxiety. But suddenly, with DID and PTSD, I was "crazy?"

I calmly replied. "You were in love with me from 2008 to about early 2011?"

"Yes," Starlight Boy wrote. "I would have married you. If you'd been single, you would have been my wife. I loved you. And part of me still loves some of those memories we made."

My heart ached a bit, but I had to end this. "Do you want to remain friends?"

"Well, yes. I don't really have anyone in my life right now. I need someone."

And that's when I knew I was over it. Even better, I could hear Ruby. She was finished, too. She'd had enough of his manipulation and need.

"That's not good enough for me," I said. "I don't want to be a backup friend just because you feel lonely. Maybe we had love once. I'm certain we did. But that's over now. A part of me will always miss you, but otherwise—goodbye, Starlight Boy."

I blocked him from contacting me, shut my computer, and reclined on the couch.

I knew that it was finally over. The memories could haunt me. But his absence would not.

RADIATION GAVE ME HEADACHES, DIZZINESS, AND SOME NAUSEA, BUT otherwise, I tolerated it. When my parents invited Toby, James, and I down to their new house in St. Michaels—something they'd bought and renovated—we accepted. We'd leave right after Christmas.

But I hadn't been in a car for two and a half hours in years. I started having panic attacks. Dr. Housel gave me a few extra Valium, and Dr. E told me to focus on something other than the car. I could sing, or talk, or remember that I'd be standing by the bay.

Instead, as we crossed the bridge to the Eastern Shore, I dissociated and let Carmen handle it. But luckily, no one caught on. She stayed quiet, and when I came to, I was staring at crystal-clear water. The smell was in the air. It wasn't the beach, but it was another type of home.

Being in St. Michaels was a dream. It had everything I wanted, and the hospital was only twenty minutes away. My parents' new house was gorgeous, and their property overlooked a large portion of water leading directly out into the Chesapeake Bay. I sat in the living room, staring out the window, watching the water lap against the shore.

And despite how sick I felt, Toby and I visited the local coffee shop and the winery. We explored the town, and I knew I had to write about it. I had to tell its story.

"Think we can move here some day?" I asked him. "I finally feel at home."

"Only if you sell enough books," he joked.

The New Year greeted us, and Toby, my parents, and I raised glasses of rich Chocolate Zinfandel in the air and talked about the future.

I was still alive. And I was told I'd be dead by the end of 2015.

"You're a walking miracle," a friend of mine said. "Keep proving them wrong."

And that was exactly what I intended to keep doing.

JANUARY 1, 2016–SEPTEMBER 10, 2016

On the return from St. Michaels, James asked us if he could ride home with my parents. They agreed, and that gave Toby and I time to talk about what we wanted to do in the new year.

"Live," I said. "And watch *Battlestar Galactica* again. But, mostly, live."

He laughed. "Then keep proving your doctors wrong. You have a million reasons to live."

And I did. "But if I'm going to live," I said, "some things have to change. And they have to change this year."

"Oh? Big things?"

"Yes."

And so I made my list—not of resolutions, but of things that I would make sure would happen.

First, I would finish radiation treatments. Maybe I wouldn't be cured, but I would finish treatments. Then, I would get my doctors to approve me to begin exercising. I wanted to lose the sixty pounds cancer had given me. I needed to reclaim my body. I would also cut down on how much sugar I put into my coffee and try to stick to the things that made me feel healthy—limited choices, but still, I had a few options. And above all, I would make sure that James had a fantastic year. He'd have a healthier, fun mom. We'd go do something together. It was time.

When radiation treatments finished in late January, my endocrinologist told me I'd had enough. If that wouldn't eradicate the remaining tissue or help with the enlarged lymph nodes, nothing would. As long as I kept fighting, I'd keep living on borrowed time—and that could be a month to ten years. She didn't know.

"Am I still incurable?" I asked.

"I don't like that word," she said. "I think you have cancer and need to be careful. And be grateful for whatever time you have."

I already was, but I made a point of going to church to express my gratitude to the universe at large. I sang in the choir, my voice stronger again. I was able to perform a few solos. And then, after speaking to my regular doctor, I was given the green light: I could walk on a treadmill for twenty minutes a day.

Toby and I had started to do some more work inside the house—painting the rooms, mostly, to reflect our style—so the idea of walking on a treadmill for twenty minutes after painting a kitchen seemed like nothing. I went out, found the cheapest treadmill I could buy, and Toby carted it home and placed it in the cool basement.

I could tell my TSH was off. But I didn't care. I got on the treadmill, and I walked.

But I only lasted ten minutes. Discouraged, I hopped on the scale.

I weighed one hundred and ninety pounds. I'd never been so heavy in my entire life.

"Sixty-five pounds," I said to myself. "You will do this by October, on your thirty-fifth birthday."

And I climbed back on the treadmill and walked another ten minutes.

James was doing very well in school, but I started to notice that he was withdrawing on an emotional level. When I asked why, he mentioned that a kid in his class, who was a year older, gave him a hard time. But when I confronted the teacher, she said, "Oh, boys will be boys. The Lord made them all to be good."

Clearly, this teacher had never met some of the boys I'd known.

I vowed to keep an eye on the situation, and I bonded with my friend Rob online about how amazing *Battlestar Galactica* was. I'd taken a recent picture with my blond, curly hair, and he deemed me to be the ultimate copy of the seductive Cylon Six. It was a flattering comment, considering I needed to lose one third of my entire body weight to even be close to her size.

But every night, when I climbed on the treadmill, I thought about Starbuck's strength and Six's measures to unite the galaxy. "They wouldn't give up," I told myself. "No matter how cold or sick I am, I won't give up, either." My heart rate often jumped to 160 beats per minute, and I was disgusted when I saw my flesh—why hadn't anyone told me what had become of me?—but I kept walking.

I lost twelve pounds in the first month.

A friend of mine was getting married that July and asked me to be in the wedding party. I agreed, and we all went shopping for brides-maid's dresses. Those twelve pounds took me from a size fourteen to a size ten, but that wasn't good enough for me. I bought the dress and took a picture in it. The plan was to have it tailored to a size six by the wedding. I had four months.

However, as I was forming my team for my third miraculous year of Relay For Life, I started feeling ill. And at the same time, Ritty, my beloved cat, started throwing up blood. At one in the morning, I took her to the emergency vet, where she was diagnosed with a few infec-tions—nothing serious, I was promised—and then, the vet looked at me.

"You are the palest person I've ever seen," she said. "I think maybe you need a hospital more than your cat does."

I drove Ritty home with her medication, and when I climbed out of the car, I noticed blood dripping down my legs. But I wasn't preg-nant: there was no chance of that now. Something else was wrong. I rushed Ritty inside, and when Toby saw me, he said he'd call 911. But I told him no—I'd go to the hospital myself. I had to do it alone.

When I walked through the doors of the ER, I collapsed.

But I'd only passed out, and when I came to, I was on a stretcher in a room.

"You are tremendously anemic," a doctor said to me. "You need an iron infusion."

"Why am I bleeding?"

"I have no idea. I checked and—there's nothing that would cause you to bleed. But you had a nosebleed, too, when you fainted."

"I have thyroid cancer that spread to my lymph nodes, and my TSH is about one hundred," I said. "Could any of that cause this?"

"Maybe. But that would be an extreme reaction."

I stayed in the hospital for the infusion and some antibiotics, and then, eight hours later, was sent home. "Take it easy" was what the doctor ordered. I wasn't to do anything that could stress my body for at least four weeks.

Screw that, I thought the next night as I climbed onto the treadmill. It's my body. And I'm the only one who can keep it alive now.

In March, as Toby and I were leaving a school function that James' class had put on, I received a phone call from my endocrinologist.

"I don't know what to tell you," she said. "But I've never seen anything like this. Ever."

I grabbed Toby's arm and prepared myself. "What did you find?"

"Your TSH. For the first time in five years, it's at a three. It's within normal range."

"I'm putting you on speaker," I said. "Say that again?"

And when she did, I almost screamed. I don't know how it had happened—probably years of high doses of Synthroid, or maybe cutting down some of the sugar in my body, I honestly had no clue—but it had happened. From three hundred a year before to three. Still not the magic number of one that was the industry standard, but three was pretty perfect.

"That doesn't mean you don't have cancer," she said. "But it's still something good."

"I don't know how to react to this," I said to Toby.

"We'll go get coffee and celebrate. That's how we'll react."

Suddenly, the world seemed—normal. I was losing weight, and my body both felt and looked better. James was doing well in school. Toby's work praised him constantly for doing a great job, and he'd been flying through his Master's classes. We had summer plans. My TSH was good. I had, and saw, many amazing, loving friends. The world was giving me a chance.

And so, I kept busying myself. While James was in school, I wrote short stories and rested my body. At night, when he slept, I walked on the treadmill for an hour and spent time with Toby, or with friends online when Toby went to sleep. I met Rob's new girlfriend, whom we called K, and I fell in love with her spirit and personality. Rob planned to come visit that June.

But then my brain rebelled.

"I don't do normal," Ruby said as she came out one night. She headed into the kitchen to drink some Drano.

Toby stopped her. "You can't do this anymore," he said. "Things are good."

"Too good for you," she said. Her hatred for him was as strong as ever.

"We have to learn to get along. If you're going to be with us forever —we have to."

Eventually, his pleas got to Ruby. "I'll tolerate you."

And to us? That was fair enough.

But the next night offered a bigger surprise when I was triggered by something I'd been watching on TV. I had no memory of what happened, but according to Toby, I came into the bedroom, perched by him, and started talking in cryptic riddles.

"Who are you?" he asked.

"She shall be the one with the Lord when she's called to the light, and all will be well if you can add the three to the six and find the sequence," the new alter said. Then, she left the room.

In the morning, Toby told me about her. "She seems —otherworldly."

"I guess so. And she's part of my head. She lives in that house."

"I wonder where she's been."

"I'm more curious as to why she's coming out. Why do I need her now?"

But we couldn't figure it out. Luckily, Carmen—ever the tattletale—was enticed by a deck of cards one night and came forth to spill her secrets.

"Oh, that's The Omnipotent," she said to Toby as she beat him at a third hand of gin rummy. "She's been around the house forever. Can we go get chicken nuggets?"

"No, Carmen. The body can't have gluten, and it's two in the morning."

"I can eat chicken nuggets in my room," Carmen said, pouting.

"I'm sure you can," Toby said. "But this isn't your room or body right now."

"Oh. Yeah." Neither of us was sure how much the alters understood —or even how much I understood when they appeared—but at least, Ruby aside, no one was harmful.

"Tell me more about The Omnipotent," Toby said. "Please."

"She knows everything. She sees everyone in the house. She even knows more than Ruby does, and Ruby hates that so much. The Omnipotent protects us."

"Does she know about things that have happened?"

"Like being hurt, and having that s-e-x thing?" Carmen said. "Yeah. She knows."

"Any idea what her messages mean?"

"No. They're puzzles. They're for you, not me. Hey, can we make coffee drinks?"

Toby couldn't get Carmen to give up more information on The Omnipotent, but in the morning, when he told me what he had learned, I was stunned.

"I have—God living in my head?" I asked.

"Seems that way."

"But I don't see myself as God," I said. "Not even close."

"You might not. But wouldn't something like a god protect you?"

He had a good point, though we were both still puzzled by her message.

By the time Relay For Life approached in early May, I was ready to take to the track. The goal was to walk 10,000 steps. But before we picked up Toby's mom, who was part of our team, from the airport, I stepped on the scale.

I'd lost forty-eight pounds in five months, and was seventeen pounds away from my goal.

"I didn't starve myself," I said to Toby. He hugged me.

"I know," he said. "You're amazing."

"You know that I've never deserved you, right? That you should have left me a long time ago, well before we knew I had DID. I'm not amazing. I'm just some broken-up girl."

"But you're wrong," Toby said. "No matter what we've dealt with, we've always loved each other. I've never seen you as broken. I see you as the person who helped me find a career path, who guided me through school, and who saved me from my own broken-up life when we met in 2003."

"You don't think I'm a failure at life? Or at us?"

"No," Toby said. "I think that you, parts and all, are the person I love."

I held the banner at Relay For Life again, celebrating my third year as a cancer survivor, and walked fifteen thousand steps with Toby, my mother in law, and Lee.

Maybe this was the person I was supposed to be, I thought. Finally, I had become a better person, once the After had the right chance to begin.

EVERYTHING CHANGED A WEEK LATER.

James came home from school in tears. And when I found out what was wrong, and looked at his uniform and face, I was filled with rage. The kid who had been bullying him since February was still doing it. James had footprints on his back, mud on his face—from being pushed down and shoved into it, he told me—and a bruise on his arm.

I went into the school the next day, and the teacher again told me that "boys will be boys."

"No," I said. "Boys will be human beings. This is bullying. It stops now."

"They're just playing," she said. "It's God's way. Let them be."

"God's way is a way of kindness," I said. "I don't know what kind of God you believe in, but this? This attitude? Accepting that my kid is getting pushed around and you don't want to handle it? This is bullshit."

I went to the principal next, and while he was compassionate, he repeated the same thing. "Kids don't know how to bully when they're four," he said. "They're just playing."

"When my child comes home crying, afraid to go to school the next day, that's not playing," I said. "That's bullying."

"If it was, we wouldn't tolerate it."

"Well, you are."

"Are you accusing me of something?" he asked.

"Yes. Of being negligent. If I see one more mark on my son, I'm pulling him out of this school, and we will not be returning."

The next day, James was crying. "He called me a fat baby," James said. "And then he punched me in the stomach."

I looked at my tall, athletic, beautiful, smart, kind child, and felt rage. I put him in the car, and we drove back to the school. I marched into the principal's office, told him what James had told me, and said, "So are you going to tell me that's not bullying?"

"It's just something the child picked up at home. Have some compassion for him."

"No! My child is being hurt every day. You have compassion for *him!*"

"They'll work it out. It's the end of the year. Boys will..."

"Don't even bother. I'm withdrawing James immediately. I expect to be refunded the tuition for the rest of the month."

"But then he won't be in Pre-K!"

"He will be in the fall. At a different school."

And with that, we never returned to the campus, or the church, again.

"James," I said that evening, "no one has the right to treat you like that. This is your body. Your mind is your mind. No one can touch you without your permission. I want you to understand that and to know Daddy and I love you and trust you. You did nothing wrong."

"I am a stupid fat baby," he said and pounded his fists against his legs. "I should die."

I gathered my son—my only child, the only thing that really mattered to me—into my arms. "I love you," I said. "And while we all make mistakes, you are perfect to me. Do you understand? You're too special to die."

"But you have cancer, Mommy. Aren't you going to die?"

I hugged him again. "I know you've seen some scary things, and I'm sorry. I wish I could take them back. But look at Mommy now. She likes to run! Her hair is growing! She doesn't go to the doctor every day! Isn't that a good thing?"

"Well," James said. "I can stay alive if you can."

"That's a deal."

I took the rest of James' tuition money and hired a nanny to come three days a week from May through August. That way, I'd have time to do what I needed to do—rest, see doctors, work out, and write— while James could stay at home and play with someone else.

But where would he go to school in the fall? Toby looked at the options in our little Baltimore town. The elementary school already had a gang. The other Pre-K program filled up months ago. We had two options left: to pay twenty thousand dollars a year to send him to a top-notch private school or to drive him back and forth to my home-town, twenty miles away, five days a week.

"We can't afford to pay that kind of money for school, especially Pre-K," I said. "We'll be broke before he's in first grade."

"But we can't drive twenty miles one way just to drop him at school, either," Toby said. "You don't get up early enough to take him, and it would tear our cars apart within a year."

"Well, then, if we're going to do the right thing for James, I guess we only have one option left."

"What's that?"

I hadn't been drinking much recently, but during that conversation, I'd gone through a few bottles of gluten-free cider. I set my bottle on the table and looked at my husband.

"We move," I said. "We sell this house—the one we just fully renovated—and we go."

"Do you want to?"

"I don't think we have a choice. He needs a good school system. We need to be in an area where there are kids, and there aren't any in this neighborhood. And honestly, we need more space. One bathroom isn't going to cut it much longer."

"But we'll be far from the good hospitals and your doctors."

"Not if we move back to my hometown," I said.

I contacted Dan, our former mortgage broker, and we discussed options. We spoke to a good real estate agent. And by the end of May, we were set.

We were leaving Baltimore, and all the memories of my illness, behind.

THINGS WERE CALM AS WE STARTED TO PREPARE FOR THE MOVE, BUT then, a couple of events occurred that almost put me back into a psychiatric facility.

As we were staging the house—putting most of our pictures, books, and prized belongings into myriad storage units—Ritty started getting sicker. She left blood everywhere she walked. I rushed her to the emergency vet again, and after several scans, the doctor told me that she had bladder cancer.

"Is she in pain?" I asked. But I already knew the answer. Ritty had lost twenty-five percent of her body weight in the past week. She climbed into my lap and simply sat there. The cat I had known and loved for nine years had already left us.

"She doesn't have a good quality of life," the doctor said. "Why don't you sleep on the decision tonight?"

At first, we thought she'd be okay. But the next morning, as Ritty heaved and stopped going to the bathroom, we knew what we had to do.

To shield James from her death, we had him say goodbye to her before she was given the injection. James held her and cried. "You're the best kitten ever," he said, and I sobbed, too. My child was in agony, and my heart was breaking as well.

Toby took James to dinner while the vet prepared for Ritty to pass. I held my cat and sobbed into her fur. "I'm so sorry," I said. "Cancer is a fucking bitch. I'm sorry, you know. I love you so much. I'm glad you chose me to raise you. And if you're ready to go, I understand. You don't have to be here, in pain, for me. I will always love you."

She looked into my eyes, and right before the vet prepared the injection, Ritty died in my arms.

The next few days were a blur as I sobbed and wondered why I'd missed Ritty's illness. I had cancer. Why didn't I know that she had been suffering, too?

I didn't even have time to process Ritty's death before the painters arrived to touch up a few rooms in our house. Before going on the market, we needed to brighten up some areas, and I was too emotionally drained to even consider it. I hated to throw money at the problem, but in this case, I had no qualms with doing so.

The painters arrived early, and as Toby left for work and the nanny took James out for the morning, I went into James' bedroom—one of the rooms that wouldn't be painted—to sleep.

I woke up with one of the painters on top of me, but thought it was a dream. And somehow, dizzy and feeling as though maybe that second Valium to help me sleep through the noise had been a bad idea, I fell asleep again.

The next day, I had fingerprint bruises all over my inner thighs. There were bruises on my stomach and breasts. I was sore.

When I showed Toby, he stood there in shock. But all I could say was, "Again?"

I blanked out and let Madeleine take me to the hospital. She endured the rape exam and questioning. And when enough evidence was found to prove that yes, I had been raped that morning, I was asked if I wanted to press charges.

"No," Madeleine said. "I think it's best to leave it alone. We have to do that right now."

I would have said otherwise, but since she was part of me, I had no say in the matter at that time.

But the morning-after pills, the antibiotics to prevent possible STDs, and the "comfort kit" from our local Rape Crisis center—a center my Grandmama had helped create when my mom had been harmed as a teenager—was enough to remind me that I couldn't let it go. And I couldn't let it go after I posted a picture of those items on Facebook, explaining the rising epidemic of rape and how we needed to be a more compassionate culture. When the post went viral, the flashbacks started.

The police had contacted our nanny to ask her if she'd seen anything the morning I'd been raped. She said no, and via text, quit.

I had never been so ready to move out of that house as I was then. It hadn't felt like home in a while, but now? It felt like a prison. It wouldn't let me move forward. We had to go.

AFTER THE REAL ESTATE PICTURES WERE TAKEN—DURING A CHAOTIC visit from my friend, Rob, who decided he'd spend most of his time bad-mouthing his girlfriend and trying to pull me into bed with him, claiming me to be his "thin, blond Cylon angel"—and the listing was written, we were on the market. Within the first week, we had several showings, but every potential buyer was deterred by the one bathroom.

We had to head to a different city to be in the wedding of two of our dear friends, but when we left, I felt heavy-hearted. We weren't going to sell this house. No one wanted it, despite how amazing the pictures had looked and how much work we had put into it.

My bridesmaid's dress had to be taken in, as I had hoped. When I had tried it on that February, I was barely squeezing into a size ten. But when I had it altered, the seamstress told me that it was now a size four. I stepped on the scale before departing for the wedding, and I was finally a healthy weight for my height.

I'd done it. I was seven pounds from my goal. All of that hard work —eating better, drinking less sugar in my coffee, two-hour-a-day workouts—had paid off. I was in the best shape I'd been in since 2010, and this time, I hadn't starved myself to get there. I had earned my success.

The wedding was a beautiful, lavish event, and my two friends were

396 • A.E. HAYES

so happy to finally marry one another. Everything was coordinated well, and the hotel they'd chosen was charming. Even at the rehearsal dinner the night before, when I realized we were going to an Italian restaurant and that I couldn't eat, drink, or touch anything due to my severe Celiac disease, a fellow bridesmaid got the server to hand us an unopened bottle of wine and a Styrofoam cup with a straw, and she gave it to me so I could participate in the dinner. The mood was light, and I was so grateful to be part of that fun, lovely occasion. Everything seemed perfect.

Despite some physical pain from being on my feet all day during the wedding, I smiled and pretended I was fine while I spent most of my time with Toby and James. Then, my phone rang. It was our realtor.

Toby took the call, and when he came back, he was smiling. "We have an offer," he said. "Less than three weeks to the day of the listing, and we have an offer."

We enjoyed the rest of the reception, crashed into bed that night, and called the realtor Monday morning.

And it was a lowball offer. There was no way we could accept it. We'd walk away with less than we'd spent just to update the bathroom.

We countered. And since the housing market in our area was hot—homes were selling anywhere between one and four weeks on average—the buyers accepted the deal. We'd walk out with close to enough for our down payment. Contracts were drawn, and come late August, we could move.

And we'd be homeless.

Panicked, we decided to start looking for homes in my hometown immediately. We didn't have long. And because we wanted a safe, community-oriented neighborhood for James, we toured a house in a planned suburban community. The house was a wreck—we later learned it had been abandoned for three years—but there was so much room. We could grow with this house. And so, without looking further, we put in an offer, and it was accepted.

But because the new house needed so many renovations, we couldn't live there right away. Some things we could do—paint, for instance—but busted windows, a dirty HVAC system, and a water-damaged ceiling? Those we had to leave for a contractor.

Most things went on my credit cards, and between the new house, moving from the old house, living in a hotel during some of the renovations, and buying all new appliances, carpets, and furniture that would fit the house, I found myself staring at mounds of bills.

"Okay," I said, paying some of them off that August. "Moving is expensive. But this could be worse. We had people to help us. We closed. Our neighbors are nice. James will be safe and make friends. No one cares if I'm in debt—I don't work. We will get through this."

When September arrived and we started to move some items into the house, I was relieved. The worst was past us. We were starting over. No one could hurt me here. I was thin, healthier than I'd been in years, and in a safe community for my son.

But going home again proved that it wasn't all I had hoped. And by the second week of September, the start of the disasters began to rain down upon us, and they threatened to ruin everything we'd worked so very hard to achieve.

W e were very lucky to become friendly with our neighbors when we moved in—in fact, people were thrilled that we'd purchased the old, dilapidated home and were working to restore it. It had been the community eyesore, one of our neighbors told me. They were grateful to us for taking a chance to rehabilitate it.

Toby and I quickly bonded with a couple down the road who had kids around James' age. What a perfect scenario, I thought to myself: dinners with these people as our kids play. It wasn't a long walk to their house, and in a safe neighborhood such as this one, we were lucky that our kids could go outside and roam the streets. It did take me a short bit to get over the fact that the neighbor's name was Thomas—the same name as the man who raped me when I was fourteen—but he struck me as docile, and I knew I had nothing to fear.

Up on a ladder the next day, painting one of the highest points of our ceiling, I began to smell something burning. Odd, I thought. I'd been singing along to music streaming from my iPhone, immersed in the task of making the house beautiful, and since our appliances weren't in yet, I had no idea what I was smelling. It must have been in my head.

"You're going to fall," Shilo said.

Stunned to hear her voice, I turned, as though expecting to see an actual person. But then, I felt an aura. I hadn't had a seizure in a while, but I knew what was about to happen.

And when I woke up, I was in Shock Trauma in Baltimore, with my neck in a brace.

It took hours for me to become coherent, but when I could finally talk—I couldn't feel my right leg, but at least I could speak—I asked what had happened.

"From what we could gather from your husband, you had a seizure, fell from the ladder, hit another ladder below that one, and landed on the unfinished floor of your new home," the doctor said. "You were still in the middle of a seizure when he called 911, and we had to airlift you here for treatment—the local hospital wasn't equipped to handle the extent of your fall."

"Airlift? In my neighborhood?" Nothing was adding up for me.

"No," the doctor said. "An ambulance took you to a field, and then, a helicopter flew you from there to Baltimore."

I'd been in a helicopter and had no memory of it. I'd lost several more hours of my life to injury.

And then I started to panic: did I have amnesia again?

But neurological testing, as well as a CT, revealed that I did not. I could name the month, the president, and my birthday. I could remember what I'd been doing beforehand. I knew who Toby was.

And I remembered hearing Shilo. But she'd been gone.

I needed to find a new, local psychologist soon. Something was happening to me.

Luckily, I didn't break my neck or spine, which was what the doctors originally thought. I walked—or, rather, rolled—out of Shock Trauma with a paralyzed leg, two sprained wrists, a mild concussion, and a ton of bruising. But by God or by luck, I was generally okay, and my leg would have feeling again in a few days.

Thomas, our neighbor, came over and took pity on me. He'd hang out on the porch and talk to me as I sat there, watching movers bring in beds and chairs, and listened to me as I complained about feeling helpless. It was nice to have someone to keep me company, especially since Toby was overwhelmed with trying to finish the rest of the house on his own.

And just as things had settled, and I was able to walk and lift again, it happened.

Thomas came over, drunk, and sat on the porch. He'd brought beer with him, and he offered me a can. I declined.

"I can't drink beer," I said. "I'm allergic to what's in it."

He winked at me. "Liar."

James was there, and Toby was off getting some items from storage. "Toss the ball with me!" James called to Thomas. They played catch, and as the ball flew back and forth, Thomas revealed himself to be who he truly was.

"I've been watching you," he said. "Taking walks this way, driving past your house. I know when your husband's car is gone. And a girl like you, with those tits? With that body? I know you wouldn't mind a quick fuck when he's gone."

I shouldn't have lost weight, I thought. I shouldn't have come outside. I shouldn't have moved. But I was paralyzed. I'd heard these words before, and they never ended well.

I didn't switch, though. James was there, and I was terrified of what Thomas might do.

Thomas grabbed his penis and started rubbing it in front of us. "God, just looking at you makes me hard," he said. "My wife hasn't let me fuck her in forever. Since the last baby we had. But you? You're probably tight. I would take that pussy and just hammer that tight shit."

I wanted to tell him to shut up. But the part of me that remembered the Thomas from 1996—the one who had told me he'd kill my family if I spoke up—kept me silent.

"The next time Toby's car is gone, I'll come over," Thomas said. "And we'll fuck."

Luckily, Toby arrived home right after that comment and told Thomas not to drink on our porch. I'd already asked that, but he hadn't listened to me. But with Toby it was different. "It's cool," Thomas said. "I gotta go, anyhow." Then he winked at me and strolled down the street.

That night, I told Toby what had happened.

"I'll kill him," he said. "What in the fuck?"

"I guess there's no safe neighborhood anywhere," I said. "How many places can I move to until I find peace?"

"You have to call the cops."

"And tell them what? That he's going to fuck me? He didn't—he just threatened he'd do so when you leave for work."

"He's stalking you. Call the cops."

But after talking to my dad, who told me I should have stood up for myself against Thomas, I didn't say anything. Most of the men in my life didn't understand the paralyzing fear of being told that you were only good for fucking. They didn't understand that "standing up for myself" wasn't easy after being raped and harassed so many times. When men understood this, I was grateful. When they didn't, it felt like misplaced blame. Our culture was failing.

Toby and I bought a security system for our house and agreed that if Thomas came on our property again, we'd call the police.

He didn't, but his wife did, and screamed accusations at me. I'd tried to seduce her husband, she yelled—in front of James and our across-the-street neighbors, whom we barely knew. I was some dumb blond whore. And if I didn't leave him alone, she'd call the police.

"What is this, Dr. Phil?" I said to Toby. But my heart raced. At least James was safe in Pre-K during the day, and Toby was at work, but what was going to happen to me if I was alone?

Right around that time, I found a new trauma psychologist named Dr. Forbes. She had had medical issues in the past, too, and came highly recommended by my psychiatrist, Dr. Housel, so I knew we'd be a good match. And thankfully, I was right. Immediately, we got into my trauma, past and present. We talked about my alters and how they presented.

"I've always wondered this," I said to her, "but I've been afraid to say it."

"What's that?" Dr. Forbes asked.

"How do I know I'm not an alter?" I said. "How do I know Ruby isn't really the person who was born into this body, and I'm really just the cover-up? Maybe I have never existed—I'm the fragment, and not the fragmented, so to speak."

"The alters—at least up to the point that they can, due to your amnesia and brain injury—are giving you memories that you cannot produce yourself," she said. "Or can you remember back to being fourteen?"

"No. That was Ruby's time."

"Do you feel as though you exist as yourself, as your name, and that perhaps you've been victimized so much that it's hard for you to comprehend the full nature of your trauma?"

"Maybe," I said. "But others have had it worse."

"Don't do that," Dr. Forbes said. "Someone will always have it worse. But millions have it better. And the good thing is, I think it will get better from here."

"Even with the cancer?"

She sighed. "Well, that I don't know. The body will do what it wants."

I turned thirty-five that October, and when I stepped on the scale that morning, I was at my goal weight. Despite the hatred, the hard work, the injuries and illnesses that had set me back—I was there. And to celebrate, I pulled out clothing that hadn't fit me since I was seventeen, and Toby and I went out for the evening.

A few days later, as I was getting dressed up to celebrate Halloween with James, Toby, and my family, I felt incredibly dizzy. I had to stop and sit down because I couldn't breathe. I found my rescue inhaler, took a few puffs, and closed my eyes, but nothing could stop me from feeling as though blood was rushing into my ears.

"Call the oncologist," my endocrinologist said to me the next day. "We need to know."

With trembling fingers, I dialed, and I prepared for the worst.

"YOU STILL HAVE CANCER—THAT'S CLEARLY NOT GOING INTO remission," the oncologist said as he examined me. "I want a new scan on your lymph nodes to see if they're growing. But this is something else. And it's probably caused by the cancer."

"What now?" I was so tired, and I was freezing again. November had me in two sweatshirts, a pair of leggings, a pair of sweatpants, and boots. I'd started to write a novel for National Novel Writing Month at our local Starbucks, going there every night for tons of coffee and good conversation to fuel my writing, but usually left when someone stopped me and said, "Your lips are turning blue." I just could not stay warm.

"Severe anemia," he said. "Severe iron-deficient anemia. We're skipping iron infusions and going straight to blood transfusions. You need blood immediately."

"What? It's that bad?" I shivered on the table and thought about the three hundred dollars I'd paid just to see this doctor. I couldn't afford much more. How much was my life worth, anyway?

"You aren't breathing well," he said. "I want you to see a pulmonologist. And yes, it's that bad. Your oxygen saturation is sixty percent. Your red blood cells are too wide. This could cause your heart to stop. We need to begin transfusions right away. We'll do them in the cancer center, and as long as you don't react poorly, you can just get up and drive home when you're finished."

For six weeks, I spent my time wrapped up in blankets on my couch, writing a novel at Starbucks, and receiving blood transfusions. I didn't react poorly to the transfusions, and while they gave me some energy, they didn't help the fact that I was constantly freezing.

"I don't know if that will ever stop," my endocrinologist said. "I think that's just part of who you are now."

"I'm a literal ice queen," I said. "I feel it in my bones."

"Queen Elsa, the Cylon." We both laughed. After several years together, we'd come to regard one another as friends.

We made it through a wonderful Christmas and New Year in St. Michaels—my heart set on moving there one day, as soon as I could afford it—and back at home, my soul was at peace. If 2016 had been such a good year, 2017 had to be better.

Then I stepped on the scale. I'd gained back twenty pounds in two months.

"What the fuck!" I screamed. "All that work for nothing?"

But it was my thyroid, and the lab work confirmed it. My TSH was back to sixty, and the Prednisone I'd been on to fight it wasn't helping anything, weight or otherwise.

"One more coma may be all it takes," I remembered a doctor saying to me.

I prayed that that coma wouldn't come. That couldn't happen. I'd made it to 2017—two and a half years after I was told I was supposed to die. One freezing winter would not defeat me and all I'd worked for. I'd get back on the treadmill, remember my reasons for living the way I had lived in 2016, and fight like hell.

But then my temperature dropped, my bones turned to ice, and I fell asleep for two weeks. And no one could wake me.

AT FIRST, I HAD SOME TROUBLE REMEMBERING WHAT HAD HAPPENED. Had I dissociated? Was James okay? Why was it suddenly warm out? But it was February, and we were in the middle of an odd warm spell that had people outside with their lawn mowers. I'd just lost that much time. But I had lived. Despite the cancer that I knew would always rage throughout my body, and the myxedema coma states that would plague me every winter, I was determined to live.

And once it was warmer, I was determined to drop those twenty pounds, too.

I put the finishing touches on the novel I wrote in November of 2016, and then put it aside in a briefcase. The story was about St. Michaels—a literary piece about a fictional coffee shop, the people who owned it, and the town that rallied around it. One day, I'd let my story see the light. But for now, I had to focus on resting so that I'd get through the remainder of the winter.

But toward the end of winter, we met Kara.

Toby met her, anyhow. I knew nothing of her, and her existence still plagues us to this day.

I'd been upstairs, changing, trying to find something warmer to wear when I saw Doo-Da in front of me.

"Am I dead?" I asked him. "Am I with you?"

"You're just on the floor," he said. "Sophie's here."

"You know my daughter?"

"She's beautiful. Her eyes change color like yours do, my girl. But for now, just keep singing. Don't stray from that path. And write. Make me proud."

"I promise."

"See you soon."

And then, he was gone.

But I was still gone, too, lost in some odd darkness. I had no sense of direction whatsoever.

As I wandered in a completely black headspace, Toby met Kara. He found her in the closet, and she sat up.

"Oh!" she said. "I'm not used to a body like this."

Toby helped her stand, and while she commented that the house was as she'd seen, she wasn't accustomed to taking on a "human form." Then, she spoke about the blessed child.

"What child?" Toby asked. "James?"

"Oh, yes. We all know about him. He is destined to do great things. And if he doesn't, we fear he'll die."

She left the bedroom and walked in to see James, fast asleep in his bed. He was five, big and tall, and healthy as any parent could have hoped. Kara brushed his forehead, kissed his hair, and said, "You will light the way."

Back in the bedroom with Toby, she gave him a revelation.

"I have to tell you I'm not coming back for a while," she said. "I'm only here as needed."

"You're in my wife's brain and body," Toby said. "I know how DID works."

Kara smiled. "This isn't DID," she said. "I know your grandparents —Anna and Clarence, right? They died a while back. But they're okay. They're safe."

"How would you know..."

"Shh," Kara said. "It's going to be fine now. I'll be back when I'm needed again. Take care of that child. He will suffer, but then, he will do things beyond your comprehension."

Toby said that when I returned, my eye color had changed. Something about my body looked different. And when he told me about Kara, I was confused.

"I thought I was dying," I said. "I saw Doo-Da. And he knows Sophie."

"I don't know what Kara is," Toby said, "but—I'll never be able to explain that."

"She's an alter. She has to be."

"I know, but if you had seen her, you would have thought otherwise. Her voice wasn't close to yours. The other alters have different voices, but I can still hear your tone. With her? It wasn't you. I'm telling you it wasn't."

"Then who was it?"

But we never knew. And we never saw her again.

The next day, I received a necklace in the mail—no sender, no label, nothing. It was a simple circle on a chain, and written on it was the word "harbinger."

Either someone was playing a very cruel joke on us, or we'd just been through something that we would never be able to explain.

IN THE NON-DYING AND NON-DID WORLD, OUR NEIGHBOR THOMAS was stalking me again. He'd drive by and leer. He'd find a reason to stand on our front lawn or driveway. And when we asked him to move, he grew confrontational.

That was when I had it. I went to the courthouse and filed a peace order, stating that he needed to stay off my property and leave me alone.

When the first judge heard the story of why I wanted Thomas to leave me alone, and why I needed a legal document to keep me safe, he granted it to me. "But for two weeks," he said. "Then there will be a trial, and Thomas will present his side as well."

I prepared myself. I dressed in a suit, and with my briefcase in hand —along with photos I'd captured from our security system on the house, proving he was stalking me—I entered the courtroom two weeks later.

The second judge listened to Thomas as he spouted a sob story. He'd been unfairly accused of sexual harassment and assault, he said. Girls liked him; he couldn't help it. He was a good family man. He'd just been keeping an eye on me since he knew I had a seizure disorder. Plus, his ailing, dying father-in-law who somehow made it to court that day could prove Thomas was a good, hardworking man. I wanted to roll my eyes, but I kept myself in check. I'd met Thomas' father-in-law. The man in the courtroom wasn't him. And Thomas didn't have a job. He told me he'd been fired from a sales position after he had sex with a seventeen-year-old employee—a fact he'd been proud of but that hadn't made the boss very pleased.

But when I presented my evidence, the tone changed.

"You will leave her and her child alone," the judge said. "You will not step foot on their property again. She has every right to feel safe in her home, on her deck, in her driveway. You make yourself sound like a victim, but you aren't. Stop making her one and let her live her life."

"Thank you, Your Honor," I said. And ten minutes later, I had the peace order in my hands.

I'd won. After thirty-five years of being raped, manipulated, abused, and harassed, I'd won.

And winning fueled me to go forth and start to become a better, stronger person again.

APRIL 13, 2017–PRESENT

Thomas stopped bothering me after the peace order was in full effect, with the exception of a few passive-aggressive drives past my house. But throwing his middle finger out the car window in my direction didn't mean much to me. I had a sheriff on speed dial, and I was finished taking shit from anyone who wanted to dish it out.

And one night, as I was walking out of a major retail store, I had the chance to prove it.

A man coming into the store saw me, whistled, and said, "I'm glad it's summer! Time for girls like you to show their titties! Come closer and let me see them."

"What did you say?" I asked. I let the man approach me and I studied his face. His eyes looked sickly perverse, and I knew I wasn't the only person he'd bothered today.

"I said I want to see those titties. Look at those titties!"

I stepped back, lifted my right leg, and extended it forward, kicking him swiftly in the groin.

"You bitch!" he said, dropping to his knees. "How dare you?"

"How dare *you*," I said. "Think before you speak. You have no right to treat people like objects. I am not here for your pleasure, you sick fuck."

I'd defended myself. Ruby hadn't come forward, Johnny hadn't taken over, and I hadn't been stunned into silence. I had been in charge. I simply did what needed to be done.

I committed myself to another year of Relay For Life—my fourth —and furiously collected donations and started walking to get healthy for the event. I would lose those twenty pounds. I hadn't yet, and I didn't by the time of the event, but I was more immersed in cele-brating the fact that I'd been living with cancer for four years. Once again, I was given the honor to hold the survivor's banner, and the woman who walked beside me told me she was supposed to die at thirty-five—but now, she was sixty, and felt as though she had a good, long life ahead of her.

"I'm thirty-five," I said as we walked.

"No, you aren't! You're twenty-five!"

"I wish. I was healthy then. But I'm thirty-five. My son is five— he'll be six in the fall. And I have to be there for that. For him."

"Oh, honey." She put her arm around my shoulder. "Something tells me that, despite your cancer, you're going to be around for a lot."

I cried during the remainder of the lap, and even though I hadn't lost those twenty pounds, my body was strong, and it carried me twenty thousand steps that night. Lee and I walked together during a lap, and as we linked arms, we joked about pretty nurses in hospitals and how they'd saved my life. Toby carried the caregiver's banner, and my heart melted as a young boy, barely taller than the banner, asked to carry it with him. Toby smiled and nodded, and the two of them walked together, fierce caregivers in a world that so often took away the ones they loved.

Carrie joined Toby and me for the event, and she and I held hands during one of the laps.

"It's hard to believe we've been best friends for twenty-two years," I said.

"I know," she said. "And here we are. You're still here."

"I'm still here. I love you."

"I love you, too, chica."

Toby, James, and I took another trip to St. Michaels, and while there, I was offered two chances to be published: one in a romance anthology (a genre I hadn't written before, but I had never been one to decline a challenge), and another in a horror anthology. One piece was released with a decent amount of success, and the other wasn't set to see the light until 2018. But that was okay, I thought. I have time. I'll make it to see my words, forever enclosed in books.

But with so many writing jobs coming in, and no space for me to work at home, I felt displaced. Toby and I came up with a plan, and he and I—along with an electrician and a very good carpet company—renovated the unused garage into an office. I painted it red, hung *Battlestar Galactica* posters on all the walls, and set up my desk so that I could work.

"You won't fail," Ruby said to me one night as I was researching space travel for a story.

"Did you just compliment me?" I asked her.

"I can see everything now," she said. "We won't let you fail."

Having DID meant I'd never be fully at peace. But at least Ruby and I were on some sort of common ground.

And that was more progress than we'd made in all the decades she'd existed. I was certain I had my psychologist and psychiatrist to thank for that.

I did the math. I hadn't cut or injured myself in three years. I hadn't had the need to be committed to a psychiatric facility since August 2013—right when I was diagnosed with cancer.

Cancer wasn't a blessing, but somehow, it had kept some of the worst memories from taking over my life. It had stopped me from injuring my body. The struggle to breathe, to fight the healthcare system, to win against an oppressive new government—that was what mattered now.

I'd lost two dear friends, Alia and John, to cancer right around the time of Relay For Life. Every time I felt dizzy or nauseated, I thought about them, and how we had all joked that we'd see who would stay alive the longest. Sadly, and filled with survivor's guilt, I was the only one left. But I knew they'd sense I'd continue to fight. Maybe cancer would take me in a month. Maybe it would take a year.

Perhaps it was going to just sit back and wait until I was sixty. But I was going to fight it, along with my other conditions, until I drew my last breath.

James finished Pre-K at the top of his class, doing math years ahead of other kids his age. He was dealing with anxiety problems and asked me to go see some colleges.

"You're five," I said as we drove by a local four-year college. "Don't worry about getting into college yet."

"But I want to go," he said. "And be an architect. And a writer. I want to write like you. Sometimes, I think smart people with broken brains need to write. It's what saves us."

Whoever Kara was or had been, she'd been right. This child was out to change the world. And I loved everything about him in a way that was helping me repair the trauma of my past.

James went with my parents to the Outer Banks for a week—sadly, I hadn't seen the ocean in years, but vowed I would, once my lungs functioned properly again and I stopped passing out frequently—and Toby and I returned to the hotel where our friends had had their lavish wedding the year before.

"I wish I could remember our own wedding," I said to him as we unpacked in the large suite we'd booked for two nights. "I can't remember much at all."

"We can change that," he said, smiling.

I smiled back. "We can change that."

The next day, after we'd had a fun night in the hotel bar and spent far too much money in the shops across the street, we met with the hotel's event planner. She gave us some prices, and told us that a ten-year wedding vow renewal in 2018 sounded lovely.

"Ten years together," she said. "You guys must have it all figured out by now!"

Toby and I glanced at each other and smiled. We had nothing figured out. We'd been through illness, injury, fire, death, cancer, pregnancy loss, an affair, being so broke that we were almost homeless, and DID. He'd seen me in psych wards, banging my head against the wall, and when I came out, he still loved me.

But we had *one* thing figured out. After almost fourteen years together, we still knew how to love one another. And we couldn't wait to start preparing for a wedding that I would remember.

Amnesia and DID—and the trauma of it all—took so much from my life. But it gave me a purpose. It gave me a need to educate others on how DID wasn't a silly genre movie, or a soap opera plot. Amnesia isn't just for a storyline filler. People live with these conditions. People like myself deal with them every day, and will until death. The stigma that plagues those with any sort of mental illness bothered me, and I needed to talk about it. I needed to find a way to say that life was worth it. No matter the situation or how bad things felt, there was some way to hold on, to ask for help, to connect, and to live proudly, despite the illness and fear and darkness.

One night in my office, I sat down and stared at a blank page. And I decided to write a memoir—the story of a random girl with mental health problems, who struggled with madness and moods and multiple personalities, and all the ways that she would forever battle the angels and devils associated with the good and bad things in her life.

There was no choice in the matter, Ruby told me. It had to be written.

It was the right thing to do.

ACKNOWLEDGMENTS

Writing this memoir—going through tons of old journals; gathering old documents such as police reports, psych evals, and medical records from doctors; and talking to friends and family who helped me piece my life together—has been an incredibly painful experience. But at the same time, it has been a rich and rewarding one. Here is a record of my life, in which I am not always the victim, but sometimes the villain. Here is the story of my life, the full truth of my existence, out for all to see. Here is the proof of who I was and who I can still be.

I could not have written this—or even lived to tell this story—without the following people:

I'd be an utter fool if I did not thank my amazing publisher, Terra Publishing/Stars and Stone Books for allowing me to release this darkness and redemption into the world. The genius behind the company, Cara McKinnon—a brilliant businessperson, writer, and an even more brilliant friend—cannot be overlooked. Thank you (for reasons).

Michael Dell at EditOneNine took this wayward beast of a manuscript and breathed some beauty (as well as direction and sense) into it. For that, I am eternally grateful. Thank you for seeing the things I was unable to see, and for giving this massive text a fighting chance.

My hair and makeup artist, Lindsay Mack, and my photographer, Katie Venezia, took my face and body and provided me with a much-needed, updated look (as well as a lot of confidence) for everything regarding the publicity surrounding this book. Thank you for making me feel like a human being (even if I'm secretly a Cylon, ha-ha).

James was cared for by our wonderful nanny and friend, Emily, during the research and writing of this memoir. Thank you so much for filling his days and nights with fun and love.

My medical doctors throughout the years have provided comfort, care, and quality of life, and I would not be here without their assistance. I have no way to name every single one, but I would like to thank Dr. V, Dr. L, Dr. H, Dr. G, Dr. K, Dr. Gr, Dr. F, Dr. A, Dr. M, Dr. W, Dr. R, and Dr. I for your attention to detail—the business of keeping me, and many others, alive.

My psychiatric doctors throughout the years have kept me alive and (passably) sane. A huge thank you goes out to Dr. Housel, who has stuck by me for seven years, always believing that I can find a way to live a good life despite the madness. Dr. Forbes, my wonderful psychologist, helps me find reason within the past and guides me toward a better future. She is warm and compassionate, and gives me a good reason to wake up in the morning. Dr. Palmisano, the first psychologist to diagnose me with a personality disorder, was a kind, reasonable man, and he allowed me to comprehend why I'd randomly wake up in places without any memory of how I got there. He also laughed at inspirational posters with me and gave me a pen that imitated how to correct erectile dysfunction, so, thank you for all of that. There are tons of other doctors to thank as well: Dr. E, Dr. M, Dr. V, Dr. A, Dr. R, Dr. L—a veritable alphabet soup of psychologists, trauma specialists, and psychiatrists, without whom I would have died two decades ago. I am grateful for all of you.

To the hospitals that have kept me alive (and, mostly, to the nurses who have sat by my bedside, giving me reasons to push through the pain)—thank you for your dedication and amazing work. The teams at Johns Hopkins Hospital, GBMC, Sinai Hospital, University of Maryland, Shock Trauma, Northwest Hospital, Carroll Hospital Center,

Sheppard Pratt, Brook Lane, and others I am certain I am forgetting are why I am here to live this life. Thank you all.

I was a college-hopper and never found my academic homes until I studied at three very specific, diverse places: York College, Hood College, and Johns Hopkins University. I sang passionately at York, made lifelong friends and learned proper literary critique at Hood, and wrote with fervor at Hopkins. I am so thankful for those opportunities.

Dr. G, my writing professor at Hood, always believed that I'd be recognized for my writing one day. She even entrusted me to teach one of her classes, and invited me into her home. Her warmth, fortitude, intellect, and passion are things I will forever try to emulate.

Dr. C, my Senior Seminar professor at Hood, pushed me to a reasonable breaking point in order to restore my sanity. During my darkest moments, she gave me Eliot and Woolf, and told me to keep reading, writing, and surviving. I did. I'm glad she never gave up on me, even when I gave her nine hundred reasons to push me away.

Dr. F, my advisor at Johns Hopkins University, stood by me in sickness and in health (in a purely academic way) and encouraged me to keep writing despite the pain. I did, and this is the result. I could not have written such an honest work without his knowledge and kindness.

To all the bands, musicians, and artists who inspired me, either through my writing or throughout my life, I owe you my sincerest gratitude. I would be dead without Coheed and Cambria—Claudio Sanchez, if you ever read this, make sure you know that your amazing story saved my life. Also, the birthday wish from 2009 is still appreciated, ha-ha. The same goes for Green Day, for giving the world *American Idiot* (and giving me a chance to understand living with another personality), and for Disturbed, for fueling my writing and personal life with passion and meaning (as well as awareness about the world around us). Other bands/artists I wish to thank: Snow Patrol, Queens of the Stone Age, Billy Joel, Spin Doctors, Nirvana, Soundgarden (Chris Cornell, I miss you, buddy), Madonna, Stone Temple Pilots, Live, Counting Crows, Kansas, Collective Soul, Alanis Morissette, Edwin McCain, Barenaked Ladies, Linkin Park (Chester, I miss you, too),

Santana, Five for Fighting, Jimmy Eat World, Incubus, Matchbox Twenty, Vertical Horizon, Christina Aguilera, Michelle Branch, The Used, My Chemical Romance, The All-American Rejects, Goo Goo Dolls, Tool, A Perfect Circle, Blink-182, Amy Lee, Jason Mraz, Default, Keane, Breaking Benjamin, Brand New, Dredg, Coldplay, 311, 10 Years, Blue October (Justin, keep fighting the good fight with me!), The Fray, Silversun Pickups, Within Temptation, R.E.M., Killswitch Engage, Middle Distance Runner, Yellowcard, Muse, Third Eye Blind, 30 Seconds to Mars, Christina Perri, Rise Against, Gotye, Fall Out Boy, Imagine Dragons, Sam Smith, Hozier, twenty one pilots, Missio, A Great Big World, and countless others. Thank you for giving me some of my memories back.

This may seem silly at first, but it's not: I have to give an enormous shout-out to the crew (old and new) at the Starbucks in Westminster, MD. You all provided a safe haven for conversation, writing, and attempting to solve every problem in the world. I've written parts of three novels—this memoir included—with you, and am so fortunate for all the laughter and coffee (always Trenta, sadly always decaf, and always with sugar in the raw). I'm sure I'll forget some names by accident, but Cat, Jade, Sara, Amber, Sarah, Tyler, Beth, Nikki, Sami, Paige, Emma, Paula, Linda, Bridgette, Nathan, Heather, Rachel, Korey, Dom, Jace, Cookie, and Nutty make/made my life—my writing life and my personal life—tolerable. You are all amazing.

This may also sound silly as well, but again, it's not: without the amazing writing, directing, acting, and music of the spectacular television series *Battlestar Galactica*, I would not be the person I am today. The series aired from 2004-2009 (I'm a fan of the remake and not the original; my apologies to anyone I've just offended), but even today, I still laugh, cry, and ache with the crew aboard the BSG, as well as with the Cylons. Who would I be without Six, Starbuck, Adama, Roslin, Baltar, Helo, Boomer, Anders, Apollo, and the others? I honestly don't know. I'm grateful that shows like this provided—and still provide—such inspiration and motivation. So Say We All.

Speaking of—hey, my dear friend, Lee? What do you hear? Thank you for being my oldest (in time, not in age!) Starbucks friend and, after all these years, family member. The fact you were willing to visit my sorry, sick, dying brain in the ICU more than once speaks volumes about how awesome you are. Let's have a coffee/hot chocolate date again soon. I'm buying this round.

Faith and Lance—or, as I like to call them, the F. Scotts—have been good, solid, loving friends, both before and after the amnesia. It's been more than ten years now, and I'm still so grateful that we get together for coffee, cards, and conversation as regularly as we can. Thank you for standing by our family, and for all of your love and support.

In my healthier years, I was very fortunate to have a lot of friends who would constantly deal with my craziness—during softball games as a child, or sleepovers as teenagers, or at parties as adults. I'll never be able to list every name, but I am so grateful for Melinda, Danie, Erin, Matt, Mike, Brian, Pete, Phil, Allen, Bob, Lee S, Bev, Eric, Tim, Jason, Jim, Lisanne, Catie, and many others. You all gave—and give—me so much love. My life is richer for that.

It's nice that a lot of my beta readers happen to be good friends, both in real life and online (the world is such a connected place these days). Thanks to the following people for reading, loving, and supporting me, and for asking for updates about everything from my health to the newest pieces I'm writing: Kia, Amy, Brian L, Nicole R, Emily G, Emily M, Jennifer E, Beth S, Beth C, Derrick C, Fiona T, Jack B, Laura B, Gary D, Tracy C, Othella M, Tori U, Willow T, Wolf Q, Jo T, T.H., Amanda H, Alia D (RIP), Morgan G, J.H., Cricket H, John H, Ashleah Y, Davinia F, John B, Ashley V, Marie K, April F, Paige S, John M (RIP), Jenny B, Dom M, Lauren W, Stacey L, Jen T, Jeff G, Jodie L, Jenn M, Sarah R, Ivy S, Monika D, Dana F, Connie M, Kathi B, Jaime K, Dotty D, Debbi B, Dan P, Sarah F, Monica S, Scott S, Milton L, Susan T, Krys R, Jackie B, O.H., Jessica D, Nicole B, Kerry C, Emily K, Emily M, Allie F, Ash W, Laura F, Jamie M, Rebecca M, Jaymz K, David W, Joe N, Destiny L, Samy E.N, Michael C, Cassidy D, Tracie B, Tea B, Etan W, Brittany L, Alyce W, and Peter F. If I've forgotten you, I apologize—it wasn't intentional. Blame amnesia!

To Shayne P and Rachel K—thank you for making the impossible possible. I love you both.

Carrie is my sister in every sense of the word, and after twenty-two years as best friends, I couldn't feel more blessed. You are my forever family, chica, and I love you, Steve (the GOOD Steve, ha-ha), and the kids so very much. Thank you for being the best former roommate, supporter, and duet partner possible. Thanks for the gluten-free cheesecake, the 3:00 a.m. conversations, being one of the only people I can cry in front of, and, most of all, for loving me and not judging me despite a TON of past mistakes. LOVE.

Despite a lot—and if you've read this memoir in full, you know I do mean a *lot*—of past trauma and troubles, my family (aunts, cousins, and so forth) is still here, standing beside me. Not everyone has the opportunity to reconnect with their family, and I'm so incredibly grateful that my parents, M and L, love and support me now for who I am. My apologies for the times it wasn't an easy road; now that I'm a mother, I can understand why you both were confused about my behaviors. I'm sorry. You always have my love, no matter what. And thank you for believing in me and helping me while I wrote this memoir. That means more than I can ever express.

My brother, Booey, and his girlfriend (fiancée? Maybe soon? I need an update!) have been wonderful influences in my life, and it has been an honest, sincere pleasure to watch my brother grow up from a happy little boy with curly blond hair and bright blue eyes into a professional, kind-hearted, sensitive, loving man. You have an emotional fortitude I wish I could capture, Booey. Your love is a gift to the world. Thank you for continuing to love me.

My in-laws, L and C, as well as my brother-in-law, D, have been three of my biggest fans—even from the moment I first met them in 2003. Thank you for standing beside me despite the fact that I almost ruined everything for all of us. And thank you for still loving me today.

I miss my grandparents deeply, and think about them every day. Both of my grandfathers passed in 1999, and both of my grandmothers passed in 2015. I was close to all of them—I don't remember that in most cases, but I know it's true—and I'm so sad that they aren't here to see the person I've become. Even more so, I'm sad that they will never meet my son and get the chance to marvel at how wonderful he is. Doo-Da, my beloved grandfather—you flash into my memory the most. Buying sno-balls, letting me have the change in your pocket, talking openly with me about life and love, supporting me when I thought no one was on my side, and telling me to always pursue my dreams, even if everyone else thought they were farfetched—I couldn't have asked for a better grandfather. Keep playing your jazz up in Heaven. When I get there, I'll sit right beside you and sing along, just as I promised I would the night before you died.

My dear son, James—you are a gift to me and to the world. Never doubt it. And when you read this one day, and see exactly how crazy your mother was (is), I hope you know that the one thing I *never* doubted is how much I love you. That love is eternal; it burns within me forever. You are always my number one, and no matter what, I will love and support you with every inch and fiber of my being. My St. Jimmy-Jams: I love you completely, for all the days.

Toby—my true husband, my biggest supporter, and the person I know I am destined to spend my life with—what can I say to such an amazing human being? I know that this memoir wasn't an easy thing for you to read, but you supported me as I read painful passages and brought up memories of things that were clear to you but not so clear to me. You stayed with me despite the bullshit I put us through. You have kept your head held high and have set out to achieve every goal you've created. I am so incredibly fortunate to have your love. To the backend of forever—I love you, and nothing in this galaxy could ever change that.

I think that my final thank you—despite the madness—should be to my "head crew." DID has been quite the hindrance in my life, as well as in the lives of others, but the fact my alters exist means they protected me from the things I couldn't seem to handle myself. So—to the parts that are me, and yet are so much their own beings and identities—thank you to Ruby, Madeleine, Carmen, Shilo, Pandora, Green, Johnny, Alex, The Omnipotent, The Animal, Kara (though we all still wonder about you...), Nine-Nine, Sammy, and the thirty or so other names that will always bounce through my head. Thank you for making me the person I am. It has been a rough road, but it would have been worse without you. My gratitude runs deep. Thank you for your never-ending protection.

I take it back. My *final* thank you is to you—the reader of this memoir. This is a weird, dark, twisted work, rife with a roller coaster of ups and downs. Thank you for sticking through it and for sticking with me. I may not be likeable in every circumstance (hell, I know I'm not likeable in every circumstance!), but I truly and honestly appreciate that you wanted to go on this journey with me. Thank you for playing a part in it, and if, in some odd way, I was able to help you come to terms with trauma, mental illness, physical illness, or just some past issues that you haven't been able to talk about—well, I thank you for giving *me* that chance. I feel very blessed.

ABOUT THE AUTHOR

A.E. Hayes has been featured under various pseudonyms in myriad novels, anthologies, poetry collections, and music magazines. She is currently finishing her sixth fiction novel, *On Common Ground* (with a tentative release date of March 2018), as well as writing a paranormal science fiction story for the upcoming graphic novel *The Eynes Anthology*. A.E. was most recently featured in the anthologies *Love Across the Universe* and *Crazy Little Spring Called Love*. She studied English and Writing at Hood College, where she earned her B.A., and later studied Fiction Writing at The Johns Hopkins University in Baltimore. A.E. resides in Maryland with her husband and son, and when she isn't writing or singing opera, she spends her time drinking far too much coffee and staring at the water in St. Michaels, plotting ideas for her many future projects. Please visit her website for future updates and publications.

www.aehayes.com
aehayes@aehayes.com

Made in the USA
Middletown, DE
07 January 2018